D0719676

BY CLIVE BATTY

Published by Vision Sports Publishing in 2017

Vision Sports Publishing
19-23 High Street
Kingston upon Thames
Surrey
KT1 1LL

www.visionsp.co.uk

ISBN: 978-1909534-78-0

Editors: Paul Baillie-Lane and Jim Drewett
Design: Neal Cobourne
Kit images: David Moor, www.historicalkits.co.uk
All pictures: Getty Images

gettyimages®

Printed and bound in Slovakia by Neografia
A CIP catalogue record for this book is available from the British Library

All statistics in the *Vision Book of Football Records 2018* are correct up until the start of the 2017/18 season

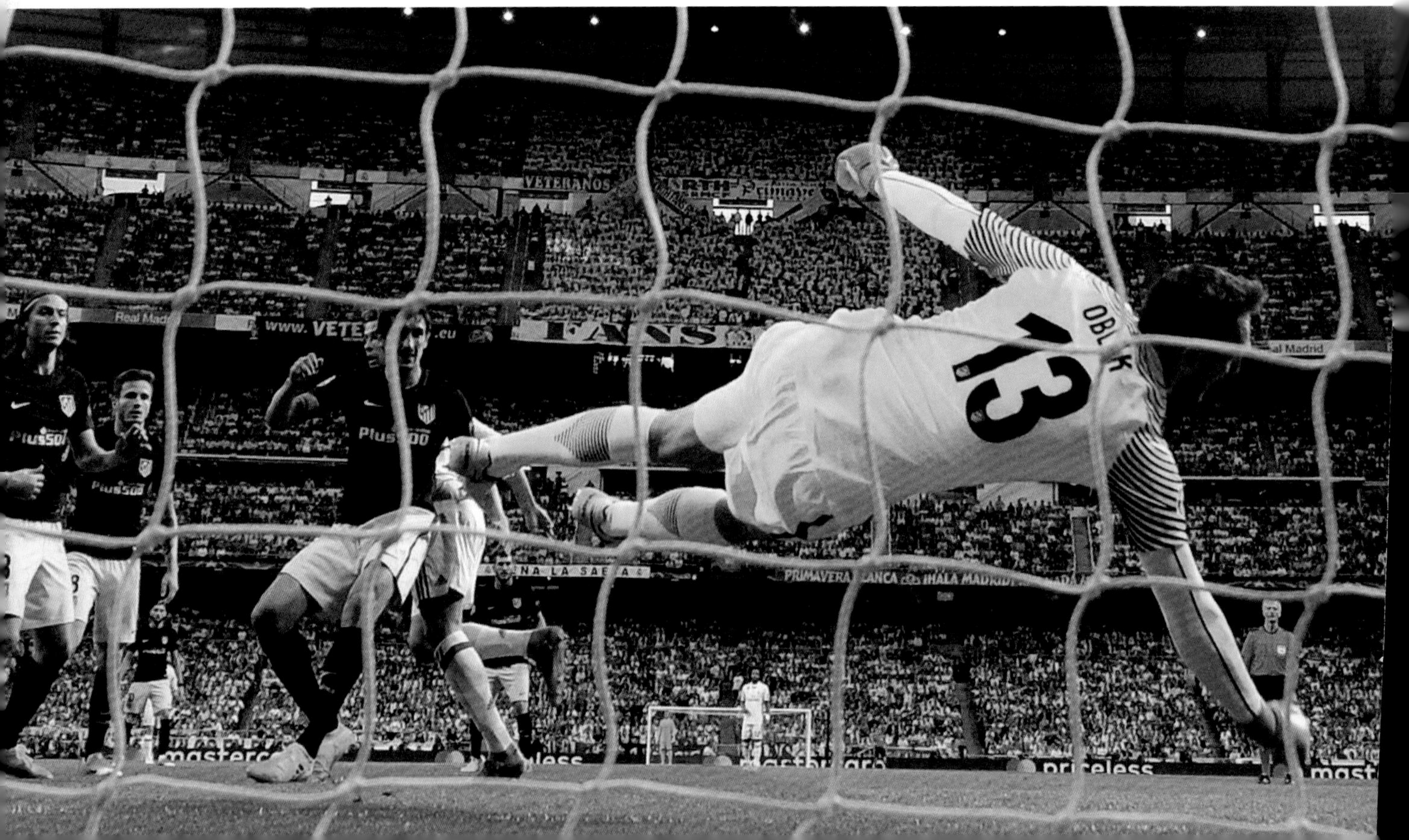

Welcome to the 2018 edition of the *Vision Book of Football Records*. Since this book last appeared on the shelves 12 months ago the football world has returned to something like normality on the pitch – although, perhaps, not off it, where transfer fees have spiralled to such an extent that even mediocre full-backs are now switching clubs for around the £50 million mark and Neymar's move from Barcelona to Paris Saint-Germain involved more cash changing hands than you'd find in most countries' central bank vault.

On the field of play, though, the mind-bogglingly crazy year of 2016 when the established order was toppled by the underdogs – led, of course, by Leicester City, whose fairytale title success captivated fans everywhere around the globe – has been filed away under the title 'Not to be repeated any time soon' as the big guns reasserted their dominance in emphatic style in 2017

In the domestic game, certainly, the roll call of clubs collecting trophies was a pretty familiar one: Chelsea, under new manager Antonio Conte, won the Premier League for a second time in three years; Arsenal lifted the FA Cup for a record 13th time; Manchester United claimed silverware in both the League Cup and the Europa League; and even the winners of the Championship, League One and League Two – Newcastle, Sheffield United and Portsmouth – are all massive clubs with large fanbases and recent histories in the top flight. In Scotland, too, the minnows were put well and truly in their place as Celtic swept the board, winning the Treble without even losing a single game. It was a similar story in Europe as the likes of Real Madrid, Bayern Munich, Juventus and Benfica all won their leagues and Real scooped up the Champions League for the third time in four years.

The 2016/17 season may not have been the rollercoaster ride of the past few years, but the various successes of the superpower clubs led to all manner of records being broken during the course of the campaign. As you'd expect, these have all been included in this latest edition along with loads of other changes, revisions and amendments. Look out, too, for new entries for the big-money signings from home and abroad who will hope to star in the Premier League in 2018 and beyond, such as Alvaro Morata, Jordan Pickford and Mohamed Salah. Alongside them there are entries for all the top players and managers, based both in Britain and the wider football world, and for some of the great legends of the past, including the likes of Stanley Matthews (ask your grandad!), George Best and the just-retired Frank Lampard.

As in previous editions, you'll also find entries for all the English league clubs (a big 'welcome' to Lincoln City and little Forest Green Rovers following their promotions to League Two), the top-flight Scottish sides and the most famous European outfits, such as Barcelona, AC Milan and Ajax. In addition, there are entries for the leading football nations, one of whom will presumably eventually lift the World Cup in Russia in 2018 (not the bravest of predictions, it has to be said, as the likes of Argentina, Brazil, Germany, Italy and Spain are all included), the most important domestic and international competitions, and individual aspects of the game such as corners, free kicks, throw-ins and penalties.

There's more too, including any number of 'wildcard' entries on subjects as varied as 'Cheating' (discover which Premier League club has collected the most yellow cards for diving in recent years), 'Draws' (can you believe that in 2015 two German clubs shared 18 goals in a ridiculous 9-9 draw?) and 'Sackings' (find out which manager got the boot after just 10 minutes in his club's hotseat).

All in all, then, you should find plenty here to keep you occupied during those rare hours when there is no actual live football on the TV. Come to think of it, with the Premier League now on Fridays, Saturdays, Sundays and Mondays, the Champions League on Tuesdays and Wednesdays and, for the truly dedicated fan, the Europa League on Thursdays, those football-free 'hours' are more like minutes, or even seconds. And to think, not so long ago the only live TV match all season was the FA Cup final!

CLIVE BATTY

ABANDONED MATCHES

Since the Premier League was formed in 1992, only six matches have had to be abandoned. The most recent was on 30th December 2006 when Watford's game with Wigan Athletic was called off after 56 minutes due to a waterlogged pitch. The score at the time was 1-1, as it was when the match was replayed later in the season.

• **The shortest ever Football League game took place in 1894, when a raging blizzard caused the match between Stoke and Wolves at the Victoria Ground to be called off after just three minutes. Only 400 hardy fans had braved the elements, and even they must have been secretly relieved when the referee, Mr Helme, called the game off.**

• The French league match between Metz and Lyon on 3rd December 2016 was abandoned after half an hour when a firecracker was thrown at Lyon goalkeeper Anthony Lopes and exploded next to him while he was receiving treatment for an injury. Lopes was taken to hospital, where he was diagnosed with temporary loss of hearing in both ears.

• **In a rare case of a football match being abandoned in summer because of bad weather, Swindon's home game with Bristol Rovers on 27th August 2016 was called off in the 60th minute due to torrential rain making the pitch unplayable.**

• Leyton Orient's final League Two home game of the season against Colchester on 29th April 2017 was 'abandoned' by the referee after O's fans invaded the pitch five minutes from the end in protest at the way their club was being run. However, once the fans had left the stadium the players returned to the pitch to play out the remaining few minutes of Colchester's 3-1 victory.

IS THAT A FACT?

In a bizarre turn of events, the Spartan South Midlands Premier League match on 29th October 2016 between Holmer Green and Edgware Town was abandoned after 13 minutes when referee Simon Higgins refused to continue after being vociferously criticised by an Edgware fan.

ABERDEEN

Year founded: 1903
Ground: Pittodrie Stadium (20,961)
Nickname: The Dons
Biggest win: 13-0 v Peterhead (1923)
Heaviest defeat: 0-9 v Celtic (2010)

Aberdeen were founded in 1903, following the amalgamation of three city clubs, Aberdeen, Orion and Victoria United. The following year the club joined the Scottish Second Division, and in 1905 the Dons were elected to an expanded First Division. Aberdeen have remained in the top flight ever since, a record shared with just Rangers and Celtic, and were runners-up in the Scottish Premiership behind Celtic in 2015, 2016 and 2017.

• **The club was originally known as the Whites and later as the Wasps or the Black and Golds after their early strips, but in 1913 became known as the Dons. This nickname is sometimes said to derive from the involvement of professors at Aberdeen University in the foundation of the club, but is more likely to be a contraction of the word 'Aberdonians', the term used to describe people from Aberdeen.**

• Aberdeen first won the Scottish title in 1955, before enjoying a trio of championship successes in the 1980s under manager Alex Ferguson. Before he moved on to even greater triumphs at Old Trafford, Fergie also led the Dons to four victories in five years in the Scottish Cup, which included a record run of 20 cup games without defeat between 1982 and 1985.

Aberdeen have lots to smile about these days

• **The club's finest hour, though, came in 1983 when the Dons became only the second Scottish club (after Rangers in 1972) to win the European Cup Winners' Cup, beating Real Madrid 2-1 in the final. Later that year Aberdeen defeated Hamburg over two legs to claim the European Super Cup and remain the only Scottish side to win two European trophies.**

• In 1984 Aberdeen became the first club outside the 'Old Firm' to win the Double, after finishing seven points clear at the top of the league and beating Celtic 2-1 in the Scottish Cup final.

• **Aberdeen's record of 16 appearances in the Scottish Cup final (including seven wins) is only bettered by Celtic and Rangers.**

• Scottish international defender Willie Miller has made more appearances for the club than any other player, an impressive 556 games between 1973 and 1990. Hotshot striker Joe Harper is the Dons' record goalscorer, with 205 during two spells at Pittodrie (1969-72 and 1976-81).

• **Diminutive Dons striker Benny Yorston scored a club record 38 league goals in the 1929/30 season but was later sacked by the club after his involvement in a betting scandal.**

• Ginger-haired central defender Alex McLeish made a club record 77 appearances for Scotland between 1980 and 1993.

HONOURS
Division 1 champions *1955*
Premier Division champions *1980, 1984, 1985*
Scottish Cup *1947, 1970, 1982, 1983, 1984, 1986, 1990*
League Cup *1956, 1977, 1986, 1990, 1996, 2014*
European Cup Winners' Cup *1983*
European Super Cup *1983*

AC MILAN

Year founded: 1899
Ground: San Siro (80,018)
Nickname: Rossoneri
League titles: 18
Domestic cups: 5
European cups: 14
International cups: 4

One of the giants of European football, the club was founded by British expatriates as the Milan Cricket and Football Club in 1899. Apart from a period during the fascist dictatorship of Benito Mussolini, the club has always been known as 'Milan' rather than the Italian 'Milano'.

• Milan were the first Italian side to win the European Cup, beating Benfica in the final at Wembley in 1963, and have gone on to win the trophy seven times – a record surpassed only by Real Madrid, with 12 victories.

• In 1986 the club was acquired by the businessman and future Italian President Silvio Berlusconi, who invested in star players like Marco van Basten, Ruud Gullit and Frank Rijkaard. Milan went on to enjoy a golden era under coaches Arrigo Sacchi and Fabio Capello, winning three European Cups and four Serie A titles between 1988 and 1994. Incredibly, the club were undefeated for 58 games between 1991 and 1993, a record run in Italian football.

• Another star of that AC Milan team was legendary defender Paolo Maldini, who made a record 647 appearances in Serie A between 1984 and 2009.

• AC Milan's Gianluigi Donnarumma became the youngest goalkeeper ever to play for Italy when he made his debut as a sub in a friendly against France aged 17 and 189 days in September 2016.

HONOURS
Italian champions *1901, 1906, 1907, 1951, 1955, 1957, 1959, 1962, 1968, 1979, 1988, 1992, 1993, 1994, 1996, 1999, 2004, 2011*
Italian Cup *1967, 1972, 1973, 1977, 2003*
European Cup/Champions League *1963, 1969, 1989, 1990, 1994, 2003, 2007*
European Cup Winners' Cup *1968, 1973*
European Super Cup *1989, 1990, 1994, 2003, 2007*
Intercontinental Cup *1969, 1989, 1990*
Club World Cup *2007*

AC Milan's Fabio Borini celebrates scoring for the 'Rossoneri'

ACCRINGTON STANLEY

Year founded: 1968
Ground: Crown Ground (5,057)
Nickname: The Stans
Biggest win: 10-1 v Lincoln United (1999)
Heaviest defeat: 2-8 v Peterborough (2008)

Accrington Stanley were founded at a meeting in a working men's club in Accrington in 1968, as a successor to the former Football League club of the same name which had folded two years earlier.

• Conference champions in 2006, Stanley were promoted to the Football League in place of relegated Oxford United and are now the longest serving members of League Two. Ironically, when a financial crisis forced the old Accrington Stanley to resign from the League in March 1962, the club that replaced them the following season was Oxford!

• Midfielder Andy Proctor made a club record 267 league appearances for the club in two spells at the Crown Ground between 2006 and 2016.

• The original town club, Accrington, were one of the 12 founder members of the Football League in 1888, but resigned from the League after just five years.

• With a capacity of just 5,057, the Stans' Crown Ground is the second smallest stadium in the Football League.

HONOURS
Conference champions *2006*

AFC WIMBLEDON

Year founded: 2002
Ground: Kingsmeadow (4,850)
Nickname: The Dons
Biggest win: 9-0 v Chessington United (2004) and v Slough Town (2007)
Heaviest defeat: 0-5 v York City (2010)

AFC Wimbledon were founded in 2002 by supporters of the former Premiership club Wimbledon, who opposed the decision of the FA to sanction the 'franchising' of their club when they allowed it to move 56 miles north from their south London base to Milton Keynes in Buckinghamshire (the club later becoming the MK Dons).

• In October 2006 an agreement was reached with the MK Dons that the honours won by the old Wimbledon would return to the London Borough of Merton. This was an important victory for the AFC fans, who view their club as the true successors to Wimbledon FC.

• In their former incarnation as Wimbledon the club won the FA Cup in 1988, beating hot favourites Liverpool 1-0 at Wembley. Incredibly, the Dons had only been elected to the Football League just 12 years earlier, but enjoyed a remarkable rise through the divisions, winning promotion to the top flight in 1986. Dubbed the 'Crazy Gang' for their physical approach on the pitch and madcap antics off it, Wimbledon remained in the Premiership until 2000.

• In 2011 the Dons gained promotion to League Two after beating Luton Town on penalties in the Conference play-off final. Then, in 2016, AFC became the first club formed in the 21st century to play in the Football League play-offs and delighted their fans by beating Plymouth Argyle 2-0 in the League Two final at Wembley.

• With a capacity of just 4,850, the club's tiny Kingsmeadow Stadium is the smallest in the Football League.

• Defender Barry Fuller has made a club record 163 league appearances for the Dons since 2013. The club's record scorer is Jack Midson with 38 league goals between 2011 and 2014.

HONOURS
Division 4 champions *1983 **(as Wimbledon FC)***
FA Cup *1988 **(as Wimbledon FC)***
FA Amateur Cup *1963 **(as Wimbledon FC)***

AFRICA CUP OF NATIONS

The Africa Cup of Nations was founded in 1957. The first tournament was a decidedly small affair consisting of just three competing teams (Egypt, Ethiopia and hosts Sudan) after South Africa's invitation was withdrawn when they refused to send a multi-racial squad to the finals. Egypt were the first winners, beating Ethiopia 4-0 in the final in Khartoum.

• With seven victories, Egypt are the most successful side in the history of the competition. In second place overall are Cameroon with five victories, the most recent of which came in 2017 when they beat Egypt 2-1 in the final in Libreville, Gabon.

• In 1970 Laurent Pokou of Ivory Coast scored a record five goals in a single match in a 6-1 demolition of Ethiopia.

• The top scorer in the history of the competition is Cameroon striker Samuel Eto'o, who hit a total of 18 goals in the tournament between 2000 and 2010. Mulamba Ndaye of Zaire holds the record for the most goals in a single tournament, with nine in 1974.

• Rigobert Song (Cameroon) made a record 33 appearances in a joint-record eight finals between 1996 and 2010.

AFRICAN FOOTBALLER OF THE YEAR

The African Footballer of the Year award was established by the Confederation of African Football in 1992. The 2016 winner was Leicester City and Algeria midfielder Riyad Mahrez.

• Ivory Coast midfielder Yaya Toure has dominated the award in recent years, with a record four wins on the trot between 2011 and 2014. Legendary Cameroon striker Samuel

The Africa Cup of Nations is always a colourful spectacle

TOP 10

YOUNGEST PREMIER LEAGUE PLAYERS

1. Matthew Briggs (Fulham, 2007)	16 years and 65 days
2. Isaiah Brown (West Bromwich Albion, 2013)	16 years and 117 days
3. Aaron Lennon (Leeds United, 2003)	16 years and 129 days
4. Jose Baxter (Everton, 2008)	16 years and 191 days
5. Rushian Hepburn-Murphy (Aston Villa, 2015)	16 years and 176 days
6. Gary McSheffrey (Coventry City, 1999)	16 years and 198 days
7. Reece Oxford (West Ham United, 2015)	16 years and 235 days
8. Jack Robinson (Liverpool, 2010)	16 years and 250 days
9. Jack Wilshere (Arsenal, 2008)	16 years and 256 days
10. Angel Gomes (Manchester United, 2017)	16 years and 263 days

Eto'o has also won the award four times, including a hat-trick between 2003 and 2005.

• The first Premier League-based player to win the award was Arsenal's Nigerian striker Kanu in 1999. Altogether, players at English clubs have won the award a record 10 times.

• Players from nine different African countries have won the award, with Ivory Coast (six wins in total) enjoying the most success.

AGE

Legendary winger Sir Stanley Matthews is the oldest player to appear in the top flight of English football. 'The Ageless Wonder' had celebrated his 50th birthday five days before playing his last match for Stoke against Fulham in February 1965.

• Matthews, though, was something of a spring chicken compared to Neil McBain, the New Brighton manager, who had to go in goal for his side's Division Three (North) match against Hartlepool during an injury crisis in 1947. He was 51 and 120 days at the time, the oldest player in the history of English football.

• Manchester City goalkeeper John Burridge became the oldest player in the Premier League when he came off the bench at half-time in City's match against Newcastle in April 1995, aged 43. The youngest player is Fulham's Matthew Briggs, who was aged 16 years and 65 days when he made his debut for the Cottagers against Middlesbrough in May 2007.

• The oldest international in British football is Wales' Billy Meredith, who played against England in 1920 at the age of 45. The youngest is Ireland's Samuel Johnston, who was aged just 15 and 154 days when he played against England in 1882.

• England's youngest ever player is Arsenal striker Theo Walcott, who was aged 17 and 75 days when he came on as a sub against Hungary at Old Trafford on 30th May 2006. The oldest player to feature for the Three Lions is winger Stanley Matthews, who was 42 and 103 days when he won his final cap against Denmark in 1957.

• The youngest player to score in the English top flight is Jason Dozzell, who was aged 16 and 57 days when he scored on his debut for Ipswich in the old First Division against Coventry on 4th February 1984. Remarkably, Dozzell's son, Andre, also scored on his Ipswich debut aged 16 (and 350 days) against Sheffield Wednesday in April 2016.

• The oldest professional footballer to score a goal is former Japan international Kazuyoshi Miura, who slotted home from inside the six-yard box for Yokohama FC against Thespa Kusatsu in the J2 League (Japanese second division) on 12th March 2017, aged 50 and 14 days.

• The youngest player to appear in international football is Lucas Knecht, who turned out for the Northern Mariana Islands against Guam two days after his 14th birthday in 2007. At the opposite end of the scale, Barrie Dewsbury was 52 and 11 days when he played in Sark's 16-0 defeat by Greenland in 2003.

SERGIO AGUERO

Born: Quilmes, Argentina, 2nd June 1988
Position: Striker
Club career:
2003-06 Independiente 54 (23)
2006-11 Atletico Madrid 175 (74)
2011- Manchester City 181 (122)
International record:
2006- Argentina 82 (33)

Manchester City striker Sergio Aguero has the best goals/minutes ratio of any player in Premier League history, averaging a goal every 109.83 minutes. His 20 goals in the 2016/17 season made him only the fifth player to reach this target in three consecutive Premier League campaigns.

Sergio Aguero, Manchester City's all-time top Premier League scorer

• Known as 'El Kun' because of his resemblance to a Japanese cartoon character, Aguero became the youngest ever player to appear in Argentina's top flight when he made his debut for Independiente in 2003 aged just 15 years and 35 days. The previous record was set by the legendary Diego Maradona, Aguero's former father-in-law.

• Aguero moved on to Atletico Madrid in 2006 aged 17, helping the Spanish club win the inaugural Europa League in 2010. The following year he joined Manchester City for £38 million, to become the second most expensive player in British football history at the time.

• The fee proved to be a bargain as Aguero banged in 23 Premier League goals – including a dramatic title-clinching winner against QPR on the last day of the season – as City topped the table for the first time since 1968. Two years later he contributed another 17 goals as City won the title again, and in 2015 he became the first Manchester City player to win the Premier League Golden Boot outright after topping the scoring charts with an impressive total of 26 goals. The following season he became only the fifth player in Premier League history to score five goals in a game, and doing so in record time – just 23 minutes and 34 seconds – in a 6-1 hammering of Newcastle.

• A quicksilver attacker who possesses excellent close control, Aguero made his international debut for Argentina in a 2006 friendly against Brazil at Arsenal's Emirates Stadium. In 2008 he was a key figure in the Argentina team that won gold at the Beijing Olympics, but he endured heartache at the 2014 World Cup and the Copa America in 2015 and 2016 when he finished on the losing side in the final all three times.

AIR CRASHES

On 28th November 2016 a plane carrying the Brazilian team Chapecoense on their way to play Colombian side Atletico Nacional in the first leg of the Copa Sudamericana finals crashed into a hillside near Medellin after running out of fuel. A total of 71 people were killed in the disaster, including 19 players and the team's coach, Luiz Carlos Saroli.

• On 6th February 1958 eight members of the Manchester United 'Busby Babes' team, including England internationals Roger Byrne, Duncan Edwards and Tommy Taylor, were killed in the Munich Air Crash. Their plane crashed while attempting to take off in a snowstorm at Munich Airport, where it had stopped to refuel after a European Cup tie in Belgrade. In total, 23 people died in the incident, although manager Matt Busby and Bobby Charlton were among the survivors. Amazingly, United still managed to reach the FA Cup final that year, but lost at Wembley to Bolton Wanderers.

• The entire first team of Torino, the strongest Italian club at the time, were wiped out in an air disaster on 4th May 1949. Returning from a testimonial match in Portugal, the team's plane crashed into the Basilica of Superga outside Turin. Among the 31 dead were 10 members of the Italian national side and the club's English manager, Leslie Lievesley. Torino fielded their youth team in their four remaining fixtures and, with their opponents doing the same as a mark of respect, won a joint-record fifth consecutive league title at the end of the season.

AJAX

Year founded: 1900
Ground: Amsterdam Arena (53,748)
Nickname: De Godenzonen (the sons of the Gods)
League titles: 33
Domestic cups: 18
European cups: 8
International cups: 2

Founded in 1900 in Amsterdam, Ajax are named after the Greek mythological hero. The club is the most successful in Holland, having won the league a record 33 times and the Dutch Cup a record 18 times.

• The Dutch side's most glorious decade was in the 1970s when, with a team featuring legends like Johan Cruyff, Johan Neeskens and Johnny Rep, Ajax won the European Cup three times on the trot, playing a fluid system known as 'Total Football'. In 1995 a young Ajax team won the trophy for a fourth time, Patrick Kluivert scoring the winner in the final against AC Milan.

• When Ajax beat Torino in the final of the UEFA Cup in 1992 they became only the second team, after Juventus, to win all three major European trophies. In 2017 Ajax reached their first European final for two decades, but lost 2-0 in the Europa League final to Manchester United.

• During the 1971/72 season Ajax won a world record 26 matches on the trot in all competitions – a run which was only finally bettered by Welsh side TNS, with 27 straight wins, in the 2016/17 season.

• Ajax were the first team to win the European Super Cup, beating Rangers 6-3 on aggregate in 1972. However, FIFA didn't officially recognise the contest as Rangers were serving a one-year ban from European competition. The following year, Ajax won the first official edition of the Super Cup, thrashing AC Milan 6-1 on aggregate.

HONOURS
Dutch League champions *1918, 1919, 1931, 1932, 1934, 1937, 1939, 1947, 1957, 1960, 1966, 1967, 1968, 1970, 1972, 1973, 1977, 1979, 1980, 1982, 1983, 1985, 1990, 1994, 1995, 1996, 1998, 2002, 2004, 2011, 2012, 2013, 2014*
Dutch Cup *1917, 1943, 1961, 1967, 1970, 1971, 1972, 1979, 1983, 1986, 1987, 1993, 1998, 1999, 2002, 2006, 2007, 2010*
European Cup/Champions League *1971, 1972, 1973, 1995*
European Cup Winners' Cup *1987*
UEFA Cup *1992*
European Super Cup *1973, 1995*
Intercontinental Cup *1972, 1995*

TOBY ALDERWEIRELD

Born: Antwerp, Belgium, 2nd March 1989
Position: Defender
Club career:
2008-13 Ajax 128 (7)
2013-15 Atletico Madrid 12 (1)
2014-15 Southampton (loan) 26 (1)
2015- Tottenham Hotspur 68 (5)
International record:
2009- Belgium 67 (3)

Belgian international centre-back Toby Alderweireld was one of Tottenham's outstanding performers in the 2016/17 season, at the end of which the north

Londoners had the best defensive record in the Premier League with just 26 goals conceded.

• Alderweireld began his career at Ajax, with whom he won three successive Dutch titles in 2011, 2012 and 2013. He then moved on to Atletico Madrid, helping the team from the Spanish capital win La Liga and reach the Champions League final a year later, where they lost to city rivals Real.

• Struggling to hold down a first-team place in Spain, Alderweireld was loaned to Southampton for the 2014/15 season. The Saints were keen to make the deal a permanent one, but were outbid by Tottenham who paid £11.5 million for the centre-back's services in July 2015.

• First capped by Belgium against the Czech Republic in 2009, Alderweireld has gone on to win nearly 70 caps for his country, playing in the same back four as his Spurs team-mate Jan Vertonghen.

Dele Alli, the 2017 PFA Young Player of the Year

DELE ALLI

Born: Milton Keynes, 11th April 1996
Position: Midfielder
Club career:
2011-15 Milton Keynes Dons 62 (18)
2015- Tottenham Hotspur 70 (28)
2015 Milton Keynes Dons (loan) 12 (4)
International record:
2015- England 19 (2)

An attacking midfielder who loves making runs into the opposition box, Dele Alli became only the fourth player to win the PFA Young Player of the Year award twice when he topped the poll in 2017, a year after his first success. The Tottenham star, who scored a career best 18 league goals in 2016/17, was also voted into the PFA Team of the Year for the second consecutive season.

• Alli joined his local club MK Dons as an 11-year-old, making his first-team debut aged just 16 in November 2012 against Cambridge City in the FA Cup. After helping the Dons win promotion to the Championship in 2015 he was voted the Football League Young Player of the Year.

• Alli moved to Tottenham for a bargain £5 million during the 2015 winter transfer window, but was loaned back to MK Dons for the rest of the season. He eventually made his Spurs debut in August 2015, scoring his first goal later that month in a 1-1 draw at Leicester. He went on to score 10 Premier League goals, including a brilliant effort against Crystal Palace at Selhurst Park that was voted the BBC's Goal of the Season.

• First capped by England at Under-17 level, Alli's eye-catching displays for Tottenham soon earned him a call up to Roy Hodgson's senior squad and he marked his first start for England in fine style with a blistering long-range strike past Spurs team-mate Hugo Lloris in a 2-0 friendly victory over France at Wembley in November 2015.

ANIMALS

The Evo-Stik Premier League match between Halesowen Town and Skelmersdale United in April 2017 was held up for six minutes when a dog scampered on to the pitch, evading numerous attempts to catch it. Eventually the dog, a beagle called Dusty, was caught by his owner – Halesowen Town defender Asa Charlton.

• The most famous dog in football, Pickles, never appeared on the pitch but, to the relief of fans around the globe, discovered the World Cup trophy which was stolen while on display at an exhibition in Central Hall, Westminster, on 20th March 1966. A black and white mongrel, Pickles found the trophy under a bush while out for a walk on Beulah Hill in south London with his owner. He was hailed as a national hero but, sadly, later that same year he was strangled by his lead while chasing after a cat.

• The World Cup also made an international celebrity of Paul, an octopus based at the Sea Life Aquarium in Oberhausen, Germany. During the 2010 finals in South Africa, the two-year-old cephalopod correctly predicted the result of all seven of Germany's games by choosing his favourite food, mussels, from one of two boxes marked with the national flag of the competing teams. Before the final between Holland and Spain, Paul's choice of breakfast snack suggested that the trophy would be heading to Madrid rather than Amsterdam... and, yet again, the amazing 'psychic' octopus was spot on!

• A Copa Peru clash between Minsa and Expreso Inambari was interrupted for a number of minutes in April 2014 when a herd of cows stampeded on to the pitch, much to the bemusement of the two sets of players.

• In an unusual double invasion, a Mexican league match between Pachuca and Jaguares in January 2017 was interrupted twice, first by a dog in the 65th minute and then by a cat in the 85th minute.

APPEARANCES

Goalkeeping legend Peter Shilton holds the record for the most Football League appearances, playing 1,005 games between 1966 and 1997. His total was made up as follows: Leicester City (286 games), Stoke City (110), Nottingham Forest (202), Southampton (188), Derby County (175), Plymouth (34), Bolton (1) and Leyton Orient (9). Shilton is followed in the all-time list by Tony Ford (931 appearances, 1975-2001), who holds the record for an outfield player.

• Manchester United winger Ryan Giggs holds the Premier League appearance record, with a total of 632 appearances between 1992 and 2014. However, West Brom midfielder Gareth Barry is closing in fast on the Welshman's tally with 628 appearances by the end of the 2016/17 season.

• Between 1946 and 1955 Harold Bell was ever present for Tranmere in a record 375 consecutive league games.

• Only four outfield players have played every minute of a Premier League title-winning campaign: Gary Pallister for Manchester United in 1992/93, John Terry for Chelsea in 2014/15, Wes Morgan for Leicester City in 2015/16, and Cesar Azpilicueta for Chelsea in 2016/17.

• Spain goalkeeper Iker Casillas holds the record for the most appearances in the Champions League with 164 for Real Madrid and Porto from 1999.

ARGENTINA

First international: Uruguay 2 Argentina 3, 1901
Most capped player: Javier Zanetti, 143 caps (1994-2011)
Leading goalscorer: Lionel Messi, 58 goals (2005-)
First World Cup appearance: Argentina 1 France 0, 1930
Biggest win: 12-0 v Ecuador, 1942
Heaviest defeat: Argentina 1 Czechoslovakia 6 (1958) and Argentina 1 Bolivia 6 (2009)

Outside Britain, Argentina is the oldest football nation on the planet. The roots of the game in this football-obsessed country go back to 1865, when the Buenos Aires Football Club was founded by British residents in the Argentine capital. Six clubs formed the first league in 1891, making it the oldest anywhere in the world outside Britain.

• Losing finalists in the first World Cup final in 1930, Argentina had to wait until 1978 before winning the competition for the first time, defeating Holland 3-1 on home soil. Another success, inspired by brilliant captain Diego Maradona, followed in 1986 and Argentina came close to retaining their trophy four years later, losing in the final to West Germany. After a 24-year wait they reached the final again in 2014, but narrowly lost to Germany.

There's no love lost between Argentina and Brazil

• Argentina's oldest rivals are neighbours Uruguay. The two countries first met in 1901, in the first official international to be played outside Britain, with Argentina winning 3-2 in Montevideo. In the ensuing years the two sides have played each other 183 times, making the Argentina-Uruguay fixture the most played in the history of international football.

• With 14 victories to their name, Argentina have the second best

record in the Copa America. In 2015 and 2016 Messi and co. had a great chance to equal Uruguay's record of 15 wins but they lost both finals to Chile on penalties.

HONOURS
World Cup winners *1978, 1986*
Copa America winners *1921, 1925, 1927, 1929, 1937, 1941, 1945, 1946, 1947, 1955, 1957, 1959, 1991, 1993*
World Cup Record
1930 Runners-up
1934 Round 1
1938 Did not enter
1950 Did not enter
1954 Did not enter
1958 Round 1
1962 Round 1
1966 Quarter-finals
1970 Did not qualify
1974 Round 2
1978 Winners
1982 Round 2
1986 Winners
1990 Runners-up
1994 Round 2
1998 Quarter-finals
2002 Round 1
2006 Quarter-finals
2010 Quarter-finals
2014 Runners-up

ARSENAL

Year founded: 1886
Ground: Emirates Stadium (60,432)
Previous name: Dial Square, Royal Arsenal, Woolwich Arsenal
Nickname: The Gunners
Biggest win: 12-0 v Ashford United (1893) and v Loughborough Town (1900)
Heaviest defeat: 0-8 v Loughborough Town (1896)

Founded as Dial Square in 1886 by workers at the Royal Arsenal in Woolwich, the club was renamed Royal Arsenal soon afterwards. Another name change, to Woolwich Arsenal, followed in 1891 when the club turned professional. Then, a year after moving north of the river to the Arsenal Stadium in 1913, the club became simply 'Arsenal'.

• One of the most successful clubs in the history of English football, Arsenal enjoyed a first golden period in the 1930s under innovative manager Herbert Chapman. The Gunners won the FA Cup for the first time in 1930 and later in the decade became only the second club to win three league titles on the trot. The first was the club Chapman managed in the 1920s, Huddersfield Town.

• Arsenal were the first club from London to win the league, topping the table in 1931 after scoring an incredible 60 goals in 21 away matches – an all-time record for the Football League.

• Arsenal are the most successful club in the history of the FA Cup with 13 victories to their name, the most recent coming in 2017 when the Gunners beat London rivals Chelsea 2-1 in the final at Wembley. Seven of those cup triumphs were achieved during the long run of boss Arsène Wenger, the best haul of any manager in FA Cup history. Wenger also led the Gunners to the Double in both 1998 and 2002, and their total of three Doubles (including an earlier triumph in 1971) is only matched by Manchester United.

• Wenger's greatest achievement, though, came in the 2003/04 season when his team were crowned Premier League champions after going through the entire campaign undefeated. Only Preston North End had previously matched this feat, way back in 1888/89, but they had only played 22 league games compared to the 38 of Wenger's 'Invincibles'.

Arsenal's new 'piggy-back' attack is a nightmare for opposition defenders

• The following season Arsenal extended their unbeaten run to 49 matches – setting an English league record in the process – before crashing to a bad-tempered 2-0 defeat against Manchester United at Old Trafford on 24th October 2004.

• One of the stars of that great Arsenal side was striker Thierry Henry, who is the Gunners' all-time leading scorer with 228 goals in all competitions in two spells at the club between 1999 and 2012. The former fans' favourite is also the most capped Arsenal player, appearing 81 times for France during his time with the club.

• In 1989 Arsenal won the closest ever title race by beating Liverpool 2-0 at Anfield in the final match of the season to pip the Reds to the championship on goals scored (the two sides had the same goal difference). But for a last-minute goal by Gunners midfielder Michael Thomas, after Alan Smith had scored with a second-half header, the title would have stayed on Merseyside.

• Irish international defender David O'Leary made a club record 722 first-team appearances for Arsenal between 1975 and 1993.

• Arsenal endured a nightmare season in 1912/13, finishing bottom of Division One and winning just one home game during the campaign – an all-time record. However, the Gunners returned to the top flight in 1919 and have stayed there ever since -- the longest unbroken run in the top tier.

• Arsenal tube station on the Piccadilly Line is the only train station in Britain to be named after a football club. It used to be called Gillespie Road, until Herbert Chapman successfully lobbied for the name change in 1932.

• Three years later, on 14th December 1935, Arsenal thrashed Aston Villa 7-1 at Villa Park. Incredibly, centre-forward Ted Drake grabbed all seven of the Gunners' goals to set a top-flight record that still stands to this day.

• Thanks in part to their decision to play Champions League games at Wembley in the late 1990s, Arsenal have played a record 52 matches at the national stadium.

• Arsenal's most expensive signing is French striker Alexandre Lacazette, who cost the Gunners £46.5 million when he joined them from Lyon in July 2017. The club's record sale is Alex Oxlade-Chamberlain, who boosted the Gunners' coffers by £35 million when he signed for Liverpool in 2017.

• On their way to the Premier League title in 2002 Arsenal won a league record 14 consecutive games and became the first club to score in every Premier League fixture in a season.

• Although the Gunners have never won the Champions League they appeared in the group stages of the competition for 19 consecutive seasons from 1998/99 to 2016/17 – a record for an English club which is only bettered by Real Madrid. However, Arsenal also hold the record for the worst defeat suffered by an English side in the competition, 10-2 on aggregate in the last 16 against Bayern Munich in 2017.

HONOURS
Division 1 champions *1931, 1933, 1934, 1935, 1948, 1953, 1971, 1989, 1991*
Premier League champions *1998, 2002, 2004*
FA Cup *1930, 1936, 1950, 1971, 1979, 1993, 1998, 2002, 2003, 2005, 2014, 2015, 2017*
League Cup *1987, 1993*
Double *1971, 1998, 2002*
Fairs Cup *1970*
European Cup Winners' Cup *1994*

ASTON VILLA

Year founded: 1874
Ground: Villa Park (42,660)
Nickname: The Villans
Biggest win: 13-0 v Wednesbury Old Athletic (1886)
Heaviest defeat: 0-8 v Chelsea (2012)

One of England's most famous and distinguished clubs, Aston Villa were founded in 1874 by members of the Villa Cross Wesleyan Chapel in Aston, Birmingham. The club were founder members of the Football League in 1888, winning their first title six years later.

• The most successful team of the Victorian era, Villa became only the second club to win the league and FA Cup Double in 1897 (Preston North End were the first in 1889). Villa's manager at the time was the legendary George Ramsay, who went on to guide the Villans to six league titles and six FA Cups – a trophy haul which has only been surpassed by Liverpool's Bob Paisley and former Manchester United boss Sir Alex Ferguson.

• Ramsay is also the second longest serving manager in the history of English football, taking charge of the Villans for an incredible 42 years between 1884 and 1926. Only West Brom's Fred Everiss has managed a club for longer, racking up 46 years' service at the Hawthorns.

• Although they slipped as low as the old Third Division in the early 1970s, Villa have spent more time in the top flight than any other club apart from Everton (105 seasons compared to the Toffees' 115). The two clubs have played each other 202 times to date, making Aston Villa v Everton the most played fixture in the history of league football.

• Villa won the last of their seven league titles in 1980/81, when manager Ron Saunders used just 14 players throughout the whole campaign – equalling Liverpool's record set in 1965/66. The following season Villa became only the fourth English club to win the European Cup when they beat Bayern Munich 1-0 in the final in Rotterdam.

• In 1961 Villa won the League Cup in the competition's inaugural season, beating Rotherham 3-2 in a two-legged final. The Villans are the joint-second most successful side in the tournament behind Liverpool with five triumphs, their most recent success coming in 1996.

• Villa's most capped international is former Republic of Ireland defender Steve Staunton, who played 64 times for his country while at Villa Park between 1991 and 1998. His team-mate Gareth Southgate, now England manager, played a club record 42 times for the Three Lions between 1991 and 2001.

• Stalwart defender Charlie Aitken made more appearances for the club than any other player, turning out in 657 games between 1959 and 1976. Villa's all-time top goalscorer is Billy Walker, who found the back of the net an incredible 244 times between 1919 and 1933.

• Walker helped Villa bang in 128 league goals in the 1930/31 season, a record for the top flight which is unlikely ever to be broken. In the same campaign, Tom 'Pongo' Waring scored a club record 49 league goals.

• **Before FA Cup semi-finals moved to Wembley, Villa Park staged a record 55 of these fixtures. The stadium has also hosted 16 England internationals and was the first venue to be used by the national team in three different centuries.**

• Villa smashed their transfer record in January 2001, splashing out £18 million on Sunderland striker Darren Bent. Belgian international Christian Benteke is the club's record sale, joining Liverpool for £32.5 million in July 2015.

HONOURS
Division 1 champions *1894, 1896, 1897, 1899, 1900, 1910, 1981*
Division 2 champions *1938, 1960*
Division 3 champions *1972*
FA Cup *1887, 1895, 1897, 1905, 1913, 1920, 1957*
Double *1897*
League Cup *1961, 1975, 1977, 1994, 1996*
European Cup *1982*
European Super Cup *1982*

ATLETICO MADRID

Year founded: 1903
Ground: Wanda Metropolitana (67,703)
Previous names: Athletic Club de Madrid, Athletic Aviacion de Madrid
Nickname: El Atleti
League titles: 10
Domestic cups: 10
European cups: 5
International cups: 1

The club was founded in 1903 by breakaway members of Madrid FC (later Real Madrid). In 1939, following a merger with the Spanish air force team, the club became known as Athletic Aviacion de Madrid before becoming plain Atletico Madrid eight years later.

• **Atletico are the third most successful club in Spanish football history with 10 La Liga triumphs under their belt. The most recent of these came in 2014 when Atleti drew 1-1 at runners-up Barcelona on the last day of the season to become the first side for a decade to break the Barca/Real Madrid duopoly.**

• Atletico have enjoyed European success in recent years, winning the Europa League in both 2010 and 2012 to become the first club to claim European football's newest competition on two occasions. Atleti also reached the Champions League final in 2014 and 2016, but lost both times to city rivals Real Madrid.

• **In May 2017 Atletico played the last match at their Vicente Calderon stadium, beating Athletic Bilbao 3-1, before moving to the near 68,000-capacity Wanda Metropolitana.**

HONOURS
Spanish League winners *1940, 1941, 1950, 1951, 1966, 1970, 1973, 1977, 1996, 2014*
Spanish Cup *1960, 1961, 1965, 1972, 1976, 1985, 1991, 1992, 1996, 2013*
European Cup Winners' Cup *1962*
Europa League *2010, 2012*
European Super Cup *2010, 2012*
Intercontinental Cup *1974*

ATTENDANCES

The Maracana Stadium in Rio de Janeiro holds the world record for a football match attendance, 199,854 spectators having watched the final match of the 1950 World Cup between Brazil and Uruguay. Most of the fans, though, went home in tears after Uruguay came from behind to win 2-1 and claim the trophy for a second time.

• **The biggest crowd at a match in Britain was for the first ever FA Cup final at Wembley in 1923. The official attendance for the match between Bolton and West Ham was 126,047, although, with thousands more fans gaining entry without paying, the actual crowd was estimated at 150,000-200,000. The record official attendance for a match in Britain is 149,547, set in 1937 for Scotland's 3-1 victory over England in the Home International Championship at Hampden Park.**

• In 1948 a crowd of 83,260 watched Manchester United entertain Arsenal at Maine Road (United's temporary home in the post-war years after Old Trafford suffered bomb damage), a record for the Football League. The following year, on 27th December 1949, the 44 Football League games played that day were watched by a record aggregate of 1,272,815 fans – an average of 28,913 per match.

• **On 15th April 1970 the biggest crowd ever to watch a European Cup tie, 135,826, crammed into Hampden Park in Glasgow to see Celtic beat Leeds United 2-1 in the semi-final second leg.**

• On 2nd November 2016 a crowd of 85,512 watched Tottenham's home Champions League group game with Bayer Leverkusen at Wembley – the biggest attendance ever for an English club's home fixture. However, it wasn't a happy night for the majority of the fans in the ground as Spurs slumped to a 1-0 defeat.

• **A record Premier League crowd of 76,098 watched Manchester United play Blackburn Rovers at Old Trafford on 31st March 2007. Less impressively, Wimbledon against Everton at Selhurst Park on 26th January 1993 attracted the lowest Premier League attendance ever, just 3,039.**

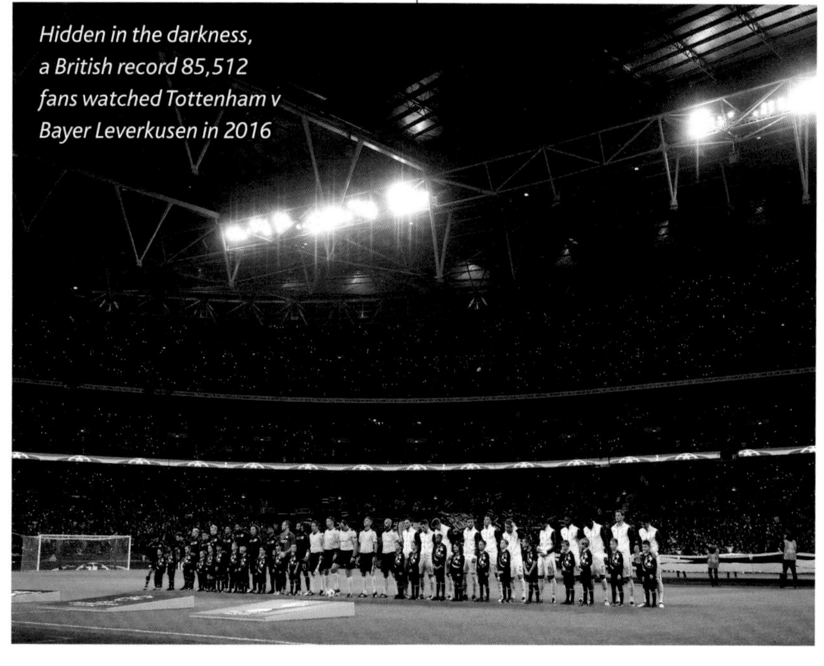

Hidden in the darkness, a British record 85,512 fans watched Tottenham v Bayer Leverkusen in 2016

GARETH BALE

Born: Cardiff, 16th July 1989
Position: Winger
Club career:
2006-07 Southampton 40 (5)
2007-13 Tottenham Hotspur 146 (22)
2013- Real Madrid 100 (54)
International record:
2006- Wales 66 (26)

Gareth Bale is the only British player to win the Champions League three times with a foreign club, completing his hat-trick when Real Madrid thrashed Juventus 4-1 in the 2017 final in his home city of Cardiff. Earlier in that season's competition, Bale scored Real's fastest ever Champions League goal when he netted after just 57 seconds against Polish side Legia Warsaw.

• Bale began his career at Southampton, where he became the second youngest player to debut for the club (behind Theo Walcott) when he appeared in a 2-0 win against Millwall in the Championship in April 2006. The following season his superb displays for the Saints earned him the Football League Young Player of the Year award.

• In the summer of 2007 Bale joined Tottenham for an initial fee of £5 million and was soon being hailed as one of the most exciting talents in the game. He enjoyed an outstanding season with Spurs in 2010/11 and at the end of the campaign he was named PFA Player of the Year – only the fourth Welshman to receive this honour. He was also the only Premier League player to be voted into the UEFA Team of the Year for 2011. He had an even better season in 2012/13, picking up both Player of the Year gongs and the PFA Young Player of the Year award – only the second player, after Cristiano Ronaldo, to collect this individual treble.

• Bale joined Real for a then world record fee of £86 million in August 2013 and has scored more goals in La Liga, 54, than any other British player. The record was previously held by Gary Lineker, who notched 43 goals for Barcelona in the 1980s.

• When Bale scored his first international goal, in a 5-1 home defeat by Slovakia in 2006, he became his country's youngest ever scorer aged 17 and 35 days. He was Wales' top scorer in their successful Euro 2016 qualifying campaign with seven goals, and at the finals he fired in another three to help his country reach the semi-finals of a major tournament for the first time.

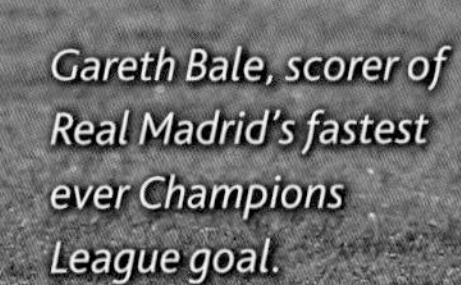

Gareth Bale, scorer of Real Madrid's fastest ever Champions League goal.

IS THAT A FACT?

Leyton Orient midfielder Liam Kelly was given a six-match ban after pushing over a ball boy in his attempt to retrieve the ball at a corner during his side's 3-2 win at Plymouth in February 2017.

BALL BOYS

Ball boys developed from a gimmick employed by Chelsea in the 1905/06 season. To emphasise the extraordinary bulk of the team's 23-stone goalkeeper, William 'Fatty' Foulke, two young boys would stand behind his goal. They soon proved themselves useful in retrieving the ball when it went out of play, and so the concept of the ball boy was born.

• Amazingly, a ball boy scored a goal in a match between Santacruzense and Atletico Sorocaba in Brazil in 2006. Santacruzense were trailing 1-0 when one of their players fired wide in the last minute. Instead of handing the ball back to the Atletico goalkeeper, the ball boy kicked it into the net and the goal was awarded by the female referee despite the angry protests of the Atletico players.

• During the South African Premier Division match between Kaizer Chiefs and Cape Town City in November 2016, a ball boy threw a ball on to the pitch when he mistakenly thought a cross had gone out of play. The referee made no allowance for the error and rather harshly sent the ball boy off!

• Seventeen-year-old Swansea ball boy Charlie Morgan helped his side reach the League Cup final in 2013 by falling on top of the ball when Chelsea's Eden Hazard wanted to take a corner kick. Frustrated at the lad's refusal to return the ball quickly, Hazard kicked it out from under him and was promptly shown a red card

that pretty much ended Chelsea's chances of overhauling a two-goal deficit from the first leg.

• In January 2017 Manchester United boss Jose Mourinho decided to change the club's usual ball boys, provided by the Manchester United Foundation, as he believed they were too slow in returning the ball to his players. Instead, he brought in youngsters from the club's academy, who made their debuts at Old Trafford for the 1-1 draw with arch rivals Liverpool.

BALLS

The laws of football specify that the ball must be an air-filled sphere with a circumference of 68-70cm and a weight before the start of the game of 410-450g. Before the first plastic footballs appeared in the 1950s, balls were made from leather and in wet conditions would become progressively heavier, sometimes actually doubling in weight.

• **Most modern footballs are made in Pakistan, especially in the city of Sialkot, and are usually stitched from 32 panels of waterproofed leather or plastic. In the past child labour was often used in the production of the balls but, following pressure from UNICEF and the International Labour Organisation, manufacturers agreed in 1997 not to employ underage workers.**

• Adidas have supplied the official ball for the World Cup since 1970. The ball for the 2014 tournament in Brazil, the Brazuca, was considered vastly superior to its predecessor, the Jabulani, which was widely thought to be the worst in the competition's history. Adidas also supplied the official ball for Euro 2016 in France, the 'Beau Jeu' ('Beautiful Game').

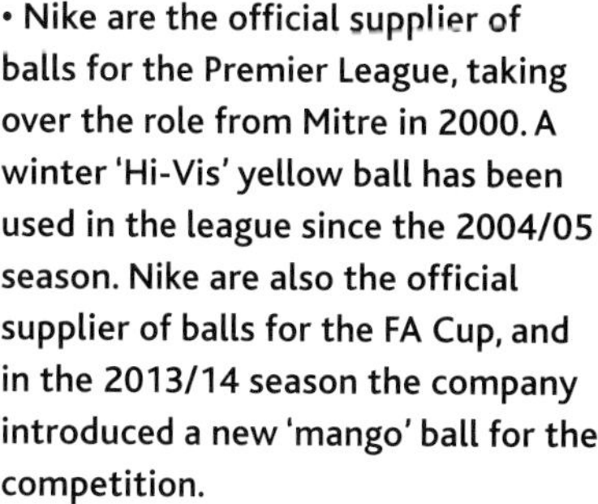

• **Nike are the official supplier of balls for the Premier League, taking over the role from Mitre in 2000. A winter 'Hi-Vis' yellow ball has been used in the league since the 2004/05 season. Nike are also the official supplier of balls for the FA Cup, and in the 2013/14 season the company introduced a new 'mango' ball for the competition.**

• The only time an orange ball has been used for the FA Cup final was in 1973, when underdogs Sunderland beat Leeds United 1-0 at Wembley.

• **A ball accidentally kicked off the pitch during a match at Scottish Under-19 side Banks O' Dee FC was discovered over 1,000 miles away on an island off Norway in April 2017. The club by the River Dee has lost numerous balls in the water, but this was the first one to turn up in the Arctic Circle.**

Cristiano Ronaldo hands the ball to Peter Crouch

BARCELONA

Year founded: 1899
Ground: Nou Camp (99,354)
Nickname: Barça
League titles: 24
Domestic cups: 29
European cups: 17
International cups: 3

One of the most famous and popular clubs in the world, Barcelona were founded in 1899 by bank worker Joan Gamper, a former captain of Swiss club Basel. The club were founder members and first winners of the Spanish championship, La Liga, in 1928 and have remained in the top flight of Spanish football ever since.

• **For the people of Catalonia, Barcelona is more like a national team than a mere club. As former manager Bobby Robson once succinctly put it, "Catalonia is a country and FC Barcelona is their army."**

• Barcelona are the only club to win the FIFA Club World Cup three times, sealing a unique hat-trick with a 3-0 defeat of Argentinian outfit River Plate in the 2015 final in Yokohama.

• With a capacity of 99,354 Barcelona's Nou Camp stadium is the largest in Europe. Among the stadium's many facilities are a museum which attracts over one million visitors a year, mini training pitches and a chapel for the players.

• For many years Barcelona played second fiddle to bitter rivals Real Madrid. Finally, in the 1990s, under former player-turned-coach Johan Cruyff, Barça turned the tables on the team from the Spanish capital by winning four La Liga titles on the trot between 1991 and 1994. Cruyff also led the Catalans to a first taste of glory in the European Cup, Barcelona beating Sampdoria at Wembley in 1992. The club have since won the Champions League on four more occasions, most recently beating Juventus 3-1 in the 2015 final to become the first European club to win the Treble twice (the first occasion was in 2009).

• Barcelona have won the Copa del Rey (the Spanish version of the FA Cup) a record 29 times, most recently beating Alaves 3-1 in the 2017 final to claim the trophy for a third consecutive year.

HONOURS

Spanish League *1929, 1945, 1948, 1949, 1952, 1953, 1959, 1960, 1974, 1985, 1991, 1992, 1993, 1994, 1998, 1999, 2005, 2006, 2009, 2010, 2011, 2013, 2015, 2016*

Spanish Cup *1910, 1912, 1913, 1920, 1922, 1925, 1926, 1928, 1942, 1951,1952, 1953, 1957, 1959, 1963, 1968, 1971, 1978, 1981, 1983, 1988, 1990, 1997, 1998, 2009, 2012, 2015, 2016, 2017*

European Cup/Champions League *1992, 2006, 2009, 2011, 2015*

European Cup Winners' Cup *1979, 1982, 1989, 1997*

Fairs Cup *1958, 1960, 1961*

European Super Cup *1992, 1997, 2009, 2011, 2015*

Club World Cup *2009, 2011, 2015*

ROSS BARKLEY

Born: Liverpool, 5th December 1993
Position: Midfielder
Club career:
2010- Everton 150 (21)
2012 Sheffield Wednesday (loan) 13 (4)
2013 Leeds United (loan) 4 (0)
International record:
2013- England 22 (2)

Compared by former England manager Roy Hodgson to a young Paul Gascoigne for his running power with the ball, Ross Barkley is one of the most exciting young English players in the Premier League.

• After joining Everton as an 11-year-old, Barkley recovered from a triple leg fracture when he was 16 to make his debut against QPR in 2011, before spending much of the next season on loan at Sheffield Wednesday and Leeds United.

• A strong player who loves to drive forward from midfield, Barkley scored

Barcelona have sometimes been criticised for losing their heads...

his first goal for Everton in a 2-2 draw at Norwich on the opening day of the 2013/14 season with a long-range strike. His eye-catching performances during the rest of the campaign saw him shortlisted for the PFA Young Player of the Year award, although he was eventually pipped to top spot by Chelsea's Eden Hazard.

• Barkley played for England at all levels from Under-16 to Under-21, helping his country win the Under-17 European Championships in 2010 after a 2-1 victory over Spain in the final. He won his first full cap as a sub against Moldova in September 2013, and two years later scored his first international goal in a 6-0 demolition of San Marino.

BARNET

Year founded: 1888
Ground: The Hive Stadium (6,205)
Previous name: Barnet Alston FC
Nickname: The Bees
Biggest win: 7-0 v Blackpool (2000)
Heaviest defeat: 1-9 v Peterborough United (1998)

Founded in 1888, Barnet spent more than a hundred years in non-league football before finally gaining promotion to the Football League after winning the Conference in 1991. The Bees have since twice suffered the agony of losing their league status, but claimed the Conference title in both 2005 and 2015 to become the first club ever to win the fifth tier of English football on three occasions.

• Barnet may not be London's most high-profile club, but some famous names have been associated with the Bees over the years. Legendary England marksman Jimmy Greaves played for Barnet at the end of his career in the late 1970s, while former Dutch international Edgar Davids was player/manager at the club from 2012 to 2014.

• On 22nd April 2017 Bees striker John Akinde became the club's all-time leading league goalscorer when he netted in a 2-0 win at Hartlepool. He ended the season one short of a half-century for Barnet.

• Defender Warren Hackett played in a club record six internationals for St Lucia while at Barnet between 1999 and 2001.

HONOURS
Conference champions *1991, 2005, 2015*
FA Amateur Cup *1946*

BARNSLEY

Year founded: 1887
Ground: Oakwell (23,009)
Previous name: Barnsley St Peter's
Nickname: The Tykes
Biggest win: 9-0 v Loughborough United (1899)
Heaviest defeat: 0-9 v Notts County (1927)

Founded as the church team Barnsley St Peter's in 1887 by the Rev. Tiverton Preedy, the club changed to their present name a year after joining the Football League in 1898.

• The Tykes have spent more seasons (75) in the second tier of English football than any other club and had to wait until 1997 before they had their first taste of life in the top flight. Unfortunately for their fans, however, it lasted just one season.

• The Yorkshiremen's finest hour came in 1912 when they won the FA Cup, beating West Bromwich Albion 1-0 in a replay. The club were nicknamed 'Battling Barnsley' that season as they played a record 12 games during their cup run, including six 0-0 draws, before finally getting their hands on the trophy. Barnsley came close to repeating this feat in 2008, but were beaten in the semi-finals by fellow Championship side Cardiff City after they had sensationally knocked out Liverpool and cup holders Chelsea.

• The youngest player to appear in the Football League is Barnsley striker Reuben Noble-Lazarus, who was 15 years and 45 days old when he faced Ipswich Town in September 2008. Afterwards, Barnsley boss Simon Davey joked Noble-Lazarus would be rewarded with a pizza as he was too young to be paid!

• Stalwart defender Barry Murphy made a club record 569 league appearances for the Tykes between 1962 and 1978.

• Barnsley received a club record £5 million when centre-back Alfie Mawson moved to Swansea City in August 2016. The Tykes' record signing was made back in 1997 when Macedonian international striker Georgi Hristov joined the club from Partizan Belgrade for £1.5 million.

HONOURS
Division 3 (N) champions *1934, 1939, 1955*
FA Cup *1912*
Football League Trophy *2016*

BAYERN MUNICH

Year founded: 1900
Ground: Allianz Arena (75,000)
Nickname: The Bavarians
League titles: 27
Domestic cups: 18
European cups: 7

The biggest and most successful club in Germany, Bayern Munich were founded in 1900 by members of a Munich gymnastics club. Incredibly, when the Bundesliga was formed in 1963, Bayern's form was so poor that they were not invited to become founder members of the league. But, thanks to the emergence in the mid-1960s of legendary players like goalkeeper Sepp Maier, sweeper Franz Beckenbauer and prolific goalscorer Gerd Muller, Bayern rapidly became the dominant force in German football. The club won the Bundesliga for the first time in 1969 and now have a record 27 German championships to their name, including a record five on the trot between 2013 and 2017.

• In 1974 Bayern became the first German club to win the European Cup, defeating Atletico Madrid 4-0 in the only final to go to a replay. Skippered by the imperious Beckenbauer, the club went on to complete a hat-trick of victories in the competition – the last time a club has won Europe's top prize three times on the spin.

• In winning the Bundesliga title in 2012/13, Bayern set numerous records, including highest points total (91), most wins (29) and best goal difference (+80). They then beat Borussia Dortmund 2-1

Thomas Muller plays for Germany's most successful club

at Wembley in the first all-German Champions League final, before becoming the first ever German team to win the Treble when they beat Stuttgart 3-2 in the final of the German Cup.

• **With 336,146 registered fans at the last count, Bayern have the largest membership of any club in the world.**

TOP 10

GERMAN CUP WINNERS

1. Bayern Munich	18 wins
2. Werder Bremen	6 wins
3. Schalke	5 wins
4. Borussia Dortmund	4 wins
4. Cologne	4 wins
4. Eintracht Frankfurt	4 wins
4. Nurnberg	4 wins
8. Borussia Monchengladbach	3 wins
Hamburg	3 wins
Stuttgart	3 wins

• Gerd Muller scored a German record 365 league goals for Bayern between 1965 and 1979, including a Bundesliga record 40 in the 1971/72 season.

HONOURS

German championship *1932, 1969, 1972, 1973, 1974, 1980, 1981, 1985, 1986, 1987, 1989, 1990, 1994,1997, 1999, 2000, 2001, 2003, 2005, 2006, 2008, 2010, 2013, 2014, 2015, 2016, 2017*

German Cup *1957, 1966, 1967, 1969, 1971, 1982, 1984, 1986, 1998, 2000, 2003, 2005, 2006, 2008, 2010, 2013, 2014, 2016*

European Cup/Champions League *1974, 1975, 1976, 2001, 2013*

European Cup Winners' Cup *1967*

UEFA Cup *1996*

European Super Cup *2013*

Club World Cup *2013*

DAVID BECKHAM

Born: Leytonstone, 2nd May 1975
Position: Midfielder
Club career:
1993-2003 Manchester United 265 (62)
1995 Preston North End (loan) 5 (2)
2003-07 Real Madrid 116 (13)
2007-12 LA Galaxy 98 (18)
2009 AC Milan (loan) 18 (2)
2010 AC Milan (loan) 11 (0)
2013 Paris Saint-Germain 10 (0)
International record:
1996-2009 England 115 (17)

One of the most famous names on the planet, David Beckham's fame extends far beyond the world of football. Yet, for all the interest in his marriage to Spice Girl Victoria Beckham, his fashion sense, his eye-catching haircuts and tattoos, it shouldn't be forgotten that his celebrity status stems primarily from his remarkable ability on the ball.

• **A superb crosser of the ball and free kick expert, at his peak Beckham was probably the best right-sided midfielder in the world. He twice came close to winning the World Player of the Year award, finishing as runner-up in 1999 and 2001 while with Manchester United.**

• Beckham enjoyed huge success during a decade-long stay at Old Trafford, winning six Premiership titles, two FA Cups and, as the final leg of the Treble, the Champions League in 1999. However, his glamorous lifestyle began to irritate United boss Sir Alex Ferguson, and the deteriorating relationship between the pair led to Beckham's departure to Spanish giants Real Madrid in 2003.

• **As one of Real's 'galacticos', Beckham was part of a team which was much hyped but frequently failed to deliver. He eventually won the Spanish title with Real in 2007, shortly before making a lucrative move to Major League Soccer in the USA with LA Galaxy, with whom he twice won the MLS championship. In 2013, shortly before announcing his retirement from the game, he enjoyed a brief spell with Paris Saint-Germain, helping them to win the French league to become the first British player to win titles in four different countries.**

• One of just nine England centurions and the only Three Lions player to have scored at three different World Cups, Beckham captained his country from 2000 to 2006. After being sent off against Argentina at the 1998 World Cup he was made the scapegoat for England's elimination from the competition, but famously bounced back to score the winning goal from the penalty spot against the same opposition at the 2002 tournament in Japan and South Korea.

• **Beckham's England career appeared to be over when he was dropped from the squad by new manager Steve McClaren in 2006. However, he was recalled the following year and was rewarded with his 100th cap by McClaren's successor, his former Real**

David Beckham, the only England player to score at three World Cups

boss Fabio Capello, against France in 2008. The following year he became England's most capped outfield player, beating the old record set by the great Bobby Moore, when he won his 109th cap against Slovakia. His total of 115 caps is only surpassed by Peter Shilton and Wayne Rooney.

BELGIUM

First international: Belgium 3 France 3, 1904
Most capped player: Jan Ceulemans, 96 caps (1977-91)
Leading goalscorer: Bernard Voorhoof, 30 goals (1928-40) and Paul Van Himst, 30 goals (1960-74)
First World Cup appearance: Belgium 2 Germany 5
Biggest win: Belgium 10 San Marino 1, 2001
Heaviest defeat: England amateurs 11 Belgium 2, 1909

A rising force in the world game, Belgium are yet to win a major trophy but they came mighty close in the 1980 European Championships in Italy. After topping their group ahead of Italy, England and Spain, Belgium went straight through to the final against West Germany where they were unfortunate to go down 2-1 in a close encounter.

• Belgium's best performance at the World Cup came in 1986 when, after beating the USSR and Spain in the earlier knock-out rounds, they lost 2-0 to a Diego Maradona-inspired Argentina in the semi-finals. After losing 4-2 in the third place match to France, Belgium had to be content with fourth spot at the tournament.

• In recent years a young Belgian side featuring the likes of Manchester City pair Vincent Kompany and Kevin De Bruyne, and Chelsea midfielder Eden Hazard, has risen to the top end of the FIFA rankings. However, they have rather under-achieved at international tournaments, bowing out of both the 2014 World Cup and Euro 2016 at the quarter-final stage.

• On 10th October 2016 Belgium scored the fastest ever goal in the World Cup, when Christian Benteke netted after just 8.1 seconds in a qualifier against Gibraltar.

World Cup Record
1930 Round 1
1934 Round 1
1938 Round 1
1950 Withdrew
1954 Round 1
1958 Did not qualify
1962 Did not qualify
1966 Did not qualify
1970 Round 1
1974 Did not qualify
1978 Did not qualify
1982 Round 2
1986 Fourth place
1990 Round 2
1994 Round 2
1998 Round 1
2002 Round 2
2006 Did not qualify
2010 Did not qualify
2014 Quarter-finals

BENFICA

Year founded: 1904
Ground: Estadio Da Luz, Lisbon (64,642)
Nickname: The Eagles
League titles: 36
Domestic cups: 29
European cups: 2

Portugal's most successful club, Benfica were founded in 1904 at a meeting of 24 football enthusiasts in south Lisbon. The club were founder members of the Portuguese league in 1933 and have since won the title a record 36 times.

• Inspired by legendary striker Eusebio, Benfica enjoyed a golden era in the 1960s when the club won eight domestic championships. In 1961 Benfica became the first team to break Real Madrid's dominance in the European Cup when they beat Barcelona 3-2 in the final. The following year, the trophy stayed in Lisbon after the Eagles sensationally beat Real 5-3 in the final in Amsterdam.

• In 1972/73 Benfica went the whole season undefeated – the first Portuguese team to achieve this feat – winning a staggering 28 and drawing just two of their 30 league matches. Along the way, Benfica set a still unbroken European record by winning 29 consecutive domestic league matches.

• In 2015/16 Benfica won the Portuguese league with a record 88 points. The following season the Eagles retained their title to move within one of FC Porto's record of five consecutive league triumphs.

• Benfica hold the record for the biggest ever aggregate win in the European Cup/ Champions League with an astonishing 18-0 thrashing of Luxembourg minnows Stade Dudelange in 1965.

HONOURS
Portuguese championship *1936, 1937, 1938, 1942, 1943, 1945, 1950, 1955, 1957,1960, 1961, 1963, 1964, 1965, 1967, 1968, 1969,1971, 1972, 1973, 1975,1976, 1977, 1981, 1983, 1984, 1987, 1989, 1991, 1994, 2005, 2010, 2014, 2015, 2016, 2017*
Portuguese Cup *1930, 1931, 1935, 1940, 1943, 1944, 1949, 1951, 952, 1953, 1955, 1957,1959, 1962, 1964, 1969, 1970, 1972, 1980,1981,1983, 1985, 1986, 1987, 1993, 1996, 2004, 2014, 2017*
European Cup *1961, 1962*

CHRISTIAN BENTEKE

Born: Kinshasa, DR Congo, 3rd December 1990
Position: Striker
Club career:
2007-09 Genk 10 (1)
2009-11 Standard Liege 18 (3)
2009-10 Kortrijk (loan) 34 (15)
2010-11 Mechelen (loan) 18 (6)
2011-12 Genk 37 (19)
2012-15 Aston Villa 88 (42)
2015-16 Liverpool 29 (9)
2016- Crystal Palace 36 (15)
International record:
2010- Belgium 32 (12)

In October 2016 Christian Benteke scored the fastest ever goal in World Cup history when he was on target for

Belgium in a qualifier against Gibraltar after just 8.1 seconds. The beefy Crystal Palace striker went on to score twice more in a 6-0 win to claim his first hat-trick for his country.

• **Benteke became Palace's record signing when he joined the south London club for £27 million (possibly rising to £32 million) from Liverpool in August 2016. He enjoyed a good first season at Selhurst Park, contributing 15 Premier League goals, including two in a surprise 2-1 win at his old Anfield stamping ground. However, he also committed more fouls, 81, than any other player in the league.**

• His best campaign, though, came in 2012/13, when his 19 league goals for Aston Villa set a record for the club in the Premier League era. Two years later he became the most expensive player ever to leave Villa Park when he joined Liverpool for £32.5 million.

• **Born in DR Congo, Benteke fled to Belgium as a child with his family to escape the dictatorial regime of President Mobutu. He played for a number of Belgian clubs, including Genk and Standard Liege, before joining Villa for £7 million from Genk in August 2012.**

Christian Benteke, Crystal Palace's record signing

GEORGE BEST

Born: Belfast, 22nd May 1946
Died: 25th November 2005
Position: Winger
Club career:
1963-74 Manchester United 361 (138)
1975 Stockport County 3 (2)
1975-76 Cork Celtic 3 (0)
1976-77 Fulham 33 (7)
1977-78 Los Angeles Aztecs 55 (27)
1978-79 Fort Lauderdale 26 (6)
1979-80 Hibernian 22 (3)
1980-81 San Jose Earthquakes 56 (28)
1983 Bournemouth 4 (0)
International record:
1964-78 Northern Ireland 37 (9)

Possibly the greatest natural talent in the history of the British game, George Best was a football genius who thrilled fans everywhere with his dazzling dribbling skills, superb ball control and goalscoring ability.

• **Best left his native Northern Ireland as a youngster to play for Manchester United, making his debut at Old Trafford in 1963 when aged just 17. His most memorable achievements were all packed into the next five years as he helped fire United to two league titles in 1965 and 1967, and to glory in the European Cup in 1968, Best scoring the vital second goal against Benfica at Wembley. In 1968 he was also named Footballer of the Year and European Footballer of the Year.**

• Dubbed 'The Fifth Beatle' for his long hair and good looks, Best was arguably the first footballer to become famous outside the game. He cashed in on his celebrity status by opening a chain of boutiques, appearing in a number of TV ads and dating a seemingly never-ending series of Miss World winners.

• **In 1970 Best scored six goals to set a still-unbeaten United record as the Red Devils thrashed Northampton 8-2 in an FA Cup fifth-round tie at the Cobblers' old County Ground. "I was so embarrassed that I played the last 20 minutes at left-back," he said years later.**

• There appeared to be no limit to what he might achieve, but Best's career nosedived in the 1970s as his hard-drinking, glamorous lifestyle inevitably took its toll. Sacked by Manchester United for repeatedly missing training sessions, Best played for a succession of lesser clubs in Britain and the USA, only occasionally showing flashes of his old brilliance. He eventually ended his playing career in the low-key environment of Dean Court, making four appearances for third-tier Bournemouth in 1983.

• **Easily the finest player ever to represent Northern Ireland, Best never appeared in the final stages of the World Cup or European Championships. Yet he remains idolised in his home country, his standing summed up by the popular Belfast saying: "Maradona good, Pelé better, George Best".**

• After a long battle with alcoholism, Best died in November 2005. His passing was marked by a minute's applause at grounds up and down the country – the first British player to receive this continental-style tribute.

BIRMINGHAM CITY

Year founded: 1875
Ground: St Andrew's (30,016)
Previous name: Small Heath Alliance, Small Heath, Birmingham
Nickname: The Blues
Biggest win: 12-0 v Nottingham Forest (1899), Walsall Town Swifts (1892) and Doncaster Rovers (1903)
Heaviest defeat: 1-9 v Blackburn Rovers (1895) and Sheffield Wednesday (1930)

Founded in 1875 as Small Heath Alliance, the club were founder members and the first champions of the Second Division in 1892. Unfortunately, Small Heath were undone at the 'test match' stage (a 19th-century version of the play-offs) and failed to gain promotion to the top flight.

• The club had to wait until 2011 for the greatest day in their history, when the Blues beat hot favourites Arsenal 2-1 in the League Cup final at Wembley, on-loan striker Obafemi Martins grabbing the winner in the final minutes to spark ecstatic celebrations among Birmingham's long-suffering fans. City had previously won the competition back in 1963 after getting the better of arch rivals Aston Villa over a two-legged final, although that achievement was hardly comparable as half the top-flight clubs hadn't even bothered to enter.

• However, on the final day of the 2010/11 season Birmingham were relegated from the Premier League. It was the 12th time in their history that the Blues had fallen through the top-flight trapdoor, a record of misery unmatched by any other club. More positively, Birmingham share the distinction with Leicester of being promoted to the top tier a record 12 times.

• Stalwart defender Frank Womack made a club record 491 league appearances for the Blues between 1908 and 1928. Incredibly, Womack played a total of 510 league games without once getting on the scoresheet – a Football League record for an outfield player.

Birmingham City, the first English club to play in Europe

• On 15th May 1955 Birmingham became the first English club to compete in Europe when they drew 0-0 away to Inter Milan in the inaugural competition of the Fairs Cup. Five years later in the same tournament, Brum became the first British club to reach a European final but were beaten 4-1 on aggregate by Barcelona.

• England international Joe Bradford scored a club record 249 league goals for the Blues between 1920 and 1935.

• In February 1979 Birmingham became the first British club to sell a player for £1 million when striker Trevor Francis left St Andrew's for Nottingham Forest. Sadly, it turned out not to be the greatest of deals for City as they were relegated from the top flight at the end of the season.

HONOURS
Division 2 champions *1893, 1921, 1948, 1955*
Second Division champions *1995*
League Cup *1963, 2011*
Football League Trophy *1991, 1995*

BLACKBURN ROVERS

Year founded: 1875
Ground: Ewood Park (31,367)
Nickname: Rovers
Biggest win: 11-0 v Rossendale United (1884)
Heaviest defeat: 0-8 v Arsenal (1933)

Founded in 1875 by a group of wealthy local residents and ex-public school boys, Blackburn Rovers joined the Football League as founder members in 1888. Two years later the club moved to a permanent home at Ewood Park, where they have remained ever since.

• Blackburn were a force to be reckoned with from the start, winning the FA Cup five times in the 1880s and 1890s. Of all league clubs Rovers were the first to win the trophy, beating Scottish side Queen's Park 2-1 in the final at Kennington Oval in 1884. The Lancashire side went on to win the cup in the two following years as well, remaining undefeated in a record 24 consecutive games in the competition between 1884 and 1886.

• Rovers won the cup again in 1890, 1891 and 1928 to make a total of six triumphs in the competition. In the first of these victories they thrashed Sheffield Wednesday 6-1 in the final, with left winger William Townley scoring three times to become the first player to hit a hat-trick in the final.

• The club have won the league title three times: in 1912, 1914 and, most memorably, in 1995 when, funded by the millions of local steel magnate Jack Walker and powered by the deadly 'SAS' strikeforce of Alan Shearer and Chris Sutton, Rovers pipped reigning champions Manchester United to the Premiership title.

• However, by 2017 Blackburn had dropped into League One to become the first Premier League winners to fall into the third tier.

• Nineteenth-century striker Jack Southworth scored a record 13 hat-tricks for Rovers, including a seasonal best of five in 1890/91.

• Derek Fazackerley made the most appearances for Blackburn, turning out in 596 games between 1970 and 1986. The club's all-time leading scorer is Simon

Garner, with 168 league goals between 1978 and 1992, although Alan Shearer's incredible record of 122 goals in just 138 games for the club is arguably more impressive.

HONOURS
Division 1 champions 1912, 1914
Premier League champions 1995
Division 2 champions 1975
FA Cup 1884, 1885, 1886, 1890, 1891, 1928
League Cup 2002

BLACKPOOL

Year founded: 1887
Ground: Bloomfield Road (17,338)
Nickname: The Seasiders
Biggest win: 10-0 v Lanerossi Vincenza (1972)
Heaviest defeat: 1-10 v Small Heath (1901)

Founded in 1887 by old boys of St John's School, Blackpool joined the Second Division of the Football League in 1896. The club merged with South Shore in 1899, the same year in which Blackpool lost their league status for a single season.

• **Blackpool's heyday was in the late 1940s and early 1950s when the club reached three FA Cup finals in five years. The Seasiders lost in the finals of 1948 and 1951 but lifted the cup in 1953 after defeating Lancashire rivals Bolton 4-3 in one of the most exciting Wembley matches ever. Although centre-forward Stan Mortensen scored a hat-trick, the match was dubbed the 'Matthews Final' after veteran winger Stanley Matthews, who finally won a winner's medal at the grand old age of 38.**

• An apprentice at the time of the 'Matthews Final', long-serving right-back Jimmy Armfield holds the record for league appearances for Blackpool, with 569 between 1952 and 1971. Now a match summariser for BBC Radio 5 Live, Armfield is also Blackpool's most capped player, having played for England 43 times. In 2011 a 9ft-high statue of the Seasiders legend was unveiled outside Bloomfield Road.

• **The club's record scorer is Jimmy Hampson, who hit 248 league goals between 1927 and 1938, including a season best 45 in the 1929/30 Second Division championship-winning campaign.**

• Blackpool were the first club to gain promotion from three different divisions via the play-offs. In total the Seasiders have played in a record seven play-off finals, most recently beating Exeter City 2-1 in the 2017 League Two decider at Wembley, and with five wins they have the best record of any club in the finals. In addition, between 2001 and 2012 the Seasiders won a record 10 consecutive play-off matches.

HONOURS
Division 2 champions 1930
FA Cup 1953
Football League Trophy 2002, 2004

BOLTON WANDERERS

Year founded: 1874
Ground: The Macron Stadium (28,723)
Previous name: Christ Church
Nickname: The Trotters
Biggest win: 13-0 v Sheffield United (1890)
Heaviest defeat: 1-9 v Preston North End (1887)

The club was founded in 1874 as Christ Church, but three years later broke away from the church after a disagreement with the vicar and adopted their present name (the 'Wanderers' part stemmed from the fact that the club had no permanent home until moving to their former stadium, Burnden Park, in 1895).

• **Bolton were founder members of the Football League in 1888, finishing fifth at the end of the campaign. The Trotters have since gone on to play more seasons in the top flight without ever winning the title, 73, than any other club. In the 2017/18 season they will play their league football in the Championship having earned promotion from League One during the previous campaign.**

• The club, though, have had better luck in the FA Cup. After defeats in the final in 1894 and 1904, Bolton won the cup for the first time in 1923 after beating West Ham 2-0 in the first Wembley final. In the same match, Bolton centre-forward David Jack enjoyed the distinction of becoming the first player to score a goal at the new stadium. The Trotters went on to win the competition again in 1926 and 1929.

• **In 1953 Bolton became the first team to score three goals in the FA Cup final yet finish as losers, going down 4-3 to a Stanley Matthews-inspired Blackpool. In 1958 Bolton won the cup for a fourth time, beating Manchester United 2-0 in the final at Wembley.**

• In 1993, while they were in the third tier, Bolton became the last club from outside the top two flights to knock out the reigning FA Cup holders when they beat Liverpool 2-0 at Anfield in a third-round replay.

• **Bolton's top scorer is legendary centre-forward Nat Lofthouse, who notched 285 goals in all competitions between 1946 and 1960. The Trotters' appearance record is held by another England international of the same era, goalkeeper Eddie Hopkinson, who turned out 578 times for the club between 1952 and 1970.**

• Bolton enjoyed their best European run in 2008, reaching the last 16 of the UEFA Cup before losing 2-1 on aggregate to Sporting Lisbon.

HONOURS
Division 2 champions 1909, 1978
First Division champions 1997
Division 3 champions 1973
FA Cup 1923, 1926, 1929, 1958
Football League Trophy 1989

BOOTS

The first record of a pair of football boots goes back to 1526 when Henry VIII, then aged 35, ordered "45 velvet pairs and one leather pair for football" from the Great Wardrobe. Whether he actually donned the boots for a royal kick-around in Hampton Court or Windsor Castle is not known.

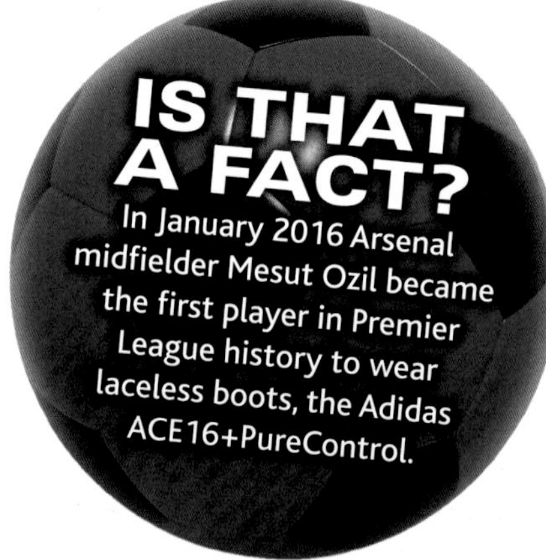

Watford's Troy Deeney took a sudden dislike to his garish orange boots

• Early leather boots were very different to the synthetic ones worn by modern players, having hard toe-caps and protection around the ankles. Studs were originally prohibited, but were sanctioned after a change in the rules in 1891. Lighter boots without ankle protection were first worn in South America, but did not become the norm in Britain until the 1950s, following the example of England international Stanley Matthews who had a lightweight pair of boots made for him by a Yorkshire company.

• Herbert Chapman, later Arsenal's manager, is believed to be the first player to wear coloured boots, sporting a yellow pair in the 1900s. White boots first became fashionable in the 1970s when they were worn by the likes of Alan Ball (Everton), Terry Cooper (Leeds) and Alan Hinton (Derby County). In 1996, Liverpool's John Barnes was the first player to wear white boots in an FA Cup final, but failed to dazzle in his side's 1-0 defeat to Manchester United.

• At the 2014 World Cup, Cesc Fabregas (Spain), Yaya Toure (Ivory Coast) and Mario Balotelli (Italy) were among the first group of players to wear mismatched boots, Puma's new 'Tricks' model featuring one pink boot and one blue one.

• Cristiano Ronaldo's incredible £1 billion lifetime sponsorship deal with boot manufacturers Nike is easily the biggest in the history of the game.

BOURNEMOUTH

Year founded: 1899
Ground: Dean Court (11,464)
Previous name: Boscombe, Bournemouth and Boscombe Athletic
Nickname: The Cherries
Biggest win: 11-0 v Margate (1970)
Heaviest defeat: 0-9 v Lincoln City (1982)

The Cherries were founded as Boscombe FC in 1899, having their origins in the Boscombe St John's club, which was formed in 1890. The club's name changed to Bournemouth and Boscombe FC in 1923 and then to AFC Bournemouth in 1971, when the team's colours were altered to red-and-black stripes in imitation of AC Milan.

• Any similarity to the Italian giants was not obvious, though, until the 2014/15 season when the Cherries won promotion to the top flight for the first time in their history, clinching the Championship title in some style with a 3-0 victory at Charlton on the final day of the campaign.

• The Cherries' attack-minded team, superbly managed by young boss Eddie Howe, set a new record for the second tier by scoring 50 goals on their travels. They also set a new club record for goals scored in a season, with 115 in total in all competitions.

• Two years later in 2016/17 Bournemouth finished ninth in the Premier League, the club's highest ever league placing. During the course of the campaign 11 English players each made at least 20 Premier League appearances for the Cherries – the first time that many home-based players had been used so regularly by a club since Aston Villa in 2000/01.

• French defender Sylvain Distin, who played 12 times for Bournemouth during the 2015/16 season, has made more Premier League appearances, 469, than any other overseas outfield player or any other uncapped player. He also holds the record for the most headed clearances in Premier League history with 1,734.

• The club recorded their biggest ever win in the FA Cup, smashing fellow seasiders Margate 11-0 at Dean Court in 1970. Cherries striker Ted MacDougall scored nine of the goals, an all-time record for an individual player in the competition. In the same season the Scot scored a club record 42 league goals.

• Bournemouth enjoyed their best ever FA Cup run as a third-tier side in 1957, knocking out Tottenham in the fifth round before losing 2-1 at home to mighty Manchester United in the quarter-finals in front of a club record attendance of 28,799.

• The club's record scorer is Ron Eyre (202 goals between 1924 and 1933), while striker Steve Fletcher pulled on the Cherries' jersey an amazing 628 times in two spells at Dean Court between 1992 and 2013.

• In June 2017 Bournemouth splashed out a club record £20 million on Chelsea defender Nathan Ake, while a year earlier the Cherries received a record £12 million when winger Matt Ritchie joined Newcastle.

HONOURS
Championship champions 2015
Division 3 champions 1987
Football League Trophy 1984

BRADFORD CITY

Year founded: 1903
Ground: Valley Parade (25,136)
Nickname: The Bantams
Biggest win: 11-1 v Rotherham United (1928)
Heaviest defeat: 1-9 v Colchester United (1961)

Bradford City were founded in 1903 when a local rugby league side, Manningham FC, decided to switch codes. The club was elected to Division Two in the same year before they had played a single match – a swift ascent into the Football League which is only matched by Chelsea.

• **City's finest hour was in 1911 when they won the FA Cup for the only time in the club's history, beating Newcastle 1-0 in a replayed final at Old Trafford. There were more celebrations in Bradford in 1929 when City won the Third Division (North), scoring 128 goals in the process – a record for the third tier.**

• Beaten in the League One play-off final in 2017, Bradford City became the first club from the fourth tier of English football to reach a major final at Wembley in 2013, losing 5-0 to Swansea City in the League Cup. Two years later the Bantams pulled off possibly the biggest FA Cup shock ever, coming back from 2-0 down to beat Chelsea 4-2 in the fourth round at Stamford Bridge.

• **Sadly, City will forever be associated with the fire that broke out in the club's main stand on 11th May 1985 and killed 56 supporters. The official inquiry into the tragedy found that the inferno had probably been caused by a discarded cigarette butt which set fire to litter under the stand. As a permanent memorial to those who died, Bradford added black trimming to their shirt collars and sleeves.**

• Saint Kitts and Nevis international defender Ces Podd made a record 502 league appearances for the Bantams between 1970 and 1984.

HONOURS
Division 2 champions 1908
Division 3 (N) champions 1929
Division 3 champions 1985
FA Cup 1911

Brazil's players are a very chatty bunch

BRAZIL

First international: Argentina 3 Brazil 0, 1914
Most capped player: Cafu, 142 caps (1990-2006)
Leading goalscorer: Pelé, 77 goals (1957-71)
First World Cup appearance: Brazil 1 Yugoslavia 2, 1930
Biggest win: Brazil 14 Nicaragua 0, 1975
Heaviest defeat: Brazil 1 Germany 7, 2014

The most successful country in the history of international football, Brazil are renowned for an exciting, flamboyant style of play which delights both their legions of drum-beating fans and neutrals alike.

• **Brazil are the only country to have won the World Cup five times. The South Americans first lifted the trophy in 1958 (beating hosts Sweden 5-2 in the final) and retained the prize four years later in Chile. In 1970, a great Brazilian side featuring legends such as Pelé, Jairzinho, Gerson and Rivelino thrashed Italy 4-1 to win the Jules Rimet trophy for a third time. Further triumphs followed in 1994 (3-2 on penalties against Italy after a dour 0-0 draw) and in 2002 (after beating Germany 2-0 in the final).**

• Brazil are the only country to have appeared at every World Cup (a total of 20) since the tournament began in 1930 and were the first country to qualify for the 2018 finals in Russia. The South Americans have also recorded the most wins (70) at the finals. Less impressively, Brazil suffered the heaviest ever defeat by a host nation when they were trounced 7-1 by Germany in the semi-finals of the 2014 tournament.

• **Between February 1993 and January 1996 Brazil set a new world record when they were undefeated for 35 consecutive internationals.**

• With eight wins to their name, Brazil are the third most successful side in the history of the Copa America (behind Uruguay and Argentina, who have won the trophy 15 and 14 times respectively). However, the South Americans flopped at the most recent tournament in 2016, failing to reach the knock-out stages after a shock 1-0 defeat to Peru.

• **Brazil have the best record of any nation in the Confederations Cup, winning the trophy four times – most recently in 2013, when they beat Spain 3-0 in the final in Rio de Janeiro.**

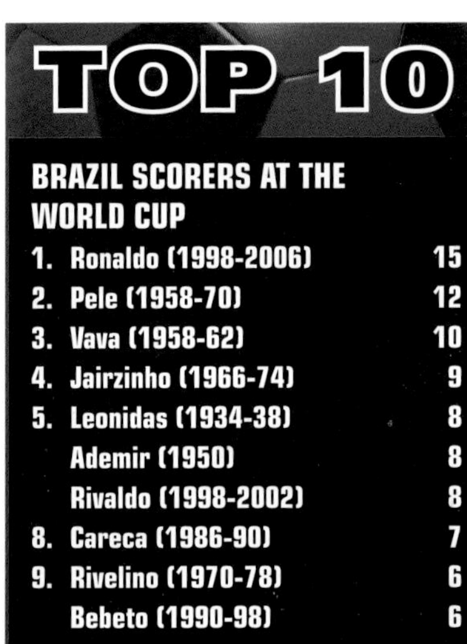

TOP 10

BRAZIL SCORERS AT THE WORLD CUP

1.	Ronaldo (1998-2006)	15
2.	Pele (1958-70)	12
3.	Vava (1958-62)	10
4.	Jairzinho (1966-74)	9
5.	Leonidas (1934-38)	8
	Ademir (1950)	8
	Rivaldo (1998-2002)	8
8.	Careca (1986-90)	7
9.	Rivelino (1970-78)	6
	Bebeto (1990-98)	6

HONOURS
World Cup winners *1958, 1962, 1970, 1994, 2002*
Copa America winners *1919, 1922, 1949, 1989, 1997, 1999, 2004, 2007*
Confederations Cup winners *1997, 2005, 2009, 2013*
World Cup Record
1930 Round 1
1934 Round 1
1938 Semi-finals
1950 Runners-up
1954 Quarter-finals
1958 Winners
1962 Winners
1966 Round 1
1970 Winners
1974 Fourth place
1978 Third place
1982 Round 2
1986 Quarter-finals
1990 Round 2
1994 Winners
1998 Runners-up
2002 Winners
2006 Quarter-finals
2010 Quarter-finals
2014 Fourth place

BRENTFORD

Year founded: 1889
Ground: Griffin Park (12,573)
Nickname: The Bees
Biggest win: 9-0 v Wrexham (1963)
Heaviest defeat: 0-7 v Swansea Town (1926), v Walsall (1957) and v Peterborough (2007)

Brentford were founded in 1889 by members of a local rowing club and, after playing at a number of different venues, the club settled at Griffin Park in 1904.

• **The club enjoyed its heyday in the decade before the Second World War. In 1929/30 Brentford won all 21 of their home games in the Third Division (South) to set a record which remains to this day. Promoted to the First Division in 1935, the Bees finished in the top six in the next three seasons before being relegated in the first post-war campaign. After plunging into the Fourth Division in 1962, Brentford became the first team to have played all the other 91 clubs in the Football League.**

• In winning promotion to the Championship in 2014 Brentford racked up a club record 94 points. The Bees shared out the goals during the campaign, too, with a club record 20 different players on target in the league.

• **The Bees paid out a club record £2.5 million when they signed Norwich midfielder Sergi Canos in January 2017. In the same month the west Londoners received a record £9 million when striker Scott Hogan joined Aston Villa.**

• In August 2014 Brentford were involved in the joint-highest scoring match in the League Cup, drawing 6-6 at Dagenham & Redbridge, before emerging victorious in the subsequent penalty shoot-out.

• **Defender Ken Coote played in a club record 514 league games for the Bees between 1949 and 1964, while his team-mate Jim Towers scored a record 153 league goals.**

HONOURS
Division 2 champions *1935*
Division 3 (S) champions *1933*
Division 4 champions *1963*
Third Division champions *1999*
League Two champions *2009*

BRIGHTON AND HOVE ALBION

Year founded: 1900
Ground: AMEX Stadium (30,750)
Previous name: Brighton and Hove Rangers
Nickname: The Seagulls
Biggest win: 10-1 v Wisbech (1965)
Heaviest defeat: 0-9 v Middlesbrough (1958)

Founded originally as Brighton and Hove Rangers in 1900, the club changed to its present name the following year. In 1920 Brighton joined Division Three as founder members, but had to wait another 38 years before gaining promotion to a higher level.

• **Brighton enjoyed the greatest achievement in their history in 2017 when, under manager Chris Hughton, they were promoted to the Premier League for the first time, finishing just one point**

The Seagulls are flying high these days

behind Championship title winners Newcastle. It was just reward for the Seagulls, who had been extremely unlucky to miss out on automatic promotion the previous season after accumulating 89 points – only Sunderland, with 90 points in 1998, have picked up more points in the second tier and not gone up.

• The club reached the final of the FA Cup for the only time in their history in 1983, holding favourites Manchester United to a 2-2 draw at Wembley. The Seagulls were unable to repeat their heroics in the replay, however, and crashed to a 4-0 defeat. In the same year Brighton were relegated from the old First Division, ending a four-season stint in the top flight.

• A decade earlier, the Seagulls were briefly managed by the legendary Brian Clough. His time in charge of the club, though, was not a successful one and included an 8-2 thrashing by Bristol Rovers – the worst home defeat in Brighton's history.

• Brighton's record scorer is 1920s striker Tommy Cook, with 114 league goals. Cult hero Peter Ward, though, enjoyed the most prolific season in front of goal for the club, notching 32 times as the Seagulls gained promotion from the old Third Division in 1976/77. Ernie 'Tug' Wilson made the most appearances for the south coast outfit, with 509 between 1922 and 1936.

• Argentinian striker Leonardo Ulloa boosted Brighton's coffers by a club record £8 million when he joined Leicester City in 2014. The Seagulls' most expensive signing is Colombia winger Jose Izquierdo, who cost £13.5 million from Belgian giants Bruges in August 2017.

• Brighton are the only club to have won the Charity Shield without ever winning the league title or FA Cup. In 1910 the Seagulls, then reigning Southern League champions, lifted the shield after beating title winners Aston Villa 1-0 at Stamford Bridge.

• Brighton's record win came in 1965 when they thrashed Wisbech Town 10-1 in the FA Cup first round.

HONOURS
Division 3 (S) champions *1958*
Second Division champions *2002*
League One champions *2011*
Division 4 champions *1965*
Third Division champions *2001*

BRISTOL CITY

Year founded: 1894
Ground: Ashton Gate (27,600)
Previous name: Bristol South End
Nickname: The Robins
Biggest win: 11-0 v Chichester City (1960)
Heaviest defeat: 0-9 v Coventry City (1934)

Founded as Bristol South End in 1894, the club took its present name when it turned professional three years later. In 1900 City merged with Bedminster, whose ground at Ashton Gate became the club's permanent home in 1904.

• The Robins enjoyed a golden decade in the 1900s, winning promotion to the top flight for the first time in 1906 after a campaign in which they won a joint-record 14 consecutive games. The following season City finished second, and in 1909 they reached the FA Cup final for the first and only time in their history, losing 1-0 to Manchester United at Crystal Palace.

• Since then the followers of Bristol's biggest club have had to endure more downs than ups. The Robins returned to the top flight after a 65-year absence in 1976, but financial difficulties led to three consecutive relegations in the early 1980s (City being the first club ever to suffer this awful fate).

• City's strikers were on fire in 1962/63 as the Robins scored 100 goals in Division Three. Sadly for their fans, however, City could only finish 14th in the league – the lowest place ever by a club hitting three figures.

• With 315 goals in 597 league games for the club between 1951 and 1966, England international striker John Atyeo is both the Robins' top scorer and record appearance maker. In the history of league football only Dixie Dean (Everton) and George Camsell (Middlesbrough) scored more goals for the same club.

• After a 2-0 victory over Walsall in the final in 2015, City became the first club to win the Football League Trophy three times.

• In June 2017 the Robins broke their transfer record to bring Senegal striker Famara Diedhiou to Ashton Gate from Angers for £5.3 million. A year earlier they sold Ivory Coast international striker Jonathan Kodjia to Aston Villa for a club record £11 million.

HONOURS
League One champions *2015*
Division 2 champions *1906*
Division 3 (S) champions *1923, 1927, 1955*
Football League Trophy *1986, 2003, 2015*
Welsh Cup *1934*

BRISTOL ROVERS

Year founded: 1893
Ground: Memorial Stadium (12,296)
Previous name: Black Arabs, Eastville Rovers, Bristol Eastville Rovers
Nickname: The Pirates
Biggest win: 15-1 v Weymouth (1900)
Heaviest defeat: 0-12 v Luton Town (1936)

Bristol Rovers can trace their history back to 1883 when the Black Arabs club was founded at the Eastville Restaurant in Bristol. The club was renamed Eastville Rovers the following year in an attempt to attract more support from the local area, later adding 'Bristol' to their name before finally settling on plain old 'Bristol Rovers' in 1898.

• Rovers have lived up to their name by playing at no fewer than nine different grounds. Having spent much of their history at Eastville Stadium, they have been based at the Memorial Stadium since 1996.

• The only Rovers player to have appeared for England while with the Pirates, Geoff Bradford, is the club's record scorer, netting 242 times in the league between 1949 and 1964. The club's record appearance maker is central defender Stuart Taylor, who turned out in 546 league games between 1966 and 1980.

• Rovers' Ronnie Dix is the youngest player ever to score in the Football League, notching against Norwich in 1928 when he was aged just 15 years and 180 days.

• Rovers have made it through to the FA Cup quarter-finals on just three occasions, most recently losing 5-1 at home to West Bromwich Albion in 2008.

HONOURS
Division 3 (S) champions *1953*
Division 3 champions *1990*

Kevin De Bruyne on the attack

KEVIN DE BRUYNE

Born: Drongen, Belgium, 28th June 1991
Position: Midfielder
Club career:
2008-12 Genk 84 (14)
2012-14 Chelsea 3 (0)
2012 Genk (loan) 13 (2)
2012-13 Werder Bremen (loan) 33 (10)
2014-15 Wolfsburg 51 (13)
2015- Manchester City 61 (13)
International record:
2010- Belgium 49 (12)

When Kevin De Bruyne moved from Wolfsburg to Manchester City for a club record £55 million in August 2015, he became the second most expensive player in British football history at the time.

• An attacking midfielder who passes the ball well and loves to strike from distance, De Bruyne enjoyed a good first season at the Etihad, although injury meant he missed out on City's League Cup final victory against Liverpool. The following campaign in 2016/17 saw him top the Premier League assists chart with 18 – a record for a City player.

• Before his move to Manchester, De Bruyne contributed a Bundesliga record 21 assists as Wolfsburg finished second in the league in 2014/15, and scored in his side's 3-1 German Cup final victory over Borussia Dortmund. After an outstanding campaign, De Bruyne was named German Footballer of the Year in 2015, the first Belgian to win this award.

• First capped in a friendly against Finland in 2010, De Bruyne was part of the Belgian team that reached the quarter-finals of both the 2014 World Cup and Euro 2016.

GIANLUIGI BUFFON

Born: Carrara, Italy, 28th January 1978
Position: Goalkeeper
Club career:
1995-2001 Parma 168
2001- Juventus 488
International record:
1997- Italy 169

Legendary goalkeeper Gianluigi Buffon is the highest-capped European ever, having played an incredible 169 times for Italy. He is also one of just three players to have featured in five squads at the World Cup finals.

• By far the most memorable of those five occasions was in 2006 when Buffon won a World Cup winners' medal with the Azzurri after Italy beat France in a penalty shoot-out in Berlin. Buffon's outstanding form – he kept five clean sheets at the tournament in seven matches – earned him the

Gianluigi Buffon, the most capped European player ever

Yashin Award for the best goalkeeper in the competition. At the end of the year he was runner-up to Italian team-mate Fabio Cannavaro in the European Footballer of the Year poll, the first goalkeeper to be ranked so highly since fellow Italian Dino Zoff also came second in 1973.

• Buffon became the world's most expensive goalkeeper at the time when he left Parma, with whom he won the UEFA Cup in 1999, for Juventus for £32.6 million in 2001. Since then he has won a joint-record eight Serie A titles with the Italian giants, including a record six on the trot between 2012 and 2017. However, he has never won Europe's biggest club prize, being one of just three players to have lost all three Champions League finals he has played in.

• Buffon holds the record for the most clean sheets in Serie A history with an impressive 282 in total. In 2016 he went an extraordinary 973 minutes without conceding a single goal to set another Italian top-flight record, and he is also second on the list of all-time appearances in Serie A with 619 – just 28 behind AC Milan's Paolo Maldini.

• A superb shot-stopper who commands his penalty area, Buffon has won the Serie A Goalkeeper of the Year award a record 11 times.

BURNLEY

Year founded: 1882
Ground: Turf Moor (21,800)
Nickname: The Clarets
Biggest win: 9-0 v Darwen (1892), v New Brighton (1957) and v Penrith (1984)
Heaviest defeat: 0-11 v Darwen (1885)

One of England's most famous old clubs, Burnley were founded in 1882 when the Burnley Rovers rugby team decided to switch to the round ball game. The club was a founder member of the Football League in 1888 and has since won all four divisions of the league – a feat matched only by four other clubs.

• Burnley have twice won the league championship, in 1921 and 1960. The first of these triumphs saw the Clarets go on a 30-match unbeaten run, the longest in a single season until Arsenal went through the whole of 2003/04 undefeated. In its own way, Burnley's 1960 title win was just as remarkable, as the Clarets only ever topped the league on the last day of the season after a 2-1 win at Manchester City.

• The club's only FA Cup triumph came in 1914 when they defeated Liverpool 1-0. After the final whistle Burnley's captain Tommy Boyle became the first man to receive the cup from a reigning monarch, King George V.

• On 16th April 2011 Burnley defender Graham Alexander became only the second outfield player in the history of English football to make 1,000 professional appearances when he came on as a sub in the Clarets' 2-1 win over Swansea City. Alexander is also the most successful penalty taker ever in the domestic game, with 78 goals in 86 attempts from the spot.

• Burnley broke their transfer record in August 2017, signing New Zealand international striker Chris Wood from Leeds for £15 million. The Clarets made

Burnley shocked champions Chelsea on the opening day of the 2017/18 season

their record sale in July 2017 when England international defender Michael Keane moved to Everton for £25 million.

• Club legend Jimmy McIlroy made a record 51 appearances for Northern Ireland between 1951 and 1962.

• Burnley are the last club to score a century of goals in consecutive top-flight seasons, hitting the back of the net 102 times in 1960/61 and 101 in 1961/62.

• England international goalkeeper Jerry Dawson made a club record 552 appearances for Burnley between 1907 and 1928. The club's record scorer is George Beel with 178 goals between 1923 and 1932.

• After two previous one-season stays in the Premier League, Burnley managed to avoid the drop in 2016/17 for the first time. The Clarets' star player was Tom Heaton, who made more saves (141) during the campaign than any other Premier League goalkeeper.

HONOURS
Division 1 champions *1921, 1960*
Division 2 champions *1898, 1973*
Championship champions *2016*
Division 3 champions *1982*
Division 4 champions *1992*
FA Cup *1914*

BURTON ALBION

Year founded: 1950
Ground: Pirelli Stadium (6,912)
Nickname: The Brewers
Biggest win: 12-1 v Coalville Town (1954)
Heaviest defeat: 0-10 v Barnet (1970)

Burton Albion were founded at a public meeting at the Town Hall in 1950. The town had previously supported two Football League clubs, Burton Swifts and Burton Wanderers, who merged to form Burton United in 1901 before folding nine years later.

• The Brewers gained promotion to the Football League for the first time in 2009, going up as Conference champions. In 2015, managed by former Chelsea striker Jimmy Floyd Hasselbaink, Burton gained promotion to the third tier for the first time after winning the League Two title with a club record 94 points.

Something tasty is brewing at Burton Albion

• The following season, Burton earned another promotion as Nigel Clough, returning for a second spell at the Pirelli Stadium, took the Brewers into the Championship after they finished runners-up to title winners Wigan Athletic.

• In 2006 Burton achieved the greatest result in their history when they held mighty Manchester United to a 0-0 draw at home in the third round of the FA Cup. A record visiting contingent at Old Trafford of 11,000 Brewers fans attended the replay, but they had little to cheer about as United strolled to an emphatic 5-0 victory.

• Brewers defender Damien McCrory has played in a record 169 league games for Burton since 2012. The club's leading scorer is striker Billy Kee, with 39 league goals between 2011 and 2014.

• With a capacity of just 6,912, Burton's Pirelli Stadium is the smallest ground in the top two tiers of English football.

HONOURS
League Two champions *2015*
Conference champions *2009*

BURY

Year founded: 1885
Ground: Gigg Lane (11,840)
Nickname: The Shakers
Biggest win: 12-1 v Stockton (1897)
Heaviest defeat: 0-10 v Blackburn Rovers (1887) and West Ham (1982)

The club with the shortest name in the Football League, Bury were founded in 1885 at a meeting at the Old White Horse Hotel in Bury, as successors to two other teams in the town, the Bury Unitarians and the Bury Wesleyans. Bury were founder members of the Lancashire League in 1889, joining the Football League five years later.

• Bury have won the FA Cup on two occasions. In 1900 the Shakers beat Southern League outfit Southampton 4-0 at Crystal Palace, and then three years later they thrashed Derby County 6-0 at the same venue to record the biggest ever victory in an FA Cup final.

• On 27th August 2005 Bury became the first club to score 1,000 goals in all four tiers of the Football League. The landmark was reached when Brian Barry-Murphy scored the first of the Shakers' goals in their 2-2 home draw with Wrexham in a League Two fixture.

• The following year Bury set a less happy record when they became the first club to be thrown out of the FA Cup for fielding an ineligible player – Stephen Turnbull, a loan signing from Hartlepool United.

• Dual international defender Bill Gorman made a club record 11 appearances for Northern Ireland and the Republic of Ireland. Rather bizarrely, in September 1946 he represented both countries against England within just three days.

HONOURS
Division 2 champions *1895*
Division 3 champions *1961*
Second Division champions *1997*
FA Cup *1900, 1903*

GARY CAHILL

Born: Dronfield, 19th December 1985
Position: Defender
Club career:
2004-08 Aston Villa 28 (2)
2004-05 Burnley (loan) 27 (1)
2007-08 Sheffield United (loan) 16 (2)
2008-12 Bolton Wanderers 130 (13)
2012- Chelsea 162 (13)
International record:
2010- England 55 (4)

After leading Chelsea to the Premier League title in 2016/17, Gary Cahill was named in the PFA Team of the Year for the third time in his career.

• An excellent all-round central defender who also poses a huge threat to the opposition at set-pieces, Cahill was signed by the Blues from Bolton Wanderers for a bargain £7 million in January 2012. He has since won all three domestic honours with the west Londoners, plus the Champions League (2012) and the Europa League (2013).

• Cahill started out with Aston Villa, before joining Bolton in 2008 in a £5 million deal. In 2010 he became only the second Bolton player – after striker Michael Ricketts – to be capped by England in 48 years. Then, the following season, he became the first Wanderers player for 52 years to score for England when he netted in a 3-0 win over Bulgaria in a Euro 2012 qualifier in Sofia.

• In the autumn of 2014 he was named England vice-captain and at Euro 2016 he was one of just three England players to play every minute of the four-match campaign.

CAMBRIDGE UNITED

Year founded: 1912
Ground: Abbey Stadium (8,127)
Previous name: Abbey United
Nickname: The U's
Biggest win: 7-0 v Morecambe (2016)
Heaviest defeat: 0-7 v Sunderland (2002)

Cambridge United were founded as Abbey United in 1912 before taking their current name two years after turning professional in 1949.

• The club was elected to the Football League in 1970 and rose to the second tier a decade later. However, the U's soon returned to the basement division after being relegated in 1984 (setting a then league record of 31 consecutive games without a win) and in 1985 (losing 35 matches to equal the league record).

• Midfielder Steve Spriggs played in a record 416 league games for Cambridge between 1975 and 1987. The club's all-time top scorer is John Taylor with 86 goals in two spells at the Abbey Stadium between 1988 and 2004.

• Two days after scoring a hat-trick against Leyton Orient, Steve Butler hit all five of Cambridge's goals in a 5-0 win at Exeter City in April 1994. No other U's player has scored as many goals in a single match.

HONOURS
Division 3 champions 1991
Division 4 champions 1977

CAPS

Legendary goalkeeper Peter Shilton has won more international caps than any other British player. 'Shilts' played for England 125 times between 1970 and 1990 and would have won many more caps if he had not faced stiff competition for the No. 1 shirt from his great rival Ray Clemence, who won 61 caps during the same period. In women's football, midfielder Fara Williams has won a record 165 caps for England since making her debut in 2001.

• The first international caps were awarded by England in 1886, following a proposal put forward by

Gary Cahill's slide tackling technique always gets England boss Gareth Southgate out of his seat

the founder of the Corinthians, N.L. Jackson. To this day players actually receive a handmade 'cap' to mark the achievement of playing for their country. England caps are made by a Bedworth-based company called Toye, Kenning & Spencer, who also provide regalia for the Freemasons.

• The most capped player in the history of the game is Egypt midfielder Ahmed Hassan, who played an astonishing 184 times for his country between 1995 and 2012. The women's record is held by Kristine Lilly, who made 354 appearances for the USA between 1987 and 2010.

• England captain Billy Wright was the first player in the world to win 100 caps, reaching his century in a 1-0 win against Scotland at Wembley in April 1959.

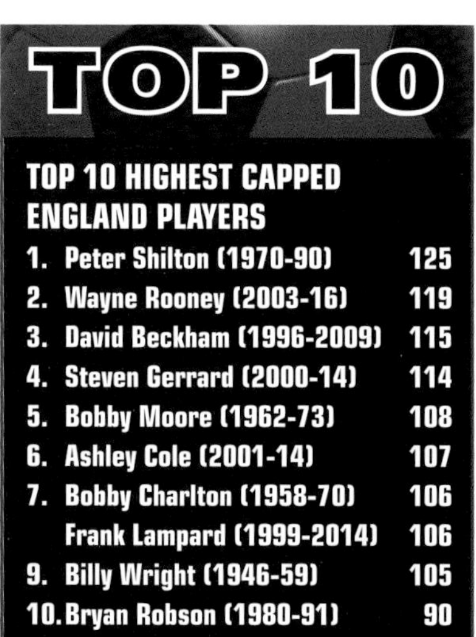

TOP 10

TOP 10 HIGHEST CAPPED ENGLAND PLAYERS

1.	Peter Shilton (1970-90)	125
2.	Wayne Rooney (2003-16)	119
3.	David Beckham (1996-2009)	115
4.	Steven Gerrard (2000-14)	114
5.	Bobby Moore (1962-73)	108
6.	Ashley Cole (2001-14)	107
7.	Bobby Charlton (1958-70)	106
	Frank Lampard (1999-2014)	106
9.	Billy Wright (1946-59)	105
10.	Bryan Robson (1980-91)	90

CARDIFF CITY

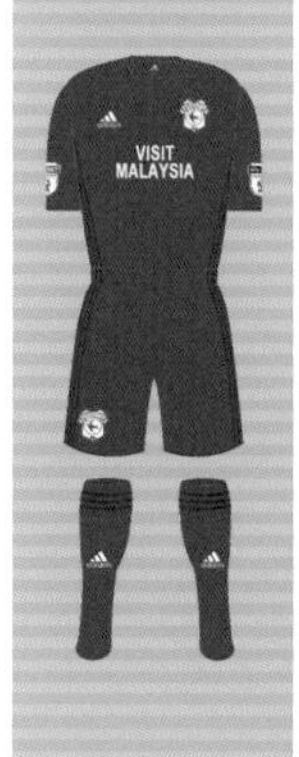

Year founded: 1899
Ground: Cardiff City Stadium (33,280)
Previous name: Riverside
Nickname: The Bluebirds
Biggest win: 16-0 v Knighton Town (1961)
Heaviest defeat: 2-11 v Sheffield United (1926)

Founded as the football branch of the Riverside Cricket Club, the club changed to its present name in 1908, three years after Cardiff was awarded city status.

• Cardiff are the only non-English club to have won the FA Cup, lifting the trophy in 1927 after a 1-0 victory over Arsenal at Wembley. Three years earlier the Bluebirds were pipped to the league title by Huddersfield on goal average, but if all-time leading scorer Len Davies had successfully converted a penalty in a 0-0 draw at Birmingham on the final day of the season the trophy would have gone to Wales.

After a brief spell in red, the Bluebirds of Cardiff are back in blue

• On 7th April 1947 a crowd of 51,621 squeezed into Cardiff's old Ninian Park Stadium for the club's match against Bristol City – an all-time record attendance for the third tier of English football.

• Cardiff have won the Welsh Cup 22 times, just one short of Wrexham's record. The Bluebirds' domination of the tournament in the 1960s and 1970s earned them regular qualification for the European Cup Winners' Cup and in 1968 they reached the semi-finals of the competition before losing 4-3 on aggregate to Hamburg.

• Cardiff's record appearance maker is midfielder Billy Hardy, who turned out 497 times for the club between 1911 and 1931.

• In the 2002/03 season Bluebirds striker Robert Earnshaw scored a club record 31 league goals. Earnshaw is the only player ever to have scored a hat-trick in the Premier League, all three divisions of the Football League, the FA Cup, the League Cup and an international match, achieving the bulk of these feats while with Cardiff between 1998 and 2004.

• Defender Alf Sherwood won a club record 39 caps for Wales while with Cardiff between 1946 and 1956.

HONOURS
Championship champions *2013*
Division 3 (S) champions *1947*
Third Division champions *1993*
FA Cup *1927*
Welsh Cup *1912, 1920, 1922, 1923, 1927, 1928, 1930, 1956, 1959, 1964, 1965, 1967, 1968, 1969, 1970, 1971, 1973, 1974, 1976, 1988, 1992, 1993*

CARLISLE UNITED

Year founded: 1903
Ground: Brunton Park (18,202)
Nickname: The Blues
Biggest win: 8-0 v Hartlepool (1928) and v Scunthorpe (1952)
Heaviest defeat: 1-11 v Hull City (1939)

Carlisle United were formed in 1903 following the merger of two local clubs, Shaddongate United and Carlisle Red Rose. The Blues joined the Third Division (North) in 1928 and were long-term residents of the bottom two divisions until 1965, when they won promotion to the second tier for the first time.

• The club's greatest moment came in 1974 when, in their one season in the top flight, they sat on top of the old First Division after the opening three games. The Cumbrians, though, were quickly knocked off their lofty perch and ended the campaign rock bottom.

• In the same season the Blues enjoyed their best ever run in the FA Cup, reaching the quarter-finals before losing 1-0 at home to eventual runners-up Fulham.

• Carlisle have appeared in the Football League Trophy final on a record six occasions, and in 1995 became the first and only team to lose an English trophy on the 'golden goal' rule when they conceded in extra-time in the final against Birmingham City.

• Scottish striker Jimmy McConnell scored a record 126 goals for Carlisle, including a seasonal best of 42 in 1928/29.

HONOURS
Division 3 champions *1965*
Third Division champions *1995*
League Two champions *2006*
Football League Trophy *1997, 2011*

PETR CECH

Born: Pilzen, Czech Republic, 20th May 1982
Position: Goalkeeper
Club career:
1999-2001 Chmel Blsany 27
2001-02 Sparta Prague 27
2002-04 Rennes 70
2004-15 Chelsea 333
2015- Arsenal 69
International record:
2002-16 Czech Republic 124

A brilliant shot-stopper who dominates his penalty area with his imposing physique, Petr Cech is the only goalkeeper and the only non-British player to have won the FA Cup five times, although he was an unused substitute for the last of these triumphs with Arsenal in 2017. He has also won the Premier League four times with Chelsea and in the first of these triumphs, in 2004/05, set a record by keeping 24 clean sheets.

Petr Cech has kept a record 190 Premier League clean sheets

• **The giant goalkeeper also has the most clean sheets, 190, in the Premier League era, with 162 of those earned with Chelsea – a record for a single club. In 2015/16 his 16 clean sheets with Arsenal earned him the Golden Glove award for a fourth time, equalling Joe Hart's record and making him the first player to win the award with two clubs.**

• Cech was a member of the Czech Republic side which reached the semi-finals of Euro 2004 before losing to eventual winners Greece. By the time he announced his retirement from international football after Euro 2016 he had taken his caps tally to a Czech record 124.

• **In October 2006 Cech suffered a depressed fracture of the skull following a challenge by Reading's Stephen Hunt. He returned to action after three months out of the game wearing a rugby-style headguard for protection, and went on to make 494 appearances in all competitions for Chelsea – a club record for an overseas player – until he joined local rivals Arsenal for around £10 million in July 2015.**

• In 2012 Cech starred in the Blues' Champions League final victory over Bayern Munich, blocking a penalty from former team-mate Arjen Robben in extra-time and then saving two more in the shoot-out. The following year he added more silverware to his collection when he helped Chelsea win the Europa League after the Blues beat Benfica in the final in Amsterdam.

CELTIC

Year founded: 1888
Ground: Celtic Park (60,411)
Nickname: The Bhoys
Biggest win: 11-0 v Dundee (1895)
Heaviest defeat: 0-8 v Motherwell (1937)

The first British team to win the European Cup, Celtic were founded by an Irish priest in 1887 with the aim of raising funds for poor children in Glasgow's East End slums. The club were founder members of the Scottish League in 1890, and have gone on to spend a record 118 seasons in the top flight.

• **Celtic have won the Scottish Cup more times than any other club, with 37 victories. The Bhoys most recently won the cup in 2017, defeating Aberdeen 2-1 in the final at Hampden Park.**

• Under legendary manager Jock Stein Celtic won the Scottish league for nine consecutive seasons in the 1960s and 1970s, with a side featuring great names like Billy McNeill, Jimmy Johnstone, Bobby Lennox and Tommy Gemmell. This extraordinary run of success equalled a world record established by MTK Budapest of Hungary in the 1920s but, painfully for Celtic fans, was later matched by bitter rivals Rangers in the 1990s.

• **The greatest ever Celtic side, managed by Stein and dubbed the 'Lisbon Lions', became the first British club to win the European Cup when they beat Inter Milan 2-1 in the Portuguese capital in 1967. Stein was central to the team's triumph, scoring an early point by sitting in Inter manager Helenio Herrera's seat and refusing to budge, and then urging his**

IS THAT A FACT?
Launched as a four-page newspaper in August 1965, *The Celtic View* is the oldest football club magazine in Britain.

A familiar sight in Scotland: another goal for Celtic!

players forward after they went a goal down to the defensive-minded Italians. Sticking to their attacking game plan, Celtic fought back with goals by Gemmell and Steve Chalmers to spark jubilant celebrations at the end among the travelling fans. Remarkably, all the 'Lisbon Lions' were born and bred within a 30-mile radius of Celtic Park.

• That 1966/67 season was the most successful in the club's history as they won every competition they entered: the Scottish league, Scottish Cup and Scottish League Cup, as well as the European Cup. To this day, no other British side has won a similar 'Quadruple'.

• The skipper of the 'Lisbon Lions' was Billy McNeill, who went on to play in a record 789 games for Celtic in all competitions between 1957 and 1975. He later managed the club, leading Celtic to the Double in their centenary season in 1987/88. The club's most capped player is goalkeeper Pat Bonner, who made 80 appearances for the Republic of Ireland between 1981 and 1996.

• Jimmy McGrory, who played for the club between 1922 and 1938, scored a staggering 397 league goals for Celtic – a British record by a player for a single club. In 1932 he hit eight goals in a 9-0 thrashing of Dunfermline, the biggest haul ever by a player in the top flight in Britain.

• In 1957 Celtic won the Scottish League Cup for the first time, demolishing Rangers 7-1 in the final at Hampden Park. The victory stands as the biggest by either side in an Old Firm match and is also a record for a major Scottish cup final. Celtic went on to enjoy more success in the League Cup, appearing in a world record 14 consecutive finals (winning six) between 1964 and 1978.

• Celtic hold the record for the longest unbeaten run in Scottish football, with 62 matches undefeated (49 wins, 13 draws) from 13th November 1915 until 21st April 1917 when Kilmarnock finally beat the men from Glasgow 2-0.

• In 2016/17 Celtic went through the entire league campaign unbeaten, only the third time this had happened in the Scottish top flight and the first time in a 38-game season. The Bhoys won the title with a record 106 points and finished an incredible 30 points clear of second-placed Aberdeen – just one point less than PSG's European record margin set a year earlier. In addition, Brendan Rodgers' 'Invincibles' were unbeaten in nine Scottish domestic cup matches as they clinched their third ever Treble.

• When Celtic signed Scott Brown from Hibs in May 2007 for £4.4 million it set a record for the most expensive transfer between two Scottish clubs which still stands today.

• During the 2013/14 season Celtic goalkeeper Fraser Forster went a Scottish league record 1,256 minutes without conceding a single goal.

HONOURS

***Division 1 champions** 1893, 1884, 1896, 1898, 1905, 1906, 1907, 1908, 1909, 1910, 1914, 1915, 1916, 1917, 1919, 1922, 1926, 1936, 1938, 1954, 1966, 1967, 1968, 1969, 1970, 1971, 1972, 1973, 1974*

***Premier Division champions** 1977, 1979, 1981, 1982, 1986, 1988, 1998*

***SPL champions** 2001, 2002, 2004, 2006, 2007, 2008, 2012, 2013*

***Premiership champions** 2014, 2015, 2016, 2017*

***Scottish Cup** 1892, 1899, 1900, 1904, 1907, 1908, 1911, 1912, 1914, 1923, 1925, 1927, 1931, 1933, 1937, 1951, 1954, 1965, 1967, 1969, 1971, 1972, 1974, 1975, 1977, 1980, 1985, 1988, 1989, 1995, 2001, 2004, 2005, 2007, 2011, 2013, 2017*

***League Cup** 1957, 1958, 1966, 1967, 1968, 1969, 1970, 1975, 1983, 1998, 2000, 2001, 2006, 2015, 2017*

***European Cup** 1967*

CHAMPIONS LEAGUE

The most prestigious competition in club football, the Champions League replaced the old European Cup in 1992. Previously a competition for domestic league champions only, runners-up from the main European nations were first admitted in 1997 and the tournament has subsequently expanded to include up to four entrants per country. In 2015 a new rule saw the Europa League winners qualify for the Champions League, with Manchester United becoming the first English club to take this route into the competition two years later.

• Spanish giants Real Madrid won the first European Cup in 1956, defeating French side Reims 4-3 in the final in Paris. Real went on to win the competition the next four years as well, thanks largely to the brilliance of their star players Alfredo Di Stefano and Ferenc Puskas. With six wins in the European Cup and another six in the Champions League, Real have won the competition a record 12 times.

• The first British club to win the European Cup was Celtic, who famously beat Inter Milan in the final in Lisbon in 1967. The following year Manchester United became the first English club to triumph, beating Benfica 4-1 at Wembley. The most successful British club in the tournament, though, are Liverpool, with five wins in 1977, 1978, 1981, 1984 and

Current holders Real Madrid have won the Champions League a record 12 times

2005, followed by Manchester United with three (1968, 1999 and 2008). Three other English clubs, Nottingham Forest (in 1979 and 1980), Aston Villa (in 1982) and Chelsea (in 2012) have also won the tournament, making England the only country to boast five different winners.

• **Portuguese superstar Cristiano Ronaldo is the leading scorer in the history of the competition with 105 goals (including a record 17 in the 2013/14 season for Real Madrid), putting him 11 ahead of his arch rival, Barcelona's Lionel Messi. Meanwhile, Porto goalkeeper Iker Casillas has appeared in a record 164 games in the tournament, keeping a record 54 clean sheets.**

• Real Madrid winger Francisco Gento is the most successful player in the history of the competition with six winner's medals (1956-60 and 1966).

• **Real legend Alfredo Di Stefano scored in a record five finals between 1956 and 1960, while Cristiano Ronaldo is the only player to have scored in three Champions League finals (2008, 2014 and 2017).**

• In 2017 Real Madrid became the first club to retain the trophy in the Champions League era, after defeating Juventus 4-1 in the final in Cardiff.

• **Real were also involved in the highest-scoring final, when they thrashed Eintracht Frankfurt 7-3 at Hampden Park in 1960.**

• Feyenoord recorded the biggest win in the competition in 1969 when they thrashed KR Reykjavik 12-2 in the first round. Benfica hold the record for the biggest aggregate victory with an 18-0 first-round humiliation of Luxembourg no-hopers Stade Dudelange in 1965.

• **In 2017 Barcelona made the best ever comeback in a two-legged tie in the competition, thrashing PSG 6-1 in the round of 16 after losing the first match in Paris 4-0.**

Champions League finals

1993 Marseille 1 AC Milan 0
1994 AC Milan 4 Barcelona 0
1995 Ajax 1 AC Milan 0
1996 Juventus 1 Ajax 1*
1997 Borussia Dortmund 3 Juventus 1
1998 Real Madrid 1 Juventus 0
1999 Man United 2 Bayern Munich 1
2000 Real Madrid 3 Valencia 0
2001 Bayern Munich 1 Valencia 1*
2002 Real Madrid 2 Bayer Leverkusen 1
2003 AC Milan 0 Juventus 0*
2004 Porto 3 Monaco 0
2005 Liverpool 3 AC Milan 3*
2006 Barcelona 2 Arsenal 1
2007 AC Milan 2 Liverpool 1
2008 Man United 1 Chelsea 1*
2009 Barcelona 2 Man United 0
2010 Inter Milan 2 Bayern Munich 0
2011 Barcelona 3 Man United 1
*2012 Bayern Munich 1 Chelsea 1**
2013 Bayern Munich 2 Borussia Dortmund 1
2014 Real Madrid 4 Atletico Madrid 1
2015 Barcelona 3 Juventus 1
2016 Real Madrid 1 Atletico Madrid 1*
2017 Real Madrid 4 Juventus 1
** Won on penalties*

CHANTS

The loudest recorded noise created by a football crowd is 131.76 decibels by Galatasaray fans during their home derby against Istanbul rivals Fenerbahce on 18th March 2011. Despite the raucous atmosphere created by the home fans, visitors Fenerbahce won the match 2-1.

• **In February 2016 the noise generated by Leicester City fans after Foxes striker Leonardo Ulloa scored a last-minute winner against Norwich City created a small earthquake measuring 0.3 on the Richter scale, according to a study carried out by geology students at the city's university.**

• Possibly the oldest football chant is 'Who ate all the pies?', which researchers at Oxford University have discovered dates back to 1894 when it was playfully directed by Sheffield United fans at their 22-stone goalkeeper William 'Fatty' Foulke. The chant stemmed from an

Galatasaray fans gear up for another deafening chant...

incident when the tubby custodian got up early at the team hotel, sneaked down into the dining room and munched his way through all the players' breakfast pies.

• In March 2017 FA chairman Greg Clarke described England fan chants during a friendly against Germany in Dortmund as "inappropriate, disrespectful and disappointing". The chants he objected to had made reference to Britain's victories over Germany in the First and Second World Wars.

CHARLTON ATHLETIC

Year founded: 1905
Ground: The Valley (27,111)
Nickname: The Addicks
Biggest win: 8-1 v Middlesbrough (1953)
Heaviest defeat: 1-11 v Aston Villa (1959)

Charlton Athletic were founded in 1905 when a number of youth clubs in the south-east London area, including East Street Mission and Blundell Mission, decided to merge. The club, whose nickname 'the Addicks' stemmed from the haddock served by a local chippy, graduated from minor leagues to join the Third Division (South) in 1921.

• Charlton's heyday was shortly before and just after the Second World War. After becoming the first club to win successive promotions from the Third to First Division in 1935/36, the Addicks finished runners-up, just three points behind league champions Manchester City, in 1937. After losing in the 1946 FA Cup final to Derby County, Charlton returned to Wembley the following year and this time lifted the cup thanks to a 1-0 victory over Burnley in the final.

• Charlton's home ground, The Valley, used to be one of the biggest in English football with a capacity of around 75,000. In 1985, though, financial problems forced Charlton to leave The Valley and the Addicks spent seven years as tenants of West Ham and Crystal Palace before making an emotional return to their ancestral home in 1992.

• Sam Bartram, who was known as 'the finest keeper England never had', played a record 623 games for the club between 1934 and 1956. Bearded striker Derek Hales is Charlton's record goalscorer, notching 168 in two spells at the club in the 1970s and 1980s.

• Charlton's transfer record was set in 2001 when striker Jason Euell signed from London rivals Wimbledon for £4.75 million. Darren Bent became the most expensive player to leave The Valley when he joined Tottenham for £16.5 million six years later.

HONOURS
First Division champions *2000*
Division 3 (S) champions *1929, 1935*
League One champions *2012*
FA Cup *1947*

SIR BOBBY CHARLTON

Born: Ashington, 11th October 1937
Position: Midfielder
Club career:
1956-73 Manchester United 606 (199)
1973-74 Preston North End 38 (8)
1975 Waterford 31 (18)
International record:
1958-70 England 106 (49)

One of English football's greatest ever players, Sir Bobby Charlton had a magnificent career with Manchester United and England. He is the second highest scorer for both club and country with 49 goals in 106 international appearances and 249 goals in all competitions for the Red Devils.

• Charlton broke into the United first team in 1956, scoring twice on his debut against Charlton Athletic. Two years later he was one of the few United players to survive the Munich air crash, after being hauled from the burning wreckage by goalkeeper Harry Gregg.

• During the 1960s Charlton won everything the game had to offer, winning the league title twice (1965 and 1967), the FA Cup (1963), the European Cup (scoring twice in the final against Benfica at Wembley in 1968) and the World Cup with England in 1966 (along with his brother, Jack). Probably his best performance for his country came in the semi-final against Portugal at Wembley, when he scored both goals (including a trademark piledriver) in a 2-1 victory.

• European Footballer of the Year in 1966, Charlton eventually left United in 1973 to become player-manager of Preston. He returned to Old Trafford as a director in 1984 and was knighted a decade later.

CHEATING

The most notorious instance of on-pitch cheating occurred at the 1986 World Cup in Mexico when Argentina's Diego Maradona punched the ball into the net to open the scoring in his side's quarter-final victory over England. Maradona was unrepentant afterwards, claiming the goal was scored by "the hand of God, and the head of Diego".

Chelsea celebrated their 2017 Premier League title win in subdued style

• In a similar incident in 2009 France captain Thierry Henry clearly handled the ball before crossing for William Gallas to score the decisive goal in a World Cup play-off against Ireland. "I will be honest, it was a handball – but I'm not the ref," a sheepish Henry admitted after the match.

• In September 2009 IFK Gothenburg goalkeeper Kim Christensen was caught by TV cameras using his feet to push the bottom of his posts a few centimetres inwards before a match against Orebro. The referee eventually spotted that the posts had been moved and pushed them back into the correct position. Christensen later admitted that he had moved the goalposts in several earlier matches.

• During the 2012/13 season Tottenham's Gareth Bale was booked a record seven times in all competitions for 'simulation' – more commonly known simply as 'diving'.

• In 2017 Victor Moses became the first player to be sent off in the FA Cup final for diving, when he picked up a second yellow card for falling theatrically in the Arsenal penalty area during Chelsea's 2-1 defeat.

• In May 2017 the FA announced that a new offence of 'successful deception of a match official' would be introduced at the start of the 2017/18 season, and that retrospective action would be taken against any offenders.

CHELSEA

Year founded: 1905
Ground: Stamford Bridge (41,631)
Nickname: The Blues
Biggest win: 13-0 v Jeunesse Hautcharage (1971)
Heaviest defeat: 1-8 v Wolves (1953)

Founded in 1905 by local businessmen Gus and Joseph Mears, Chelsea were elected to the Football League in that very same year. At the time of their election, the club had not played a single match – only Bradford City can claim a similarly swift ascent into league football.

• Thanks to the staggering wealth of their Russian owner, Roman Abramovich, Chelsea are now one of the richest clubs in the world. Since taking over the Londoners in 2003, Abramovich has pumped hundreds of millions into the club and has been rewarded with four FA Cups, three League Cups and five Premier League titles – the most recent of which, in 2016/17 under new manager Antonio Conte, saw the Blues win a record 30 league games, including a club record 13 on the trot. After watching his team come agonisingly close on numerous occasions, Abramovich finally saw Chelsea win the Champions League in 2012 when, led by caretaker manager Roberto di Matteo, the Blues beat Bayern Munich on penalties in the final.

• The following year Chelsea won the Europa League after defeating Benfica 2-1 in the final in Amsterdam. That victory meant the Blues became the first British club to win all three historic UEFA trophies, as they had previously won the European Cup Winners' Cup in both 1971 and 1998. It was in the Cup Winners' Cup that Chelsea thrashed Luxembourg minnows Jeunesse Hautcharage 21-0 in 1971 to set a European record aggregate score.

• The Blues' recent success is in marked contrast to their early history. For the first 50 years of their existence

IS THAT A FACT?
Chelsea are the only club to have won the Premier League under three different managers: Jose Mourinho (2005, 2006 and 2015), Carlo Ancelotti (2010) and Antonio Conte (2017).

Chelsea won precisely nothing, finally breaking their duck by winning the league championship in 1955. After a succession of near misses, the club won the FA Cup for the first time in 1970, beating Leeds 2-1 at Old Trafford in the first post-war final to go to a replay. Flamboyant striker Peter Osgood scored in every round of the cup run and remains the last player to achieve this feat.

• The club's fortunes declined sharply in the late 1970s and 1980s, the Blues spending much of the period in the Second Division while saddled with large debts. However, an influx of veteran foreign stars in the mid-1990s, including Gianfranco Zola, Ruud Gullit and Gianluca Vialli, sparked an exciting revival capped when the Blues won the FA Cup in 1997, their first major trophy for 26 years.

• On 26th December 1999 Chelsea became the first English club to field an entirely foreign line-up for their Premier League fixture at Southampton.

• Chelsea's arrival as one of England's top clubs was finally confirmed when charismatic manager Jose Mourinho led the Blues to the Premiership title in 2005. The club's tally of 95 points set a new record for the competition, while goalkeeper Petr Cech went a then record 1,025 minutes during the season without conceding a goal. A second Premiership title followed in 2006, and Mourinho claimed another in 2015 in his second spell at the Bridge. When the club first won the championship way back in 1955, they did so with a record low of just 52 points.

• In 2007 Chelsea won the first ever FA Cup final at the new Wembley, Ivorian striker Didier Drogba scoring the only goal against Manchester United. In the same year the Blues won the League Cup, making them just the third English team after Arsenal (1993) and Liverpool (2001) to claim a domestic cup double. The Blues also won the FA Cup in 2009 and 2010, making them the first team to retain the trophy at the new Wembley.

• Hardman defender Ron 'Chopper' Harris is Chelsea's record appearance maker, turning out an incredible 795 times for the club between 1962 and 1980. Midfielder Frank Lampard, a key figure in the club's recent successes, scored a record 211 goals in all competitions between 2001 and 2014. Legendary striker Jimmy Greaves scored the most goals in a single season, with 41 in 1960/61.

• Between 2004 and 2008 the Blues were unbeaten in 86 consecutive home league matches, a record for both the Premiership and the Football League. The impressive run was eventually ended by Liverpool, who won 1-0 at Stamford Bridge on 26th October 2008.

• Chelsea won their only league and cup Double in 2010, setting Premier League records for most goals scored (103), most home goals scored (68) and best ever goal difference (+71).

• The club's record signing is Alvaro Morata, who cost the Blues £60 million when he moved from Real Madrid to west London in July 2017. Chelsea sold Brazilian midfielder Oscar to Shanghai SIPG for a club record £60 million in January 2017.

HONOURS
Division 1 champions *1955*
Premier League champions *2005, 2006, 2010, 2015, 2017*
Division 2 champions *1984, 1989*
FA Cup *1970, 1997, 2000, 2007, 2009, 2010, 2012*
Double *2010*
League Cup *1965, 1998, 2005, 2007, 2015*
Champions League *2012*
European Cup Winners' Cup *1971, 1998*
Europa League *2013*
European Super Cup *1998*

CHELTENHAM TOWN

Year founded: 1892
Ground: Whaddon Road (7,266)
Nickname: The Robins
Biggest win: 12-0 v Chippenham Rovers (1935)
Heaviest defeat: 1-10 v Merthyr Tydfil (1952)

Cheltenham Town were founded in 1892 but had to wait over a century to join the Football League, eventually making their bow in 1999 after winning the Conference title. The Robins dropped out of the league in 2015, but bounced back the following year as the first winners of the National League.

• The Robins have twice gained promotion to the third tier via the play-offs, defeating Rushden 3-1 in the final at the Millennium Stadium in 2002 and Grimsby 1-0 four years later at the same venue, but they missed out on a hat-trick when they lost 2-0 to Crewe in the 2012 final at Wembley.

• Midfielder Dave Bird made a record 289 league appearances for the Robins between 2002 and 2012.

• Cheltenham made their record signing in January 2003, splashing out £50,000 on West Ham midfielder Grant McCann. While he was at Whaddon Road McCann won a club record four caps for Northern Ireland.

HONOURS
Conference champions *1999*
National League champions *2016*

CHESTERFIELD

Year founded: 1866
Ground: Proact Stadium (10,504)
Previous name: Chesterfield Town
Nickname: The Spireites
Biggest win: 10-0 v Glossop North End (1903)
Heaviest defeat: 0-10 v Gillingham (1987)

The fourth oldest club in the UK, Chesterfield were founded in 1866. The club was elected to the Second Division in 1899 as Chesterfield Town but lost its league status a decade later, only to return as plain Chesterfield when Division Three (North) was created in 1921.

• One-club man Dave Blakey played in a record 617 league games between 1948 and 1967. Striker Ernie Moss is the Spireites' top scorer with 162 goals in three spells at the club between 1968 and 1986.

• In the 1923/24 campaign Chesterfield goalkeeper Arthur Birch scored five goals for the club, all of them penalties – a record tally by a keeper in a single season.

• In 1997, the same year they reached the FA Cup semi-final for the only time in their history, Chesterfield sold striker Kevin Davies to Southampton for a club record £750,000. The

following year the Spireites splurged £250,000 on Watford striker Jason Lee, but their record signing proved to be a miserable flop, scoring just once in 32 appearances for the club.

• Relegated from League One in 2017, Chesterfield have won the fourth tier title on a record four occasions, most recently topping the League Two table in 2014.

HONOURS
Division 3 (N) champions 1931, 1936
Division 4 champions 1970, 1985
League Two champions 2011, 2014
Football League Trophy 2012

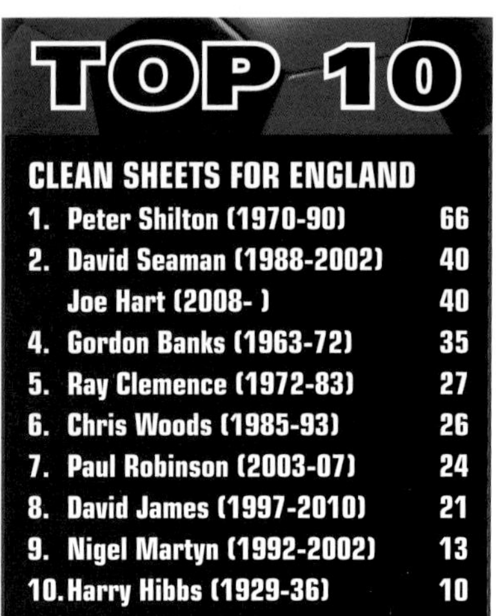

TOP 10

CLEAN SHEETS FOR ENGLAND

1.	Peter Shilton (1970-90)	66
2.	David Seaman (1988-2002)	40
	Joe Hart (2008-)	40
4.	Gordon Banks (1963-72)	35
5.	Ray Clemence (1972-83)	27
6.	Chris Woods (1985-93)	26
7.	Paul Robinson (2003-07)	24
8.	David James (1997-2010)	21
9.	Nigel Martyn (1992-2002)	13
10.	Harry Hibbs (1929-36)	10

CLEAN SHEETS

Arsenal's Petr Cech holds the Premier League clean sheet record with 190. Of these, 162 came with his former employers Chelsea – a record by a goalkeeper with a single club.

• The world record for consecutive clean sheets is held by Brazilian goalkeeper Mazaropi of Vasco de Gama, who went 1,816 minutes without conceding in 1977/78.

• Italy's long-serving goalkeeper Dino Zoff holds the international record, going 1,142 minutes without having to pick the ball out of his net between September 1972 and June 1974. Another Italian goalkeeper, Walter Zenga, holds the record for clean sheets at the World Cup, with a run of 518 minutes at the 1990 tournament. However, New Zealand's Richard Wilson did even better during the qualifying rounds for the 1982 tournament, going 921 minutes without conceding.

• England's overall clean sheet record is held by Peter Shilton, who shut out the opposition in 66 of his 125 international appearances between 1970 and 1990. The international record is held by Spain's Iker Casillas with 101 in 167 appearances.

• Former Manchester United goalkeeper Edwin van der Sar holds the British record for consecutive league clean sheets, keeping the ball out of his net for 14 Premier League games and a total of 1,311 minutes in the 2008/09 season. He was finally beaten on 4th March 2009 by Newcastle's Peter Lovenkrands in United's 2-1 victory at St James' Park.

CLUB WORLD CUP

A competition contested between the champion clubs of all six continental confederations of FIFA, the Club World Cup was first played in Brazil in 2000 but has only been an annual tournament since 2005 when it replaced the old Intercontinental Cup.

• Manchester United's participation in the first Club World Cup led to the Red Devils pulling out of the FA Cup in 2000, a tournament they had won the previous season. United's decision attracted a lot of criticism at the time, not least from many of their own fans.

• Barcelona have the best record in the competition with three triumphs, most recently beating Argentinian side River Plate 3-0 in the 2015 final in Yokohama.

• Manchester United became the first British winners of the tournament when a goal by Wayne Rooney saw off Ecuadorian side Quito in the 2008 final in Yokohama.

• Cristiano Ronaldo is the only player to have scored a hat-trick in the Club World Cup final, striking three times for Real Madrid in their 4-2 victory over Japan's Kashima Antlers in 2016.

Of all the trophies he's won, Cristiano Ronaldo particularly likes the Club World Cup...

COLCHESTER UNITED

Year founded: 1937
Ground: The Colchester Community Stadium (10,105)
Nickname: The U's
Biggest win: 9-1 v Bradford City (1961) and v Leamington (2005)
Heaviest defeat: 0-8 v Leyton Orient (1989)

Founded as the successors to amateur club Colchester Town in 1937, Colchester United joined the Football League in 1950. The club lost its league status in 1990, but regained it just two years later after topping the Conference.

• The U's enjoyed their greatest day in 1971 when they beat then-mighty Leeds United 3-2 in the fifth round of the FA Cup at their old Layer Road ground. However, a 5-0 thrashing at Everton in the quarter-finals ended their hopes of an unlikely cup triumph.

• The first brothers to be sent off in the same match while playing for the same team were Colchester's Tom and Tony English against Crewe in 1986.

• In 1971, the U's became the first English club to win a tournament in a penalty shoot-out after defeating West Brom 4-3 on penalties in the final of the Watney Cup at the Hawthorns.

• Colchester pulled in their record crowd, 19,072, at their old Layer Road ground for an FA Cup tie against Reading in November 1948. Unfortunately, the match was called off after 35 minutes due to thick fog.

HONOURS
Conference champions 1992

CHRIS COLEMAN

Born: Swansea, 10th June 1970
Managerial career:
2003-07 Fulham
2007-08 Real Sociedad
2008-10 Coventry City
2011-12 Larissa
2012- Wales

Appointed manager of Wales in January 2012 following the tragic death of his predecessor, Gary Speed, Chris Coleman led Wales to their first tournament for 58 years when they qualified for Euro 2016.

• Under Coleman Wales performed magnificently at the finals, reaching the last four after victories over Slovakia, Russia, Northern Ireland and Belgium before losing 2-0 to Portugal. When Coleman and his squad returned home they were given a heroes' reception, with thousands of proud Welsh fans lining the streets of Cardiff to greet them.

• Coleman's first experience of management came at Fulham, where he became the youngest ever Premier League manager when he was put in charge of the Cottagers, aged 32 and 10 months, in April 2003.

• After parting company with the west Londoners in 2007, Coleman managed Spanish side Real Sociedad and Coventry, where he was sacked after leading the Midlanders to their lowest position – 19th in the Championship – for 45 years in 2010.

• A tough centre-back in his playing days with Swansea, Crystal Palace, Blackburn and Fulham, Coleman won 32 caps for Wales before his career was ended by a car crash in 2002.

COLOURS

In the 19th century, players originally wore different coloured caps, socks and armbands – but not shirts – to distinguish between the two sides. The first standardised kits were introduced in the 1870s, with many clubs opting for the colours of the schools or other sporting organisations from which they had emerged.

• Thanks largely to the longstanding success of Arsenal, Liverpool and Manchester United, teams wearing red have won more trophies in England than those sporting any other colour. Teams wearing stripes have fared less well, their last FA Cup success coming in 1987 (Coventry City) and their last league triumph way back in 1936 (Sunderland).

• The only two countries to win the World Cup wearing their change strip in the final are England (red shirts, 1966) and Spain (dark blue shirts, 2010).

• Miami-based River Plate fan Dan Goldfarb has an incredible 312 different shirts belonging to the Argentinian giants - the biggest single club collection of jerseys in the world.

IS THAT A FACT?

In April 2017 Liverpool Ladies turned up at Yeovil Town Ladies without any kit, after their dozy kitman forget to pack it. The Merseysiders had to wear Yeovil's yellow away kit instead, and it seemed to suit them as they romped to a 4-1 win.

• In the summer of 2017 Wycombe Wanderers unveiled an eye-catching multi-coloured 'kaleidoscope-style' goalkeeper's kit. "I wanted to try to create a target area to draw opposition players' eyes to," revealed the Chairboys' goalkeeping coach and chief designer Barry Richardson.

Wycombe's new 'kaleidoscope' goalkeeper's kit is designed to give opposition strikers a headache!

COMMUNITY SHIELD

The Community Shield was originally known as the Charity Shield and since 1928 has been an annual fixture usually played at the start of the season between the reigning league champions and the FA Cup winners. Founded in 1908 to provide funds for various charities, the Charity Shield was initially played between the Football League First Division champions and the Southern League champions, developing into a game between select teams of amateurs and professionals in the early 1920s.

• **Manchester United were the first club to win the Charity Shield, defeating QPR 4-0 in a replay at Stamford Bridge. With 17 outright wins and four shared, United are also the most successful side in the history of the competition.**

• United also appeared in a record six consecutive Shields between 1996 and 2001, winning twice.

• **The 1974 Charity Shield between Leeds and Liverpool was the first to be held at Wembley and the first to be decided by penalties, the Reds winning 6-5. However, the game is best remembered for the dismissals of Liverpool's Kevin Keegan and Leeds' Billy Bremner for fighting, the pair becoming the first British players to be sent off at the national stadium.**

• Manchester United's Ryan Giggs is the most successful player in the history of the Shield, with nine wins in 15 appearances (another record).

COMPUTER GAMES

FIFA 13 sold more than 4.5 million copies worldwide in the first five days after its launch in 2012, leading publishers EA to claim it was the biggest selling sports video launch of all time. The FIFA series as a whole has sold well over 100 million copies since it launched in 1993, making it the best selling football video game of all time.

• **The first football video game was created in 1973 by Tomohiro Nishikado, who later designed Space Invaders. Called simply Soccer, the ball-and- paddle game allowed two players to each control a goalkeeper and a striker.**

• FIFA 16 added female players to its squad list for the first time, featuring 12 international women's teams including England, Brazil and Germany. The cover star of FIFA 17 is Borussia Dortmund's Marco Reus, who replaces Lionel Messi.

• **The longest single game of Football Manager lasted 173 days 16 hours and 51 minutes and only ended in December 2014 when a liquid spillage ruined the laptop of the player, UK-based Liverpool fan Darren Bland.**

CONFEDERATIONS CUP

The Confederations Cup is a competition held every four years contested by the holders of each of the six FIFA confederation championships – such as the European Championships and the Copa America – plus the World Cup holders and host nation.

• **Since 2005 the Confederations Cup has been held in the country that will host the following year's World Cup, acting as a dress rehearsal for the larger and more prestigious tournament.**

The Community Shield: a nice trophy for winning just one match!

• Brazil have the best record in the tournament with four victories to their name: in 1997 (after a 6-0 win over Australia in the final), in 2005 (4-1 against Argentina), 2009 (3-2 against the USA) and 2013 (3-0 against Spain). The only other country to win the Confederations Cup more than once are France (in 2001 and 2003). The holders are Germany, who beat Chile 1-0 in the 2017 final in St Petersburg.

• Ronaldo (Brazil) and Cuauhtemoc Blanco (Mexico) are the leading scorers in the competition, with nine goals each. Brazilian striker Romario scored a record seven goals at the 1997 tournament in Saudi Arabia.

ANTONIO CONTE

Born: Lecce, Italy, 31st July 1969
Managerial career:
2006-07 Arezzo
2007-09 Bari
2009-10 Atalanta
2010-11 Siena
2011-14 Juventus
2014-16 Italy
2016- Chelsea

On his way to leading Chelsea to the Premier League title in 2017 in his first season at Stamford Bridge, Antonio Conte won the Manager of the Month award in October, November and December 2016 – the first boss ever to win three consecutive awards. At the end of the season Conte was also voted Premier League Manager of the Year.

• After guiding both Bari and Siena to promotion from Serie B, Conte became manager of Juventus in 2011. He led the 'Bianconeri' to three consecutive Serie A titles, the first of which saw them go through the whole league season unbeaten – the first time this feat had been achieved since Serie A was expanded to 20 clubs.

• An intense character who possesses an explosive temper, Conte was appointed manager of Italy in 2014. His side knocked out reigning champions Spain at Euro 2016 but were then eliminated in the quarter-finals by Germany on penalties.

• A combative midfielder, Conte enjoyed a stellar career with Juventus, winning five Serie A titles, the UEFA Cup in 1993 and the Champions League three years later.

IS THAT A FACT?

Antonio Conte is one of a record four Italian managers to have won the Premier League title. The others are Carlo Ancelotti (Chelsea, 2010), Roberto Mancini (Manchester City, 2012) and Claudio Ranieri (Leicester City, 2016).

COPA AMERICA

The oldest surviving international football tournament in the world, the Copa America was founded in 1916. The first championships were held in Argentina as part of the country's independence centenary commemorations, with Uruguay emerging as the winners from a four-team field. Originally known as the South American Championship, the tournament was renamed in 1975. Previously, the Copa America was held every two years, but in 2007 it was decided to stage future tournaments at four-year intervals.

Antonio Conte's 'Saturday Night Fever' dance routine impressed the 'Strictly' judges

• Uruguay have won the tournament a record 15 times, while Argentina are second in the winners' list, lifting the trophy on 14 occasions. The holders are Chile, who won the Centenary edition of the competition in 2016 after beating Argentina on penalties in the final.

• Uruguay have played a record 197 matches in the competition, but Argentina have the most victories to their name with 120.

COPA LIBERTADORES

The Copa Libertadores is the South American equivalent of the Champions League, played annually between top clubs from all the countries in the continent (in recent years, leading clubs from Mexico have also participated). Argentine club Independiente have the best record in the competition, winning the trophy seven times, including four in a row between 1972 and 1975.

• Ecuadorian striker Albert Spencer is the leading scorer in the history of the competition with 54 goals (48 for Uruguayan club Penarol, helping them to win the first two tournaments in 1960 and 1961, and six for Ecuadorian outfit Barcelona de Guayaquil).

• Goalkeeper Hugo Almeida played in a record 113 Copa Libertadores games for Paraguayan side Olimpia between 1973 and 1990.

• In 1970 Uruguayan giants Penarol recorded the biggest victory in the history of the competition, thrashing Venezuela's Valencia 11-2. Penarol also hold the record for the most emphatic aggregate win, destroying Ecuadorian minnows Everest 14-1 in 1963.

• Argentinian clubs have won the trophy a record 24 times, while a record 10 different clubs from Brazil have raised the cup.

CORNERS

Corner kicks were first introduced in 1872, but goals direct from a corner were not allowed until 1924. The first player to score from a corner in league football was Billy Smith of Huddersfield in the 1924/25 season. On 2nd October 1924 Argentina's Cesareo Onzari scored direct from a corner against reigning Olympic champions Uruguay in Buenos Aires, the first goal of this sort in an international fixture.

• Turkish striker Sukru Gulesin holds the record for the most goals scored direct from corners with an incredible 32 between 1940 and 1954 for a variety of clubs, including Besiktas, Lazio, Palermo and Galatasaray.

• The only player to score direct from a corner at the World Cup finals is Colombia's Marcus Coll, who was on target against the Soviet Union in a 4-4 draw in Chile in 1962.

• On 21st January 2012 Coleraine's Paul Owens became the first player ever to score two goals direct from a corner in the same match when his wind-assisted efforts sailed over the Glenavon goalkeeper in his team's 3-1 Irish Premiership win.

• During the 2016/17 Premier League season Manchester City won more corners (280) than any other team, while Burnley conceded the most (263).

DIEGO COSTA

Born: Lagarto, Brazil, 7th October 1988
Position: Striker
Club career:
2006 Braga 0 (0)
2006 Penafiel (loan) 13 (5)
2007-09 Atletico Madrid 0 (0)
2007 Braga (loan) 7 (0)
2007-08 Celta (loan) 30 (5)
2008-09 Albacete (loan) 34 (9)
2009-10 Valladolid 34 (8)
2010-14 Atletico Madrid 94 (43)
2012 Rayo Vallecano (loan) 16 (10)
2014- Chelsea 89 (52)
International record:
2013 Brazil 2 (0)
2014- Spain 16 (6)

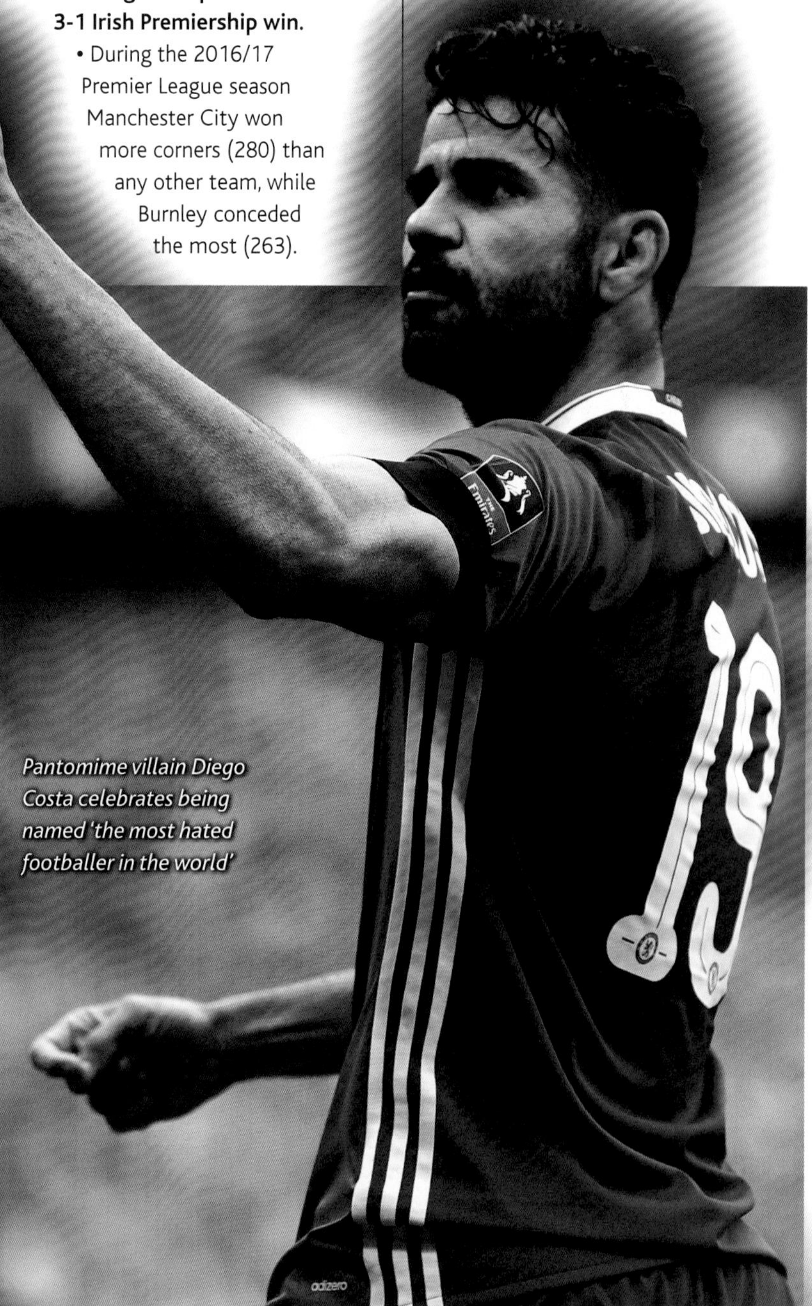

Pantomime villain Diego Costa celebrates being named 'the most hated footballer in the world'

Fiery striker Diego Costa was Chelsea's most important player in the whole of the 2016/17 Premier League campaign, his 20 goals earning the Blues 15 points they otherwise would not have won on their way to a second title success in three seasons.

• **After a fairly undistinguished start to his career, Costa gradually developed into one of Europe's deadliest forwards after rejoining Atletico Madrid from Valladolid in 2010. Three years later he scored a vital goal in the Copa del Rey final as Atleti beat Real Madrid 2-1 to record their first victory over their glitzy city rivals since 1999.**

• The following season Costa was third-top scorer in La Liga with 27 goals – only Cristiano Ronaldo and Lionel Messi were more prolific – as Atletico surprised everyone by lifting the title. Costa also helped Atleti reach the final of the Champions League for the first time, but had to limp out of the showpiece event against Real with a hamstring injury after just eight minutes. Later that summer he moved to Chelsea for £32 million.

• **Costa won the first of two caps for Brazil in 2013, but later that year gained Spanish citizenship and declared his intention to play for his adopted nation, much to the disgust of Brazilian fans. He made his debut for Spain in a 1-0 friendly win over Italy in March 2014 but wasn't selected for his country's Euro 2016 squad after scoring just once in his first 10 internationals.**

• In December 2015 Costa was named by French sports newspaper *L'Equipe* as the most hated footballer in the world, because of his 'provocative, aggressive and violent' style of play.

THIBAUT COURTOIS

Born: Bree, Belgium, 11th May 1992
Position: Goalkeeper
Club career:
2009-11 Genk 41
2011- Chelsea 93
2011-14 Atletico Madrid (loan) 111
International record:
2011- Belgium 49

Rated by many as one of the most accomplished goalkeepers in world football, Thibaut Courtois was a key member of the Chelsea team which won the Premier League title in both 2015 and 2017. In the second of these campaigns he won the Premier League Golden Glove award for the first time.

• **A tall and well-built stopper who is especially adept at plucking crosses from the sky, Courtois came through the youth ranks at Genk to help the Belgian outfit win the league title in 2011, a season in which he was voted Goalkeeper of the Year.**

• Courtois joined Chelsea for around £5 million in July 2011, but was immediately moved out on loan to Atletico Madrid. He enjoyed three great seasons with the Spanish outfit, helping Atletico win the Europa League in 2012, the Copa del Rey in 2013 and the league title in 2014. In addition, he became the first Atletico goalkeeper ever to retain the Ricardo Zamora trophy – awarded to the goalkeeper with the best goals-to-games ratio – when he topped the poll in both 2013 and 2014.

• **However, like most of his Chelsea team-mates he had a season to forget in 2015/16. Sent off in home matches against Swansea City and Manchester City, Courtois became only the sixth goalkeeper to pick up two red cards in the same Premier League campaign.**

• Courtois is the youngest ever goalkeeper to have played for Belgium, making his debut as a 19-year-old in a 0-0 friendly draw with France in 2011.

PHILIPPE COUTINHO

Born: Rio de Janeiro, Brazil, 12th June 1992
Position: Midfielder
Club career:
2009-10 Vasco de Gama 19 (1)
2010-13 Inter Milan 28 (3)
2012 Espanyol (loan) 16 (5)
2013- Liverpool 138 (34)
International record:
2010- Brazil 27 (7)

Skilful Liverpool midfielder Philippe Coutinho is the highest-scoring Brazilian player in the history of the Premier League with 34 goals, passing Middlesbrough legend Juninho's old

Philippe Coutinho, the highest-scoring Brazilian in Premier League history

benchmark of 29 goals in a 2-1 victory at Stoke in April 2017. Nearly half of his strikes, 15, have come from outside the penalty area - more than any other player during his four and a half seasons in the Premier League.

• Coutinho helped the Reds reach two cup finals during the 2015/16 season, scoring Liverpool's equaliser in the League Cup final against Manchester City at Wembley. However, he missed from the spot in the subsequent penalty shoot-out and had to settle for a runners-up medal, and he was again disappointed in the Europa League final when the Reds lost to Sevilla.

• Coutinho moved to Italian giants Inter Milan from Vasco de Gama when he was just 18, but struggled to adapt to Serie A. However, a loan spell at Spanish outfit Espanyol in 2012 proved a turning point in his career and the following January he joined Liverpool in a £8.5 million deal.

• A typical Brazilian number 10 who combines vision, flair and creativity in equal measure, Coutinho made his debut for his country in a 3-0 friendly win against Iran in 2010 when he was aged just 18. After years in the international wilderness he was called up by new boss Dunga for the 2015 Copa America in Chile and two years later scored in a 3-0 defeat of Paraguay that secured Brazil's qualification for the 2018 World Cup.

COVENTRY CITY

Year founded: 1883
Ground: Ricoh Arena (32,609)
Previous name: Singers FC
Nickname: The Sky Blues
Biggest win: 9-0 v Bristol City (1934)
Heaviest defeat: 2-11 v Berwick Rangers (1901)

Coventry were founded in 1883 by workers from the local Singer's bicycle factory and were named after the company until 1898. The club was elected to the Second Division in 1919, but their league career started unpromisingly with a 5-0 home defeat to Tottenham Hotspur.

• A club with a history of ups and downs, Coventry were the first team to play in seven different divisions: Premier, Division One, Two, Three, Four, Three (North) and Three (South). They have also played in the Championship, League One and, after suffering relegation from the third tier, will begin the 2017/18 season in League Two.

Coventry will need to get off their knees to escape from League Two

• Coventry's greatest moment came in 1987 when the club won the FA Cup for the only time, beating Tottenham 3-2 in an exciting Wembley final. Two years later, though, the Sky Blues were dumped out of the cup by non-league Sutton United in one of the competition's biggest ever upsets.

• In July 2000 the Sky Blues made their record sale when striker Robbie Keane joined Inter Milan for £13 million. The following month Coventry forked out a club record fee of £6.5 million for Norwich striker Craig Bellamy.

• Long-serving goalkeeper Steve Ogrizovic played in a club record 504 league games between 1984 and 2000. Sky Blues legend Clarrie Bourton scored a club record 173 league goals between 1931 and 1937, including a season's best 49 goals in 1931/32.

• Coventry's highest-capped international is goalkeeper Magnus Hedman, who played 44 times for Sweden between 1997 and 2002.

HONOURS
Division 2 champions *1967*
Division 3 champions *1964*
Division 3 (S) champions *1936*
FA Cup *1987*
FA Trophy *2017*

CRAWLEY TOWN

Year founded: 1896
Ground: Broadfield Stadium (6,134)
Nickname: The Red Devils
Biggest win: 8-0 v Droylsden (2008)
Heaviest defeat: 0-7 v Bath City (2000)

Founded in 1896, Crawley Town started out in the West Sussex League, eventually rising to the Conference in 2004. Dubbed the 'Manchester City of non-league', Crawley splashed out more than £500,000 on new players at the start of the 2010/11 season, an investment which paid off when the club

won promotion to the Football League at the end of the campaign.

• **Runaway Conference champions, Crawley's haul of 105 points set a new record for the division, while they also equalled the records for fewest defeats (3), most wins (31) and best goal difference (63). The following season Crawley enjoyed a second successive promotion, after finishing third in League Two behind Swindon and Shrewsbury.**

• Crawley reached the fifth round of the FA Cup for the first time in their history in 2011 after knocking out Swindon, Derby and Torquay. To their fans' delight they were then paired with Manchester United, and their team did them proud, only losing 1-0 at Old Trafford.

• **On 14th February 2015 striker Izale McLeod became the first Crawley player to hit a hat-trick in the Football League when he scored three goals in a 5-1 thrashing of Barnsley at Broadfield Stadium.**

HONOURS
Conference champions 2011

CREWE ALEXANDRA

Year founded: 1877
Ground: Gresty Road (10,153)
Nickname: The Railwaymen
Biggest win: 8-0 v Rotherham (1932)
Heaviest defeat: 2-13 v Tottenham Hotspur (1960)

Founded by railway workers in 1877, the Crewe Football Club added 'Alexandra' to their name in honour of Princess Alexandra, wife of the future king, Edward VII. The club were founder members of the Second Division in 1892, although they lost their league status four years later before rejoining the newly formed Third Division (North) in 1921.

• **Club legend Herbert Swindells scored a record 126 goals for Crewe between 1927 and 1937. Crewe's appearance record is held by Tommy Lowry, who turned out in 475 games between 1966 and 1977.**

• Alex fans endured a miserable spell in the mid-1950s when their club failed to win away from home for a record 56 consecutive matches. The depressing run finally ended with a 1-0 win at Southport in April 1957.

• **Prolific striker Frank Lord scored a club record eight hat-tricks for Crewe, including four in the 1960/61 season.**

• Trinidad and Tobago goalkeeper Clayton Ince won a club record 31 international caps while at Crewe between 1999 and 2005.

HONOURS
Football League Trophy 2013
Welsh Cup 1936, 1937

JOHAN CRUYFF

Born: Amsterdam, Netherlands, 5th April 1947
Died: 24th March 2016
Position: Midfielder/striker
Club career:
1964-73 Ajax 240 (190)
1973-78 Barcelona 142 (48)
1979-80 Los Angeles Aztecs 27 (16)
1980-81 Washington Diplomats 32 (12)
1981 Levante 10 (2)
1981-83 Ajax 36 (14)
1983-84 Feyenoord 33 (11)
International record:
1966-78 Netherlands 48 (33)

Arguably the greatest European player ever, Johan Cruyff was captain of the brilliant Netherlands side which reached the final of the 1974 World Cup and of the outstanding Ajax team which won the European Cup three times on the trot in the early 1970s.

• **Unquestionably the best player in the world at the time, Cruyff became the first man to win the European Player of the Year award three times, topping the poll in 1971, 1973 and 1974.**

• Fast, skilful, creative and a prolific scorer, Cruyff was also a superb organiser on the pitch. His talents prompted Barcelona to shell out a world record £922,000 fee to bring him to the Nou Camp in 1973 and the following year Cruyff helped the Catalans win their first title for 14 years.

• **After his retirement, Cruyff coached both Ajax and Barcelona. He led the Spanish giants to four consecutive league titles between 1991 and 1994 and, in 1992, guided them to their first ever European Cup success, with a 1-0 victory over Sampdoria at Wembley.**

The residents of this Amsterdam block of flats spend hours every day staring at their lovely Johan Cruyff wall mural

Even MI5 have no idea what goes on inside the secretive Crystal Palace 'huddle'!

CRYSTAL PALACE

Year founded: 1905
Ground: Selhurst Park (26,255)
Nickname: The Eagles
Biggest win: 9-0 v Barrow (1959)
Heaviest defeat: 0-9 v Burnley (1909) and v Liverpool (1989)

The club was founded in 1905 by workers at the then cup final venue at Crystal Palace, and was an entirely separate entity to the amateur club of the same name which was made up of groundkeepers at the Great Exhibition and reached the first ever semi-finals of the FA Cup in 1872.

• After spending their early years in the Southern League, Palace were founder members of the Third Division (South) in 1920. The club had a great start to their league career, going up to the Second Division as champions in their first season.

• Crystal Palace are only the second club (after Scottish outfit Queen's Park in 1885) to reach two FA Cup finals and lose on both occasions to the same club. In 1990 the Eagles held Manchester United to a thrilling 3-3 draw at Wembley before losing 1-0 in the replay. Then, in 2016, the south London club endured more agony at the hands of United when they went down to a 2-1 defeat in extra-time despite taking the lead through substitute Jason Puncheon.

• Pre-war striker Peter Simpson is the club's all-time leading scorer with 153 league goals between 1930 and 1936. Rugged defender Jim Cannon holds the club appearance record, turning out 660 times between 1973 and 1988.

• Palace are the only club to have been promoted to the top flight four times via the play-offs, most recently in 2013. The Eagles are also the only club to have won play-off finals at four different venues: Selhurst Park (1989), old Wembley (1997), Millennium Stadium (2004) and new Wembley (2013).

• Less happily for their fans, Palace have been relegated a joint-record four times from the Premier League, including a particularly unfortunate occasion in 1993 when they went down with a record 49 points (from 42 games). However, after surviving in the Premier League for a fourth consecutive season in 2016/17, the Eagles are enjoying their longest ever spell in the English top flight.

• The club made their record signing in August 2016, when Belgium striker Christian Benteke signed from Liverpool for £27 million. In the same month the Eagles sold DR Congo winger Yannick Bolasie to Everton for a club record £25 million.

• A record fourth-tier crowd of 37,774 watched Palace's home match with Millwall on 31st March 1961,

but it proved to be a disappointing afternoon for the Selhurst faithful as the Eagles slumped to a 2-0 defeat.

• The Eagles have played just one tie in European football, losing 4-0 on aggregate to Turkish outfit Samsunspor in the Intertoto Cup in 1998.

HONOURS
Division 2 champions 1979
First Division champions 1994
Division 3 (S) champions 1921

CUP WINNERS' CUP

A competition for the domestic cup winners of all European countries, the European Cup Winners' Cup ran for 39 seasons from 1960/61 until 1998/99. Barcelona have the best record in the competition with four wins (in 1979, 1982, 1989 and 1997).

• In 1963 Tottenham Hotspur became the first British club to win the competition and the first to win a major European trophy, when they thrashed Atletico Madrid 5-1 in Rotterdam – a record score for a European final.

• English clubs won the cup eight times – a figure unmatched by any other country. England's successful teams were Tottenham (1963), West Ham (1965), Manchester City (1970), Chelsea (1971 and 1998), Everton (1985), Manchester United (1991) and Arsenal (1994).

• In 1963 Sporting Lisbon tonked APOEL Nicosia 16-1 in a second-round, first-leg tie to record the biggest ever win in any European fixture. Two-time winners Chelsea hold the competition record for the biggest aggregate victory, smashing Luxembourg side Jeunesse Hautcharage 21-0 in 1971.

• Feyenoord's De Kuip stadium hosted the final of the competition on a record five occasions.

TOP 10

CUP WINNERS' CUP VICTORIES

1. **Sporting Lisbon 16 APOEL Nicosia 1, 1963**
2. **Chelsea 13 Jeunesse Hautcharage 0, 1971**
3. **Swansea City 12 Sliema Wanderers 0, 1982**
4. **Levski Spartak 12 Lahden Reipas 2, 1976**
5. **Malmo 11 Pezoporikos 0, 1973**
   Liverpool 11 Stromsgodset 0, 1974
7. **Sparta Prague 10 Anorthosis Famagusta 0, 1964**
   Aberdeen 10 KR Reykjavik 0, 1967
   PSV 10 Ards 0, 1974
   Rangers 10 Valetta 0, 1983
   Maribor 10 Norma Tallinn 0, 1994
   Roda 10 Hapoel Be'er Sheva 0, 1997

The Cup Winners' Cup was won a record eight times by English clubs, including Arsenal in 1994

KENNY DALGLISH

Born: Glasgow, 4th March 1951
Position: Striker
Club career:
1968-77 Celtic 204 (112)
1977-90 Liverpool 354 (118)
International record:
1971-87 Scotland 102 (30)

The last player to score 100 league goals in both the Scottish and English leagues, Kenny Dalglish began his career at Celtic, winning nine major trophies before moving to Liverpool in 1977 for a then British record fee of £440,000. A true Anfield legend, Dalglish won nine championships, two FA Cups and four League Cups with the Reds, plus the European Cup in 1978, 1981 and 1984. He was voted Footballer of the Year in 1979 and 1983.

• A clever striker with a superb first touch, Dalglish won a record 102 caps for Scotland and scored 30 goals – a figure matched only by Denis Law. He represented his country at three World Cups in 1974, 1978 and 1982.

• In 1986 he became the first player-manager to lead a club to the title when he won the championship with Liverpool, and he secured two more titles in 1988 and 1990 before suddenly resigning in 1991.

• Eight months later he took over at Blackburn and in 1995 steered Rovers to the Premiership title, becoming the last of just four managers to win the title with two different clubs. In 1997 Dalglish became Newcastle manager, but was sacked after a poor start to the 1998/99 season.

• He was briefly manager of Celtic but was out of the game for nine years before going back to Liverpool in 2009, initially as youth academy coach. In January 2011 Dalglish replaced Roy Hodgson as manager but, despite winning the Carling Cup the following year and guiding the Reds to the 2012 FA Cup final, the Kop legend was sacked at the end of the 2011/12 season after a poor league campaign.

DEATHS

The first recorded death as a direct result of a football match came in 1889 when William Cropper of Derbyshire side Staveley FC died of a ruptured bowel sustained in a collision with an opponent.

• In 1931 Celtic's brilliant young international goalkeeper John Thompson died in hospital after fracturing his skull in a collision with Rangers forward Sam English. Some 40,000 fans attended his funeral, many of them walking the 55 miles from Glasgow to Thompson's home village in Fife. In the same decade two other goalkeepers, Jimmy Utterson of Wolves and Sunderland's Jimmy Thorpe, also died from injuries sustained on the pitch. Their deaths led the Football Association to change the rules so that goalkeepers could not be tackled while they had the ball in their hands.

• In March 2017 Estevao Albert Gino, a 19-year-old defender with Mozambique second division side Atletico Mineiro de Tete, was snatched and killed by a 16ft crocodile while training by the banks of the river Zambezi.

• In May 2009 Oroboa Adan, of Nigerian side Warri Wolves, was attacked by fans of Enugu Rangers shortly before the teams were due to play each other. The goalkeeper suffered internal bleeding and died three days later.

• On 11th November 1923 Aston Villa centre-half Tommy Ball was shot dead by his neighbour, becoming the first and last Football League player to be murdered. Ball's killer, George Stagg, was sentenced to life imprisonment and later declared to be insane.

• In a tragic incident in October 2014 Indian player Peter Biaksangzuala died after injuring his spine while performing a somersault to celebrate a goal he had scored for his club, Bethlehem Vengthlang.

• In June 2017 former Newcastle midfielder Cheick Tiote collapsed and died while training with Chinese club Beijing Enterprises.

IS THAT A FACT?
Over 280 Football League and Scottish League players were killed in action during the First World War, including nine from Bradford City and seven from Hearts.

DEBUTS

Aston Villa striker Howard Vaughton enjoyed the best England debut ever, scoring five goals in a 13-0 rout of Ireland in 1882. The last England player to score a hat-trick on his debut was Luther Blissett, who smashed three past Luxembourg in a 9-0 win at Wembley in 1982.

• The worst ever international debut was by American Samoa goalkeeper Nicky Salapu against Fiji in 2001. He conceded 13 goals in that game, and then another 44 within a week in three matches against Samoa, Tonga and Australia.

• Freddy Eastwood scored the fastest goal on debut, netting after just seven seconds for Southend against Swansea in 2004.

• The fastest goal by an England player on debut was by future Tottenham boss Bill Nicholson after just 19 seconds against Portugal at Goodison Park in 1951.

• After scoring for Manchester United against Bournemouth on 14th August 2016, much-travelled striker Zlatan Ibrahimovic became the first player ever to hit the target on his debuts in the Premier League, Serie A, La Liga, Ligue 1 and the Champions League.

• The fastest Premier League goal on debut was scored by West Brom's Congolese striker Thievy Bifouma after 36 seconds during a substitute appearance against Crystal Palace at Selhurst Park in February 2014.

DERBIES

So called because they matched the popularity of the Epsom Derby horserace, 'derby' matches between local sides provoke intense passions among fans and players alike.

• Celtic v Rangers is the most played derby in world football – the two teams having met an incredible 407 times, including six times in the 2016/17 campaign (Celtic winning five

and drawing once). In the 2010/11 season the two teams met a record seven times, the clashes provoking so many violent incidents in Glasgow that the chairman of the Scottish Police Federation called for future Old Firm matches to be banned.

• Famous derbies in England include Liverpool (89 wins in total) v Everton (66 wins), Arsenal (75 wins) v Tottenham (56 wins), Manchester City (50 wins) v Manchester United (71 wins) and Newcastle (53 wins) v Sunderland (50 wins).

• England and Scotland have met in the world's oldest international derby 114 times, England leading the way with 48 wins to 41 wins. Seven players have scored a hat-trick in the fixture, but none since Jimmy Greaves in England's 9-3 win at Wembley in 1961.

• The biggest win in a derby match in England was Nottingham Forest's 12-0 thrashing of east Midland rivals Leicester City in the old First Division in 1909. In the Premier League era Chelsea recorded the most emphatic derby win when they smashed Arsenal 6-0 at Stamford Bridge in March 2014.

• Arsenal's Thierry Henry scored a record 43 goals in 59 Premier League London derbies between 1999 and 2007.

Even the ball has some bruises at the end of the Old Firm derby!

DERBY COUNTY

Year founded: 1884
Ground: Pride Park (33,597)
Nickname: The Rams
Biggest win: 12-0 v Finn Harps (1976)
Heaviest defeat: 2-11 v Everton (1890)

Derby were formed in 1884 as an offshoot of Derbyshire Cricket Club and originally wore an amber, chocolate and blue strip based on the cricket club's colours. Perhaps wisely, they changed to their traditional black-and-white colours in the 1890s.

• The club were founder members of the Football League in 1888 and seven years later moved from the ground they shared with the cricketers to the Baseball Ground (so named because baseball was regularly played there in the 1890s). Derby had to oust a band of gypsies before they could move in, one of whom is said to have laid a curse on the place as he left. No doubt, then, the club was pleased to leave the Baseball Ground for Pride Park in 1997... although when Derby's first game at the new stadium had to be abandoned due to floodlight failure, there were fears that the curse had followed them!

• Runners-up in the FA Cup final in 1898, 1899 and 1903, Derby reached their last final in 1946. Before the match the club's captain, Jack Nicholas, visited a gypsy encampment and paid for the old curse to be lifted. It worked, as Derby beat Charlton 4-1 after extra-time.

• Under charismatic manager Brian Clough, Derby took the top flight by storm after winning promotion to the First Division in 1969. Three years later they won the league in one of the closest title races ever. Having played all their fixtures ahead of their title contenders, Derby's players were actually sitting on a beach in Majorca when they heard news of their victory. The following season Derby reached the semi-finals of the European Cup and, in 1975 under the management of former skipper Dave Mackay, they won the championship again.

• The Rams' last season in the top flight in 2007/08 was an utter disaster as they managed just one win in the whole campaign, equalling a Football League record set by Loughborough in 1900. Even worse, between September 2007 and September 2008 Derby went a record 36 league games without a win, including a record 32 games in the Premier League and another four in the Championship.

• Derby made their record signing in August 2016 when Watford striker Matej Vydra moved to Pride Park for £12.5 million. In the same month the Rams sold midfielder Jeff Hendrick to Burnley for a club record £10.5 million.

• Derby's best ever goalscorer was one of the true greats of the game in the late 19th and early 20th centuries, Steve Bloomer. He netted an incredible 332 goals in two spells at the club between 1892 and 1914. Striker Kevin Hector, a two-time title winner with the club in the 1970s, played in a record 485 league games for the Rams during two spells at the Baseball Ground.

HONOURS
***Division 1 champions** 1972, 1975*
***Division 2 champions** 1912, 1915, 1969, 1987*
***FA Cup** 1946*

ERIC DIER

Born: Cheltenham, 15th January 1994
Position: Defender/midfielder
Club career:
2012-14 Sporting Lisbon B 16 (2)
2012-14 Sporting Lisbon 27 (1)
2014- Tottenham Hotspur 101 (7)
International record:
2015- England 19 (2)

A versatile player who is normally employed as a defensive midfielder but is equally effective at right-back or at centre-back, Eric Dier was one of Tottenham's most consistent performers as the north Londoners finished a best ever second in the Premier League in 2017.

• Born in Cheltenham, Dier moved to Portugal with his parents aged seven and came through the ranks of the Sporting Lisbon academy while also spending 18 months on loan at Everton as a teenager. After breaking into the Sporting first team in 2012 he moved on to Tottenham in a £4 million deal two years later.

• Dier scored the winner on his Spurs debut in a 1-0 victory at West Ham on the opening day of the 2014/15 campaign. Later that season he played in the League Cup final at Wembley, which Spurs lost 2-0 to London rivals Chelsea.

• Capped by England at all age groups from Under-18s onwards, Dier made his full international debut as a sub in a 2-0 friendly defeat against Spain in November 2015. Four months later he scored his first England goal, heading the winner in a famous 3-2 friendly victory away to Germany, and he was also on target at Euro 2016 with a superb free kick in a 1-1 draw with Russia.

'Hiding your face behind a mask...I'm sorry, Pedro, but that's a straight red card!'

His name may be Dier, but he's far from dire!

DISCIPLINE

Yellow and red cards were introduced into English league football on 2nd October 1976, and on the same day Blackburn's David Wagstaffe received the first red card during his side's match with Leyton Orient. Five years later cards were withdrawn by the Football Association as referees were getting 'too flashy', but the system was re-introduced in 1987.

• A stormy last 16 match between the Netherlands and Portugal in 2006 was the most ill-disciplined in the history of the World Cup. Russian referee Valentin Ivanov was the busiest man on the pitch as he pulled out his yellow card 16 times and his red one four times, with the match ending as a nine-a-side affair.

• West Brom midfielder Gareth Barry has been shown a record 121 yellow cards in the Premier League, while Watford's Jose Holebas equalled the record for the most yellows in a season with 14 in 2016/17. Richard Dunne, Duncan Ferguson and Patrick Vieira share the record for receiving the most red cards in Premier League matches, with eight each.

• Former Colombian international Gerardo Bedoya was sent off a record 46 times in his playing career. In March 2016 in his first match as a senior coach with Independiente Santa Fe, the man dubbed 'the world's dirtiest footballer' was shown a red card in the first half.

• Former Arsenal midfielder Patrick Vieira is the only player to be sent off in the Champions League for three different clubs, seeing red with the Gunners, Juventus and Inter Milan.

• When a mass brawl erupted in the middle of the pitch during a match

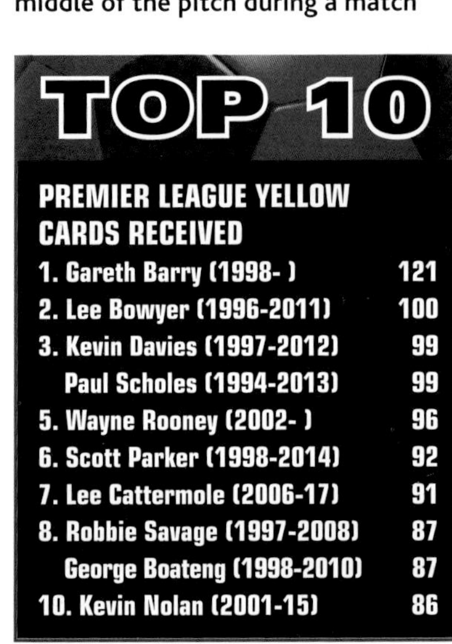

TOP 10

PREMIER LEAGUE YELLOW CARDS RECEIVED

1. Gareth Barry (1998-)	121
2. Lee Bowyer (1996-2011)	100
3. Kevin Davies (1997-2012)	99
Paul Scholes (1994-2013)	99
5. Wayne Rooney (2002-)	96
6. Scott Parker (1998-2014)	92
7. Lee Cattermole (2006-17)	91
8. Robbie Savage (1997-2008)	87
George Boateng (1998-2010)	87
10. Kevin Nolan (2001-15)	86

between Argentinian sides Victoriano Arenas and Claypole on 26th February 2011, referee Damian Rubino showed red cards to all 22 players and 14 substitutes as well as coaches and technical staff. The total of 36 players sent off set a new world record, smashing the previous 'best' of 20!

• In a bizarre incident in January 2017 PSG's Marco Verratti was shown the yellow card for 'trickery' after stooping to the ground to head the ball back to his goalkeeper Kevin Trapp. Almost as strangely, Barcelona star Neymar was booked for tying his bootlaces while opponents Malaga were waiting to take a free kick in March 2017.

DONCASTER ROVERS

Year founded: 1879
Ground: Keepmoat Stadium (15,231)
Nickname: The Rovers
Biggest win: 10-0 v Darlington (1964)
Heaviest defeat: 0-12 v Small Heath (1903)

Founded in 1879 by Albert Jenkins, a fitter at Doncaster's Great Northern Railway works, Doncaster turned professional in 1885 and joined the Second Division of the Football League in 1901.

• Remarkably, Doncaster hold the record for the most wins in a league season (33 in 1946/47) and for the most defeats (34 in 1997/98).

• Midfield stalwart James Coppinger has played in a club record 472 league games since signing from Exeter City in 2004.

• In 1946 Doncaster were involved in the longest ever football match, a Third Division (North) cup tie against Stockport County at Edgeley Park which the referee ruled could extend beyond extra-time in an attempt to find a winner. Eventually, the game was abandoned after 203 minutes due to poor light.

• Promoted from League Two in 2017, Doncaster have won the third tier a record four times, most recently winning the League One title in 2013.

• Defender Len Graham won a club record 14 caps for Northern Ireland between 1951 and 1958.

HONOURS
Division 3 (North) champions *1935, 1947, 1950*
League One champions *2013*
Division 4 champions *1966, 1969*
Third Division champions *2004*
Football League Trophy *2007*

DOUBLES

The first club to win the Double of league championship and FA Cup were Preston North End, in the very first season of the Football League in 1888/89. The Lancashire side achieved this feat in fine style, remaining undefeated in the league and keeping a clean sheet in all their matches in the FA Cup.

• Arsenal and Manchester United have both won the Double a record three times. The Red Devils' trio of successes all came within a five-year period in the 1990s (1994, 1996 and 1999), with the last of their Doubles comprising two-thirds of a legendary Treble which also included the Champions League. Arsenal first won the Double in 1971, and since then the Gunners have twice repeated the feat under manager Arsène Wenger in 1998 and 2002.

• Perhaps, though, the most famous Double of all was achieved by Tottenham Hotspur in 1961 as it was the first such success in the 20th century. Under manager Bill Nicholson, Spurs clinched the most prized honour in the domestic game with a 2-0 victory over Leicester City in the FA Cup final. The other English clubs to win the Double are Aston Villa (1897), Liverpool (1986) and Chelsea (2010).

• Linfield have won a world record 24 Doubles, the most recent coming in 2017. The Northern Ireland outfit are followed by Hong Kong's South China (22) and Rangers (18).

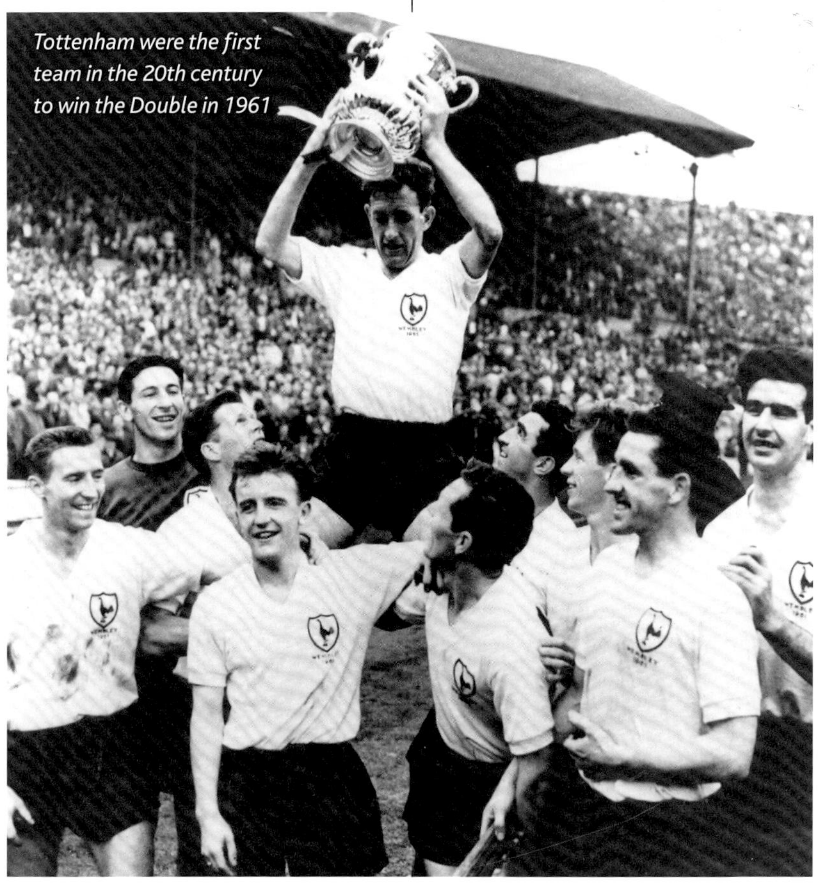

Tottenham were the first team in the 20th century to win the Double in 1961

DRAWS

Preston North End have drawn more league matches than any other club, having finished on level terms 1,246 times. Bootle FC have drawn the fewest league matches, just three in their single season in the Second Division in 1892/93.

• The highest scoring draw in the top division of English football was 6-6, in a match between Leicester City and Arsenal in 1930. In an incredible match in the fourth qualifying round of the FA Cup in November 1929, Dulwich Hamlet and Wealdstone drew 7-7 before Dulwich won the replay 2-1.

• The highest scoring draw in Premier League history came on the last day of

the 2012/13 season at the Hawthorns when West Brom and Manchester United drew 5-5 in Sir Alex Ferguson's last game in charge of the Red Devils.

• In the 2016/17 season Manchester United equalled the record for home Premier League draws with 10 Old Trafford stalemates. Newcastle hold the record for away draws with 10 in in 2003/04.

• Everton have drawn a record 277 Premier League games. Even the Toffees, though, can't match Norwich City's record of 23 draws in a single season, set in the First Division in 1978/79.

• During the 1997/98 season Tranmere Rovers really put their fans through the mill, drawing a record five consecutive league matches 0-0.

DUNDEE

Year founded: 1893
Ground: Dens Park (11,506)
Nickname: The Dee
Biggest win: 10-0 v Alloa (1947), v Dunfermline (1947) and v Queen of the South (1962)
Heaviest defeat: 0-11 v Celtic (1895)

Dundee were founded in 1893 after the merger of two local clubs, Dundee Our Boys and Dundee East End.

• The club's greatest ever moment was in 1962 when the Dee won the Scottish title under the managership of Bob Shankly, brother of the legendary Bill. The following season Dundee reached the semi-finals of the European Cup, before bowing out to eventual winners AC Milan.

• In April 2010 Dundee goalkeeper Bobby Geddes became the oldest man ever to appear in a Scottish league game when he came on as a first-half substitute during a 1-0 defeat against Raith Rovers just four months short of his 50th birthday.

• Future Tottenham hero Alan Gilzean scored a club record 113 league goals for the Dee between 1957 and 1964, including a season's best 52 in 1963/64.

• Dundee made their record signing in 2000 when Paraguayan striker Fabian Caballero signed from Club Sol de America for £600,000. In the same year the Dee sold goalkeeper Robert Douglas to Celtic for a record £1.2 million.

• Dundee's Dens Park is situated just a few hundred yards from Dundee United's Tannadice Park, making the two clubs the closest neighbours in British football.

HONOURS
Division 1 champions *1962*
Division 2 champions *1947*
First Division champions *1979, 1992*
Championship champions *2014*
Scottish Cup *1910*
Scottish League Cup *1952, 1953, 1974*

DUNDEE UNITED

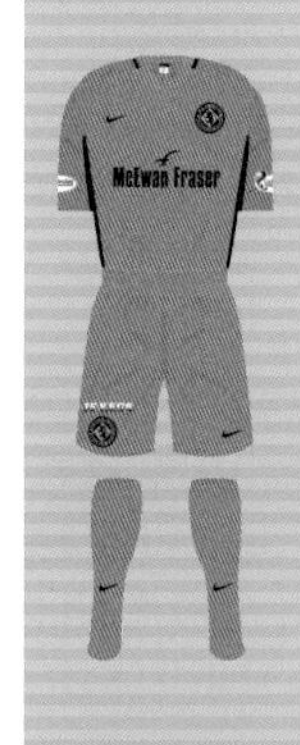

Year founded: 1909
Ground: Tannadice Park (14,223)
Previous name: Dundee Hibernian
Nickname: The Terrors
Biggest win: 14-0 v Nithsdale Wanderers (1931)
Heaviest defeat: 1-12 v Motherwell (1954)

Originally founded as Dundee Hibernian by members of the city's Irish community in 1909, the club changed to its present name in 1923 to attract support from a wider population.

• The club emerged from relative obscurity to become one of the leading clubs in Scotland under long-serving manager Jim McLean in the 1970s and 1980s, winning the Scottish Premier Division in 1983. The club's success, allied to that of Aberdeen, led to talk of a 'New Firm' capable of challenging the 'Old Firm' of Rangers and Celtic for major honours.

OK, it's only the Irn Bru Scottish Challenge Cup but Dundee United don't care!

• Relegated to the Scottish Championship in 2016, United reached the semi-finals of the European Cup in 1984 and the final of the UEFA Cup in 1987, where they lost 2-1 on aggregate to Swedish side Gothenburg. The club's European exploits also include four victories over Barcelona – a 100 per cent record against the Catalans which no other British team can match.

• After being losing finalists on six previous occasions, Dundee United finally won the Scottish Cup in 1994 when they beat Rangers 1-0 in the final. They won the trophy for a second time in 2010, following a comfortable 3-0 win against shock finalists Ross County, but went down in the 2014 final to surprise winners St Johnstone.

• Maurice Malpas turned out in a club record 617 league games for the Terrors between 1981 and 2000. The defender also played in a record 55 internationals for Scotland during his long Tannadice career.

• In the 1964/65 season Danish striker Finn Dossing scored in 13 consecutive league games – just one short of the British record set by Falkirk's Evelyn Morrison in 1928/29.

HONOURS
Premier League champions *1983*
Division 2 champions *1925, 1929*
Scottish Cup *1994, 2010*
Scottish League Cup *1980, 1981*

ENGLAND

First international: Scotland 0 England 0, 1872
Most capped player: Peter Shilton, 125 caps (1971-90)
Leading goalscorer: Wayne Rooney, 53 goals (2003-16)
First World Cup appearance: England 2 Chile 0, 1950
Biggest win: England 13 Ireland 0, 1882
Heaviest defeat: Hungary 7 England 1, 1954

England, along with their first opponents Scotland, are the oldest international team in world football. The two countries met in the first official international in Glasgow in 1872, with honours being shared after a 0-0 draw. The following year, William Kenyon-Slaney of Wanderers FC scored England's first ever goal in a 4-2 victory over Scotland at the Kennington Oval.

• **With a team entirely composed of players from England, Great Britain won the first Olympic Games football tournament in 1908 and repeated the feat in 1912.**

• England did not lose a match on home soil against a team from outside the British Isles until 1953 when they were thrashed 6-3 by Hungary at Wembley. The following year England went down to their worst ever defeat to the same opposition, crashing 7-1 in Budapest.

• **Although Walter Winterbottom was appointed as England's first full-time manager in 1946, the squad was picked by a committee until Alf Ramsey took over in 1963. Three years later England hosted and won the World Cup – the greatest moment in the country's football history by some considerable margin.**

• There were many heroes in that 1966 team, including goalkeeper Gordon Banks, skipper Bobby Moore and striker Geoff Hurst, who scored a hat-trick in the 4-2 victory over West Germany in the final at Wembley. Ramsey, too, was hailed for his part in the success and was knighted soon afterwards.

• **Since then, however, England fans have experienced more than their fair share of disappointment. A second appearance in the World Cup final was within the grasp of Bobby Robson's team in 1990 but, agonisingly, they lost on penalties in the semi-final to the eventual winners, West Germany.**

• In 1996 England hosted the European Championships and were again knocked out on penalties by Germany at the semi-final stage. England have lost four more times on penalties at major tournaments, to leave them with the worst shoot-out record (one win in seven) of any country in the world.

• **Long-serving goalkeeper Peter Shilton won a record 125 caps for England, keeping a record 66 clean sheets. With 53 goals for England, Wayne Rooney is the leading scorer for the Three Lions.**

• Legendary winger Stanley Matthews holds the record for the longest England

TOP 10

TOP 10 ENGLAND GOALSCORERS

1.	Wayne Rooney (2003-16)	53
2.	Bobby Charlton (1958-70)	49
3.	Gary Lineker (1984-92)	48
4.	Jimmy Greaves (1959-67)	44
5.	Michael Owen (1998-2008)	40
6.	Tom Finney (1946-58)	30
	Nat Lofthouse (1950-58)	30
	Alan Shearer (1992-2000)	30
9.	Vivian Woodward (1903-11)	29
	Frank Lampard (1999-2014)	29

England: the quest for a first trophy since 1966 goes on...and on

career - an incredible 22 years and 228 days from 1934 to 1957.

• **David Beckham won a record 55 England caps while outside the English league system during his time with Real Madrid, LA Galaxy and AC Milan.**

• The most number of goals scored in a match by one England player is five. The last of the four players to achieve this feat was Malcolm Macdonald, who netted all the Three Lions' goals in a 5-0 win over Cyprus in 1975.

• **The highest number of appearances by an England player without once finishing on the winning side is six, by Bolton defender Tommy Banks in 1958.**

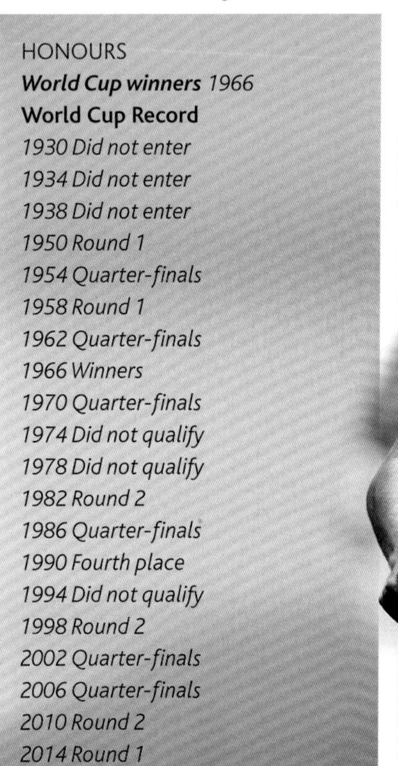

HONOURS
***World Cup winners** 1966*
World Cup Record
1930 Did not enter
1934 Did not enter
1938 Did not enter
1950 Round 1
1954 Quarter-finals
1958 Round 1
1962 Quarter-finals
1966 Winners
1970 Quarter-finals
1974 Did not qualify
1978 Did not qualify
1982 Round 2
1986 Quarter-finals
1990 Fourth place
1994 Did not qualify
1998 Round 2
2002 Quarter-finals
2006 Quarter-finals
2010 Round 2
2014 Round 1

CHRISTIAN ERIKSEN

Born: Middelfart, Denmark, 14th February 1992
Position: Midfielder
Club career:
2010-13 Ajax 113 (25)
2013- Tottenham Hotspur 134 (34)
International record:
2010- Denmark 69 (14)

Silky Tottenham Hotspur midfielder Christian Eriksen was a stand-out performer for Spurs in the 2016/17 season, contributing a club record 15 assists, a total only bettered by Manchester City's Kevin De Bruyne. The Dane also had an incredible 133 shots on goal, a figure only bettered by City striker Sergio Aguero, and took more corners (195) than any other player.

• **As a youth player with Odense Boldklub, Eriksen was a transfer target for numerous top European clubs, but after trials with Chelsea, Manchester United, Barcelona and Real Madrid, he decided to join Ajax as a 16-year-old in 2008. It proved to be a wise move, as the youngster soon cemented a place in the Dutch giants' side and went on to win three league titles before joining Spurs for £11 million in 2013. He was a key figure in Tottenham's run to the 2015 League Cup final, scoring both goals in a 2-2 draw at Sheffield United in the second leg of the semi-final that secured Spurs a 3-2 aggregate win.**

A rare image of Christian Eriksen not taking a corner or free kick

• When he made his international debut in 2010 against Austria, aged 18, Eriksen became the fourth youngest Danish player ever to appear for the national team. He then became the youngest Danish player ever to score in a European Championship qualifier when he netted in a 2-0 win against Iceland the following year.

• **Eriksen is the only player to be named Danish Footballer of the Year three years running, collecting the award in 2014, 2015 and 2016.**

EUROPA LEAGUE

In 2016 Sevilla became the first club to win the same European trophy three years on the trot since Bayern Munich in the 1970s when they beat Liverpool 3-1 in the Europa League final in Basle. The Spanish side's success was all the more remarkable as they had started the season in the Champions League as their reward for winning the Europa League in 2015.

• **In 2011, a year after the competition was rebranded as the Europa League, Porto beat Braga 1-0 in Dublin in the first ever all-Portuguese European final. Porto's match-winner was Colombian striker Radamel Falcao, whose goal in the final was his 17th in the competition that season – a record for the tournament.**

• The competition is now in its third incarnation, having previously been known as the Fairs Cup (1955-71) and the UEFA Cup (1971-2009). The tournament was originally established in 1955 as a competition between cities, rather than clubs. The first winners were Barcelona, who beat London 8-2 on aggregate in a final which, bizarrely, did not take place until 1958! Sevilla have the best overall record in the competition with five wins in total, all of their triumphs coming since 2006.

• **The first team to win the newly named UEFA Cup were Tottenham Hotspur in 1972, who beat Wolves 3-2 on aggregate in the only all-English final. Following Manchester United's triumph in the 2017 Europa League final against Ajax, English clubs have**

The Europa League trophy is a heavy old piece of silverware, as Paul Pogba discovered in 2017

won the competition 12 times... an impressive record, although Spanish teams lead the way with 16 victories.

• Swedish striker Henrik Larsson is the leading scorer in the history of the UEFA Cup with 40 goals for Feyenoord, Celtic and Helsingborg between 1993 and 2009.

• In 1980 all four semi-finalists came from the same nation, Germany – the only time this has happened in European competition. After dispensing with Bayern Munich and Schalke respectively, Eintracht Frankfurt beat Borussia Monchengladbach in the final on the away goals rule.

EUROPEAN CHAMPIONSHIPS

Originally called the European Nations Cup, the idea for the European Championships came from Henri Delaunay, the then secretary of the French FA. The first championships in 1960 featured just 17 countries (the four British nations, Italy and West Germany were among those who declined to take part). The first winners of the tournament were the Soviet Union, who beat Yugoslavia 2-1 in the final in Paris.

• Germany have the best record in the tournament, having won the trophy three times (in 1972, 1980 and 1996) and been runners-up on a further three occasions. Spain have also won the championships three times (1964, 2008 and 2012) and are the only country to retain the trophy following a 4-0 demolition of Italy in the final at Euro 2012 – the biggest win in any European Championships or World Cup final.

• In the biggest win at the finals the Netherlands thrashed FR Yugoslavia 6-1 in 2000.

• French legend Michel Platini and Portugal's Cristiano Ronaldo are the leading scorers in the finals of the European Championships with nine goals each. Platini's goals all came in 1984, setting a record for a single tournament.

• Including qualifying matches, Cristiano Ronaldo is the leading scorer in the competition with 29 goals and is the only player to have scored at four finals (2004, 2008, 2012 and 2016). Ronaldo has also made a record 21 appearances at the finals.

• In the qualifying tournament for the 2008 finals, Germany recorded the biggest ever win in the history of the competition, thrashing minnows San Marino 13-0 on their home patch.

• Real Madrid starlet Martin Odegaard is the youngest player to feature in the qualifying tournament, coming on as a sub for Norway against Bulgaria in October 2014 aged 15 and 300 days.

European Championships finals

1960 USSR 2 Yugoslavia 1 (Paris)
1964 Spain 2 USSR 1 (Madrid)
1968 Italy 2 Yugoslavia 0 • (Rome)
1972 West Germany 3 USSR 0 (Brussels)
*1976 Czechoslovakia 2 * West Germany 2 (Belgrade)*
1980 West Germany 2 Belgium 1 (Rome)
1984 France 2 Spain 0 (Paris)
1988 Netherlands 2 USSR 0 (Munich)
1992 Denmark 2 Germany 0 (Gothenburg)
1996 Germany 2 Czech Republic 1 (London)
2000 France 2 Italy 1 (Rotterdam)
2004 Greece 1 Portugal 0 (Lisbon)
2008 Spain 1 Germany 0 (Vienna)
2012 Spain 4 Italy 0 (Kiev)
2016 Portugal 1 France 0 (Paris)
*• After 1-1 draw   * Won on penalties*

EUROPEAN GOLDEN BOOT

Now officially known as the European Golden Shoe, the European Golden Boot has been awarded since 1968 to the leading scorer in league matches in the top division of every European league. Since 1997 the award has been based on a points system which gives greater weight to goals scored in the leading European leagues.

• World superstars Lionel Messi and Cristiano Ronaldo are the only players to have won the award four times, the Barcelona man topping the charts in 2016/17 with 37 goals. Messi also holds the record for the most goals scored by a Golden Shoe winner, with an incredible 50 in 2011/12.

Wayne Rooney is delighted to hear that Everton have spent more seasons in the top flight than any other club

• The first British winner of the award was Liverpool's Ian Rush in 1984, and the most recent was Sunderland's Kevin Phillips in 2000. Since then, Thierry Henry (in 2004 and 2005), Cristiano Ronaldo (in 2008) and Luis Suarez (jointly with Cristiano Ronaldo in 2014) have won the Golden Shoe after topping both the Premier League and European goalscoring charts. When Ronaldo first won the Golden Shoe with Real Madrid in 2011, he became the first player to win the award in two different countries.
• Players based in the Spanish league have won the award a record 13 times.

EUROPEAN SUPER CUP

Founded in 1972 as a two-legged final between the winners of the European Cup and the European Cup Winners' Cup, the European Super Cup trophy is now awarded to the winners of a one-off match between the Champions League and Europa League holders.
• AC Milan and Barcelona have won the trophy a record five times each. Liverpool are the most successful English club in the competition with three victories (in 1977, 2001 and 2005).
• Liverpool's Terry McDermott (against Hamburg in 1977) and Atletico Madrid's Radamel Falcao (against Chelsea in 2012) are the only two players to have ever scored a hat-trick in the European Super Cup.
• Monaco's Stade Louis II has hosted the final a record 16 times, including for 15 consecutive years between 1998 and 2012.
• Spanish clubs have won the Super Cup a record 14 times, while German clubs have the poorest record with just one win in eight appearances.

EVERTON

Year founded: 1878
Ground: Goodison Park (39,572)
Previous name: St Domingo
Nickname: The Toffees
Biggest win: 11-2 v Derby County (1890)
Heaviest defeat: 0-7 v Sunderland (1934), v Wolves (1939) and v Arsenal (2005)

The club was formed as the church team St Domingo in 1878, adopting the name Everton (after the surrounding area) the following year. In 1888 Everton joined the Football League as founder members, winning the first of nine league titles three years later.
• One of the most famous names in English football, Everton hold the proud record of spending more seasons, 115, in the top flight than any other club. Relegated only twice, in 1930 and 1951, they have spent just four seasons in total outside the top tier.
• The club's unusual nickname, the Toffees, stems from a local business called Ye Ancient Everton Toffee House which was situated near Goodison Park. In the early 1930s Everton's precise style of play earned the club the tag 'The School of Science', a nickname which lingers to this day.
• The club's record goalscorer is the legendary Dixie Dean, who notched an incredible total of 383 goals in all competitions between 1925 and 1937. Dean's best season for the club was in the Toffees' title-winning campaign in 1927/28 when his 60 league goals set a Football League record that is unlikely ever to be beaten. Then, in 1930/31, he scored in a Football League record 12 consecutive games. Dean's total of 349 league goals is a record for a player with the same club.
• Everton's most capped player is long-serving goalkeeper Neville Southall, who made a record 92 appearances for Wales in the 1980s and 1990s. He is also the club's record appearance maker, turning out in 578 league games.
• In 1931 Everton won the Second Division title, scoring 121 goals in the process. The following season the Toffees banged in 116 goals on their way to lifting the First Division title, becoming the first club to find the net 100 times in consecutive seasons.

• The club's most successful decade, though, was in the 1980s when, under manager Howard Kendall, they won the league championship (1985 and 1987), FA Cup (1984) and the European Cup Winners' Cup (in 1985, following a 3-1 win over Austria Vienna in the final). Since those glory days Everton have had to play second fiddle to city rivals Liverpool, although the Toffees did manage to win the FA Cup for a fifth time in 1995, beating Manchester United in the final thanks to a single goal by striker Paul Rideout.

• The club's record signing is Icelandic midfielder Gylfi Sigurdsson, who moved to Merseyside from Swansea City for £45 million in August 2017. A month earlier the Toffees' Belgian striker Romelu Lukaku joined Manchester United for £75 million in the most expensive transfer deal between two Premier League clubs.

• In 1893 Everton's Jack Southworth became the first player in Football League history to score six goals in a match when he fired a double hat-trick in a 7-1 victory against West Bromwich Albion.

• Everton's Louis Saha scored the fastest ever goal in the FA Cup final, when he netted after just 25 seconds against Chelsea at Wembley in 2009. However, the Toffees were unable to hold on to their lead and were eventually beaten 2-1 – one of a record eight times Everton have lost in the final.

• The oldest ground in the Premier League, Goodison Park is the only stadium in the world to have a church, St Luke the Evangelist, inside its grounds.

• Everton were the first club to win a penalty shoot-out in the European Cup, beating German outfit Borussia Monchengladbach 4-3 at Goodison Park in 1970.

• Everton have scored a record 6,923 goals in the top flight of English football.

HONOURS
Division 1 champions *1891, 1915, 1928, 1932, 1939, 1963, 1970, 1985, 1987*
Division 2 champions *1931*
FA Cup *1906, 1933, 1966, 1984, 1995*
European Cup Winners' Cup *1985*

EXETER CITY

Year founded: 1904
Ground: St James Park (8,541)
Nickname: The Grecians
Biggest win: 14-0 v Weymouth (1908)
Heaviest defeat: 0-9 v Notts County (1948) and v Northampton Town (1958)

Exeter City were founded in 1904 following the amalgamation of two local sides, Exeter United and St Sidwell's United. The club were founder members of the Third Division (South) in 1920 and remained in the two lower divisions until they were relegated to the Conference in 2003. Now owned by the Exeter City Supporters' Trust, the club rejoined the Football League in 2008.

• The Grecians have twice reached the quarter-finals of the FA Cup, losing to Sunderland in a replay in 1931 and to eventual winners Tottenham in 1981.

• Club legend Arnie Mitchell played a record 516 games for Exeter between 1952 and 1966. The Grecians' record scorer is Tony Kellow with 129 league goals in three spells at St James Park between 1976 and 1988.

• On a tour of South America in 1914 Exeter became the first club side to play the Brazilian national team. The Grecians lost 2-0 but the occasion has gone into club folklore, with Exeter fans delighting in taunting their opponents by chanting, "Have you ever, have you ever, have you ever played Brazil?"

HONOURS
Division 4 champions *1990*

EXTRA-TIME

Normally consisting of two halves of 15 minutes each, extra-time has been played to produce a winner in knock-out tournaments since the earliest days of football, although to begin with the playing of the additional time had to be agreed by the two captains. Extra-time was first played in an FA Cup final in 1875, Royal Engineers and the Old Etonians drawing 1-1 (Royal Engineers won the replay 2-0). In all, extra-time has been played in 20 finals, the most recent in 2016 when Manchester United beat Crystal Palace 2-1 despite being reduced to 10 men after Chris Smalling was sent off.

• The first World Cup final to go to extra-time was in 1934, when hosts Italy and Czechoslovakia were tied 1-1 at the end of 90 minutes. Seven minutes into the additional period, Angelo Schiavio scored the winner for Italy. Since then, six other finals have gone to extra-time, most recently in 2014 when Germany's Mario Gotze scored the winner against Argentina with just seven minutes left to play.

• In an attempt to encourage attacking football and reduce the number of matches settled by penalty shoot-outs, FIFA ruled in 1993 that the first goal scored in extra-time would win the match. The first major tournament to be decided by the so-called 'golden goal' rule was the 1996 European Championships, Germany defeating the Czech Republic in the final thanks to a 94th-minute strike by Oliver Bierhoff. The 2000 final of the same competition was also decided in the same manner, David Trezeguet scoring a stunning winner for France against Italy in the 103rd minute.

• Concerns that the 'golden goal' put too much pressure on referees led UEFA to replace it with the 'silver goal' in 2002. Under this rule, which was used at Euro 2004 but scrapped afterwards, only the first half of extra-time was played if either team led at the interval.

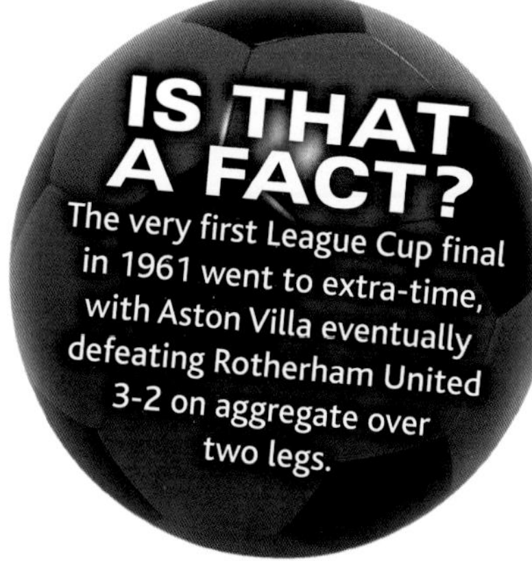

FA CUP

The oldest knock-out competition in the world, the FA Cup dates back to 1871 when it was established under the control of the Football Association. The first round of the first FA Cup was played on 11th November 1871, Clapham Rovers' Jarvis Kenrick scoring the very first goal in the competition in a 3-0 win over Upton Park.

• **The following year Wanderers beat Royal Engineers at Kennington Oval in the first ever FA Cup final. The only goal of the game was scored by Morton Peto Betts, who played under the pseudonym A.H. Chequer. Uniquely, Wanderers, as holders, were given a bye all the way through to the following year's final, and they took full advantage by beating Oxford University 2-1.**

• The FA Challenge Cup – the competition's full title – has always retained the same name despite being sponsored in recent years by Littlewoods (1994-98), AXA (1998-2002), E.ON (2006-11), Budweiser (2011-14) and Emirates (2015-).

TOP 10 FA CUP FINAL WINS

1.	Arsenal	13
2.	Manchester United	12
3.	Tottenham Hotspur	8
4.	Aston Villa	7
	Chelsea	7
	Liverpool	7
7.	Blackburn Rovers	6
	Newcastle United	6
9.	Everton	5
	Manchester City	5
	Wanderers	5
	West Bromwich Albion	5

• **There have, however, been five different trophies. The first trophy – known as the 'little tin idol' – was stolen from a Birmingham shop window in September 1895 where it was on display, having been won by Aston Villa a few months earlier. Sixty years later the thief revealed that the trophy was melted down and turned into counterfeit coins. A second trophy was used until 1910 when it was presented to the FA's long-serving President and former five-time cup winner, Lord Kinnaird.**

Arsenal have won the FA Cup a record 13 times

A new, larger trophy was commissioned by the FA from Fattorini and Sons Silversmiths in Bradford – and, by a remarkable coincidence, was won in its first year by Bradford City in 1911. This trophy was used until 1992, when it was replaced with an exact replica. In 2014 a new trophy, with an identical design to the 1911 one, was presented to that year's winners, Arsenal.

• The most successful club in the competition is Arsenal, who won the cup for a record 13th time in 2017 when they beat Chelsea 2-1 in the final. The only league team to have won the FA Cup in three consecutive years are Blackburn Rovers, who lifted the trophy in 1884, 1885 and 1886.

• **In 2000 Manchester United became the first holders not to defend their title when they failed to enter the FA Cup, opting instead to take part in the inaugural FIFA Club World Championship in Brazil.**

• Five years later United were involved in the first FA Cup final to be decided by penalties, losing 5-4 to Arsenal after a 0-0 draw at the Millennium Stadium, Cardiff. In 2007 the final returned to Wembley, Chelsea becoming the first club to lift the trophy at the new national stadium after a 1-0 victory over Manchester United.

• **Tottenham Hotspur are the only non-league side to win the competition since the formation of the Football League in 1888, lifting the trophy for the first time in 1901 while members of the Southern League. West Ham were the last team from outside the top flight to win the cup, beating Arsenal 1-0 in the 1980 final.**

• The only non-English club to win the FA Cup are Cardiff City, who beat Arsenal 1-0 in 1927. Previously, Scottish club Queen's Park reached the final in 1884 and 1885 but lost on both occasions to Blackburn Rovers.

• **In 1887 Preston North End recorded the biggest win in the history of the competition when they thrashed Hyde 26-0 in a first-round tie. In the same season, Preston's Jimmy Ross scored a record 19 goals in the competition.**

• Ashley Cole has won the FA Cup a record seven times. Three of his triumphs came with Arsenal (in 2002, 2003 and 2005), and he also enjoyed four successes with Chelsea (in 2007,

2009, 2010 and 2012). Arsenal boss Arsène Wenger has won the cup a record seven times as a manager between 1998 and 2017.

• The leading scorer in the FA Cup is Notts County's Henry Cursham, who banged in 49 goals between 1877 and 1888. Liverpool's Ian Rush scored a record five goals in three appearances in the final in 1986, 1989 and 1992, but Chelsea's Didier Drogba is the only player to have scored in four finals (2007, 2009, 2010 and 2012).

• In the 2016/17 season Lincoln City became the first non-league team since QPR in 1914 to reach the quarter-finals of the FA Cup, but their hopes of a Wembley appearance were dashed when they lost 5-0 at Arsenal.

FAMILIES

The first brothers to win the World Cup together were West Germany's Fritz and Ottmar Walter in 1954. England's Bobby and Jack Charlton famously repeated the feat in 1966, when the Three Lions beat West Germany 4-2 in the final at Wembley.

• The only time two sets of brothers have played in the FA Cup final was in 1876 when the victorious Wanderers side included Frank and Hubert Heron, while losers Old Etonians' line-up featured Alfred and Edward Lyttelton.

• Between 1995 and 2007 Gary and Phil Neville won a total of 144 caps for England, a record for a pair of brothers, and played in a record 31 matches together. The Nevilles also played in a record total of 903 Premier League matches, the majority of them for Manchester United.

• The first time a father and son both played in the same international match was in 1996 when 17-year-old Eidur Gudjohnsen came on for his father Arnor, 34, in Iceland's 3-0 win over Estonia. At the 2010 World Cup, brothers opposed each other in an international for the first time when Jerome Boateng (Germany) lined up against Kevin-Prince Boateng (Ghana).

• The last time three brothers lined up on the same side in the English top flight was on 9th September 1989 when Danny, Ray and Rod Wallace played in Southampton's 4-4 draw at Norwich City.

• On 24th October 2015 Jordan Ayew (Aston Villa) and Andre Ayew (Swansea City) became the first brothers to score for different sides in the same Premier League match. Andre ended up the happier, though, as the Swans won 2-1 at Villa Park.

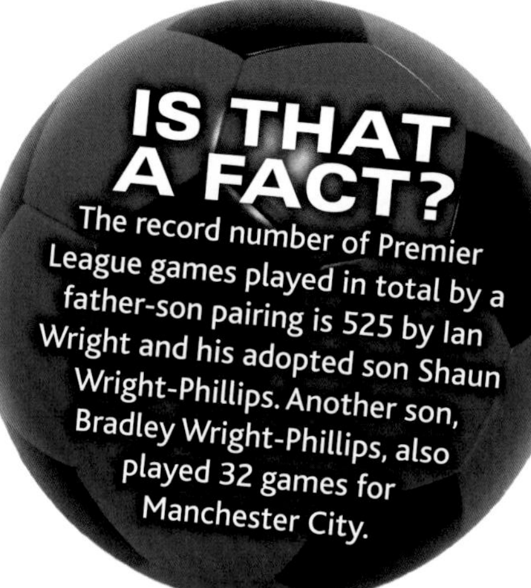

SIR ALEX FERGUSON

Born: Govan, 31st December 1942
Managerial career:
1974 East Stirling
1974-78 St Mirren
1978-86 Aberdeen
1985-86 Scotland (caretaker)
1986-2013 Manchester United

Sir Alex Ferguson is the most successful British manager in the history of the game. Over his long career he won 38 major trophies and is the only manager from these shores to win the Champions League on two occasions.

• Ferguson's reputation was forged at Aberdeen between 1978 and 1986 where he transformed the Dons into Scotland's leading club, breaking the domination of the Glasgow Old Firm in the process. Under Fergie, Aberdeen won three Premier Division titles, four Scottish Cups, one League Cup and the European Cup Winners' Cup in1983, making him easily the most successful boss in the club's history.

• He moved to Manchester United in 1986 and, after some difficult early years, established the Reds as the dominant force of the 1990s and the new millennium. With United Ferguson won a record 13 Premier League titles, five FA Cups, three League Cups, the European Cup Winners' Cup (in 1991) and the Champions League in both 1999 and 2008.

• Fergie's 26-year and 1,500-game tenure at Old Trafford from November 1986 until his retirement in May 2013 included a record 625 top-flight wins and made him the Premier League's and Manchester United's longest serving manager, ahead of the 24-year stint of another Scot, Sir Matt Busby.

• Ferguson is the only man to guide both Scottish and English clubs to success in all three domestic competitions and in Europe. He is also the only manager to win the English championship in three consecutive seasons with the same club twice, achieving this feat with United (1999-2001 and 2007-09). In the first of those years Fergie also won the FA Cup and Champions League to pull off an unprecedented Treble.

• A committed but not especially skilful striker in his playing days in the 1960s and early 1970s, Ferguson scored over 150 goals for a number of Scottish clubs including Dunfermline, Rangers and Falkirk.

• Knighted for services to football in 1999, Ferguson was named Premier League Manager of the Year on a record 11 occasions, claiming the award for the last time at the end of the 2012/13 season. Following the announcement of his retirement from the game, tributes flooded in from far and wide, with then Prime Minister David Cameron describing Ferguson as "a remarkable man in British football".

FEYENOORD

Year founded: 1908
Ground: De Kuip (51,117)
Previous names: Wilhelmina, Hellesluis, Celeritas, Feijenoord
Nickname: The club aan de Maas (The club on the Meuse)
League titles: 15
Domestic cups: 12
European cups: 3
International cups: 1

One of the 'Big Three' clubs in the Netherlands along with arch rivals Ajax and PSV Eindhoven, Feyenoord were founded in 1908 as Wilhelmina by a Dutch mining businessman. After two early name changes, the club settled on 'Feijenoord' in 1912 after the local district where it was based in Rotterdam. In an effort to help foreigners pronounce the club's name correctly, the spelling was changed to Feyenoord in 1974.

Feyenoord really quite enjoyed winning the Dutch league title in 2017...

• In 1970 Feyenoord became the first Dutch club to win a European trophy when they beat Celtic 2-1 in the final of the European Cup in Milan. The club can also boost two triumphs in the UEFA Cup, against Tottenham in 1974 and Borussia Dortmund in 2002 when Feyenoord had the advantage of playing the final on home turf.

• The club's stadium, De Kuip ('The Tub'), is famous for the fiercely partisan atmosphere created by the home fans, who are known as Het Legioen ('The Legion'). In recognition of their fans' unwavering support the number 12 shirt is never worn by a Feyenoord player but is officially awarded to Het Legioen instead.

• During the North Sea floods of 1953 thousands of Rotterdam residents took refuge in De Kuip until the waters retreated. Around 2,000 Dutch people were killed in the floods, while over 30,000 animals also perished.

• Feyenoord have won the Dutch title 15 times, a record only surpassed by Ajax and PSV. The club's most recent triumph came in 2017 when they led the league from start to finish and clinched their first title for 18 years with a final-day 3-1 victory against Heracles.

HONOURS
Dutch League champions *1924, 1928, 1936, 1938, 1940, 1961, 1962, 1965, 1969, 1971, 1974, 1984, 1993, 1999, 2017*
Dutch Cup *1930, 1935, 1965, 1969, 1980, 1984, 1991, 1992, 1994, 1995, 2008, 2016*
European Cup/Champions League *1970*
UEFA Cup *1974, 2002*
Intercontinental Cup *1970*

FIFA

FIFA, the Federation Internationale de Football Association, is the most important administrative body in world football. It is responsible for the organisation of major international tournaments, notably the World Cup, and enacts law changes in the game.

• Founded in Paris in 1904, FIFA is now based in Zurich and has 211 members, 18 more than the United Nations. The President is Gianni Infantino, who was elected in February 2016 after his long-serving predecessor, Sepp Blatter, was banned from any role in FIFA for six years for making unauthorised payments to then UEFA President Michel Platini. Infantino has promised to clean up an organisation whose reputation has been badly damaged in recent years by allegations that high-ranking FIFA officials have been involved in serious criminal activity, including racketeering and money laundering.

• Law changes that FIFA have introduced into the World Cup include the use of substitutes (1970), penalty shoot-outs to settle drawn games (1982) and three points for a group-stage win (1994).

• The British football associations have twice pulled out of FIFA. First, in 1918 when they were opposed to playing matches against Germany after the end of the First World War, and in 1928 over the issue of payments to amateurs. This second dispute meant that none of the British teams were represented at the first World Cup in 1930.

• In 1992 FIFA decided to introduce a ranking index for all its member countries. As of September 2017 the top-ranked nation was Brazil, followed by Germany and Argentina.

ROBERTO FIRMINO

Born: Maceio, Brazil, 2nd October 1991
Position: Midfielder/striker
Club career:
2009-10 Figueirense 38 (8)
2010-15 1899 Hoffenheim 140 (35)
2015- Liverpool 66 (21)
International record:
2014- Brazil 15 (5)

Roberto Firmino became Liverpool's third most expensive signing at the time when he joined the Reds from Hoffenheim in the summer of 2015 for a cool £29 million. He has since paid back a good slice of that fee by reaching double figures in the Premier League in both his seasons at Anfield, and helping Liverpool qualify for the Champions League in 2016/17.

• An attacking midfielder who is often used as a centre forward for his pressing ability, Firmino also

'Here's another funny one. Why did the chicken cross the road?...'

possesses good vision, technical skills and an eye for goal. He joined his first club, Figueirense, as a youngster after being spotted by a local football-loving dentist, and he helped Figueirense gain promotion from the Brazilian second tier in 2010, before moving to Germany in January 2011.

• After taking a while to settle with Hoffenheim, Firmino enjoyed a sensational campaign in 2013/14 when he was named the Bundesliga's 'Breakthrough Player' after scoring 16 league goals – a total only bettered by three other players.

• His fine form saw him earn a first cap for Brazil in November 2014 and later that month he scored his first international goal in a friendly against Austria. The following year he was in the Brazil squad that reached the semi-finals of the Copa America in Chile.

FLEETWOOD TOWN

Year founded: 1997
Ground: Highbury Stadium (5,327)
Previous names: Fleetwood Wanderers, Fleetwood Freeport
Nickname: The Trawlermen
Biggest win: 13-0 v Oldham Town (1998)
Heaviest defeat: 0-7 v Billingham Town (2001)

Established in 1997 as the third incarnation of a club which dates back to 1908, Fleetwood Town have enjoyed a remarkable rise in recent years. In 2012 the Trawlermen were promoted to the Football League as Conference champions, and just two years later they went up to the third tier after beating Burton Albion 1-0 in the League Two play-off final. Another promotion beckoned in 2017, until Fleetwood were narrowly beaten by Bradford City in the League One play-off semi-final.

• The Trawlermen's highest capped international is right-back Conor McLaughlin, who won 22 caps for Northern Ireland between 2012-17.

• In May 2012 Fleetwood sold striker Jamie Vardy to Leicester City for £1 million – a record fee for a non-league club.

• Since making his debut for Fleetwood in the North West Counties Football League Division One in 2003, long-serving defender Nathan Pond has played for the Trawlermen in seven different divisions – a world record for a player at the same club.

• In their short period in the Football League Fleetwood striker David Ball is the club's top scorer with 41 league goals.

HONOURS
Conference champions 2012

FLOODLIGHTS

The first ever floodlit match was played at Bramall Lane between two representative Sheffield sides on 14th October 1876 in front of a crowd of 10,000 people (around 8,000 of whom used the cover of darkness to get in without paying). The pitch was illuminated by four lamps, powered by dynamos driven by engines located behind the goals.

• For many years the Football Association banned floodlit football, so the first league match played under lights did not take place until 1956, when Newcastle beat Portsmouth 2-0

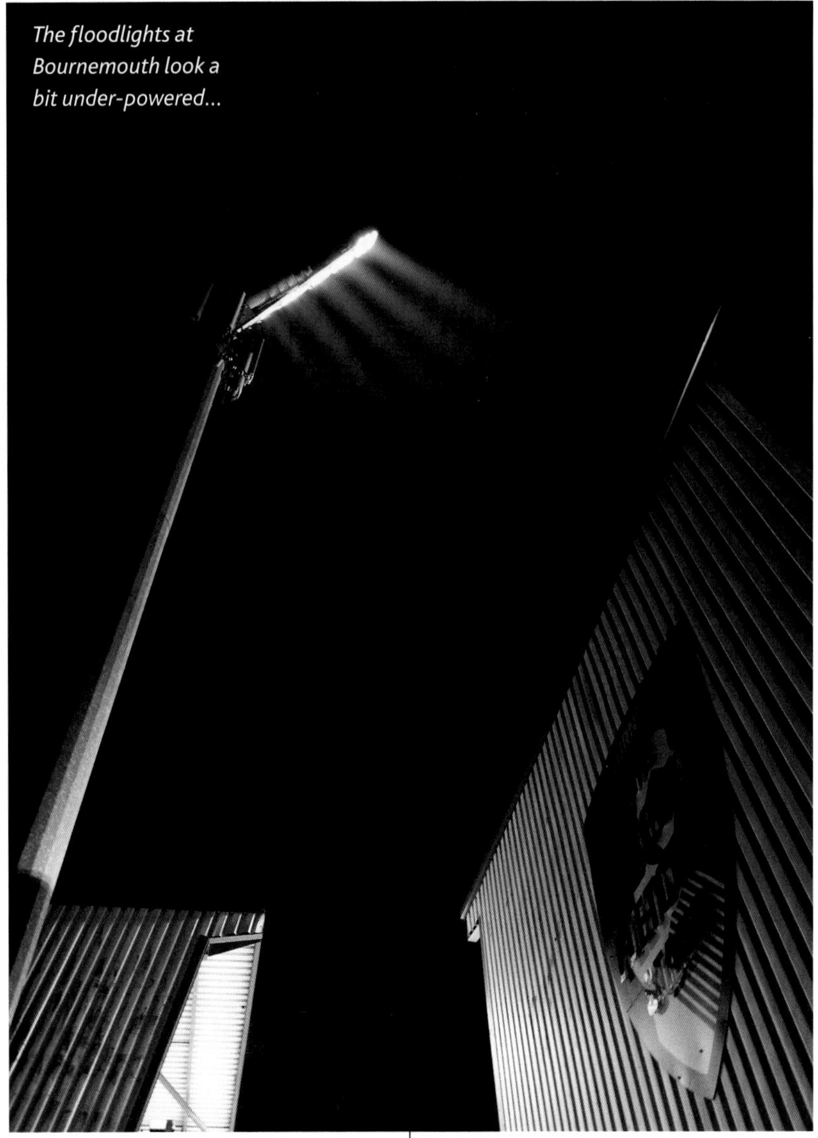

The floodlights at Bournemouth look a bit under-powered...

at Fratton Park. It was hardly the most auspicious of occasions, though, as floodlight failure meant the kick-off was delayed for 30 minutes.

• Arsenal became the first top-flight club in England to install floodlights in 1951 – some 20 years after legendary Gunners manager Herbert Chapman had advocated their use. Chesterfield were the last Football League club to install floodlights, finally putting up a set in 1967.

• In the winter of 1997 two Premier League games, at West Ham and Wimbledon, were abandoned because of floodlight failure. What seemed to be an unfortunate coincidence was eventually revealed to be the work of a shadowy Far Eastern betting syndicate, four members of whom were eventually arrested and sentenced to three years each in prison.

• The first club in Scotland to stage a match under modern floodlights were Stenhousemuir in November 1951. Almost exactly 30 years later Stranraer's Stair Park became the last senior ground in Britain to install floodlights.

FOOTBALL ASSOCIATION

Founded in 1863 at a meeting at the Freemasons' Tavern in central London, the Football Association is the oldest football organisation in the world and the only national association with no mention of the country in its name.

• The first secretary of the FA was Ebenezer Cobb Morley of Barnes FC, nicknamed 'The Father of Football', who went on to draft the first set of laws of the game. The most controversial of the 14 laws he suggested outlawed kicking an opponent, known as 'hacking'. The first match to be played under the new laws was between Barnes and Richmond in 1863.

• In 1871 the then secretary of the FA, Charles Alcock, suggested playing a national knock-out tournament similar to the competition he had enjoyed as a schoolboy at Harrow School. The idea was accepted by the FA and the competition, named the FA Challenge Cup, has been running ever since. The FA Cup, as it is usually called, has long been the most famous national club competition in world football.

• Since 1992, the FA has run the English game's top division, the Premier League, which was formed when the old First Division broke away from the then four-division Football League.

• The FA is also responsible for the appointment of the management of the England men's and women's football teams. The FA's main asset is Wembley Stadium, which it owns via its subsidiary, Wembley National Stadium Limited.

• Among the innovations the FA has fought against before finally accepting are the formation of an international tournament, the use of substitutes and the use of floodlights.

FOOTBALL LEAGUE

The Football League was founded at a meeting at the Royal Hotel, Piccadilly, Manchester in April 1888. The prime mover behind the new body was Aston Villa director William McGregor, who became the league's first President.

• The 12 founder members were Accrington, Aston Villa, Blackburn Rovers, Bolton Wanderers, Burnley, Derby County, Everton, Notts County, Preston North End, Stoke City, West Bromwich Albion and Wolverhampton Wanderers. At the end of the inaugural 1888/89 season, Preston were crowned champions.

• In 1892 a new Second Division, absorbing clubs from the rival Football Alliance, was added to the league and by 1905 the two divisions were made up of a total of 40 clubs. After the First World War, the league was expanded again to include a Third Division (later split between North and South sections).

• A further expansion after 1945 took the number of clubs playing in the league to its long-time total of 92. The formation of the Premier League in 1992 reduced the Football League to three divisions – now known as the Championship, League One and League Two.

• As well as being the governing body for the three divisions, the Football League also organises two knock-out competitions: the League Cup (now the

EFL Cup) and the Football League Trophy (now the EFL Trophy).

• In May 2016 the Football League (rebranded as the 'English Football League' for the start of the 2016/17 season) announced plans to reduce the Championship, League One and League Two to 20 clubs each and to form another professional division, League Three, also of 20 clubs. If approved, the revamped format will be established for the start of the 2019/20 season.

FOOTBALL LEAGUE TROPHY

Rebranded as the EFL Trophy in 2016 and known as the Checkatrade Trophy for sponsorship reasons, the Football League Trophy was established in 1983 as a knock-out competition for the 48 League One and League Two clubs.

• The most successful team in the competition are Bristol City with three victories in the final, against Bolton in 1986, Carlisle United in 2003 and Walsall in 2015.

• The competition was expanded in the 2016/17 season to include 16 Premier League and Championship academy teams. Swansea City performed best out of the academies, reaching the quarter-finals before losing on penalties to eventual winners Coventry City.

• However, the new format did not appeal greatly to fans with an all-time competition low attendance of just 274 turning out for the match between West Brom academy and Gillingham at the Hawthorns in November 2016.

FOOTBALLER OF THE YEAR

Confusingly, there are two Footballer of the Year awards in England and Scotland. The Football Writers' Association award was inaugurated in 1948, and the first winner was England winger Stanley Matthews. In 1974 the Professional Footballers' Association (PFA) set up their own award, Leeds hard man Norman 'Bites Yer Legs' Hunter being the first to be honoured by his peers.

• Liverpool midfielder Terry McDermott was the first player to win both awards in the same season after helping Liverpool retain the title in 1980. A total of 18 different players have won both Footballer of the Year awards in the same season, most recently Chelsea midfielder N'Golo Kante in 2017. Former Arsenal striker Thierry Henry won a record five awards, landing the 'double' in both 2003 and 2004, and also carrying off the Football Writers' award in 2006.

• Liverpool players have won the Football Writers' Association award a record 12 times, while Manchester United lead the way in the PFA category with 12 wins.

Football Writers' Player of the Year (Premier League era)

1993 Chris Waddle (Sheffield Wednesday)
1994 Alan Shearer (Blackburn Rovers)
1995 Jurgen Klinsmann (Tottenham)
1996 Eric Cantona (Manchester Utd)
1997 Gianfranco Zola (Chelsea)
1998 Dennis Bergkamp (Arsenal)
1999 David Ginola (Tottenham)
2000 Roy Keane (Manchester Utd)
2001 Teddy Sheringham (Manchester Utd)
2002 Robert Pires (Arsenal)
2003 Thierry Henry (Arsenal)
2004 Thierry Henry (Arsenal)
2005 Frank Lampard (Chelsea)
2006 Thierry Henry (Arsenal)
2007 Cristiano Ronaldo (Manchester Utd)
2008 Cristiano Ronaldo (Manchester Utd)
2009 Steven Gerrard (Liverpool)
2010 Wayne Rooney (Manchester Utd)
2011 Scott Parker (West Ham Utd)
2012 Robin van Persie (Arsenal)
2013 Gareth Bale (Tottenham)
2014 Luis Suarez (Liverpool)
2015 Eden Hazard (Chelsea)
2016 Jamie Vardy (Leicester City)
2017 N'Golo Kante (Chelsea)

Winners of the Football League Trophy – like Coventry City in 2017 – are obliged to wear jesters' hats

PFA Footballer of the Year (Premier League era)
1993 Paul McGrath (Aston Villa)
1994 Eric Cantona (Manchester Utd)
1995 Alan Shearer (Blackburn Rovers)
1996 Les Ferdinand (Newcastle Utd)
1997 Alan Shearer (Newcastle Utd)
1998 Dennis Bergkamp (Arsenal)
1999 David Ginola (Tottenham)
2000 Roy Keane (Manchester Utd)
2001 Teddy Sheringham (Manchester Utd)
2002 Ruud van Nistelrooy (Manchester Utd)
2003 Thierry Henry (Arsenal)
2004 Thierry Henry (Arsenal)
2005 John Terry (Chelsea)
2006 Steven Gerrard (Liverpool)
2007 Cristiano Ronaldo (Manchester Utd)
2008 Cristiano Ronaldo (Manchester Utd)
2009 Ryan Giggs (Manchester Utd)
2010 Wayne Rooney (Manchester Utd)
2011 Gareth Bale (Tottenham)
2012 Robin van Persie (Arsenal)
2013 Gareth Bale (Tottenham)
2014 Luis Suarez (Liverpool)
2015 Eden Hazard (Chelsea)
2016 Riyad Mahrez (Leicester City)
2017 N'Golo Kante (Chelsea)

FOREST GREEN ROVERS

Year founded: 1889
Ground: The New Lawn (5,141)
Previous names: Forest Green, Nailsworth & Forest Green United, Stroud FC
Nickname: Rovers
Biggest win: 8-0 v Hyde (2013)
Heaviest defeat: 0-10 v Gloucester (1900)

Now owned by green energy tycoon Dale Vince, Forest Green Rovers were founded in Nailsworth, Gloucestershire by a local church minister in 1889 and five years later were founder members of the mid-Gloucestershire league. During more than a century in the non-league wilderness the club was briefly renamed Nailsworth & Forest Green United (1911) and Stroud FC (1989).

• **A year after losing 3-1 to Grimsby Town in the National League play-off final, Rovers were finally promoted to the Football League following a 3-1 win against Tranmere Rovers in the 2017 final at Wembley.**

• In 2009 Rovers reached the third round of the FA Cup for the first time in their history, losing 4-3 to Championship side Derby County in front of a record crowd of 4,836 at their New Lawn stadium.

• **In November 2014 Rovers hosted the world's first ever vegan football match (selling no animal-based products) and the following year Rovers officially became a vegan football club.**

• With a population of just 5,794 Nailsworth is the smallest place ever to have a Football League club.

FRANCE

First international: Belgium 3 France 3, 1904
Most capped player: Lilian Thuram, 142 caps (1994-2008)
Leading goalscorer: Thierry Henry, 51 goals (1997-2010)
First World Cup appearance: France 4 Mexico 1, 1930
Biggest win: France 10 Azerbaijan 0, 1995
Heaviest defeat: France 1 Denmark 17, 1908

The fourth most successful European football nation ever, France won the World Cup for the first and only time on home soil in 1998 with a stunning 3-0 victory over Brazil in the final in Paris. Midfield genius Zinedine Zidane was the star of the show, scoring two goals.

• **Two years later France became the first World Cup holders to go on to win the European Championships when they overcame Italy in the final in Rotterdam. This, though, was a much closer affair with the French requiring a 'golden goal' by striker David Trezeguet in extra-time to claim the trophy.**

• France had won the European Championships once before, in 1984. Inspired by the legendary Michel Platini, who scored a record nine goals in the tournament, Les Bleus beat Spain 2-0 in the final in Paris. In 2016 France had another chance to win the trophy on home soil but surprisingly lost 1-0 in the final to Portugal after extra-time.

• **French striker Just Fontaine scored an all-time record 13 goals at the 1958 World Cup finals in Sweden. His remarkable strike rate helped his country finish third in the tournament.**

• When World Cup holders France were beaten 1-0 by Senegal in the 2002 World Cup, it was one of the biggest shocks in the history of the tournament. Les Bleus slumped out of the competition in the first round on that occasion, but bounced back to reach the final again in 2006... only to suffer the agony of a penalty shoot-out defeat at the hands of Italy.

Formidable! France's Ousmane Dembele shows off his best moves

In 2010, though, the French endured another nightmare campaign, internal disputes between leading players and coach Raymond Domenech contributing to a humiliating first-round exit in South Africa.

• Former Bordeaux defender Franck Jurietti set a record for the shortest international career ever when he came on for the last five seconds of France's 4-0 win over Cyprus in October 2005 and never played for his country again.

HONOURS
***World Cup winners** 1998*
***European Championships winners** 1984, 2000*
***Confederations Cup winners** 2001, 2003*
World Cup Record
1930 Round 1
1934 Round 1
1938 Round 2
1950 Did not qualify
1954 Round 1
1958 Third place
1962 Did not qualify
1966 Round 1
1970 Did not qualify
1974 Did not qualify
1978 Round 1
1982 Fourth place
1986 Third place
1990 Did not qualify
1994 Did not qualify
1998 Winners
2002 Round 1
2006 Runners-up
2010 Round 1
2014 Quarter-finals

FREE KICKS

A method for restarting the game after an infringement, free kicks may either be direct (meaning a goal can be scored directly) or indirect (in which case a second player must touch the ball before a goal can be scored).

• Famous free kick goals include Paul Gascoigne's superb effort for Tottenham in the FA Cup semi-final against Arsenal in 1991, David Beckham's last-minute equaliser for England against Greece in 2001, Didier Drogba's winner for Chelsea in the 2010 FA Cup final against Portsmouth, and two stunners by Scotland's Leigh Griffiths against England in a World Cup qualifier at Hampden Park in 2017.

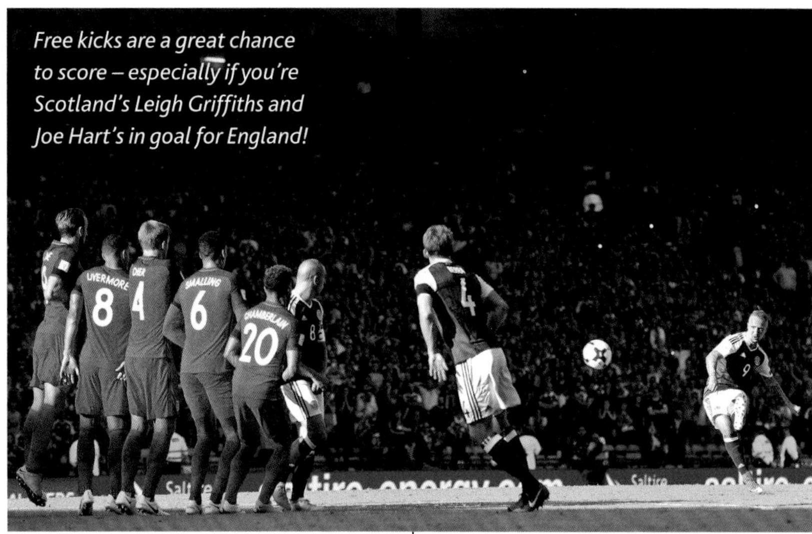
Free kicks are a great chance to score – especially if you're Scotland's Leigh Griffiths and Joe Hart's in goal for England!

• Tottenham goalkeeper Paul Robinson scored the longest-range free kick in Premier League history when he walloped one in from an incredible 96 yards against Watford on 17th March 2007.

• Brazilian midfielder Juninho Pernambucano holds the world record for the most goals scored direct from a free kick with 76, most of them coming during his time at French club Lyon between 2001 and 2009. Incredibly, the record for the most free kicks scored by a player for just one club is held by a goalkeeper, Rogerio Ceni of Sao Paulo with 61.

• David Beckham holds the record for the most Premier League goals direct from free kicks with 15 for Manchester United between 1993 and 2003.

• Vanishing spray from an aerosol can to mark the 10 yards defenders must retreat from an attacking free kick was introduced to the Premier League at the start of the 2014/15 season. The spray was first used at an international tournament in the 2011 Copa America and made its debut at the World Cup in Brazil in 2014.

FRIENDLIES

The first official international friendly took place on 30th November 1872 between Scotland and England at the West of Scotland Cricket Ground, Partick, Glasgow. The Scottish side for the match, which ended in a 0-0 draw, was made up entirely of players from the country's leading club, Queen's Park.

• England's first ever friendly against continental opposition was on 6th June 1908 against Austria in Vienna. England won that match 6-1 and went on to win a record 12 friendlies on the trot before drawing 2-2 with Belgium in 1923.

• On 6th February 2007 London played host to a record four international friendlies on the same night – and England weren't even one of the eight teams in action! At the Emirates Stadium Portugal beat Brazil 2-0, Ghana thrashed Nigeria 4-1 at Brentford's Griffin Park, South Korea beat European champions Greece 1-0 at Craven Cottage, while at Loftus Road Denmark were 3-1 winners over Australia.

• England played a record eight international friendlies in the calendar year 1966. A member of the team at the time, midfielder George Eastham, played in a record 19 matches for England without once appearing in a competitive fixture.

• Then England manager Sven-Goran Eriksson became the first Three Lions boss to substitute all 11 starters in a 2-1 friendly defeat to Italy in 2002. However, two years later FIFA ruled that the maximum number of substitutes that could be used in an international friendly would be limited to six per team.

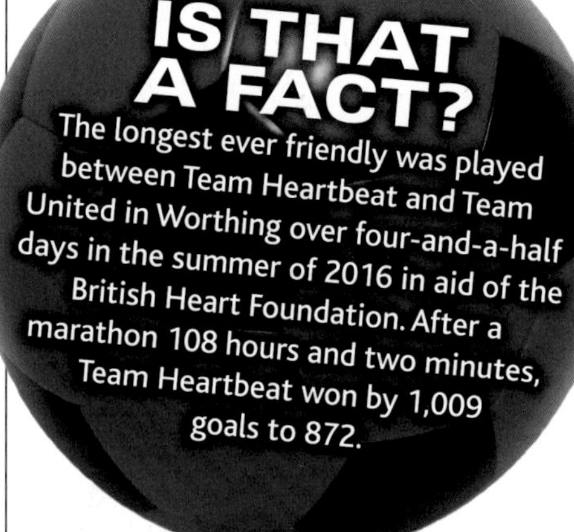

FULHAM

Year founded: 1879
Ground: Craven Cottage (25,700)
Previous name: Fulham St Andrew's
Nickname: The Cottagers
Biggest win: 10-1 v Ipswich Town (1963)
Heaviest defeat: 0-10 v Liverpool (1986)

London's oldest club, Fulham were founded in 1879 by two clergymen. Originally known as Fulham St Andrew's, the club adopted its present name nine years later. After winning the Southern League in two consecutive seasons Fulham were elected to the Football League in 1907.

• **Before moving to Craven Cottage in 1896, Fulham had played at no fewer than 11 different grounds. Including a stay at Loftus Road from 2002-04 while the Cottage was being redeveloped, Fulham have played at 13 venues, a total only exceeded by QPR.**

• The proudest moment in the club's history came in May 2010 when Fulham met Atletico Madrid in Hamburg in the first Europa League final. Sadly for their fans, the Cottagers lost 2-1 in extra-time despite putting up a spirited fight.

• **In 1975 Fulham reached the FA Cup final for the first (and so far only) time, losing 2-0 to West Ham. The Cottagers have appeared in the semi-final six times, including a forgettable occasion in 1908 when they were hammered 6-0 by Newcastle, to this day the biggest ever winning margin at that stage of the competition.**

• Midfield legend Johnny Haynes holds the club's appearance record, turning out in 594 league games between 1952 and 1970. 'The Maestro', as he was known to Fulham fans, is also the club's most honoured player at international level, with 56 England caps. Welsh international striker Gordon Davies is Fulham's top scorer with 159 league goals in two spells at the club between 1978 and 1991.

• **Beaten in the Championship play-off semi-finals in 2017, Fulham made their record signing when they bought Konstantinos Mitroglou from Olympiakos for £12.4 million in January 2014. However, it proved to be a waste of money as the Greek striker failed to score a single goal for the Cottagers, and at the end of the season they were relegated from the Premier League after using a record 39 different players during the campaign.**

• Fulham's biggest ever win, 10-1 against Ipswich on Boxing Day 1963, was the last time a team scored double figures in the English top flight.

• **Rene Meulensteen's 75-day reign at the Cottage in 2013/14 was the second shortest by a permanent manager in the Premier League era.**

HONOURS
Division 2 champions *1949*
First Division champions *2001*
Division 3 (S) champions *1932*
Second Division champions *1999*

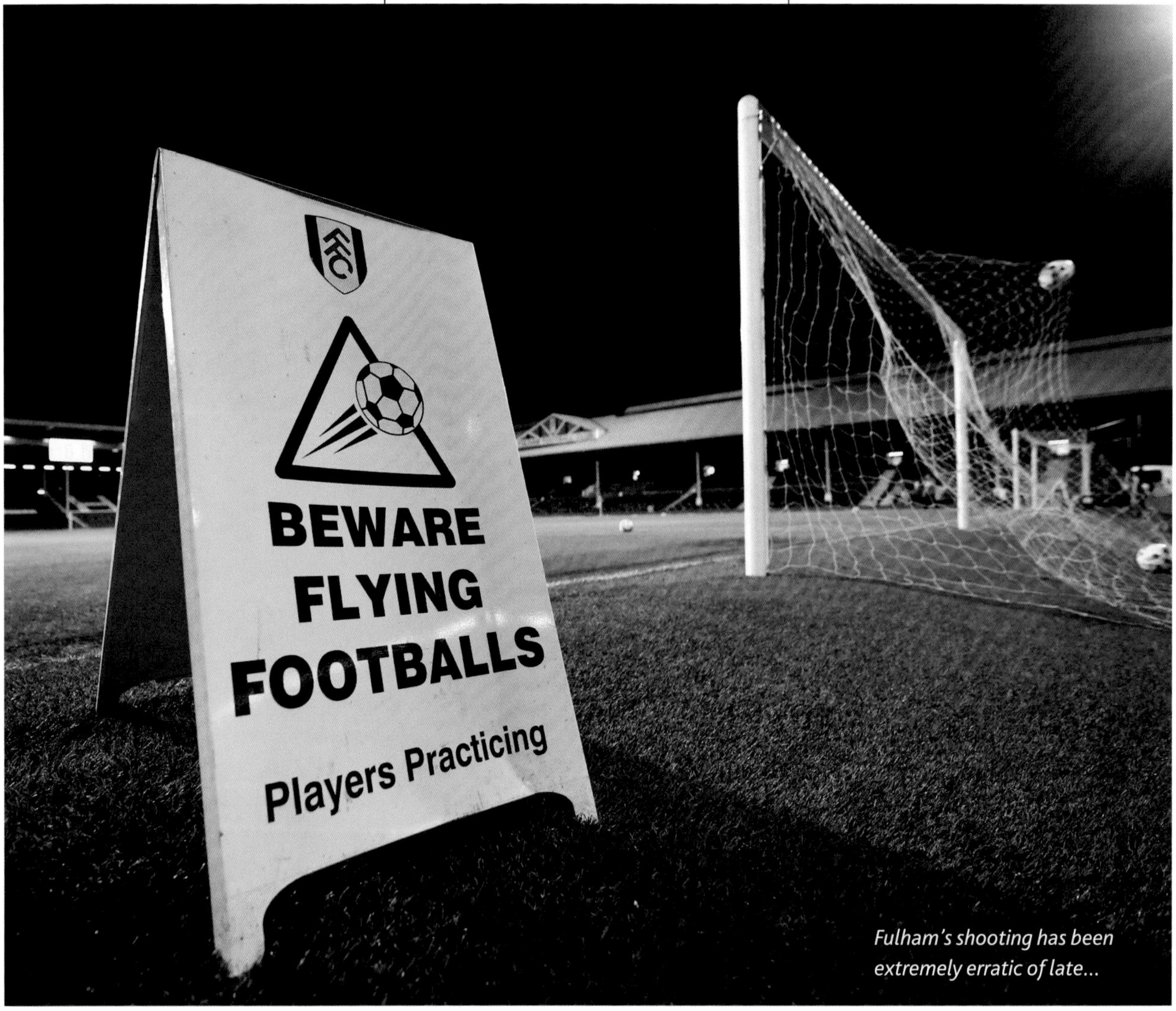

Fulham's shooting has been extremely erratic of late...

DAVID DE GEA

Born: Madrid, 7th November 1990
Position: Goalkeeper
Club career:
2008-09 Atletico Madrid B 35
2009-11 Atletico Madrid 57
2011- Manchester United 200
International record:
2014- Spain 21

When he moved from Atletico Madrid to Manchester United for around £18 million in June 2011 David De Gea was the most expensive goalkeeper in the British game, although he has since slipped to third on the list behind Everton's Jordan Pickford (£25 million) and Manchester City's Ederson Moraes (£35 million).

• After coming through the youth ranks at Atletico, De Gea enjoyed a great first season with the Madrid club, helping them win the Europa League following a 2-1 victory against Fulham in the final in Hamburg. At the start of the next campaign he starred in Atletico's UEFA Super Cup victory over Champions League holders Inter Milan, saving a late penalty from Uruguayan striker Diego Milito.

• Following some unconvincing early performances for United De Gea was dropped by then manager Sir Alex Ferguson, but after winning his place back his form soon improved. In 2013 he helped United win the Premier League title and was voted into the PFA Team of the Year for the first time – he has since been selected four times in total to set a record for a goalkeeper in the Premier League era. In 2016 he helped United win the FA Cup and the following year he added the League Cup and Europa League to his list of honours, although he was on the bench for the last of these finals.

• De Gea has won the BBC's 'Save of the Season' an incredible four times since it was introduced in 2013, finally losing his crown to Burnley's Tom Heaton in 2017. Manchester United's Player of the Year in 2014, 2015 and 2016, De Gea is the only player in the club's history to win this award three times on the trot.

• De Gea made his first appearance for Spain in a 2-0 friendly win against El Salvador in 2014. Two years later he was his country's first-choice goalkeeper at Euro 2016, but couldn't prevent the reigning champions going out of the tournament in the last 16.

With his beard and quiff, David De Gea has perfected the 'hipster' look

GERMANY

First international: Switzerland 5 Germany 3, 1908
Most capped player: Lothar Matthaus, 150 caps (1980-2000)
Leading goalscorer: Miroslav Klose, 71 goals (2001-14)
First World Cup appearance: Germany 5 Belgium 2, 1934
Biggest win: Germany 16 Russian Empire 0, 1912
Heaviest defeat: Austria 6 Germany 0, 1931

Germany (formerly West Germany) have the joint second best record in the World Cup behind Brazil, having won the tournament four times and reached the final on a record eight occasions. They have also won the European Championships a joint-record three times and been losing finalists on another three occasions.

• The Germans recorded their fourth World Cup triumph in Brazil in 2014, when they beat Argentina 1-0 in the final thanks to Mario Gotze's extra-time goal. Perhaps more remarkable,

BIGGEST EUROPEAN CHAMPIONSHIPS AND WORLD CUP (UEFA SECTION) QUALIFYING VICTORIES

1. San Marino 0 Germany 13, 2006
2. West Germany 12 Cyprus 0, 1969
3. Spain 12 Malta 1, 1983
4. Netherlands 11 San Marino 0, 2011
5. Liechtenstein 1 Macedonia 11, 1996
6. Finland 0 Soviet Union 10, 1957
   France 10 Azerbaijan 0, 1995
   Poland 10 San Marino 0, 2009
9. Belgium 10 San Marino 1, 2001
10. Luxembourg 0 England 9, 1960*
   *First of 10 9-0 wins

though, was their performance in the semi-final when they massacred the hosts 7-1 – the biggest ever win at that late stage of the competition and one of the most amazing World Cup scorelines ever. Germany's other victories came in 1954 (against Hungary), on home soil in 1974 (against the Netherlands) and at Italia 90 (against Argentina).

• Lothar Matthaus, a powerhouse in the German midfield for two decades, played in a record 25 matches at the World Cup in five tournaments between 1982 and 1998. His total of 150 caps for Germany is also a national record.

• Germany striker Miroslav Klose is the all-time leading scorer at the World Cup with a total of 16 goals, one ahead of Brazil's Ronaldo and two better than fellow German Gerd 'the Bomber' Muller.

• Between 10th July 2010 and 22nd June 2012 Germany won a world record 15 competitive matches on the trot – a run which ended when they lost 2-1 to Italy in the semi-final of Euro 2012.

• Germany hold the record for the biggest win in the European Championship qualifiers (13-0 against San Marino in 2006) and the UEFA section of the World Cup qualifiers (12-0 against Cyprus in 1969).

HONOURS
World Cup winners 1954, 1974, 1990, 2014
European Championships winners 1972, 1980, 1996
Confederations Cup winners 2017

World Cup Record
1930 Did not enter
1934 Third place
1938 Round 1
1950 Did not enter
1954 Winners
1958 Fourth place
1962 Quarter-finals
1966 Runners-up
1970 Third place
1974 Winners
1978 Round 1
1982 Runners-up
1986 Runners-up
1990 Winners
1994 Quarter-finals
1998 Quarter-finals
2002 Runners-up
2006 Third place
2010 Third place
2014 Winners

STEVEN GERRARD

Born: Whiston, 30th May 1980
Position: Midfielder
Club career:
1998-2015 Liverpool 504 (120)
2015-16 LA Galaxy 34 (5)
International record:
2000-14 England 114 (21)

Now Liverpool youth coach, Anfield legend Steven Gerrard is the only player to have scored in the FA Cup final, the League Cup final, the UEFA Cup final and the Champions League final. He achieved this feat between 2001 and 2006 while winning all four competitions with the Reds (and, indeed, earning winner's medals in the FA Cup and League Cup on two occasions). His 41 goals for the Reds in European football is a record for a British player.

• Famed for his surging runs and thunderous shooting, Gerrard broke into the Liverpool team in 1998 and, five years later, then Anfield boss Gerard Houllier made the Kop idol his skipper – and he retained the armband until he decided to move on to LA Galaxy in 2015. By then he had made more than 500 Premier League appearances for the Reds, one of just three players (along with Ryan Giggs and former team-mate Jamie Carragher) to reach that milestone with one club.

• In the 2006 FA Cup final Gerrard scored two stunning goals against West Ham, including a last-minute equaliser which many rate as the best ever goal in the final. Liverpool went on to win the match on penalties and Gerrard's heroics were rewarded with the 2006 PFA Player of the Year award. Three years later he was voted Footballer of the Year by the football writers. Then, in 2014, he was voted into the PFA Team of the Year for a record eighth time.

• Gerrard made his international debut for England against Ukraine in 2000 and scored his first goal for his country with a superb 20-yarder in the famous 5-1 thrashing of Germany in Berlin in 2001. In the absence of regular skipper Rio Ferdinand, he captained England at the 2010 World Cup and, after being appointed the permanent captain by new boss Roy Hodgson, he led his country at the 2012 European Championships and the 2014 World Cup.

• With 114 caps to his name before he announced his retirement from international football in July 2014, Gerrard is fourth on the list of England's all-time appearance makers behind Peter Shilton, David Beckham and Wayne Rooney.

GIANT-KILLING

Many of the most remarkable instances of giant-killing have occurred in the FA Cup, with teams from lower down the football pyramid beating supposedly superior opposition. The first shock of this type occurred in 1888 when non-league Warwick County beat First Division Stoke City 2-1 in the first qualifying round of the competition.

• Only two non-league teams have beaten Premier League outfits in the FA Cup, Luton Town sensationally beating Norwich City 1-0 in the fourth round in 2013 and Lincoln City surprising Burnley by the same score in the fifth round in 2017.

• In their non-league days Yeovil Town beat a record 20 league teams in the FA Cup. The Glovers' most famous win came in the fourth round in 1949 against First Division Sunderland, who they defeated 2-1 on their notorious sloping pitch at Huish Park.

• After two incredible feats of giant-killing Rochdale (in 1962) and Bradford City (in 2013) both reached the League Cup final. Neither minnow, though, was able to get their hands on the trophy.

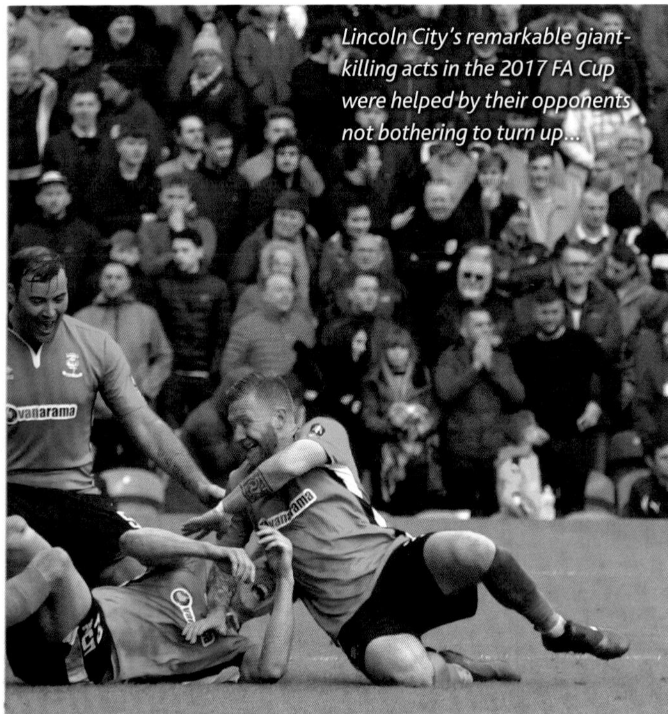
Lincoln City's remarkable giant-killing acts in the 2017 FA Cup were helped by their opponents not bothering to turn up...

• Giant-killings also happen at international level. Among the shocks at the World Cup, for example, are the USA beating England 1-0 in 1950, North Korea defeating Italy 1-0 in 1966 and holders France going down 1-0 to Senegal in 2002.

RYAN GIGGS

Born: Cardiff, 29th November 1973
Position: Winger/midfielder
Club career:
1991-2014 Manchester United 672 (114)
International record:
1991-2007 Wales 64 (12)

In a glorious career with Manchester United, Ryan Giggs became the most decorated player in English football history. Between 1991 and 2014, when he announced his retirement from the game, he won 22 major honours: a record 13 Premier League titles, four FA Cups, three League Cups and two Champions League trophies. In 2009 he was voted PFA Player of the Year by his fellow professionals.

• Giggs scored at least one goal in a record 21 Premier League seasons before drawing a blank in the 2013/14 campaign. He also holds the Premier League appearance record, 632 games, has played in the most wins (407) and has played more games in the top flight for the same club, 672, than any other player.

• A one-club man who briefly filled in as caretaker manager in 2014, Giggs made a record 963 appearances for United in all competitions – 205 more than the previous record holder, Sir Bobby Charlton.

• Giggs enjoyed his best ever year in 1999 when he won the Premiership, FA Cup and Champions League with United. His goal against Arsenal in that season's FA Cup semi-final, when he dribbled past four defenders before smashing the ball into the roof of the net from a tight angle, was voted the best of the past 50 years by *Match of the Day* viewers in 2015.

• A tremendous crosser of the ball, Giggs made a record 162 assists in the Premier League and also holds the record for Champions League assists, with 30. His total of 159 European appearances in the Champions League and UEFA cup is a record for a British player.

TOP 10

PREMIER LEAGUE ASSISTS

1.	Ryan Giggs (1992-2014)	162
2.	Cesc Fabregas (2003-)	107
3.	Frank Lampard (1996-2015)	102
4.	Wayne Rooney (2002-)	101
5.	Dennis Bergkamp (1995-2006)	94
6.	Steven Gerrard (1998-2015)	92
7.	David Beckham (1993-2003)	80
8.	Teddy Sheringham (1992-2006)	76
9.	James Milner (2002-)	75
10.	Thierry Henry (1999-2012)	74

• Once Wales' youngest ever player, Giggs previously played for England Schoolboys under the name Ryan Wilson (the surname being that of his father, a former Welsh rugby league player). However, having no English grandparents, Giggs was ineligible to play for the England national team and was proud to represent Wales on 64 occasions before retiring from international football in 2007.

GILLINGHAM

Year founded: 1893
Ground: Priestfield Stadium (11,582)
Previous name: New Brompton
Nickname: The Gills
Biggest win: 12-1 v Gloucester City (1946)
Heaviest defeat: 2-9 v Nottingham Forest (1950)

Founded by a group of local businessmen as New Brompton in 1893, the club changed to its present name in 1913. Seven years later Gillingham joined the new Third Division but in 1938 were voted out of the league in favour of Ipswich Town. They eventually returned in 1950.

• Goalkeeper John Simpson played in a record 571 league games for the Gills between 1957 and 1972, while his team-mate Brian Yeo scored a club record 136 goals.

• Gillingham made their record signing in 1998 when striker Carl Asaba moved from Reading for £600,000. The following year the club received a record £1.5 million from Manchester City for striker Robert Taylor.

• In their 1995/96 promotion campaign Gillingham only conceded 20 goals – a record for a 46-game season in the Football League.

• Winger Luke Freeman became the youngest ever player in the FA Cup proper when he came on as a sub for Gillingham against Barnet in 2007 aged just 15 years and 233 days.

HONOURS
Division 4 champions *1964*
League Two champions *2013*

OLIVIER GIROUD

Born: Chambery, France, 30th September 1986
Position: Striker
Club career:
2005-08 Grenoble 23 (2)
2007-08 Istres (loan) 33 (14)
2008-10 Tours 44 (24)
2010-12 Montpellier 73 (33)
2010 Tours (loan) 17 (6)
2012- Arsenal 164 (69)
International record:
2011- France 64 (27)

With a total of three wins in the FA Cup (in 2014, 2015 and 2017) Olivier Giroud is just one more triumph away from equalling Didier Drogba's record for an overseas outfield player in the competition.

• A tall, powerful striker who finishes well on the ground and in the air, Giroud first came to the fore when he was top scorer in the French second division with Tours in 2009/10, his goalscoring feats also earning him the Ligue 2 Player of the Year award.

• A move to Montpellier followed, and in only his second season with the club Giroud helped the southern French side win the league for the first time in their history. The striker's 21 goals during the campaign made him the league's joint-top scorer and were instrumental in Montpellier's surprise success.

• Later that summer he joined Arsenal for £9.6 million and he has gone on to become a hugely consistent force for the Gunners, hitting double figures in the Premier League in all five of his seasons at the Emirates.

• Giroud won his first cap for France in a 1-0 friendly win over the USA in 2011. He represented his country at the 2014 World Cup and at Euro 2016, and in June 2017 became the first player to score a hat-trick for his country for 17 years when he hit a treble in a 5-0 demolition of Paraguay.

'I can feel a scorpion kick coming on...'

GOAL CELEBRATIONS

Elaborate and sometimes spectacular goal celebrations have been a feature of English football since the mid-1990s when the Premier League started opening its doors to large numbers of overseas players. Middlesbrough striker Fabrizio Ravanelli, for instance, was famed for pulling his shirt over his head after scoring, and soon players were removing their shirts altogether, sometimes to reveal personal, political or religious messages written on a t-shirt.

• In 2003 FIFA decided that things had got out of hand and ruled that any player removing his shirt would be booked. The first player to be sent off after falling foul of this new law was Everton's Tim Cahill, who was shown a second yellow against Manchester City in 2004.

• In 2013 West Brom striker Nicolas Anelka was fined a record £80,000 by the FA and banned for five matches after celebrating a goal at West Ham by placing his arm across his chest in a gesture known as the 'quenelle' which, especially in Anelka's native France, carries anti-semitic connotations. The former France star was subsequently sacked by his club for gross misconduct.

• In May 2017 three players from Indonesian club Bali United won worldwide praise when they celebrated a goal against Borneo FC by adopting the prayer positions of their respective religions, Islam, Christianity and Hinduism, in a bid to promote peace and harmony in their country.

• In September 2014 Cameroonian striker Joel of Brazilian side Coritiba celebrated a goal against Sao Paulo by jumping over an advertising hoarding – only to fall down a hole leading to an underground stairwell. "I've made a fool of myself," he reflected afterwards.

• In a bizarre goal celebration in Argentina in September 2015, Mariano Gorosito of third division side Lujan jumped into a pitchside ambulance and pretended to drive it after scoring against Merlo. The ref was unamused and showed him a yellow card.

IS THAT A FACT?

When Jamie Vardy scored for England against Spain at Wembley in November 2016, he froze like a statue with team-mates Raheem Sterling and Theo Walcott, the trio reflecting the popular internet video trend 'the mannequin challenge'.

• Many players refuse to celebrate goals against their former clubs. Famous examples include Denis Law for Manchester City against Manchester United in 1974, Cristiano Ronaldo for Real Madrid against United in the Champions League in 2013 and Frank Lampard for Manchester City against Chelsea in 2014.

GOAL OF THE SEASON

The Goal of the Season award has been awarded by the BBC's flagship football programme *Match of the Day* since 1971 (apart from the years 2001-04 when, for broadcasting rights reasons, the award was given by ITV). The first winner was Coventry City's Ernie Hunt, whose spectacular volley against Everton at Highfield Road topped the poll.

• Manchester United striker Wayne Rooney is the only player to win the award three times, most recently in 2011 for an acrobatic overhead kick against local rivals Manchester City. Liverpool's John Aldridge (in 1988 and 1989) and Arsenal's Jack Wilshere (in 2014 and 2015) are the only two players to have won the award in consecutive seasons.

• Incredibly, in 1988 all 10 shortlisted goals were scored by players from Liverpool, that season's league champions. The award was won by John Aldridge for his volley in the FA Cup semi-final against Nottingham Forest.

• Liverpool players have claimed the award a record seven times, the most recent winner being Emre Can in 2017, whose spectacular overhead kick against Watford just pipped a stunning 'scorpion kick' goal by Arsenal's Olivier Giroud.

GOALKEEPERS

• On 27th March 2011 Sao Paulo's Rogerio Ceni became the first goalkeeper in the history of football to score 100 career goals when he netted with a free kick in a 2-1 win against Corinthians. His unlikely century was made up of 56 free kicks and 44 penalties. By the time he retired in 2015 Ceni had taken his career goals total to 131 – better than countless outfield players!

• Just five goalkeepers have scored in the Premier League: Peter Schmeichel (Aston Villa), Brad Friedel (Blackburn Rovers), Paul Robinson (Tottenham), Tim Howard (Everton) and Asmir Begovic (Stoke City). Begovic's goal after just 13 seconds against Southampton in November 2013 is the fastest ever by a goalkeeper in English football history and was scored at a greater distance (91.9 metres) than any goal ever.

• David James has played more Premier League games in goal than any other player with a total of 572 between 1992 and 2010, while Petr Cech holds the clean sheet record with 190 for Chelsea and Arsenal.

• In a long career for Derby County and Bradford Park Avenue between 1907 and 1925, Ernie Scattergood scored eight penalties – a record number of goals for a goalkeeper in the Football League.

• The most expensive goalkeeper in world football is Ederson Moraes, who cost Manchester City £35 million when he joined the club from Benfica in July 2017.

GOAL-LINE TECHNOLOGY

Goal-line technology was introduced to the Premier League for the first time in the 2013/14 season after the league agreed to adopt the Hawk-Eye system, which uses seven cameras per goal and notifies the match officials whether or not the ball has crossed the line via a vibration and optical signal sent to the officials' watches within one second of the incident.

• In July 2012 FIFA's International Football Association Board, which determines the laws of the game, agreed to the principle of using goal-line technology at future FIFA tournaments. The following year Goal Control, a similar system to Hawk-Eye, was used at the 2013 Confederations Cup and again at the 2014 World Cup in Brazil.

• For many years then FIFA President Sepp Blatter was opposed to the introduction of goal-line technology, believing that it would undermine the authority of the match officials. However, he changed his mind after the 2010 World Cup, during which a number of questionable goal-line decisions were made, most notably the denying of a goal to England when Frank Lampard's shot clearly crossed the line in his country's last 16 match with Germany.

• In 2016 the Video Assistant Referee (VAR) system was trialled in America, allowing a referee's decision to be reviewed by an official watching video footage of the incident. On 1st September 2016 the system was used for the first time in an international match, between Italy and France in Bari, and it will also be in place at the 2018 World Cup in Russia.

TOP 10

TOTAL PREMIER LEAGUE GOALS SCORED

	Club	Goals
1.	Manchester United	1,856
2.	Arsenal	1,698
3.	Chelsea	1,645
4.	Liverpool	1,601
5.	Tottenham Hotspur	1,406
6.	Everton	1,259
7.	Manchester City	1,173
8.	Newcastle United	1,168
9.	Aston Villa	1,117
10.	West Ham United	964

GOALS

Manchester United have scored more Premier League goals than any other English club. Up to the start of the 2017/18 season, the Red Devils had managed an impressive 1,856 goals. Tottenham have conceded the most goals in the Premier League, 1,231.

• Peterborough United hold the record for the most league goals in a season, banging in 134 in 1960/61 on their way to claiming the Fourth Division title. Less impressively, Darwen conceded a record 141 goals in the Second Division in 1898/99 and promptly resigned from the Football League.

• Aston Villa hold the top-flight record, with 128 goals in 1930/31. Despite their prolific attack, the Villans were pipped

Just one of the record 1,856 Premier League goals Manchester United have scored

to the First Division title by Arsenal (amazingly, the Gunners managed 127 goals themselves). Title-winners Chelsea became the first team to score a century of goals in the Premier League era in 2009/10, the Blues taking their tally to 103 with an 8-0 thrashing of Wigan on the final day of the season.

• Arthur Rowley scored a record 434 Football League goals between 1946 and 1965, notching four for West Brom, 27 for Fulham, 251 for Leicester City and 152 for Shrewsbury. Former Republic of Ireland international John Aldridge is the overall leading scorer in post-war English football, with an impressive total of 476 goals in all competitions for Newport County, Oxford United, Liverpool and Tranmere between 1979 and 1998.

• Joe Payne set an English Football League record for goals in a game by scoring 10 times for Luton against Bristol Rovers on 13th April 1936. Earlier in the decade, Sheffield United striker Jimmy Dunne scored in a record 12 consecutive league games in the 1931/32 season. The Premier League record is held by Leicester City star Jamie Vardy, who scored in 11 games on the trot in 2015/16.

• The most goals scored in a Football League match is 17 on Boxing Day 1935 when Tranmere hammered Oldham 13-4 in Division Three (North). The Premier League record is a mere 11, when Portsmouth beat Reading 7-4 at Fratton Park in 2007. Neither of these games, though, was anything like as goal-filled as the 1887 FA Cup first-round clash between Preston and Hyde which contained 26 goals – all scored by Preston!

• The biggest win in international football saw Vanuatu hammer Micronesia 46-0 in an Olympic qualifier in July 2015.

• Germany have scored the most goals at the World Cup (224) and at the European Championships (72).

ANTOINE GRIEZMANN

Born: Macon, France, 21st March 1991
Position: Forward
Club career:
2009-14 Real Sociedad 179 (46)
2014- Atletico Madrid 111 (60)
International record:
2014- France 43 (16)

Antoine Griezmann's total of six goals at Euro 2016 helped him win the Player of the Tournament award and was the best return for a player since fellow Frenchman Michel Platini hit a record nine goals at the 1984 tournament.

• However, the nippy forward had to be satisfied with a runners-up medal after the hosts lost in the final to Portugal, and he also finished on the losing side in the 2016 Champions League final after his club, Atletico Madrid, lost on penalties to city rivals Real – a match in which Griezmann missed from the spot in normal time. The Frenchman thus became only the second player (after Michael Ballack in 2008) to lose in both finals in the same season.

• After being rejected by a number of clubs in his native France for being too small, Griezmann began his career with Real Sociedad, helping the Basque outfit win the Segunda Division in his debut campaign in 2009/10. A £24 million move to Atletico Madrid followed in 2014, and in his first season in the Spanish capital Griezmann was voted into the Team of the Year after scoring 22 league goals – a record for a French player in a single La Liga campaign. Following another fine season in 2015/16 he came third in the inaugural Best FIFA Men's Player award.

• After representing his country at Under-19, 20 and 21 level, Griezmann made his senior international debut in 2014 and went on to play for France at that year's World Cup in Brazil.

'Oh no, I've got one of my boots muddled up with somebody else's!'

GRIMSBY TOWN

Year founded: 1878
Ground: Blundell Park (9,027)
Previous name: Grimsby Pelham
Nickname: The Mariners
Biggest win: 8-0 v Darlington (1885) and v Tranmere Rovers (1925)
Heaviest defeat: 1-9 v Phoenix Bessemer (1882) and v Arsenal (1931)

The club was founded at the Wellington Arms in 1878 as Grimsby Pelham (the Pelhams being a local landowning family), becoming plain Grimsby Town a year later and joining the Second Division as founder members in 1892. After losing their Football League place in 2010, the Mariners returned to League Two in 2016 after beating Forest Green Rovers 3-1 in the National League play-off final at Wembley.

• Grimsby enjoyed a glorious decade in the 1930s, when they were promoted to the top flight and reached two FA Cup semi-finals, losing to Arsenal in 1936 and Wolves three years later.

• In 1909 Grimsby's Walter Scott became the first goalkeeper to save three penalties in a match. However, his heroics were in vain as the Mariners still lost 2-0 to Burnley.

• Striker Pat Glover scored a club record 180 league goals for the Mariners between 1929 and 1939, and also won a club best seven caps for Wales.

HONOURS
Division 2 champions *1901, 1934*
Division 3 (North) champions *1926, 1956*
Division 3 champions *1980*
Division 4 champion *1972*
Football League Trophy *1998*

PEP GUARDIOLA

Born: Santpedor, Spain, 18th January 1971
Managerial career:
2007-08 Barcelona B
2008-12 Barcelona
2013-16 Bayern Munich
2016- Manchester City

Manchester City manager Pep Guardiola is the only coach to lead a club to six trophies in a calendar year, claiming an amazing Sextuple in 2009 when his former charges Barcelona won the Spanish title, the Copa del Rey, the Champions League, the Spanish Super Cup, the UEFA Super Cup and, finally, the FIFA Club World Cup.

• When Barcelona won the Champions League in 2009, following a 2-0 win over Manchester United in the final in Rome, the 38-year-old Guardiola became the youngest coach ever to win the trophy.

• After winning 14 trophies in four years – an impressive haul unmatched by any other Barcelona manager – Guardiola quit the Catalan club in 2012, citing "tiredness" as the main reason for his decision. A year later he took over the reins at Bayern Munich and in his first season with the German giants in 2013/14 won the league and cup Double, the FIFA Club World Cup and the European Super Cup.

• He claimed two more Bundesliga titles with Bayern before moving to Manchester in July 2016. In his first season at the Etihad he guided City to Champions League qualification, but also endured the worst ever run of his managerial career when his new team went six games without a win in the autumn of 2016.

Pep Guardiola was delighted with his cunning plan to use two tiny balls instead of one large one

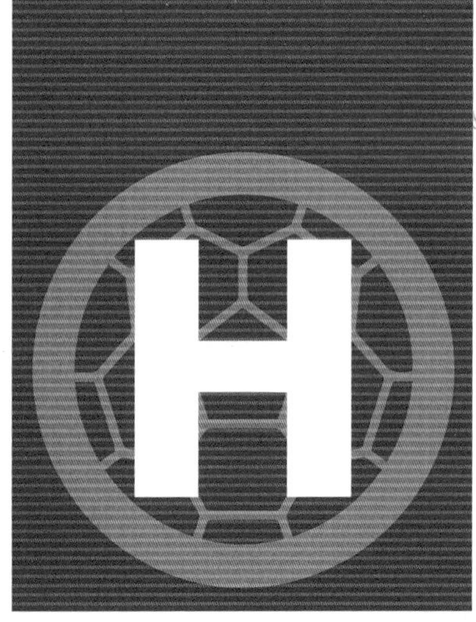

HAMILTON ACADEMICAL

Year founded: 1874
Ground: SuperSeal Stadium (5,510)
Nickname: The Accies
Biggest win: 11-1 v Chryston (1885)
Heaviest defeat: 1-11 v Hibernian (1965)

Founded in 1874 by the Rector and pupils of Hamilton Academy, Hamilton Academical is the only professional club in Britain to have originated from a school team. Shortly after the start of the 1897/98 season, the Accies joined the Scottish League in place of Renton, who were forced to resign for financial reasons.

• Hamilton fans have had little to cheer over the years, but the club did reach the Scottish Cup final in 1911 (losing to Celtic after a replay) and again in 1935 (losing to Rangers).

• English striker David Wilson scored a club record 246 goals for the Accies between 1928 and 1939, including a seasonal best of 34 in 1936/37.

Hamilton's Alex Gogic

• With a capacity of just 5,510, Hamilton's ground (now known as the SuperSeal stadium for sponsorship reasons) is the smallest in the Scottish Premiership. It is also one of just two in the top flight, along with Kilmarnock's Rugby Park, to have an artificial pitch.

• In 2014 Hamilton became the first club to be promoted to the Scottish Premier League via the new play-off system. Three years later the Accies preserved their Premiership status after beating Dundee United 1-0 on aggregate in the play-off final.

HONOURS
First Division champions 1986, 1988, 2008
Division 2 champions 1904
Third Division champions 2001

JOE HART

Joe Hart, a record four times winner of the Golden Glove award

Born: Shrewsbury, 19th April 1987
Position: Goalkeeper
Club career:
2003-06 Shrewsbury Town 54
2006- Manchester City 266
2007 Tranmere Rovers (loan) 6
2007 Blackpool (loan) 5
2009-10 Birmingham City (loan) 36
2016–17 Torino (loan) 36
2017- West Ham United (loan)
International record:
2008- England 71

Along with Petr Cech, Joe Hart has won the Premier League Golden Glove award for keeping the most clean sheets in the division a record four times, claiming the honour in 2011, 2012, 2013 and 2015. His consistent performances for City helped them win the title in both 2012 and 2014, but after losing his place in the Mancunians' side in 2016 he was loaned out to Torino to become the first ever English goalkeeper to play in Serie A. One year later he joined West Ham on loan.

• Hart began his career with his hometown club, Shrewsbury Town. His assured displays with the Shrews soon attracted the attention of bigger clubs and in 2006 he moved to City for an initial £600,000 fee. After loan spells at Tranmere Rovers, Blackpool and Birmingham City, where his superb displays earned him a place in the 2010 PFA Team of the Year, he returned to the Etihad to claim the keeper's jersey ahead of Irish international Shay Given.

• Hart became a regular for England during the Euro 2012 qualifiers and since then he has become established as his country's No. 1. His total of 40 clean sheets for England is only bettered by Peter Shilton (66).

• However, he had a miserable time at Euro 2016, conceding poor goals against Wales in the group stage and Iceland in England's shock last 16 defeat. A year later, Hart was also criticised after conceding two late free kicks against Scotland in a World Cup qualifier at Hampden Park.

HAT-TRICKS

Geoff Hurst is the only player to have scored a hat-trick in a World Cup final, hitting three goals in England's 4-2 defeat of West Germany at Wembley in 1966.

• Eighteen-year-old Tony Ross scored the fastest hat-trick in football history in 1964, taking just 90 seconds to complete a treble for Ross County in a Highland League match against Nairn County.

• In 2004 Bournemouth's James Hayter scored the fastest hat-trick in Football League history, finding the net three times against Wrexham in just two minutes and 20 seconds. Sadio Mane holds the record for the fastest hat-trick in Premier League history, hitting a quick-fire treble for Southampton in a 6-1 rout of Aston Villa on 16th May 2015 in just two minutes and 56 seconds.

• The legendary Dixie Dean scored a record 37 hat-tricks during his career, while his contemporary George Camsell scored a record nine hat-tricks for Middlesbrough in the 1925/26 season.

• Japanese international Masashi Nakayama of Jubilo Iwata scored a world record four consecutive hat-tricks in the J League in April 1998.

• Argentina's Gabriel Batistuta is the only player to have scored hat-tricks at two World Cups, firing trebles past Greece in 1994 and Jamaica four years later.

• Lionel Messi and his arch rival Cristiano Ronaldo have both scored a record seven hat-tricks in the Champions League.

• Alan Shearer scored a record 11 Premier League hat-tricks for Blackburn and Newcastle. In 2017 Tottenham's Harry Kane became only the fifth player to hit hat-tricks in consecutive Premier League matches, filling his boots against Leicester City and Hull City.

TOP 10

PREMIER LEAGUE HAT-TRICKS BY CLUB

	Club	
1.	Arsenal	38
2.	Liverpool	36
3.	Manchester United	32
4.	Chelsea	22
5.	Tottenham Hotspur	21
6.	Blackburn Rovers	17
7.	Manchester City	16
8.	Everton	14
9.	Newcastle United	13
10.	Aston Villa	10
	Leeds United	10

EDEN HAZARD

Born: Louviere, Belgium, 7th January 1991
Position: Midfielder
Club career:
2007-12 Lille 147 (36)
2012- Chelsea 175 (57)
International record:
2008- Belgium 76 (17)

A creative midfielder who possesses wonderful dribbling skills, Eden Hazard was voted into the PFA Team of the Year for the fourth time in five seasons after helping Chelsea win the Premier League title in 2017. Two years earlier the Belgian was instrumental in another title success for the Blues, topping both the PFA and Football Writers' Player of the Year polls.

• The son of footballers – his father played in the Belgian second tier, while his mother was a striker in the women's league – Hazard joined Lille when he was 14, making his debut for the first team just two years later. In his first full season, 2008/09, he became the first non-French player to win the Young Player of the Year award. He scooped the award again the following season to become the first player to win it twice.

• In 2011, after completing a league and cup Double with Lille, Hazard was voted Player of the Year – aged 20, he was the youngest player to win the award. The following year he became only the second player to retain the trophy.

• After signing for Chelsea for £32 million in May 2012, Hazard's eye-catching performances in his first

Hazard a guess who this is?

season at Stamford Bridge helped power the Blues to Europa League glory. However, his temperament was questioned by some pundits after he was stupidly sent off in the League Cup semi-final against Swansea for kicking the ball from underneath the body of a time-wasting ball boy. The following year, though, saw him up his game another notch and he was voted PFA Young Player of the Year and second behind Liverpool's Luis Suarez in the main poll.

• Hazard was first capped by Belgium, aged 17, against Luxembourg in 2008 and has gone on to win nearly 80 caps. He captained his country at Euro 2016, scoring one of the goals of the tournament against Hungary in the last 16.

HEADERS

In September 2011 Jone Samuelsen of Odd Grenland scored with a header from 58.13 metres in a Norwegian top-flight match against Tromso to set a record for the longest distance headed goal. He was helped, though, by the fact that the Tromso goalkeeper had gone upfield for a corner, leaving his goal unguarded.

• Huddersfield striker Jordan Rhodes scored the fastest headed hat-trick in Football League history in 2009, nodding in three goals against Exeter City in eight minutes and 23 seconds to smash a record previously held by Everton legend Dixie Dean.

• Stoke's giraffe-like striker Peter Crouch holds the record for the most headed goals in Premier League history, with 50.

• Just two players have scored a hat-trick of headers at the World Cup: Tomas Skuhravy for Czechoslovakia against Costa Rica in 1990, and Miroslav Klose for Germany against Saudi Arabia in 2002.

• Only two players have scored headed hat-tricks in the Premier League: Duncan Ferguson for Everton against Bolton in 1997, and Salomon Rondon for West Brom against Swansea in 2016.

Heading the ball is a hair-raising experience for Bournemouth's Nathan Ake

IS THAT A FACT?

Swansea City striker Fernando Llorente was the most effective performer in the air in the 2016/17 season, with an impressive eight headed goals. Arsenal topped the team chart with a total of 17 headers, including six from powerful striker Olivier Giroud.

HEART OF MIDLOTHIAN

Year founded: 1874
Ground: Tynecastle (17,480)
Nickname: Hearts
Biggest win: 21-0 v Anchor (1880)
Heaviest defeat: 1-8 v Vale of Leven (1883)

Hearts were founded in 1874, taking their unusual and romantic-sounding name from a popular local dance hall which, in turn, was named after the famous novel *The Heart of the Midlothian* by Sir Walter Scott. The club were founder members of the Scottish League in 1890, winning their first title just five years later.

• The club enjoyed a golden era in the late 1950s and early 1960s, when they won two league championships and five cups. In the first of those title triumphs in 1958 Hearts scored 132 goals, many of them coming from the so-called 'Terrible Trio' of Alfie Conn, Willie Bauld and Jimmy Wardhaugh. The total is still a record for the top flight in Scotland. In the same year Hearts conceded just 29 goals, giving them the best ever goal difference in British football, an incredible 103.

• In 1965 Hearts came agonisingly close to winning the championship again when they were pipped by Kilmarnock on goal average after losing 2-0 at home to their title rivals on the last day of the season. Twenty-one years later they suffered a similar fate, losing the title on goal difference to Celtic after a surprise last-day defeat against Dundee. Annoyingly for their fans, on both occasions Hearts would have won the title if the alternative method for separating teams level on points had been in use.

• The club's record goalscorer is John Robertson with 214 goals between 1983 and 1998. Midfielder

'I'm sure I saw the ball around here somewhere...'

Gary Mackay made a record 640 appearances for Hearts between 1980 and 1997.

• Hearts won the Scottish Cup in 2012, thrashing local rivals Hibs 5-1 in the final at Hampden Park – the biggest victory in the final since Hearts themselves were tonked by the same score by Rangers in 1996. It was the eighth time that Hearts had won the Scottish Cup, making them the fourth most successful club in the competition after Celtic, Rangers and Queen's Park.

• A dual international with the USA and Scotland, prolific striker Barney Battles scored a club record 44 league goals in 1930/31, including hat-tricks in three consecutive matches.

• Relegated from the Premiership in 2014, Hearts bounced back by winning the Championship in fine style the following season with a second-tier record 91 points.

HONOURS
Division 1 champions *1895, 1897, 1958, 1960*
First Division champions *1980*
Championship champions *2015*
Scottish Cup *1891, 1896, 1901, 1906, 1956, 1998, 2006, 2012*
League Cup *1955, 1959, 1960, 1963*

JORDAN HENDERSON

Born: Sunderland, 17th June 1990
Position: Midfielder
Club career:
2008-11 Sunderland 71 (4)
2009 Coventry City (loan) 10 (1)
2011- Liverpool 180 (20)
International record:
2010- England 32 (0)

A dynamic and hardworking midfielder who can also score the occasional spectacular goal from the edge of the box, Jordan Henderson joined Liverpool for around £20 million from Sunderland in 2011.

• A product of the Black Cats' academy, Henderson was twice voted Sunderland Young Player of the Year after making his debut for his hometown club in a forgettable 5-0 defeat at Chelsea in November 2008.

• He helped Liverpool win the League Cup in 2012, although he was substituted before the Reds' penalty shoot-out victory over Cardiff City in the final, and later that year played in Liverpool's 2-1 defeat by Chelsea in the FA Cup final. After being made Liverpool captain in 2015, Henderson led the Reds to the League Cup final the following year, but lost on penalties to Manchester City. He missed the Europa League final against Sevilla later in the season through injury.

• First capped by England in 2010, Henderson was named his country's Under-21 Player of the Year in 2012. He has since represented his country at Euro 2012, the 2014 World Cup and Euro 2016 but is yet to register his first England goal.

THIERRY HENRY

Born: Paris, 17th August 1977
Position: Striker
Club career:
1994-98 Monaco 105 (20)
1999 Juventus 16 (3)
1999-2007 Arsenal 254 (174)
2007-10 Barcelona 80 (35)
2010-2014 New York Red Bulls 122 (51)
2012 Arsenal (loan) 4 (2)
International record:
1997-2010 France 123 (51)

Arguably Arsenal's greatest ever player, Thierry Henry is the Gunners' all-time top goalscorer. During an eight-year stay in north London after signing from Juventus for a bargain £10.5 million in 1999 he scored 224 goals, many of them memorable. He briefly returned to Arsenal on loan from New York Red Bulls in 2012, adding two more goals to his Gunners account.

• Frighteningly quick and a reliably clinical finisher, Henry started out with Monaco and helped the club win the French title in 1997. He was even more successful at Arsenal, winning two league titles and three FA Cups, and in 2006 became the first ever player to win the Footballer of the Year award three times. The following year he joined Barcelona, with whom he won the Spanish league title and the Champions League in 2009.

• A two-time winner of the European Golden Boot, Henry's total of 175 league goals for Arsenal puts him fifth in the list of all-time Premier League scorers. The Frenchman was also a great provider of goals, creating a Premier League record of 20 assists in 2002/03.

• A member of the French squad that won the World Cup in 1998, Henry collected a European Championships winner's medal two years later. In 2006 he had to settle for a runners-up medal in the World Cup final.

Hibs are thrilled to be back in the Scottish top flight

HIBERNIAN

Year founded: 1875
Ground: Easter Road (20,421)
Previous name: Hibernians
Nickname: Hibs
Biggest win: 22-1 v 42nd Highlanders (1881)
Heaviest defeat: 0-10 v Rangers (1898)

Founded in 1875 by Irish immigrants, the club took its name from the Roman word for Ireland, Hibernia. After losing many players to Celtic the club disbanded in 1891, but reformed and joined the Scottish League two years later.

• **Hibs won the Scottish Cup for the first time in 1887 and lifted the same trophy again in 1902. However, they then had to wait 114 years before winning the cup again, beating Rangers 3-2 in a thrilling final in 2016 – the first ever between two clubs from outside the top flight. The following season Hibs returned to the big time after topping the Scottish Championship table.**

• The club enjoyed a golden era after the Second World War, winning the league championship in three out of five seasons between 1948 and 1952 with a side managed by Hugh Shaw that included the 'Famous Five' forward line of Bobby Johnstone, Willie Ormond, Lawrie Reilly, Gordon Smith and Willie Turnbull. All of the Famous Five went on to score 100 league goals for Hibs, a feat only achieved for the club since by Joe Baker.

• **In 1955 Hibs became the first British side to enter the European Cup, having been invited to participate in the new competition partly because their Easter Road ground had floodlights. They did Scotland proud, reaching the semi-finals of the competition before falling 3-0 on aggregate to French side Reims.**

• Hibs hold the British record for the biggest away win, thrashing Airdrie 11-1 on their own patch on 24th October 1959. As if to prove that the astonishing result was no fluke, they also hit double figures at Partick later that season, winning 10-2.

• **When Joe Baker made his international debut against Northern Ireland in 1959 he became the first man to represent England while playing for a Scottish club. In the same season Baker scored an incredible 42 goals in just 33 league games to set a club record.**

• Lawrie Reilly scored a club record 185 league goals for Hibs between 1946 and 1958, and is also the Edinburgh outfit's most decorated international with 38 caps for Scotland.

HONOURS
Division 1 champions *1903, 1948, 1951, 1952*
Division 2 champions *1894, 1895, 1933*
First Division champions *1981, 1999*
Championship champions *2017*
Scottish Cup *1887, 1902, 2016*
League Cup *1972, 1991, 2007*

GONZALO HIGUAIN

Born: Brest, France, 10th December 1987
Position: Striker
Club career:
2005-07 River Plate 35 (13)
2007-13 Real Madrid 190 (107)
2013-16 Napoli 104 (71)
2016- Juventus 38 (24)
International record:
2009- Argentina 68 (31)

Prolific striker Gonzalo Higuain became the most expensive player ever to transfer between two clubs in the same league when he joined Juventus from Napoli in the summer of 2016 for a staggering £75 million. He immediately repaid some of that fee by banging in an impressive 24 league goals as Juve claimed a record sixth Serie A title on the trot.

Juve striker Gonzalo Higuain in typical pose

• A pacy forward who specialises in hard, low shots, Higuain began his career with River Plate in Argentina. In January 2007 he moved to Real Madrid for around £11 million, and went on to win three La Liga titles with the Spanish giants before switching to Napoli in 2013.

• In his first season with the southern Italian side Higuain won the Coppa Italia, but his best campaign came in 2015/16 when he topped the Serie A scoring charts with 36 goals – equalling an Italian top-flight record set by Torino's Gino Rossetti way back in 1928/29.

• Higuain was born in France and at one point seemed destined to play for Les Bleus. However, he eventually chose to represent Argentina and after scoring on his debut against Peru in 2009 has gone on to feature at two World Cups and three Copa Americas, helping his country to three second-place finishes in total.

HOME AND AWAY

Brentford hold the all-time record for home wins in a season. In 1929/30 the Bees won all 21 of their home games at Griffin Park in Division Three (South). However, their away form was so poor that they missed out on promotion to champions Plymouth.

• Chelsea hold the record for the longest unbeaten home run in the league, remaining undefeated at Stamford Bridge between February 2004 and October 2008. Ironically, the Blues' 86-game run was eventually broken by Liverpool, the previous holders of the same record.

• Arsenal hold the record for the most consecutive away wins, with 12 in the Premier League in 2013. The highest number of straight home wins is 25, a record set by Bradford Park Avenue in the Third Division (North) in 1926/27.

• Stockport's 13-0 win over Halifax in 1934 is the biggest home win in Football League history (equalled by Newcastle against Newport in 1946). Sheffield United hold the record for the most emphatic away win, thrashing Port Vale 10-0 way back in 1892.

• On their way to winning the title in 2009/10, Chelsea scored a record 68 Premier League goals at home. Liverpool hold the away record with an impressive 48 in 2013/14.

• When Liverpool won 4-0 at West Ham's Olympic Stadium on 14th May 2017, it was the 52nd different away ground that the Reds had won at in the Premier League – a record unmatched by any other club.

TOP 10

TOP-FLIGHT HOME GOALS IN A SEASON

1.	Aston Villa (1930/31)	86
2.	Everton (1931/32)	84
3.	Arsenal (1934/35)	74
4.	Sheffield United (1925/26)	72
	Burnley (1962/63)	72
6.	Sunderland (1935/36)	71
7.	Sunderland (1926/27)	70
	Arsenal (1932/33)	70
	Tottenham Hotspur (1955/56)	70
	Wolverhampton Wanderers (1955/56)	70

The Terriers of Huddersfield are making a lot of noise in the Premier League

HUDDERSFIELD TOWN

Year founded: 1908
Ground: John Smith's Stadium (24,500)
Nickname: The Terriers
Biggest win: 11-0 v Heckmondwike (1909)
Heaviest defeat: 1-10 v Manchester City (1987)

Huddersfield Town were founded in 1908 following a meeting held at the local Imperial Hotel some two years earlier – it took the club that long to find a ground to play at! The club were elected to the Second Division of the Football League two years later.

• The Terriers enjoyed a golden era in the 1920s when, under the shrewd

management of the legendary Herbert Chapman, they won three consecutive league titles between 1924 and 1926 – no other club had matched this feat at the time and only three have done so since. The Terriers also won the FA Cup in 1922, beating Preston 1-0 at Stamford Bridge.

• Huddersfield won the first of their league titles in 1924 by pipping Cardiff City on goal average, the first time the champions had been decided by this method.

• After 45 years outside the top flight Huddersfield finally returned to the big time when they beat Reading in the 2017 Championship play-off final. It was a close run thing, though, with the Terriers triumphing 4-3 on penalties after a tense 0-0 draw. Huddersfield's unlikely promotion to the Premier League meant that they became only the second club (after Blackpool) to win three different divisional play-offs.

• In 1932 prolific striker Dave Mangnall scored in 11 consecutive games for Huddersfield – just one game short of the record set by Sheffield United's Jimmy Dunne and Everton's Dixie Dean the previous season.

• Outside left Billy Smith made a record 521 appearances, scoring 114 goals, for Huddersfield between 1913 and 1934. Smith and his son, Conway, who started out with the Terriers before playing for QPR and Halifax, were the first father and son to both hit a century of goals in league football.

• However, Huddersfield's record scorer is England international George Brown, who notched 159 goals in all competitions between 1921 and 1929.

• The Terriers broke their transfer record in July 2017 when they paid out £11.4 million for Montpellier striker Steve Mounie, an international with Benin. The club's coffers were boosted by a record £8 million in 2012 when prolific striker Jordan Rhodes joined Blackburn.

• Defender Mally Brown made a club record 259 consecutive appearances between 1978 and 1983.

HONOURS
Division 1 champions *1924, 1925, 1926*
Division 2 champions *1970*
Division 4 champions *1980*
FA Cup *1922*

HULL CITY

Year founded: 1904
Ground: KC Stadium (24,450)
Nickname: The Tigers
Biggest win: 11-1 v Carlisle United (1939)
Heaviest defeat: 0-8 v Wolves (1911)

Hull City were formed in 1904, originally sharing a ground with the local rugby league club. The Tigers joined the Football League in 1905 but failed to achieve promotion to the top flight until 2008.

• Hull enjoyed their best ever moment when they reached their first ever FA Cup final in 2014. The Tigers roared into a shock 2-0 lead against favourites Arsenal at Wembley, but eventually went down 3-2 after extra-time.

• In 2008 Hull first made it into the top flight thanks to a play-off final victory over Bristol City, with local boy Dean Windass scoring the vital goal. The triumph meant that the Tigers had climbed from the bottom tier to the top in just five seasons – a meteoric rise only bettered in the past by Fulham, Swansea City and Wimbledon.

• The club's record goalscorer is Chris Chilton, who banged in 193 league goals in the 1960s and 1970s. His sometime team-mate Andy Davidson has pulled on a Hull shirt more than any other player at the club, making 520 league appearances between 1952 and 1968.

• In his first spell at Hull between 1991 and 1996, goalkeeper Alan Fettis played a number of games as a striker during an injury crisis. He did pretty well too, scoring two goals!

• In August 2016 Hull splashed a club record £13 million on Spurs midfielder Ryan Mason. The Tigers received a club record £17 million when central defender Harry Maguire moved to Leicester City in June 2017.

• Hull were the first team in the world to lose in a penalty shoot-out, Manchester United beating them 4-3 on spot-kicks in the semi-final of the Watney Cup in 1970.

• The Tigers briefly topped the Premier League table in August 2016 but finished the season being relegated – only the third time a club has experienced this particular combination of fleeting high and crushing low.

HONOURS
Division 3 (North) champions *1933, 1949*
Division 3 champions *1966*

SIR GEOFF HURST

Born: Ashton-under-Lyme, 8th December 1941
Position: Striker
Club career:
1959-72 West Ham United 410 (180)
1972-75 Stoke City 108 (30)
1975-76 West Bromwich Albion 10 (2)
1976 Seattle Sounders 24 (9)
International record:
1966-72 England 49 (24)

Geoff Hurst is the only player to have scored a hat-trick in the World Cup final. His famous treble against West Germany at Wembley helped England to an iconic 4-2 triumph in 1966, although his second goal remains one of the most controversial of all time as the Germans claimed the ball didn't cross the line after Hurst's shot bounced down off the underside of the crossbar.

• Along with Ian Rush, Hurst is the leading scorer in the history of the League Cup with an impressive total of 49 goals. He is also the last player to hit six goals in a top-flight league match, netting a double hat-trick in West Ham's 8-0 thrashing of Sunderland at Upton Park in 1968. Hurst's total of 252 goals in all competitions for West Ham is only bettered by Vic Watson, with 326 between 1920 and 1935.

• A well-built centre-forward who was strong in the air and possessed a powerful shot, Hurst won an FA Cup winner's medal with West Ham in 1964 and, the following year, helped the Hammers win the European Cup Winners' Cup when they beat Munich 1860 in the final at Wembley.

• In 1979 he was appointed manager of Second Division side Chelsea, but was sacked two years later after a dismal run of results. However, Hurst's great achievements on the pitch remain part of English folklore and earned him a knighthood in 1998.

ZLATAN IBRAHIMOVIC

Born: Malmo, Sweden, 3rd October 1981
Position: Striker
Club career:
1999-2001 Malmo 40 (16)
2001-04 Ajax 74 (35)
2004-06 Juventus 70 (23)
2006-09 Inter Milan 88 (57)
2009-11 Barcelona 29 (16)
2010-11 AC Milan (loan) 29 (14)
2011-12 AC Milan 32 (28)
2012-16 Paris Saint-Germain 122 (113)
2016- Manchester United 28 (17)
International record:
2001-16 Sweden 116 (62)

A tremendously gifted striker with a uniquely individualistic style of play, Zlatan Ibrahimovic is the only player to have won league titles with six different European clubs.

• **His incredible run began with Ajax, who he had joined from his first club Malmo in 2001, when the Amsterdam giants won the Dutch league in 2004. Ibrahimovic's golden touch continued with his next club, Juventus, where he won back-to-back Serie A titles, although these were later scrubbed from the record books following Juve's involvement in a match-fixing scandal.**

• At his next club, Inter Milan, Ibrahimovic fared even better, helping the Nerazzurri win a hat-trick of titles in 2007, 2008 and 2009. He then moved to Barcelona and, despite failing to see eye-to-eye with Barca boss Pep Guardiola, won a La Liga title medal in 2010. Returning to Italy, his astonishing run of success continued with AC Milan, who were crowned Serie A champions in 2011.

• **In the summer of 2012 Ibrahimovic was transferred to newly moneyed Paris Saint-Germain for £31 million, taking his combined transfer fee up to a then world record £150 million. In four years with PSG, he won four league titles, two French cups, was voted Ligue 1 Player of the Year three times, topped the Ligue 1 scoring charts three times and became the club's all-time leading scorer after banging in 156 goals in all competitions, including a season's best 50 in 2015/16.**

• Sweden's all-time leading goalscorer and the only player to score four times against England in a match, Ibrahimovic enjoyed yet more success with Manchester United in 2016/17. He scored twice in the Red Devils' 3-2 defeat of Southampton in the League Cup final and helped his new club reach the Europa League final, although he missed their win over Ajax through injury.

IS THAT A FACT?

Zlatan Ibrahimovic is the only player to have scored in the Champions League for six different clubs: Ajax, Juventus, Inter Milan, Barcelona, AC Milan and Paris Saint-Germain.

The famous 'Zlatan stare' has terrified many a defender...

INTER MILAN

Year founded: 1908
Ground: San Siro (80,018)
Nickname: Nerazzurri (The black and blues)
League titles: 18
Domestic cups: 7
European cups: 6
International cups: 3

Founded in 1908 as a breakaway club from AC Milan, Internazionale (as they are known locally) are the only Italian team never to have been relegated from Serie A and have spent more seasons in the top flight, 85, than any other club.

• **Inter were the first Italian club to win the European Cup twice, beating the mighty Real Madrid 3-1 in the 1964 final before recording a 1-0 defeat of Benfica the following year. They had to wait 45 years, though, before making it a hat-trick with a 2-0 defeat of Bayern Munich in Madrid in 2010 – a victory that, with the domestic league and cup already in the bag, secured Inter the first ever Treble by an Italian club.**

Inter Milan, never relegated from Serie A

• Under legendary manager Helenio Herrera, Inter introduced the 'catenaccio' defensive system to world football in the 1960s. Playing with a sweeper behind two man-markers, Inter conceded very few goals as they powered to three league titles between 1963 and 1966.

• The club endured a barren period domestically until they were awarded their first Serie A title for 17 years in 2006 after Juventus and AC Milan, who had both finished above them in the league table, had points deducted for their roles in a match-fixing scandal. Inter went on to win the championship in more conventional style in the following four years – the last two of these triumphs coming under Jose Mourinho – winning an Italian record 17 consecutive league games in 2006/07.

• Inter's San Siro stadium, which they share with city rivals AC Milan, is the largest in Italy, with a capacity of over 80,000. The stadium has hosted the European Cup/Champions League final on four occasions, a record only surpassed by Wembley.

HONOURS
Italian champions *1910, 1920, 1930, 1938, 1940, 1953, 1954, 1963, 1965, 1966, 1971, 1980, 1989, 2006, 2007, 2008, 2009, 2010*
Italian Cup *1939, 1978, 1982, 2005, 2006, 2010, 2011*
European Cup/Champions League *1964, 1965, 2010*
UEFA Cup *1991, 1994, 1998*
Intercontinental Cup/Club World Cup *1964, 1965, 2010*

ISCO

Born: Benalmadena, Spain, 21st April 1992
Position: Midfielder
Club career:
2009-11 Valencia B 52 (16)
2010-11 Valencia 4 (0)
2011-13 Malaga 69 (14)
2013- Real Madrid 127 (25)
International record:
2013- Spain 20 (3)

Isco always looks good on the ball – even in purple!

With his superb close control and dazzling dribbling skills, attacking midfielder Isco has been an instrumental figure in the Real Madrid side which has won the Champions League three times since 2014.

• Born Francisco Roman Alarcon Suarez in 1992, Isco got his big break with Valencia before moving to Malaga in 2011. The following year his eye-catching performances earned him the Golden Boy award, given to the most impressive footballer in Europe aged under 21, and helped propel Malaga into the Champions League for the first time in their history.

• In June 2013 Isco signed for Real Madrid for around £25 million and immediately endeared himself to fans at the Bernabeu by scoring a late winner on his debut in a 2-1 home victory against Real Betis.

• Isco played for Spain at every age level

from Under-16 upwards to make his senior debut in a 3-1 friendly win against Uruguay in February 2013. Later that year he played in the European Under-21 Championship final, scoring from the spot in Spain's 4-2 victory over Italy in Jerusalem.**

IPSWICH TOWN

Year founded: 1878
Ground: Portman Road (30,311)
Nickname: The Blues, The Tractor Boys
Biggest win: 10-0 v Floriana (1962)
Heaviest defeat: 1-10 v Fulham (1963)

The club was founded at a meeting at the town hall in 1878 but did not join the Football League until 1938, two years after turning professional.

• Ipswich were the last of just four clubs to win the old Second and First Division titles in consecutive seasons, pulling off this remarkable feat in 1962 under future England manager Sir Alf Ramsey. The team's success owed much to the strike partnership of Ray Crawford and Ted Phillips, who together scored 61 of the club's 93 goals during the title-winning campaign.

• Two years after that title win, though, Ipswich were relegated after conceding 121 goals – only Blackpool in 1930/31 (125 goals against) have had a worse defensive record in the top flight. The Blues' worst defeat in a season to forget was a 10-1 hammering at Fulham, the last time a team has conceded double figures in a top-flight match.

• However, the club enjoyed more success under their longest serving boss Bobby Robson, another man who went on to manage England, in the following two decades. In 1978 Ipswich won the FA Cup, beating favourites Arsenal 1-0 in the final at Wembley, and three years later they won the UEFA Cup with midfielder John Wark contributing a then record 14 goals during the club's continental campaign.

• Ipswich have the best home record in European competition of any club, remaining undefeated at Portman Road in 31 games (25 wins and six draws) since making their debut in the European Cup in 1962 with a 10-0 hammering of Maltese side Floriana – the Blues' biggest win in their history.

• With 203 goals for the Tractor Boys between 1958 and 1969, Ray Crawford is the club's record goalscorer. Mick Mills is the club's record appearance maker, turning out 591 times between 1966 and 1982.

• The club are the longest serving members of the Championship, having resided in the second tier since being relegated from the Premiership in 2002.

HONOURS
Division 1 champions *1962*
Division 2 champions *1961*
Division 3 (S) champions *1954, 1957*
FA Cup *1978*
UEFA Cup *1981*

ITALY

First international: Italy 6 France 2, 1910
Most capped player: Gianluigi Buffon, 169 caps (1997-)
Leading goalscorer: Luigi Riva, 35 goals (1965-74)
First World Cup appearance: Italy 7 USA 1, 1934
Biggest win: Italy 11 Egypt 3, 1928
Heaviest defeat: Hungary 7 Italy 1, 1924

Italy have the joint best record of any European nation at the World Cup, having won the tournament four times (in 1934, 1938, 1982 and 2006). Only Brazil, with five wins, have done better in the competition.

• The Azzurri, as they are known to their passionate fans, are the only country to have been involved in two World Cup final penalty shoot-outs. In 1994 they lost out to Brazil, but in 2006 they beat France on penalties after a 1-1 draw in the final in Berlin.

• Italy's Vittorio Pozo is the only coach to win the World Cup twice, guiding the Azzurri to victory on home soil in 1934 and again in France four years later.

• The most humiliating moment in Italy's sporting history came in 1966 when they lost 1-0 to minnows North Korea at the World Cup in England. The Italians had a remarkably similar embarrassment at the 2002 tournament when they were knocked out by hosts South Korea after a 2-1 defeat. Fortunately for the Azzurri, neither 'East Korea' or 'West Korea' exist as independent countries!

• With 169 appearances for Italy, goalkeeper Gianluigi Buffon is the highest-capped European player ever and the fifth highest in the history of world football.

• Italy have won the European Championships just once, beating Yugoslavia 2-0 in a replayed final in Rome in 1968 after a 1-1 draw. They reached the final again in 2000 but lost 2-1 to France on the 'golden goal' rule in Rotterdam, and endured more disappointment in 2012 when they were hammered 4-0 by Spain in the final in Kiev.

IS THAT A FACT?

Aged 40 and 133 days when he helped the Azzurri win the trophy in 1982, Italy goalkeeper Dino Zoff is the oldest player to appear in the World Cup final.

HONOURS
World Cup winners *1934, 1938, 1982, 2006*
European Championships winners *1968*

World Cup Record
1930 Did not enter
1934 Winners
1938 Winners
1950 Round 1
1954 Round 1
1958 Did not qualify
1962 Round 1
1966 Round 1
1970 Runners-up
1974 Round 1
1978 Fourth place
1982 Winners
1986 Round 2
1990 Third place
1994 Runners-up
1998 Quarter-finals
2002 Round 2
2006 Winners
2010 Round 1
2014 Round 1

JUVENTUS

Year founded: 1897
Ground: Juventus Stadium (41,254)
Nickname: The Zebras
League titles: 33
Domestic cups: 12
European cups: 8
International cups: 2

The most famous and successful club in Italy, Juventus were founded in 1897 by pupils at a school in Turin – hence the team's name, which means 'youth' in Latin. Six years later the club binned their original pink shirts and adopted their distinctive black-and-white-striped kit after an English member of the team had a set of Notts County shirts shipped out to Italy.

• Juventus emerged as the dominant force in Italian football in the 1930s when they won a best ever five titles in a row. They have a record 33 titles to their name and are the only team in Italy allowed to wear two gold stars on their shirts, signifying 20 Serie A victories. In 2016/17 Juve became the first Italian club to win the Serie A title six times on the trot and the first ever to win three consecutive Doubles.

• When, thanks to a single goal by their star player Michel Platini, Juventus beat Liverpool in the European Cup final in 1985 they became the first ever club to win all three European trophies. However, their triumph at the Heysel Stadium in Brussels was overshadowed by the death of 39 of their fans, who were crushed to death as they tried to flee from crowd trouble before the kick-off.

• Juventus won the trophy again in 1996, beating Ajax on penalties in Rome, but since then have lost five Champions League finals, most recently going down 4-1 to Real Madrid in Cardiff in 2017. The club's total of seven defeats in the final is a record for the competition.

• Juventus have won the Coppa Italia a record 12 times, most recently beating Lazio 2-0 in the 2017 final to claim the trophy for a record third consecutive time.

• In 2014 Juventus won the Serie A title with a record 102 points, winning a record 33 league games.

HONOURS
Italian champions *1905, 1926, 1931, 1932, 1933, 1934, 1935,1950, 1952, 1958, 1960, 1961, 1967, 1972, 1973, 1975, 1977, 1978, 1981, 1982, 1984, 1986, 1995, 1997, 1998, 2002, 2003, 2012, 2013, 2014, 2015, 2016, 2017*
Italian Cup *1938, 1942, 1959, 1960, 1965, 1979, 1983, 1990, 1995, 2015, 2016, 2017*
European Cup/Champions League *1985, 1996*
European Cup Winners' Cup *1984*
UEFA Cup *1977, 1990, 1993*
European Super Cup *1984, 1996*
Club World Cup *1985, 1996*

HARRY KANE

Born: Chingford, 28th July 1993
Position: Striker
Club career:
2011- Tottenham Hotspur 113 (78)
2011 Leyton Orient (loan) 18 (5)
2012 Millwall (loan) 22 (7)
2012-13 Norwich City (loan) 3 (0)
2013 Leicester City (loan) 13 (2)
International record:
2015- England 19 (8)

Top scorer in the Premier League with 29 goals in 2016/17, Harry Kane became only the fifth player to retain the Golden Boot after winning the award the previous season for the first time with a haul of 25 goals. Kane also became only the fourth player to score at least 20 goals in three consecutive Premier League seasons, having first hit this benchmark in 2014/15.

• Kane's fine form saw him nominated for the PFA Player of the Year award, but he missed out on top spot for the second year running. However, he did collect the PFA Young Player of the Year award in 2015 after scoring a total of 31 goals in all competitions over the course of the campaign – the best haul by a Tottenham player since Gary Lineker banged in 35 in 1991/92.

• A clever player who can create as well as score goals, Kane came through the Tottenham youth system and spent time on loan with Leyton Orient, Millwall, Norwich and Leicester before finally establishing himself in the Spurs first team in 2014. The following year he helped the north Londoners reach the League Cup final, but had to settle for a loser's medal after a 2-0 defeat to Chelsea at Wembley.

• An England international at Under-17, Under-19, Under-20 and Under-21 level, Kane made his senior debut against Lithuania in a Euro 2016 qualifier at Wembley in March 2015. His international career got off to a dream start, too, as he came off the bench to score with a header after just 78 seconds – the third fastest goal by an England player on debut. In June 2017 he captained his country for the first time, and celebrated by scoring a last-minute equaliser in a 2-2 draw with Scotland at Hampden Park.

TOP 10

PREMIER LEAGUE GOALSCORERS 2016/17

1.	Harry Kane (Tottenham Hotspur)	29
2.	Romelu Lukaku (Everton)	25
3.	Alexis Sanchez (Arsenal)	24
4.	Sergio Aguero (Manchester City)	20
	Diego Costa (Chelsea)	20
6.	Dele Alli (Tottenham Hotspur)	18
7.	Zlatan Ibrahimovic (Manchester United)	17
8.	Eden Hazard (Chelsea)	16
	Joshua King (Bournemouth)	16
10.	Christian Benteke (Crystal Palace)	15
	Jermain Defoe (Sunderland)	15
	Fernando Llorente (Swansea City)	15

N'Golo Kante just beats Harry Kane to the ball... even though he's flying!

N'GOLO KANTE

Born: Paris, France, 29th March 1991
Position: Midfielder
Club career:
2011-13 Boulogne 38 (3)
2013-15 Caen 75 (4)
2015-16 Leicester City 37 (1)
2016- Chelsea 35 (1)
International record:
2016- France 17 (1)

After helping Chelsea win the Premier League title in 2017, N'Golo Kante became the first outfield player to lift the trophy in consecutive seasons with two different clubs, having starred in the Leicester City team which surprisingly claimed the top spot the previous year. Kante's unstinting efforts for the Blues also saw him win both the PFA Player of the Year award and the Footballer of the Year gong.

• A tenacious midfielder who loves to make surging forward runs from deep, Kante started out with Boulogne in the third tier of French football, before moving to Caen in 2013. In his first season with his new club he played in every match as Caen won promotion to Ligue 1.

• After a £5.6 million transfer to Leicester in the summer of 2015, Kante was soon gaining plaudits for his hard-working, unselfish style of play which helped propel the Foxes to the top of the table. His excellent campaign, which saw him make a season best 175 tackles, ended with him being nominated for the PFA Player of the Year award and named in the PFA Team of the Year before he moved to Stamford Bridge for £32 million, then a record for a player leaving the King Power Stadium.

• Kante was rewarded with his first French cap in March 2016, coming on as a half-time sub in a 3-2 win against the Netherlands in Amsterdam. Later that month he made his first start for Les Bleus, scoring in a 4-2 win against Russia in Paris.

ROBBIE KEANE

Born: Dublin, 8th July 1980
Position: Striker
Club career:
1997-99 Wolves 74 (24)
1999-2000 Coventry City 31 (12)
2000-01 Inter Milan 6 (0)
2001 Leeds United (loan) 18 (9)
2001-02 Leeds United 28 (4)
2002-08 Tottenham Hotspur 197 (80)
2008-09 Liverpool 19 (5)
2009-11 Tottenham Hotspur 41 (11)
2010 Celtic (loan) 16 (12)
2011 West Ham United (loan) 9 (2)
2011-16 LA Galaxy 125 (83)
2012 Aston Villa (loan) 6 (3)
International record:
1998-2016 Republic of Ireland 146 (68)

Republic of Ireland striker Robbie Keane is his country's all-time top scorer and highest appearance maker. His total of 68 goals for the Irish puts him in third place in the all-time list of European international goalscorers, behind Hungary legend Ferenc Puskas and German goalpoacher Miroslav Klose. Keane also holds the record for the most goals in European Championship qualifiers with 23.

• **Keane began his club career with Wolves, for whom he scored twice on his debut against Norwich in 1997. Two years later, aged 19, he joined Coventry City for £6 million – then a record fee for a teenager.**

• After brief spells with Inter Milan and Leeds, Keane moved to Tottenham in 2002. While at White Hart Lane he finally won the first trophy of his career, the Carling Cup in 2007/08 – a season in which he hit a personal best 23 goals in all competitions.

• **His goals record prompted Liverpool to pay £20 million for him in the summer of 2008. It was a dream move for Keane, a childhood fan of the Reds, but he was used irregularly by then Liverpool boss Rafa Benitez and, in the January 2009 transfer window, he returned to Tottenham for £15 million. However, he soon found himself surplus to requirements at White Hart Lane and, after loan spells at Celtic and West Ham, Keane signed for LA Galaxy in a £3.5 million deal in the summer of 2011. In 2014 he scored Galaxy's winning goal against New England Revolution as they won the MLS Cup for a record fifth time.**

KICK-OFF

Scottish club Queen's Park claim to have been the first to adopt the traditional kick-off time of 3pm on a Saturday, which allowed those people who worked in the morning time to get to the match.

• **The fastest ever goal from a kick-off was scored in just two seconds by Nawaf Al Abed, a 21-year-old striker for Saudi Arabian side Al Hilal in a cup match against Al Shoalah in 2009. After a team-mate tapped the ball to him, Al Abed struck a fierce left-foot shot from the halfway line which sailed over the opposition keeper and into the net.**

• Ledley King scored the fastest goal in Premier League history, striking just 9.9 seconds after the kick-off for Tottenham against Bradford City on 9th December 2000.

• **The fastest goal in Football League history was scored after just four seconds by Jim Fryatt for Bradford Park Avenue against Tranmere Rovers on 25th April 1964.**

• From the start of the 2016/17 season a rule change allowed for the ball to be kicked in any direction from the kick-off, whereas previously it had to be played forwards.

IS THAT A FACT?
For the first time ever, the Premier League kicked off on a Friday night in 2017 when Arsenal hosted Leicester City at the Emirates on 11th August.

KILMARNOCK

Year founded: 1869
Ground: Rugby Park (17,889)
Nickname: Killie
Biggest win: 13-2 v Saltcoats Victoria (1896)
Heaviest defeat: 1-9 v Celtic (1938)

The oldest professional club in Scotland, Kilmarnock were founded in 1869 by a group of local cricketers who were keen to play another sport during the winter months. Originally, the club played rugby (hence the name of Kilmarnock's stadium, Rugby Park) before switching to football in 1873.

• **That same year Kilmarnock entered the inaugural Scottish Cup and on 18th October 1873 the club took part in the first ever match in the competition, losing 2-0 in the first round to Renton.**

• Kilmarnock's greatest moment was back in 1965 when they travelled to championship rivals Hearts on the last day of the season requiring a two-goal win to pip the Edinburgh side to the title on goal average. To the joy of their travelling fans, Killie won 2-0 to claim the title by 0.04 of a goal.

• **Two years later Kilmarnock had their best ever run in Europe, when they reached the semi-finals of the Fairs Cup before losing 4-2 on aggregate to Leeds United.**

Kilmarnock are the oldest professional club in Scotland

• Alan Robertson played in a club record 607 games for Kilmarnock between 1972 and 1989. Killie's top scorer is Willie Culley, who notched 149 goals between 1911 and 1923.

• **Kilmarnock have won the Scottish Cup three times, most recently defeating Falkirk 1-0 in the 1997 final. The club won the League Cup for the first time in 2012, after a 1-0 win against Celtic in the final.**

• Killie defender Joe Nibloe played in a club record 11 games for Scotland between 1929 and 1932.

HONOURS
Division 1 champions *1965*
Division 2 champions *1898, 1899*
Scottish Cup *1920, 1929, 1997*
Scottish League Cup *2012*

KIT DEALS

In May 2016 Barcelona signed the biggest ever kit deal in football history with American company Nike. The deal, which starts at the beginning of the 2018/19 campaign, will see Barcelona paid £1 billion over 10 seasons in return for wearing Nike supplied training and playing kit. Real Madrid's 10-year deal with Adidas signed in 2015 is not far behind, being worth around £850 million.

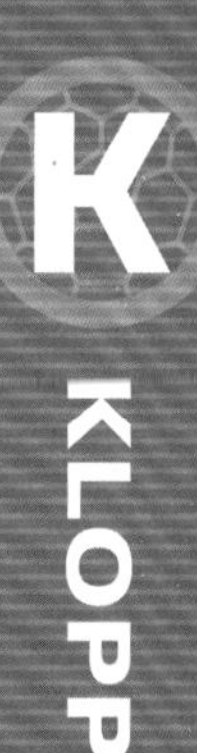

Barcelona's record kit deal with Nike produced smiles all round at the Nou Camp

• **Manchester United's £75 million per year kit deal with Adidas is the most lucrative in the Premier League, followed by Chelsea's new £60 million per year deal with Nike.**

• Puma are the most popular kit suppliers in the Premier League in 2017/18, providing playing gear for five clubs: Arsenal, Burnley, Huddersfield Town, Leicester City and Newcastle United. However, Nike can boast that they supply kit to the top three clubs of the 2016/17 season – Chelsea, Tottenham and Manchester City – along with newcomers Brighton.

JURGEN KLOPP

Born: Stuttgart, Germany, 16th June 1967
Managerial career:
2001-08 Mainz 05
2008-15 Borussia Dortmund
2015- Liverpool

After replacing Brendan Rodgers as Liverpool manager in October 2015, Jurgen Klopp has made steady progress with the Reds, culminating in the club qualifying for the Champions League in 2017. In his previous season on Merseyside he took his side to the League Cup final and the Europa League final. However, Klopp's men lost both matches, meaning that the unfortunate German has been beaten in his last five cup finals.

• **Klopp took his first steps in management in 2001 with Mainz 05, the club he had previously turned out for more than 300 times as a striker-turned-defender. By the time he left Mainz in 2008 he was the club's longest serving manager.**

• An engaging character who is rarely seen without a big smile on his face, Klopp made his reputation with Borussia Dortmund, who he led to consecutive Bundesliga titles in 2011 and 2012. In the second of those years Dortmund also claimed their first ever domestic Double after thrashing Bayern Munich 5-2 in the final of the German Cup.

• **The following year Klopp took Dortmund to the final of the Champions League after they overcame Jose Mourinho's Real Madrid in the semi-finals. Again, their opponents in the final were Bayern, but this time the Bavarian side exacted revenge with a 2-1 victory at Wembley. Klopp then endured more agony when Dortmund lost the 2014 and 2015 German Cup finals to Bayern and Wolfsburg, respectively.**

• Klopp was named German Manager of the Year in 2011 and 2012, the first man to win this award in two consecutive years.

• **A popular figure with the general public, Klopp has appeared in numerous TV adverts, including ones for sportswear manufacturers Puma, German car makers Opel and gambling outfit Bet Victor.**

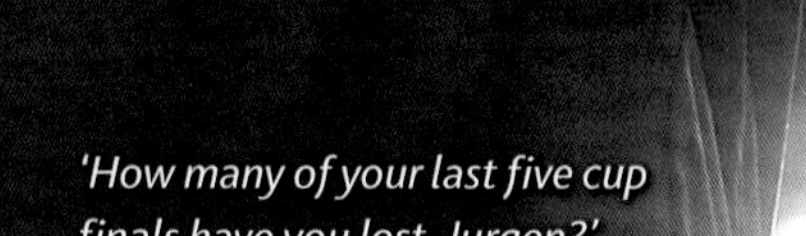
'How many of your last five cup finals have you lost, Jurgen?'

ADAM LALLANA

Born: St Albans, 10th May 1988
Position: Midfielder
Club career:
2006-14 Southampton 235 (48)
2007 Bournemouth (loan) 3 (0)
2014- Liverpool 88 (17)
International record:
2013- England 33 (3)

Liverpool midfielder Adam Lallana is the only player to have been voted into the PFA Team of the Year for the three top divisions: League One, the Championship and the Premier League.

• An intelligent player who can spot a defence-splitting pass while also carrying a goal threat himself, Lallana came through the ranks at Southampton to make his debut as an 18-year-old in a 5-2 defeat of Yeovil Town in the League Cup in August 2006. He became a regular for the Saints in the 2009/10 season, during which he became the first Southampton midfielder since club legend Matt Le Tissier in 1994/95 to score 20 goals in a season in all competitions.

• After enjoying successive promotions with Southampton in 2011 and 2012, and being made captain in 2012, Lallana quickly demonstrated that he was more than comfortable playing at the highest level, with his dynamic displays earning him a nomination for the PFA Player of the Year in 2014. That summer he moved on to Liverpool for £25 million, Southampton's record sale at the time. In his second season at Anfield he came within a whisker of landing his first silverware with the Reds, but finished on the losing side in both the League Cup and Europa League finals.

Adam Lallana, England Player of the Year in 2016

• Lallana won his first England cap in November 2013, gaining rave reviews for his vibrant performance in a friendly against Chile at Wembley. He scored his first goal for his country three years later against Slovakia in a World Cup qualifier and after further strikes against Scotland and Spain was voted England Player of the Year for 2016.

FRANK LAMPARD

Born: Romford, 20th June 1978
Position: Midfielder
Club career:
1996-2001 West Ham United 148 (24)
1995-96 Swansea City (loan) 9 (1)
2001-14 Chelsea 429 (147)
2014-16 New York City 29 (15)
2014-15 Manchester City (loan) 32 (6)
International record:
1999-2014 England 106 (29)

With 177 goals to his name, Frank Lampard is the highest scoring midfielder in Premier League history and, along with Wayne Rooney, one of just two players to hit double figures in the league in 10 consecutive seasons (2004-13). A model of consistency, his total of 609 Premier League appearances is only bettered by Ryan Giggs and Gareth Barry.

• Lampard, who joined Chelsea from his first club West Ham for £11 million in 2001, is the highest goalscorer in the Blues' history with an impressive total of 211 goals in all competitions for the club, who he served for 13 highly successful years. In June 2014 he joined New York City, before spending the following season on loan at Chelsea's main title rivals, Manchester City.

• Lampard won the league three times and the FA Cup four times during his time with the Blues, including the Double in 2010. After numerous near misses, he finally won the Champions League with Chelsea in 2012, scoring one of his team's penalties in the shoot-out victory over Bayern Munich in the final. The following year he skippered the Blues to success in the Europa League after the Londoners beat Benfica in the final.

• Lampard played in a then record 164 consecutive Premier League games until illness forced him out of Chelsea's visit to Manchester City in

December 2005. Goalkeepers David James and Brad Friedel have since passed his total, but Lampard still holds the Premier League record for an outfield player.

• The son of former England and West Ham defender Frank senior, Lampard made his international debut in 1999. He starred at the European Championships in 2004, scoring in three of his country's four games, but fared less well at the 2006 World Cup where he was one of three England players to miss a penalty in the quarter-final shoot-out defeat at the hands of Portugal. His luck was also out at the 2010 tournament in South Africa, when the officials failed to spot that his shot in England's second-round defeat by Germany had clearly crossed the line after bouncing down off the crossbar. His total of 29 goals for his country is a record for an England midfielder, while his total of nine converted penalties is also a Three Lions record.

DENIS LAW

Born: Aberdeen, 24th February 1940
Position: Striker
Club career:
1956-60 Huddersfield Town 81 (16)
1960-61 Manchester City 44 (21)
1961-62 Torino 27 (10)
1962-73 Manchester United 309 (171)
1973-74 Manchester City 24 (9)
International record:
1958-74 Scotland 55 (30)

Along with Kenny Dalglish, Denis Law is Scotland's leading scorer with 30 international goals. Law, though, scored his goals in roughly half the number of games as 'King Kenny'.

• Law made his international debut in 1958, scoring in a 3-0 win against Wales. Aged 18, he was the youngest player to appear for Scotland since before the Second World War. He went on to represent Scotland for 16 years, taking his bow at the 1974 World Cup in Germany.

• On two occasions Law was sold for fees that broke the existing British transfer record. In 1960 he moved from Huddersfield to Manchester City for a record £55,000, and two years later his £115,000 transfer from Torino to Manchester United set a new benchmark figure.

• With United, Law won two league titles and the FA Cup in 1963, but he missed out on the club's European Cup triumph in 1968 through a knee injury. He remains the only Scottish player to have been voted European Footballer of the Year, an award he won in 1964.

• The last goal Law scored, a clever backheel for Manchester City against United at Old Trafford in 1974, gave him no pleasure at all as it condemned his old club to relegation to the Second Division. "I have seldom felt so depressed as I did that weekend," he remarked later.

• In 2002 a statue of Law was unveiled at Old Trafford, scene of many of his greatest triumphs. The following year the Scottish Football Association marked UEFA's Jubilee by naming him as Scotland's 'Golden Player' of the previous 50 years.

TOP 10

SCOTLAND GOALSCORERS

1.	Denis Law (1958-70)	30
2.	Kenny Dalglish (1971-86)	30
3.	Hughie Gallacher (1924-35)	23
4.	Lawrie Reilly (1948-57)	22
5.	Ally McCoist (1986-98)	19
6.	Kenny Miller (2001-13)	18
7.	Robert Hamilton (1899-1911)	15
	James McFadden (2002-10)	15
9.	Mo Johnston (1984-91)	14
10.	Robert Smith McColl (1896-1908)	13
	Andrew Wilson (1920-23)	13

LAWS

Thirteen original laws of association football were adopted at a meeting of the Football Association in 1863, although these had their roots in the 'Cambridge Rules' established at Cambridge University as far back as 1848.

• No copy of those 1848 rules now exist, but they are thought to have included laws relating to throw-ins, goal-kicks, fouls and offside. They even allowed for a length of string to be used as a crossbar.

• Perhaps the most significant rule change occurred in 1925 when the offside law was altered so that an attacking player receiving the ball would need to be behind two opponents, rather than three. The effect of this rule change was dramatic, with the average number of goals per game in the Football League rising from 2.55 in 1924/25 to 3.44 in 1925/26.

• The laws of the game are governed by the International Football Association Board, which was founded in 1886 by the four football associations of the United Kingdom. Each of these associations still has one vote on the IFAB, with FIFA having four votes. Any changes to the laws of the game require a minimum of six votes.

• In recent years the most important change to the laws of the game was the introduction of the 'back pass' rule in 1992, which prevented goalkeepers from handling passes from their own team-mates. The rule was introduced to discourage time-wasting and overly defensive play, following criticisms of widespread negative tactics at the 1990 World Cup.

LEAGUE CUP

With eight wins to their name, Liverpool are the most successful club in League Cup history. The Reds have also appeared in a record number of finals, 12, most recently losing the 2016 final to Manchester City on penalties.

• The competition has been known by more names than any other in British football. Originally called the Football League Cup (1960-81), it has subsequently been rebranded through sponsorship deals as the Milk Cup (1981-86), Littlewoods Cup (1986-90), Rumbelows Cup (1990-92), Coca-Cola Cup (1992-98), Worthington Cup (1998-2003), Carling Cup (2003-12), the Capital One Cup (2012-16) and the Carabao Cup (from 2017).

• Ian Rush won a record five winner's medals in the competition with Liverpool (1981-84 and 1995) and, along with Geoff Hurst, is also the leading scorer in the history of the League Cup with 49 goals. In the 1986/87 season Tottenham's Clive Allen scored a record 12 goals in the competition.

• Oldham's Frankie Bunn scored a record six goals in a League Cup match when Oldham thrashed Scarborough 7-0 on 25th October 1989.

• Liverpool won the competition a record four times in a row between 1981 and 1984, going undefeated for an unprecedented 25 League Cup matches.

• In 1983 West Ham walloped Bury 10-0 to record the biggest ever victory in the history of the League Cup. Three years later Liverpool equalled the Hammers' tally with an identical thrashing of Fulham.

Manchester United's Zlatan Ibrahimovic heads home the winner against Southampton in the 2017 League Cup final

• In 1985 Barry Venison became the youngest ever player to captain a team in a Wembley final when he skippered Sunderland in the League Cup final against Norwich aged 20 and 220 days. However, he finished on the losing side after the Canaries won 1-0.
• Swansea City recorded the biggest ever win in the final, thrashing Bradford City 5-0 in 2013, although the Bantams were the first side from the fourth tier of English football to reach a major Wembley final.
• The first League Cup final to be played at Wembley was between West Brom and QPR in 1967. QPR were then a Third Division side and pulled off a major shock by winning 3-2. Prior to 1967, the final was played on a home and away basis over two legs.
• On two occasions a League Cup match has featured a record 12 goals: Arsenal's 7-5 win at Reading in 2012, and Dagenham's 6-6 draw with Brentford two years later.
• A competition record 32 penalties were taken when Derby County beat Carlisle United 14-13 in a first round shoot-out in August 2016.

LEEDS UNITED

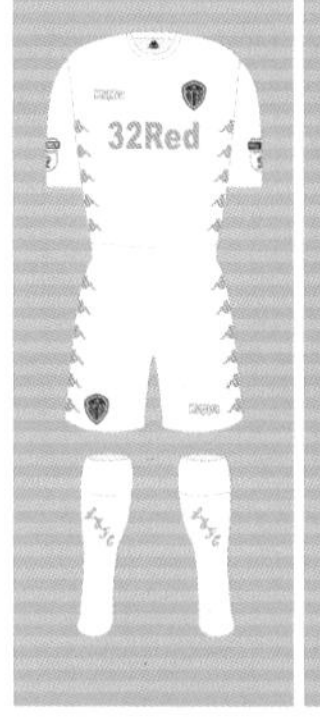

Year founded: 1919
Ground: Elland Road (37,890)
Nickname: United
Biggest win: 10-0 v Lyn Oslo (1969)
Heaviest defeat: 1-8 v Stoke City (1934)

Leeds United were formed in 1919 as successors to Leeds City, who had been expelled from the Football League after making illegal payments to their players. United initially joined the Midland League before being elected to the Second Division in 1920.
• Leeds' greatest years were in the 1960s and early 1970s under legendary manager Don Revie. The club were struggling in the Second Division when he arrived at Elland Road in 1961 but, building his side around the likes of Jack Charlton, Billy Bremner and Johnny Giles, Revie soon turned Leeds into a formidable force.
• During the Revie years Leeds won two league titles in 1969 and 1974, the FA Cup in 1972, the League Cup in 1968, and two Fairs Cup in 1968 and 1971. In the last of those triumphs Leeds became the first club to win a European trophy on the away goals rule after they drew 2-2 on aggregate with Italian giants Juventus.
• Leeds also reached the final of the European Cup in 1975, losing 2-0 to Bayern Munich. Sadly, rioting by the club's fans resulted in Leeds becoming the first English club to be suspended from European competition. The ban lasted three years.
• Peter Lorimer, another Revie-era stalwart, is the club's leading scorer, hitting 168 league goals in two spells at Elland Road (1962-79 and 1983-86). Lorimer is also the club's youngest ever player, making his debut against Southampton in 1962 aged 15 and 289 days.
• England World Cup winner Jack Charlton holds the club appearance record, turning out in 773 games in total between 1952 and 1973.
• In 1992 Leeds pipped Manchester United to the title to make history as the last club to win the old First Division before it became the Premiership. Ironically, Leeds' star player at the time, Eric Cantona, joined the Red Devils the following season. The club remained a force over the next decade, even reaching the Champions League semi-final in 2001, but financial mismanagement saw them plummet to League One in 2007 – a season in which Leeds used a club record 44 players – before they climbed back into the Championship three years later.
• Striker Gordon Hodgson scored a club record five goals in an 8-2 thrashing of Leicester City in October 1938.
• Former England captain Rio Ferdinand is both Leeds' record buy and record sale, joining the club from West Ham for £18 million in 2000 before leaving for Manchester United for a then British record £29.1 million two years later.

HONOURS
Division 1 champions *1969, 1974, 1992*
Division 2 champions *1924, 1964, 1990*
FA Cup *1972*
League Cup *1968*
Fairs Cup *1968, 1971*

LEICESTER CITY

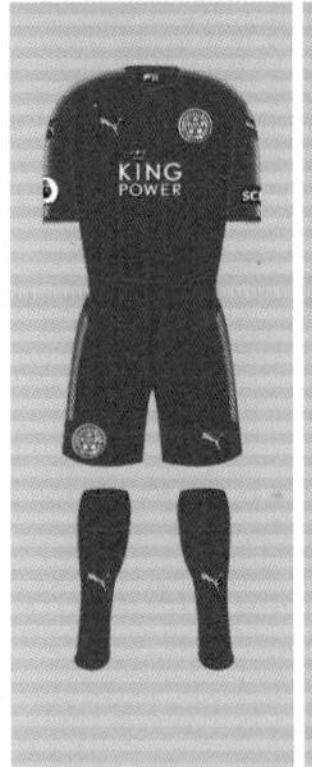

Year founded: 1884
Ground: King Power Stadium (32,312)
Previous name: Leicester Fosse
Nickname: The Foxes
Biggest win: 13-0 v Notts Olympic (1894)
Heaviest defeat: 0-12 v Nottingham Forest (1909)

Founded in 1884 as Leicester Fosse by old boys from Wyggeston School, the club were elected to the Second Division a decade later. In 1919 they changed their name to Leicester City, shortly after Leicester was given city status.

• **Leicester enjoyed their greatest success in 2015/16 when, under the leadership of popular manager Claudio Ranieri, they won the Premier League title in one of the greatest upsets in sporting history. The Foxes were 5,000-1 outsiders at the start of the campaign, but defied the odds thanks in part to the goals of striker Jamie Vardy, who set a new Premier League record by scoring in 11 consecutive matches.**

• The following season Leicester enjoyed their best ever European campaign, reaching the quarter-finals of the Champions League before losing 2-1 on aggregate to Atletico Madrid.

• **Leicester have won the second-tier championship seven times – a record only matched by Manchester City. On the last of these occasions in 2013/14 the Foxes set a number of significant club records, including highest number of points (102) and most league games won (33).**

• In 1909, while still known as Leicester Fosse, the club suffered their worst ever defeat, losing 12-0 to East Midlands neighbours Nottingham Forest – still a record score for a top-flight match. It later emerged that the Leicester players had been celebrating the wedding of a team-mate for two full days before the game, which might have contributed to their pitiful performance!

• **Leicester City are the only club to have played in four FA Cup finals and lost them all. Beaten in 1949, 1961 and 1963, they were defeated again by Manchester City in 1969 – the same season in which they were relegated from the top flight. Previously, only Manchester City (in 1926) had suffered this bitter double blow. The Foxes, though, have had more luck in the League Cup, winning the trophy three times.**

IS THAT A FACT?

Leicester City's defence of their Premier League title in 2016/17 was the worst in the competition's history, the Foxes finishing 12th after a disappointing campaign which saw manager Claudio Ranieri leave the club. The change worked, though, with new man Craig Shakespeare winning his first five league games to set a new record for a British manager.

• Leicester made their record signing in August 2016, when Algerian striker Islam Slimani joined the club from Sporting Lisbon for £30 million. A year later the Foxes received a club record £35 million when midfielder Danny Drinkwater signed for Chelsea.

• **Arthur Chandler holds the club goalscoring record, netting 259 times between 1923 and 1935. The club's appearance record is held by defender and ex-Leicestershire county cricketer Graham Cross, who turned out 599 times in all competitions for the Foxes between 1960 and 1976.**

• When, in 2005, Ashley Chambers made his debut for the Foxes in a League Cup tie against Blackpool aged 15 and 203 days, he became the youngest ever player in the history of the competition.

• **Long-serving midfielder Andy King has won 39 caps for Wales since making his international debut in 2009, equalling the club record set by Northern Ireland defender John O'Neill in the 1980s.**

Leicester's recent successes have got Jamie Vardy shouting from the rooftops

HONOURS
Premier League champions *2016*
Division 2 champions *1925, 1937, 1954, 1957, 1971, 1980*
Championship champions *2014*
League One champions *2009*
League Cup *1964, 1997, 2000*

The prolific Robert Lewandowski counts up the goals he's scored since kick-off

ROBERT LEWANDOWSKI

Born: Warsaw, Poland, 21st August 1988
Position: Striker
Club career:
2005 Delta Warsaw 10 (4)
2005-06 Legia Warsaw II 5 (2)
2006-08 Znicz Pruszkow 59 (36)
2008-10 Lech Poznan 58 (32)
2010-14 Borussia Dortmund 131 (74)
2014- Bayern Munich 96 (77)
International record:
2008- Poland 87 (46)

On 22nd September 2015 Robert Lewandowski scored five goals for Bayern Munich against Wolfsburg in just eight minutes and 59 seconds – the fastest five-goal haul ever in any major European league. Incredibly, the pacy Polish striker had begun the match on the bench!

• After starting out in the Polish lower leagues, Lewandowski made his name at Lech Poznan. In only his second season in the top flight, in 2009/10, he led the scoring charts with 18 goals as Poznan won the title.

• In the summer of 2010 Lewandowski moved on to Dortmund for around £4 million. The fee proved to be a bargain as Lewandowski's goals helped his club win two league titles and the German Cup in 2012, the Pole scoring a hat-trick in Dortmund's 5-2 demolition of Bayern Munich in the final. The following season Lewandowski set a new club record when he scored in 12 consecutive league games, and he also became the first player to score four goals in a Champions League semi-final, achieving this record in Dortmund's shock 4-1 defeat of Real Madrid.

• After topping the Bundesliga scoring charts in 2013/14 he moved on to Bayern Munich, with whom he has since won three titles. In 2015/16 Lewandowski became the first player for 39 years to score 30 goals in a Bundesliga campaign and the following season he was even more prolific, hitting a career-best 54 goals in total for club and country.

• Lewandowski first played for Poland aged 20 in 2008, coming off the bench to score in a World Cup qualifier against San Marino to become his country's second ever youngest goalscorer on his debut. In June 2015 he scored a four-minute hat-trick in a Euro 2016 qualifier against Georgia – the second fastest treble in the history of the European Championships – and he is now his country's second highest scorer ever with 46 goals.

LINCOLN CITY

Year founded: 1884
Ground: Sincil Bank (10,120)
Nickname: The Imps
Biggest win: 11-1 v Crewe Alexandra (1951)
Heaviest defeat: 3-11 v Manchester City (1895)

Lincoln City were founded in 1884 as the successors to Lincoln Rovers and are the oldest club never to have played in the top flight. The Imps have endured a fair amount of misery over the years, suffering a record five demotions from the Football League but always bouncing back, most recently winning the National League championship in 2017.

• In the same year Lincoln made headline news when they became the first non-league club since 1914 to reach the quarter-finals of the FA Cup after thrilling wins against Championship duo Ipswich and Brighton, and Premier League Burnley. However, with Wembley in their sights the Imps' cup dreams were crushed by Arsenal, who beat them 5-0 at the Emirates.

• In 1976, under the stewardship of future England boss Graham Taylor, Lincoln won the old Division 4 title with a record 74 points (the highest ever total until 1981/82 when wins earned an additional point).

• The Imps set an unwanted record between 2003 and 2007 when they reached the fourth tier play-offs in five consecutive seasons without once gaining promotion, losing three semi-finals and two finals.

• In three spells at Sincil Bank between 1950 and 1961, club legend Andy Graver scored a record 143 goals for the Imps.

HONOURS
Division 3 (North) champions *1932, 1948, 1952*
Division 4 champions *1976*
Conference champions *1988*
National League champions *2017*

GARY LINEKER

Born: Leicester, 30th November 1960
Position: Striker
Club career:
1978-85 Leicester City 194 (95)
1985-86 Everton 41 (30)
1986-89 Barcelona 103 (43)
1989-92 Tottenham Hotspur 105 (67)
1992-94 Nagoya Grampus Eight 23 (9)
International record:
1984-92 England 80 (48)

Now a popular television presenter, Gary Lineker is England's third highest scorer with 48 goals. He had a great chance to set a new benchmark, but failed to score in any of his final six matches and even missed a penalty against Brazil in 1992 that would have equalled Bobby Charlton's then record tally of 49 goals.

• He is, though, England's leading scorer at the finals of the World Cup with 10 goals. At the 1986 tournament

in Mexico Lineker scored six goals to win the Golden Boot, and he added another four at Italia '90.

• Lineker is the only player to have twice scored all four England goals in a match, grabbing all his side's goals in 4-2 away wins over Spain in 1987 and Malaysia in 1991. In all, he hit five hat-tricks for the Three Lions – just one behind Jimmy Greaves' record.

• At club level Lineker won the European Cup Winners' Cup with Barcelona in 1989 and the FA Cup with Spurs two years later. He was also voted PFA Player of the Year in 1986 after a single goal-filled season with Everton.

• In his last international, against Sweden at the 1992 European Championships, Lineker was controversially substituted by England boss Graham Taylor. The move backfired, however, as England lost the match and were eliminated.

• In August 2016 Lineker presented *Match of the Day* in just his underpants after promising his 5 million Twitter followers he would do exactly that if his beloved Leicester City won the Premier League.

LIVERPOOL

Year founded: 1892
Ground: Anfield (44,742)
Nickname: The Reds
Biggest win: 11-0 v Stromsgodset (1974)
Heaviest defeat: 1-9 v Birmingham City (1954)

Liverpool were founded as a splinter club from local rivals Everton following a dispute between the Toffees and the landlord of their original ground at Anfield, John Houlding. When the majority of Evertonians decided to decamp to Goodison Park in 1892, Houlding set up Liverpool FC after his attempts to retain the name 'Everton' had failed.

• With 18 league titles to their name, including the Double in 1986, Liverpool are the second most successful club in the history of English football behind deadly rivals Manchester United – although their last championship success came way back in 1990. The Reds' total of 103 seasons in the top flight is only surpassed by Aston Villa (105) and Everton (115).

Jurgen Klopp's Reds are the toughest gang on the streets of Liverpool these days

• Liverpool dominated English football in the 1970s and 1980s after the foundations of the club's success were laid by legendary manager Bill Shankly in the previous decade. Under Shankly's successor, Bob Paisley, the Reds won 13 major trophies – a haul only surpassed by Sir Alex Ferguson.

• As their fans love to remind their rivals Liverpool are the most successful English side in Europe, having won the European Cup/ Champions League on five occasions. The Reds first won the trophy in 1977, beating Borussia Monchengladbach 3-1 in Rome, and the following year became the first British team to retain the cup (after a 1-0 win in the final against Bruges at Wembley, club legend Kenny Dalglish grabbing the all-important goal). Liverpool have also won the UEFA Cup three times, giving them a total of eight European triumphs.

• Liverpool have won the League Cup a record eight times, including four times in a row between 1981 and 1984, and are the only club to win the trophy twice on penalties (in 2001 and 2012). Reds striker Ian Rush is the joint-leading scorer in the history of the competition with 49 goals, hitting all but one of these for Liverpool in two spells at the club in the 1980s and 1990s.

• Rush also scored a record five goals in three FA Cup finals for Liverpool in 1986, 1989 and 1992 – all of which were won by the Reds. In all, the Merseysiders have won the trophy seven times, most recently in 2006 when they became only the second team (after Arsenal the previous year) to claim the cup on penalties.

• When the Reds recorded their biggest ever victory, 11-0 against Norwegian no-hopers Stromsgodset in the Cup Winners' Cup in 1974, no fewer than nine different Liverpool players got on the scoresheet to set a British record for the most scoring players in a competitive match.

IS THAT A FACT?

When James Milner blasted home from the penalty spot in Liverpool's 1-1 draw with Manchester City at the Etihad on 19th March 2017, he set a new record for the most Premier League games (47) in which a player has scored a goal without once ending up on the losing side.

• At the 2014 World Cup Liverpool provided England with a record six players for a match at a major tournament. Steven Gerrard, Jordan Henderson, Glen Johnson, Raheem Sterling and Daniel Sturridge all started the 2-1 defeat to Uruguay, while Rickie Lambert was a late substitute.

• England international striker Roger Hunt is the club's leading scorer in league games, with 245 goals between 1958 and 1969. His team-mate Ian Callaghan holds the Liverpool appearance record, turning out in 640 league games between 1960 and 1978.

• Pacy winger Mohamed Salah is the club's record signing, joining the Reds from Roma for £36.9 million in June 2017. In the summer of 2014 Uruguayan striker Luis Suarez left Anfield for Barcelona in a club record £75 million deal.

• Between 1976 and 1983 Liverpool full-back Phil Neal played in 365 consecutive league games – a record for the top flight of English football.

• Kop legend Steven Gerrard won a club record 114 international caps for England between 2000 and 2014, and scored a British record 41 goals in European competition.

• Young striker Ben Woodburn became Liverpool's youngest ever scorer at 17 and 45 days when he netted in a 2-0 victory against Leeds United in the quarter-final of the League Cup in November 2016.

HONOURS
Division 1 champions *1901, 1906, 1922, 1923, 1947, 1964, 1966, 1973, 1976, 1977, 1979, 1980, 1982, 1983, 1984, 1986, 1988, 1990*
Division 2 champions *1894, 1896, 1905, 1962*
FA Cup *1965, 1974, 1986, 1989, 1992, 2001, 2006*
League Cup *1981, 1982, 1983, 1984, 1995, 2001, 2003, 2012*
Double *1986*
European Cup/Champions League *1977, 1978, 1981, 1984, 2005*
UEFA Cup *1973, 1976, 2001*
European Super Cup *1977, 2001, 2005*

HUGO LLORIS

Born: Nice, France, 26th December 1986
Position: Goalkeeper
Club career:
2004-06 Nice B 20
2005-08 Nice 72
2008-12 Lyon 146
2012- Tottenham Hotspur 169
International record:
2008- France 90

Tottenham skipper Hugo Lloris enjoyed his best season to date in 2016/17, the acrobatic goalkeeper being part of a resolute Spurs defence which conceded just 26 goals – the best record of any club in the Premier League.

• After starting out with his hometown club Nice, Lloris made his name with Lyon. During a four-year stint with the French giants, Lloris was voted Ligue 1 Goalkeeper of the Year three times, but only managed to win one piece of silverware – the French Cup in 2012, following a 1-0 victory in the final over third-tier US Quevilly.

Hugo Lloris' impression of a flying banana was coming along a treat

• Famed for his superb reflexes and his ability to rush out to the edge of the box to snuff out dangerous opposition attacks, Lloris won the European Under-19 Championship with France in 2005. He was awarded his first senior cap in 2008, keeping a clean sheet in a 0-0 draw with Uruguay, and he skippered his country for the first time in a 2-1 friendly win against England at Wembley in November 2010. He has since gone on to captain his country a record 66 times.

• At Euro 2016 Lloris was in fine form, especially in France's 2-0 win against Germany in the semi-final. However, in the final he was beaten by a low 20-yard shot from Portugal's Eder in extra-time and finished on the losing side.

DAVID LUIZ

Born: Diadema, Brazil, 22nd April 1987
Position: Defender
Club career:
2006-07 Vitoria 26 (1)
2007 Benfica (loan) 10 (0)
2007-11 Benfica 72 (4)
2011-14 Chelsea 81 (6)
2014-16 Paris Saint-Germain 53 (3)
2016- Chelsea 33 (1)
International record:
2010- Brazil 56 (3)

In the first season of his second spell at Chelsea, flamboyant centre-back David Luiz added the Premier League title to an already impressive collection of medals, while his consistent performances in the Blues' back three also earned him a place in the Premier League Team of the Year for the first time.

• The frizzy-haired Brazilian had returned to Chelsea from Paris Saint-Germain in a surprise £32 million deal on transfer deadline day in August 2016. Previously, when Luiz left London for Paris in June 2014 it was for £50 million, making him the world's most expensive defender at the time.

'Look, say I've got silly hair again, and you'll get a slap!'

• An occasionally erratic performer in his earlier career, Luiz answered his critics in the best possible manner by playing a starring role in Chelsea's run to the 2012 Champions League final and then bravely stepping up to score one of his team's penalties in the shoot-out victory over Bayern Munich which brought the trophy to London for the first time. The following year he helped the Blues become the first British side to win the Europa League, after victory over his former club Benfica in the final.

• In 2010 Luiz made his debut for Brazil in a 2-0 friendly win over the USA, and two years later he captained his country for the first time in a 1-0 win against South Africa. He had mixed fortunes at the World Cup in 2014, scoring a thunderous free kick in the quarter-final against Colombia but ending the tournament in tears after Brazil were hammered 7-1 by Germany in the semi-final.

ROMELU LUKAKU

Born: Antwerp, Belgium, 13th May 1993
Position: Striker
Club career:
2009-11 Anderlecht 73 (33)
2011-14 Chelsea 10 (0)
2012-13 West Bromwich Albion (loan) 35 (17)
2013-14 Everton (loan) 31 (15)
2014-17 Everton 110 (53)
2017- Manchester United
International record:
2010- Belgium 57 (20)

In July 2017 Romelu Lukaku joined Manchester United from Everton for £75 million (potentially rising to a British record £90 million) in the most expensive ever transfer between two English clubs.

• Lukaku's 25 goals in 2016/17 put him second behind Harry Kane in the race for the Golden Boot and was the best ever haul by an Everton player in the Premier League era – as is his total of 53 league goals for the Toffees. During the campaign Lukaku scored

'Please Lord, let me score in every match for Manchester United and win the Premier League Golden Boot!'

in nine consecutive home games to equal a club record set by the legendary Dixie Dean in 1934.

• Powerfully built, strong, quick and athletic, Lukaku enjoyed a great first season with his original club, Anderlecht, scoring 15 league goals as they won the Belgian championship in 2010. The following season he was the top scorer in Belgium with 20 goals in all competitions.

• Chelsea snapped up Lukaku for £10 million in 2011 but he struggled to make an impact at Stamford Bridge and the following season was loaned out to West Brom. The young striker thrived at the Hawthorns, netting 17 goals – the most ever in a single season by a Baggies player in the Premier League era. After another successful loan season at Everton, Lukaku joined the Toffees in a permanent deal for £28 million in July 2014, making him the club's most expensive ever player at the time.

• The son of a former Zaire (now DR Congo) international, Lukaku made his bow for Belgium in March 2010 while still only 16. He represented his country at the 2014 World Cup in Brazil and at Euro 2016, scoring twice in a 3-0 group stage defeat of the Republic of Ireland. His younger brother, Jordan, is also a Belgian international.

IS THAT A FACT?
Romelu Lukaku scored Everton's fastest ever Premier League goal when he netted after just 31 seconds of the Toffees' 6-3 home win against Bournemouth on 4th February 2017.

LUTON TOWN

Year founded: 1885
Ground: Kenilworth Road (10,356)
Nickname: The Hatters
Biggest win: 15-0 v Great Yarmouth Town (1914)
Heaviest defeat: 0-9 v Small Heath (1898)

Founded in 1885 following the merger of two local sides, Luton Town Wanderers and Excelsior, Luton Town became the first professional club in the south of England five years later.

• The club's greatest moment came in 1988 when they beat Arsenal 3-2 in the League Cup final. The Hatters returned to Wembley for the final the following year, but lost to Nottingham Forest – the same club which beat them in their only FA Cup final appearance in 1959.

• In 1936 Luton striker Joe Payne scored a Football League record 10 goals in a Third Division (South) fixture against Bristol Rovers. The Hatters won the match 12-0 to record their biggest ever league victory.

• Midfielder Bob Morton made a record 495 league appearances for the Hatters between 1946 and 1964, while his team-mate Gordon Turner scored a record 243 goals for the club.

• In January 2013, while they were languishing in the Football Conference, Luton became the first ever non-league team to beat a Premier League outfit in the FA Cup when they won 1-0 at Norwich City in a fourth-round tie.

HONOURS
Division 2 champions *1982*
Division 3 (South) champions *1937*
League One champions *2005*
Division 4 champions *1968*
Conference champions *2014*
League Cup *1988*
Football League Trophy *2009*

MANAGER OF THE YEAR

Former Manchester United boss Sir Alex Ferguson won the FA Premier League Manager of the Year award a record 11 times. He also won the old Manager of the Year award in 1993, giving him a total of 12 triumphs.

• **Arsène Wenger (in 1998, 2002 and 2004) and Jose Mourinho (2005, 2006 and 2015) are the only other managers to win the award more than once since it was introduced in the 1993/94 season.**

• Just two English managers have won the award: Harry Redknapp (Tottenham Hotspur) in 2010 and Alan Pardew (Newcastle United) in 2012.

• **Tony Pulis topped the poll in 2014 despite his club, Crystal Palace, only finishing 11th in the Premier League – the lowest ever placing for a manager collecting the award.**

• Chelsea are the only club to have two managers who have won the award: Jose Mourinho on three occasions, and Antonio Conte in 2017 after guiding the Blues to the title in his first season in the Premier League.

MANCHESTER CITY

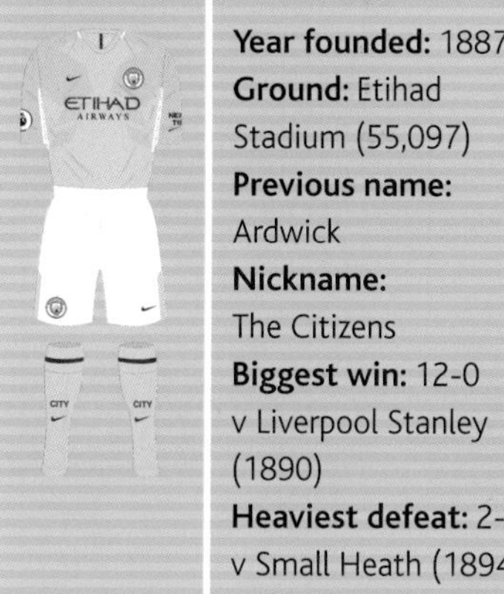

Year founded: 1887
Ground: Etihad Stadium (55,097)
Previous name: Ardwick
Nickname: The Citizens
Biggest win: 12-0 v Liverpool Stanley (1890)
Heaviest defeat: 2-10 v Small Heath (1894)

City have their roots in a church team which was renamed Ardwick in 1887 and became founder members of the Second Division five years later. In 1894, after suffering financial difficulties, the club was reformed under its present name.

Manchester City have come a long way from their Ardwick days

• **Now owned by Sheikh Mansour of the Abu Dhabi Royal Family, City are one of the richest clubs in the world. Following a massive spending spree on the likes of David Silva and Yaya Toure, the Sheikh received the first return on his huge investment in 2011 when City won the FA Cup, their first trophy for 35 years, after beating Stoke City 1-0 in the final at Wembley. More silverware followed the next season as City won the Premier League, their first league title since 1968, after pipping arch rivals Manchester United on goal difference. In 2014 City won the Premier League for a second time, Chilean boss Manuel Pellegrini becoming the first non-European manager to win the title.**

• Prior to the modern era, the late 1960s were the most successful period in City's history, a side featuring the likes of Colin Bell, Francis Lee and Mike Summerbee winning the league title (1968), the FA Cup (1969), the League Cup (1970) and the European Cup Winners' Cup (also in 1970), and for a short time usurping Manchester United as the city's premier club.

• **City also won the league title in 1937. Incredibly, the following season they were relegated to the Second Division despite scoring more goals than any other side in the division. To this day they remain the only league champions to suffer the drop in the following campaign. Almost as bizarrely, City were demoted from the top flight in 1983 after spending just the final four minutes of the season in the relegation zone.**

• Eric Brook, an ever-present in that initial title-winning season, is City's joint leading scorer (along with 1920s marksman Tommy Johnson) with 158 league goals between 1928 and 1940. The club's record appearance maker is Alan Oakes, who turned out 564 times in the sky blue shirt between 1958 and 1976.

• **The club have won the League Cup four times, most recently beating Liverpool in 2016 on penalties after City keeper Willy Caballero became the first goalkeeper to save three spot-kicks in a final shoot-out. City have won the FA Cup five times and, in 1926, were the first club to reach the final and be relegated in the same season. A 1-0 defeat by Bolton at Wembley ensured a grim campaign ended on a depressing note.**

• In January 1961 Denis Law scored a club record six goals in an FA Cup tie at Luton. Unfortunately, the match was abandoned due to a waterlogged pitch with City leading 6-2, and although Law was again on target when the game was replayed City went down to a 3-1 defeat.

• **City have won the title for the second tier of English football a joint-record seven times, most recently in 2002 when they returned to the Premiership under then manager**

Kevin Keegan. Four years earlier the club experienced their lowest ever moment when they dropped into the third tier for the first and only time in their history – the first European trophy winners to sink this low.

• The club's most expensive purchase is Belgian midfielder Kevin De Bruyne, who signed from Wolfsburg for £55 million in August 2015. In August 2017 City received a club record £25 million when they sold Nigeria international striker Kelechi Iheanacho to Leicester City.

• Mercurial midfielder David Silva is the club's highest capped international, having played 65 times for Spain since he joined the Citizens in 2010.

• Sergio Aguero is City's all-time leading scorer in European competitions with 29 goals in total.

HONOURS
Division 1 champions *1937, 1968*
Premier League champions *2012, 2014*
Division 2 champions *1899, 1903, 1910, 1928, 1947, 1966*
First Division champions *2002*
FA Cup *1904, 1934, 1956, 1969, 2011*
League Cup *1970, 1976, 2014, 2016*
European Cup Winners' Cup *1970*

MANCHESTER UNITED

Year founded: 1878
Ground: Old Trafford (75,643)
Previous name: Newton Heath
Nickname: Red Devils
Biggest win: 10-0 v Anderlecht (1956)
Heaviest defeat: 0-7 v Blackburn (1926), Aston Villa (1930) and v Wolverhampton Wanderers (1931)

The club was founded in 1878 as Newton Heath, a works team for employees of the Lancashire and Yorkshire Railway. In 1892 Newton Heath (who played in yellow-and-green-halved shirts) were elected to the Football League but a decade later went bankrupt, only to be immediately reformed as Manchester United with the help of a local brewer, John Davies.

• United are the most successful club in the history of English football, having won the league title a record 20 times. The Red Devils have been the dominant force of the Premier League era, winning the title a record 13 times under former manager Sir Alex Ferguson.

• United were the first English club to win the Double on three separate occasions, in 1994, 1996 and 1999. The last of these triumphs was particularly memorable as the club also went on to win the Champions League, beating Bayern Munich 2-1 in the final in Barcelona thanks to late goals by Teddy Sheringham and Ole Gunner Solskjaer, to record English football's first ever Treble.

• Under legendary manager Sir Matt Busby United became the first ever English club to win the European Cup in 1968, when they beat Benfica 4-1 in the final at Wembley. Victory was especially sweet for Sir Matt who, a decade earlier, had narrowly survived the Munich air crash which claimed the lives of eight of his players as the team returned from a European Cup fixture in Belgrade. United also won European football's top club prize in 2008, beating Chelsea in the Champions League final on penalties in Moscow.

• When United won the Europa League in 2017 – after beating Dutch outfit Ajax 2-0 in the final in Stockholm – they became only the second British club (after Chelsea) to win all three historic European trophies, having previously won the Cup Winners' Cup in 1991.

• United won the FA Cup for the first time in 1909, beating Bristol City 1-0 in the final. The club's total of 12 wins in the competition is only bettered by Arsenal. In 2000 the Red Devils became the first holders not to defend the cup when they played in the first FIFA Club World Cup Championship instead.

• Old Trafford has the highest capacity of any dedicated football ground bar Wembley in Britain but, strangely, when United set an all-time Football League attendance record of 83,260 for their home game against Arsenal on 17th January 1948 they were playing at Maine Road, home of local rivals Manchester City. This was because Old Trafford was badly damaged by German bombs during the Second World War, forcing United to use their neighbours' ground in the immediate post-war period.

• United's leading appearance maker is Ryan Giggs, who played in an incredible 963 games in all competitions for the club

Manchester United, still the most successful club in English football

between 1991 and 2014. Winger Steve Coppell played in a club record 206 consecutive league games between 1977 and 1981.

• The club's highest goalscorer is Wayne Rooney, who banged in a total of 253 goals in all competitions having joined the club from Everton in 2004. Rooney is also United's most capped international, with 110 appearances for England in his time at Old Trafford.

• United provided a record seven players for the England team for a World Cup qualifier away to Albania in March 2001. David Beckham, Nicky Butt, Andy Cole, Gary Neville and Paul Scholes all started the match, while Wes Brown and Teddy Sheringham came off the bench in England's 3-1 win.

• In 1999/2000 United won the Premier League with a record 18-point margin over runners-up Arsenal. Three years earlier, in 1996/97, they won the title with the fewest points in the Premier League era, just 75.

• Known for many years as a big-spending club, United's record signing is French midfielder Paul Pogba, who cost a then world record £89.3 million when he moved from Juventus in August 2016. The club's most expensive sale is former Old Trafford hero Cristiano Ronaldo, who joined Real Madrid for a then world record £80 million in 2009.

• United hold the record for the biggest ever Premier League victory, thrashing Ipswich Town 9-0 at Old Trafford in March 1995. Andy Cole scored five goals in that game to set a record for the league that was matched by Dimitar Berbatov, against Blackburn in November 2010.

TOP 10

TOTAL PREMIER LEAGUE WINS

1.	Manchester United	604
2.	Arsenal	525
3.	Chelsea	516
4.	Liverpool	478
5.	Tottenham Hotspur	400
6.	Everton	349
7.	Manchester City	327
8.	Newcastle United	322
9.	Aston Villa	316
10.	West Ham United	265

• With around 84 million followers on Facebook and Twitter, Manchester United have more fans worldwide than any other English club.

HONOURS

Division 1 champions *1908, 1911, 1952, 1956, 1957, 1965, 1967*
Premier League champions *1993, 1994, 1996, 1997, 1999, 2000, 2001, 2003, 2007, 2008, 2009, 2011, 2013*
Division 2 champions *1936, 1975*
FA Cup *1909, 1948, 1963, 1977, 1983, 1985, 1990, 1994, 1996, 1999, 2004, 2016*
League Cup *1992, 2006, 2009, 2010, 2017*
Double *1994, 1996, 1999*
European Cup/Champions League *1968, 1999, 2008*
European Cup Winners' Cup *1991*
Europa League *2017*
European Super Cup *1991*
Intercontinental Cup/Club World Cup *1999, 2008*

SADIO MANE

Born: Sedhiou, Senegal, 10th April 1992
Position: Striker/winger
Club career:
2011-12 Metz 22 (2)
2012-14 Red Bull Salzburg 63 (31)
2014-16 Southampton 67 (21)
2016- Liverpool 27 (13)
International record:
2012- Senegal 45 (13)

Senegal international Sadio Mane became the most expensive African player ever when he joined Liverpool from Southampton for £34 million in June 2016, although he has since ceded that title to Anfield team-mate Mohamed Salah. In an excellent first season at Anfield Mane scored 13 league goals. earning himself a place in the PFA Team of the Year.

Sadio Mane holds the record for the fastest Premier League hat-trick

• A speedy attacker who generally finishes with calm confidence, Mane started out with French club Metz before coming to the fore with Red Bull Salzburg, with whom he won the Austrian Double in 2014. In the same year he joined Southampton for £11.8 million.

• In May 2015 Mane made headlines when he hit the fastest Premier League hat-trick ever, scoring three times in a 6-1 rout of Aston Villa in an incredible two minutes and 56 seconds. The following season he was the Saints' top scorer in all competitions with 15 goals.

• Mane made his debut for Senegal in 2012, representing his country at that year's Olympics in London. In 2017 he helped Senegal reach the quarter-finals of the Africa Cup of Nations but missed a penalty in the shoot-out defeat against Cameroon.

MANSFIELD TOWN

Year founded: 1897
Ground: One Call Stadium (9,186)
Previous names: Mansfield Wesleyans, Mansfield Wesley
Nickname: The Stags
Biggest win: 9-2 v Rotherham United (1932)
Heaviest defeat: 1-7 v Reading (1932), v Peterborough United (1966) and v QPR (1966)

The club was founded as Mansfield Wesleyans, a boys brigade team, in 1897, before becoming Mansfield Town in 1910. The Stags eventually joined the Football League in 1931, remaining there until relegation to the Conference in 2008. Five years later the club bounced back to League Two as Conference champions with a club record 95 points.

• In 1950/51 Mansfield were the first club ever to remain unbeaten at home in a 46-game season, but just missed out on promotion to the old Second Division. The Stags finally reached the second tier in 1977, but were relegated at the end of the campaign.

• Already Sheffield United's all-time top scorer, striker Harry Johnson arrived at Mansfield in 1932 and in just three seasons scored 104 league goals to set a record for the Stags that still stands. Goalkeeper Rod Arnold played in a club record 440 league games for the Stags between 1971 and 1984.

• Mansfield's Field Mill ground (now known as the One Call Stadium for sponsorship purposes) is the oldest in the world hosting professional football, the first match having been played there in 1861.

HONOURS
Division 3 champions *1977*
Division 4 champions *1975*
Conference champions *2013*
Football League Trophy *1987*

DIEGO MARADONA

Born: Buenos Aires, Argentina, 30th October 1960
Position: Striker/midfielder
Club career:
1976-80 Argentinos Juniors 167 (115)
1980-82 Boca Juniors 40 (28)
1982-84 Barcelona 36 (22)
1984-91 Napoli 186 (83)
1992-93 Sevilla 25 (4)
1995-97 Boca Juniors 29 (7)
International record:
1977-94 Argentina 91 (34)

The best player in the world in the 1980s, Diego Maradona is considered by many to be the greatest footballer ever.

• During his career in his native Argentina, then in Spain and Italy, he smashed three transfer records. First, his £1 million move from Argentinos Juniors to Boca Juniors in 1980 was a world record for a teenager. Then he broke the world transfer record when he joined Barcelona from Boca for £4.2 million in 1982, and again when he signed for Napoli for £6.9 million in 1984.

• A superb dribbler who used his low centre of gravity to great effect, Maradona was almost impossible to mark. He was idolised at Napoli, who he led to a first ever Italian title in 1987 and a first European trophy two years later, when they won the UEFA Cup.

• He made his international debut aged 16 in 1977 and went on to play at four World Cups, captaining his country in a record 16 games at the finals. His greatest triumph came in 1986 when, after scoring the goals that beat England (including the infamous 'Hand of God' goal which he punched into the net) and Belgium in the quarter and semi-finals, he skippered Argentina to victory in the final against West Germany. He also led his side to the 1990 final against the same opponents.

• However, Maradona's international career ended in disgrace when he was thrown out of the 1994 World Cup in the USA after failing a drugs test. He had previously been hit with a worldwide 15-month ban from football in 1991 after testing positive for cocaine.

• Despite these blots on his reputation, Maradona was voted 'The Player of the Century' by more than half of those who took part in a worldwide FIFA internet poll in 2000. In 2008 he became head coach of Argentina, but resigned two years later after his side were thrashed 4-0 by Germany in the World Cup quarter-finals.

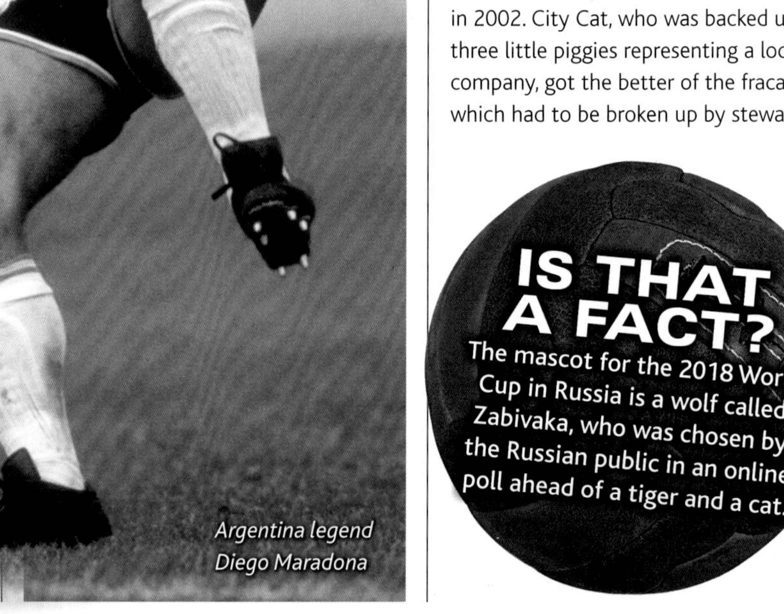

Argentina legend Diego Maradona

MASCOTS

In December 2016 then Crystal Palace manager Sam Allardyce fumed that Watford mascot Harry the Hornet was 'out of order' after the 7ft insect mocked Eagles winger Wifried Zaha by diving behind him at the end of the match – a cheeky reference to an incident late on in the 1-1 draw which saw the Ivory Coast international booked for diving in the Watford penalty area.

• Swansea mascot Cyril the Swan was fined a record £1,000 in 1999 for celebrating a goal against Millwall in the FA Cup by running on to the pitch and pushing the referee. Two years later Cyril was in trouble again when he pulled off the head of Millwall's Zampa the Lion mascot and drop-kicked it into the crowd.

• In one of the most bizarre football sights ever, Wolves mascot Wolfie traded punches with his Bristol City counterpart City Cat during a half-time penalty shoot-out competition at Ashton Gate in 2002. City Cat, who was backed up by three little piggies representing a local company, got the better of the fracas which had to be broken up by stewards.

IS THAT A FACT?
The mascot for the 2018 World Cup in Russia is a wolf called Zabivaka, who was chosen by the Russian public in an online poll ahead of a tiger and a cat.

Watford mascot Harry the Hornet packs a bit of a sting

• Schalke mascot Erwin, a giant sporting a blue-and-white cap, was warned by the German FA in May 2017 after running on to the pitch to show a red card to the referee, who had just denied the home side a last-gasp penalty in their local derby with Borussia Dortmund.

• Charlton fan Daniel Boylett was jailed for 21 months and banned from attending football matches for six years after attempting to punch Crystal Palace's mascot, a live eagle called Kayla, during the south London rivals' League Cup tie in September 2015. Kayla, though, had the last laugh as the Eagles ran out 4-1 winners.

• A recent survey found that 11 out of 20 Premier League clubs charged children to be mascots at their home matches. West Ham were the most expensive of the bunch, charging a hefty £600 per mascot.

MATCH-FIXING

The first recorded incidence of match-fixing occurred in 1900 when Jack Hillman, goalkeeper with relegation-threatened Burnley, was alleged to have offered a bribe to the Nottingham Forest captain. Hillman was found guilty of the charges by a joint Football Association and Football League commission and banned for one year.

• Nine players received bans after Manchester United beat Liverpool at Old Trafford in April 1915. A Liverpool player later admitted the result had been fixed in a Manchester pub before the match. For his part in the scandal, United's Enoch West was banned for life – although the punishment was later waived... when West was 62!

• In the mid-1960s English football was rocked by a match-fixing scandal when former Everton player Jimmy Gauld revealed in a newspaper interview that a number of games had been rigged as part of a betting coup. Gauld implicated three Sheffield Wednesday players in the scam, including England internationals Tony Kay and Peter Swan. The trio were later sentenced to four months in prison and banned for life from football. Ringleader Gauld received a four-year prison term.

• In November 2015 five members of the Nepal national team were charged with treason after being arrested on suspicion of match-fixing in a number of World Cup qualifiers.

• In 2011 former Roma director Riccardo Viola admitted his club had paid French referee Michel Vautrot £50,000 ahead of the Italian side's European Cup semi-final second leg at home to Dundee United in 1984. Roma won the match 3-0 to go through to the final 3-2 on aggregate.

• A match in the Swedish top flight between Gothenburg and AIK Stockholm in May 2017 was postponed after allegations that an AIK player had been offered a considerable sum of money to ensure his team lost the match.

SIR STANLEY MATTHEWS

Born: Stoke, 1st February 1915
Died: 23rd February 2000
Position: Winger
Club career:
1932-47 Stoke City 259 (51)
1947-61 Blackpool 379 (17)
1961-65 Stoke City 59 (3)
International record:
1934-57 England 54 (11)

Nicknamed 'the Wizard of the Dribble' for his magnificent skills on the ball, Stanley Matthews was one of the greatest footballers of all time. His club career spanned a record 33 years and, incredibly, he played his last game in the First Division for Stoke City five days after his 50th birthday. He remains the oldest player to appear in the top flight.

• Matthews' England career was almost as lengthy, his 54 appearances for his country spanning 23 years between 1934 and 1957. He made his last appearance for the Three Lions at the age of 42, setting another record.

• A brilliant winger who possessed superb close control, Matthews inspired Blackpool to victory in the 1953 FA Cup final after the Seasiders came back from 3-1 down to beat Bolton 4-3. Despite a hat-trick by his team-mate Stan Mortensen, the match is remembered as 'the Matthews final'. He had never won an FA Cup winner's medal before and the whole country (outside of Bolton) was willing Matthews to succeed.

• The first player to be voted Footballer of the Year (in 1948) and European Footballer of the Year (in 1956), Matthews was knighted in 1965 – the only footballer to be so honoured while still playing. When he died in 2000 more than 100,000 people lined the streets of Stoke to pay tribute to one of the true legends of world football.

LIONEL MESSI

Born: Rosario, Argentina, 24th June 1987
Position: Striker/winger
Club career:
2004- Barcelona 382 (349)
International record:
2005-16 Argentina 118 (58)

Rated by many as the best player in the world, Lionel Messi is Barcelona's all-time leading scorer with 507 goals in all competitions. No fewer than 349 of those came in La Liga, making the diminutive Argentinian the competition's leading all-time scorer.

• Life, though, could have been very different for Messi, who suffered from a growth hormone deficiency as a child in Argentina. However, his outrageous talent was such that

The magical Lionel Messi is the all-time top scorer in La Liga

Barcelona were prepared to move him and his family to Europe when he was aged just 13 and pay for his medical treatment.

• Putting these problems behind him, he has flourished to the extent that in 2009 he was named both World Player of the Year and European Player of the Year, and in 2010 he was the inaugural winner of the FIFA Ballon d'Or – an award, following his most recent triumph in 2015, he has won a record four times. A brilliant dribbler who possesses mesmeric ball skills, in 2012 Messi became the first player to be top scorer in four consecutive Champions League campaigns (2009-12) and he also set another record for the competition when he struck five goals in a single game against Bayer Leverkusen. In 2015 he helped Barcelona become the first European club to win the Treble of league, cup and Champions League twice, scoring twice in the Copa del Rey final against Athletic Bilbao.

• Messi scored a world record 91 goals in the calendar year of 2012 for club and country, and the following year became the first player to score against every other La Liga club in consecutive matches. In 2017 he claimed the European Golden Shoe for a joint-record fourth time after netting 37 goals in la Liga.

• Messi made his international debut in 2005 but it was a forgettable occasion – he was sent off after just 40 seconds for elbowing a Hungarian defender who was pulling his shirt. Happier times followed in 2007 when he was voted Player of the Tournament at the Copa America and in 2008 when he won a gold medal with the Argentine football team at the Beijing Olympics.

• At the 2014 World Cup he won the Golden Ball as the tournament's outstanding player, but had to be satisfied with a runners-up medal after Argentina's defeat by Germany in the final. The following year he turned down the Player of the Tournament award at the Copa America following Argentina's defeat to hosts Chile in the final and after his country's defeat in the final to the same opposition in 2016 he announced his retirement from international football.

• However, a huge public campaign calling for him to change his mind was successful, and he marked his return with the winning goal against old foes Uruguay in a World Cup qualifier in September 2016. With 58 goals for his country, Messi is Argentina's all-time top scorer.

MIDDLESBROUGH

Year founded: 1876
Ground: Riverside Stadium (34,746)
Nickname: Boro
Biggest win: 11-0 v Scarborough (1890)
Heaviest defeat: 0-9 v Blackburn Rovers (1954)

Founded by members of the Middlesbrough Cricket Club at the Albert Park Hotel in 1876, the club turned professional in 1889 before reverting to amateur status three years later. Winners of the FA Amateur Cup in both 1895 and 1898, the club turned pro for a second time in 1899 and was elected to the Football League in the same year.

• In 1905 Middlesbrough became the first club to sign a player for a four-figure transfer fee when they forked out £1,000 for Sunderland and England striker Alf Common. On his Boro debut Common paid back some of the fee by scoring the winner at Sheffield United... the Teesiders' first away win for two years!

• The club had to wait over a century before winning a major trophy, but finally broke their duck in 2004 with a 2-1 victory over Bolton in the League Cup final at the Millennium Stadium, Cardiff.

• Two years later Middlesbrough reached the UEFA Cup final, after twice overturning three-goal deficits earlier in the competition. There was no happy ending, though, as Boro were thrashed 4-0 by Sevilla in the final in Eindhoven.

• In 1997 the club were deducted three points by the FA for calling off a Premier League fixture at Blackburn at short notice after illness and injury ravaged their squad. The penalty resulted in Boro being relegated from the Premier League at the end of the season. To add to their supporters' disappointment the club was also beaten in the finals of the League Cup and FA Cup in the same campaign.

• **Goalkeeper Mark Schwarzer is Boro's highest capped international, playing 51 times for Australia while at the Riverside between 1997 and 2008.**

• In 1926/27 striker George Camsell hit an astonishing 59 league goals, including a record nine hat-tricks, as the club won the Second Division championship. His tally set a new Football League record and, although it was beaten by Everton's Dixie Dean the following season, Camsell still holds the divisional record. An ex-miner, Camsell went on to score a club record 325 league goals for Boro – a tally only surpassed by Dean's 349 goals for Everton.

• **The Teesiders have been promoted to the Premier League a joint-record four times, but have also been relegated from the league a joint-record four times, most recently in 2017. Ironically, when Boro set a Premier League record for scoring the fewest Premier League goals away from home, just eight in 1995/96, they finished in mid-table.**

HONOURS
Division 2 champions *1927, 1929, 1974*
First Division champions *1995*
League Cup *2006*
FA Amateur Cup *1895, 1898*

MILLWALL

Year founded: 1885
Ground: The Den (20,146)
Previous name: Millwall Rovers
Nickname: The Lions
Biggest win: 9-1 v Torquay (1927) and v Coventry (1927)
Heaviest defeat: 1-9 v Aston Villa (1946)

The club was founded as Millwall Rovers in 1885 by workers at local jam and marmalade factory, Morton and Co. In 1920 they joined the Third Division, gaining a reputation as a club with some of the most fiercely partisan fans in the country.

• **In 1988 Millwall won the Second Division title to gain promotion to the top flight for the first time in their history. The Lions enjoyed a few brief weeks at the top of the league pyramid in the autumn of 1988 but were relegated two years later.**

• The club's greatest moment, though, came in 2004 when they reached their first FA Cup final. Despite losing 3-0 to Manchester United, the Lions made history by becoming the first club from outside the top flight to contest the final in the Premier League era, while substitute Curtis Weston set a new record for the youngest player to appear in the final (17 years and 119 days).

• **Lions boss Neil Harris is the club's all-time leading scorer with 125 goals in two spells at the Den between 1998 and 2011. In 2017 he cemented his place in the hearts of Lions fans by leading Millwall out of League One and into the Championship after a 1-0 play-off final win against Bradford City.**

• On their way to winning the Division Three (South) championship in 1928 Millwall scored 87 goals at home, an all-time Football League record. Altogether, the Lions managed 127 goals that season – a figure only ever bettered by three clubs.

• **In 1974 Millwall hosted the first league match to be played on a Sunday. To get around the law at the time, admission for the Lions' game with Fulham was by 'programme only' – the cost of the programme being the same as a match ticket.**

Millwall's cup is overflowing after their 2017 play-off win

HONOURS
Division 2 champions *1988*
Division 3 (S) champions *1928, 1938*
Second Division champions *2001*
Division 4 champions *1962*

MILTON KEYNES DONS

Year founded: 2004
Ground: Stadium MK (30,500)
Nickname: The Dons
Biggest win: 7-0 v Oldham (2014)
Heaviest defeat: 0-6 v Southampton (2015)

The club was effectively formed in 2004 when Wimbledon FC were controversially allowed to re-locate to Milton Keynes on the ruling of a three-man FA commission despite the opposition of the club's supporters, the Football League and the FA.

• **Despite pledging to Wimbledon fans that they would not change their name, badge or colours, within a few seasons all three of these things had happened, reinforcing the impression amongst many in the game that the MK Dons are English football's first 'franchise'.**

• The MK Dons have since handed back to Merton Council all the honours and trophies won by Wimbledon FC and claimed by AFC Wimbledon, the club started up by angry Wimbledon supporters which was promoted to the Football League in 2011 despite the claim by the FA commission that the creation of such a team would "not be in the wider interests of football".

• The greatest day in the club's short history came in 2015 when they were promoted to the Championship after thrashing Yeovil Town 5-1 on the last day of the season. However, the following season the Dons were relegated back to the third tier.

• In January 2015 MK Dons sold dynamic midfielder Dele Alli to Tottenham for a club record £5 million.

• Club captain Dean Lewington, the son of former England coach Ray, has made a record 551 league appearances for the Dons since making his debut in 2004.

HONOURS
League Two champions 2008
Football League Trophy 2008

HENRIKH MKHITARYAN

Born: Yerevan, Armenia, 21st January 1989
Position: Midfielder
Club career:
2006-09 Pyunik 70 (30)
2009-10 Metalurh Donetsk 37 (12)
2010-13 Shakhtar Donetsk 72 (38)
2013-16 Borussia Dortmund 90 (23)
2016- Manchester United 24 (4)
International record:
2007- Armenia 64 (22)

Soon after joining Manchester United from Borussia Dortmund for around £27 million in July 2016, Henrikh Mkhitaryan became the first ever Armenian to play in the Premier League. After a slow start to his Old Trafford career, Mkhitaryan gradually began to show his class and he finished the season in fine style by scoring in United's 2-0 victory over Ajax in the Europa League final in Stockholm.

• An attacking midfielder who can both score and create goals, Mkhitaryan won four league titles with Armenian side FC Pyunik before moving to Ukrainian outfit Metalurh Donetsk in 2009, where he was made the club's youngest ever captain aged 21. With his next club, Shakhtar Donetsk, Mkhitaryan won three domestic Doubles and set a record for the most goals scored in a single Ukrainian Premier League season with 25 in 2012/13.

• His star continued to shine at Borussia Dortmund, who he joined for a club record £21.5 million in July 2013, and in 2016 Mkhitaryan was voted Bundesliga Players' Player of the Season after topping the assists poll with 15.

• First capped by Armenia in 2007, Mkhitaryan is now his country's all-time leading scorer with 22 goals. In a friendly in 2016 he became the first ever Armenian to score an international hat-trick in a 7-1 rout of Guatemala.

LUKA MODRIC

Born: Zagreb, Croatia, 9th September 1985
Position: Midfielder
Club career:
2003-08 Dinamo Zagreb 112 (31)
2003 Zrinjski Mostar (loan) 22 (8)
2004 Inter Zapresic (loan) 18 (4)
2008-12 Tottenham Hotspur 127 (13)
2012- Real Madrid 140 (8)
International record:
2006- Croatia 97 (11)

After helping Real Madrid win the Champions League in 2014, 2016 and 2017, floppy-haired midfielder Luka Modric became the first Croatian player to win the trophy three times.

• Modric started out with Croatian side Dinamo Zagreb, winning three league titles and the national Player of the Year award with his hometown club before joining Tottenham in 2008. He recovered from a broken leg to help Spurs qualify for the Champions League for the first time in 2010, but the following summer he agitated for a move to Chelsea until being forced to honour his contract by Tottenham chairman Daniel Levy. He finally left White Hart Lane in 2012, joining Real for around £33 million.

• A gifted playmaker who is known as 'the Croatian Cruyff' in his home

Henrikh Mkhitaryan, the first Armenian to play in the Premier League

Luka Modric, the only Croatian to win the Champions League three times

country, Modric made his international debut in 2006 and two years later starred at Euro 2008, where he was voted into the Team of the Tournament after some magnificent displays – only the second Croatian player ever to achieve this honour. He is now the captain of his country and closing in on a century of caps.

• **When he scored a superb volleyed winner in a Euro 2016 group stage game against Turkey, Modric became the first Croatian player to score at two European Championships.**

MONACO

Year founded: 1924
Ground: Stade Louis II (26,768)
Nickname: Les rouge et blanc (The red and whites)
League titles: 8
Domestic cups: 5

AS Monaco were founded in 1924, following the merger of a number of small clubs in the principality and the surrounding region. In 2011 the club was bought by an investment group led by Russian billionaire Dmitry Rybolovlev and they have since splashed the cash on some big-name players, including a then French record £51 million on Colombian striker Radamel Falcao from Atletico Madrid in 2013.

• **The club enjoyed a golden period in the early 1960s, winning two league titles under iconic manager Lucien Leduc. More recently, they were managed by a young Arsène Wenger between 1987 and 1994, a team including former Tottenham midfielder Glenn Hoddle claiming the French title in thrilling style in 1988.**

• Monaco have never won a European trophy, but they came close in 2004 when they reached the Champions League final, only to lose 3-0 to Jose Mourinho's Porto. The red and whites also reached the Cup Winners' Cup final in 1992, but went down 2-0 to German outfit Werder Bremen.

• **Monaco have never lost to an English club in the knock-out stages of the Champions League, beating Manchester United (1998), Chelsea (2004), Arsenal (2015) and Manchester City (2017).**

• Monaco won the French league for the first time in 17 years in 2017, along the way setting a new record for Ligue 1 with 12 consecutive victories.

HONOURS
French League champions *1961, 1963, 1978, 1982, 1988, 1997, 2000, 2017*
French Cup *1960, 1963, 1980, 1985, 1991*

MONEY

The Premier League is easily the richest league in world football. In the 2015/16 season the league's revenues hit a record £3.6 billion, with domestic and worldwide TV rights accounting for more than half of that money. However, the 20 clubs still made a combined pre-tax loss of £110 million as wages rose to a record total of £2.3 billion.

• **Real Madrid and Portugal star Cristiano Ronaldo is the world's richest footballer with an estimated wealth of around $450 million, taking into account all streams of revenue, including club wages, image rights, and income from endorsements, advertising and his 'CR7' fashion range. He is followed in the rich list by Lionel Messi ($350 million) and Neymar, who has to scrape by on just $148 million.**

• According to Forbes, Manchester United are the most valuable club in the world, worth £2.86 billion in 2016. The Red Devils lead the way ahead of Spanish giants Barcelona (£2.82 billion) and Real Madrid (£2.77 billion), while fellow Premier League clubs Arsenal, Chelsea, Liverpool and Tottenham also feature in the top 10.

• **Jose Mourinho is the wealthiest manager in the world, earning £24.2 million in 2016/17, taking into account his gross salary at Manchester United, bonuses and advertising revenues.**

TOP 10

CLUB VALUATIONS IN 2015/16

	Club	Valuation
1.	Manchester United	£2.86 billion
2.	Barcelona	£2.82 billion
3.	Real Madrid	£2.77 billion
4.	Bayern Munich	£2.10 billion
5.	Manchester City	£1.61 billion
6.	Arsenal	£1.50 billion
7.	Chelsea	£1.43 billion
8.	Liverpool	£1.15 billion
9.	Juventus	£976 million
10.	Tottenham Hotspur	£821 million

BOBBY MOORE

Born: Barking, 12th April 1941
Died: 24th February 1993
Position: Defender
Club career:
1958-74 West Ham United 544 (22)
1974-77 Fulham 124 (1)
1976 San Antonio Thunder 24 (1)
1978 Seattle Sounders 7 (0)
International record:
1962-73 England 108 (2)

The first and only Englishman to lift the World Cup, Bobby Moore captained England on 90 occasions – a record shared with Billy Wright. When he skippered the team for the first time against Czechoslovakia in 1963 he was aged just 22 and 47 days, making him England's youngest ever captain.

• **Moore's total of 108 caps was a record until it was surpassed by Peter Shilton in 1989, but he was England's most capped outfield player until David Beckham passed him in 2009.**

• At club level, Moore won the FA Cup with West Ham in 1964 and the European Cup Winners' Cup the following year. Then, in 1966, he made it a Wembley treble when England beat West Germany in the World Cup final. England boss Sir Alf Ramsey later paid tribute to his skipper and most reliable defender, saying, "He was the supreme professional. Without him England would never have won the World Cup."

• In the same year Moore was voted the BBC Sports Personality of the Year – the first footballer to win the honour.

• The world of football mourned Moore's death when he died of cancer in 1993, but he has not been forgotten. A decade later he was selected by the FA as England's 'Golden Player' of the previous 50 years and, in 2007, a huge bronze statue of England's greatest captain was unveiled outside the new Wembley.

ALVARO MORATA

Born: Madrid, Spain, 23rd October 1992
Position: Striker
Club career:
2010-13 Real Madrid B 83 (45)
2010-14 Real Madrid 37 (10)
2014-16 Juventus 63 (15)
2016-17 Real Madrid 26 (15)
2017- Chelsea
International record:
2014- Spain 20 (9)

Spain international Alvaro Morata became Chelsea's record signing when he moved from Real Madrid to west London for a cool £60 million in July 2017.

• A hard-working striker who possesses excellent movement, Morata came through Real's youth system to score on his first start for the Spanish giants against Rayo Vallecano in February 2012. Two years later he came on as a sub for Real in their 4-1 defeat of city rivals Atletico Madrid in the 2014 Champions League final.

• That summer he moved on to Juventus for around £16 million, and in his first season in Turin scored in his team's Champions League final defeat against Barcelona. In October 2015 he equalled a club record held by Juve legend Alessandro Del Piero when he scored in a fifth consecutive Champions League match against Sevilla.

• After helping Juve win two league titles and scoring the winner in the 2016 Coppa Italia final against AC Milan, Morata returned to Real in a £27 million deal. He contributed 15 league goals as Real won La Liga in 2017 and also made a brief substitute appearance in their Champions League final victory against Juventus.

• After helping Spain win the 2013 European Under-21 Championship, Morata made his senior debut against Belarus in 2014. Two years later he played at the 2016 Euros, scoring twice in a 3-0 win against Turkey.

Chelsea's record signing Alvaro Morata

MORECAMBE

Year founded: 1920
Ground: Globe Arena (6,476)
Nickname: The Shrimps
Biggest win: 8-0 v Fleetwood Town (1993)
Heaviest defeat: 0-7 v Chesterfield (2016)

Founded in 1920 after a meeting at the local West View Hotel, Morecambe joined the Lancashire Combination League that same year and subsequently spent the next 87 years in non-league football.

• The greatest moment in the club's history came in 2007 when the Shrimps beat Exeter 2-1 in the Conference play-off final at Wembley to win promotion to the Football League.

• Veteran midfielder Stewart Drummond made a club record 280 appearances for the Shrimps before retiring in 2015. The club's top scorer is Kevin Ellison with 64 goals between 2011 and 2017.

• Morecambe have reached the FA Cup third round on just three occasions, most recently in 2003 when they lost 4-0 away to Ipswich Town.

MOTHERWELL

Year founded: 1886
Ground: Fir Park (13,677)
Nickname: The Well
Biggest win: 12-1 v Dundee United (1954)
Heaviest defeat: 0-8 v Aberdeen (1979)

Motherwell were founded in 1886 following the merger of two local factory-based sides, Alpha and Glencairn. The club turned pro in 1893 and, in the same year, joined the newly formed Scottish Second Division.

• The club enjoyed its heyday in the 1930s, winning the league title for the first and only time in 1932 and finishing as runners-up in the Scottish Cup three times in the same decade.

• Striker Willie McFadyen scored a remarkable 52 league goals for the Well when they won the title in 1931/32, a Scottish top-flight record that still stands today. His team-mate Bob Ferrier played in a Scottish record 626 league games between 1917 and 1937.

• Motherwell had to wait until 1952 before they won the Scottish Cup for the first time, and they did it in some style by thrashing Dundee 4-0 in the final. Another success followed in 1991, the Well beating Dundee United 4-3 in an exciting final.

• Striker Jamie Murphy scored a club record seven goals in European competition, including a hat-trick in Motherwell's best ever Europa League victory, 8-1 against Albanian side Flamurtari in 2009.

• In May 2010 Motherwell were involved in the highest scoring game ever in the SPL, coming from 6-2 down to draw 6-6 with Hibs.

HONOURS
Division 1 champions *1932*
First Division champions *1982, 1985*
Division 2 champions *1954, 1969*
Scottish Cup *1952, 1991*
League Cup *1951*

JOSE MOURINHO

Born: Setubal, Portugal, 26th January 1963
Managerial career:
2000 Benfica
2001-02 Uniao Leiria
2002-04 Porto
2004-07 Chelsea
2008-10 Inter Milan
2010-13 Real Madrid
2013-15 Chelsea
2016- Manchester United

In 2016/17 Jose Mourinho enjoyed the best ever debut season of a Manchester United manager as his team won both the League Cup, beating Southampton 3-2 in the final, and the Europa League, following a 2-0 win against Ajax in the final.

• Mourinho started out as Bobby Robson's assistant at Sporting Lisbon, Porto and Barcelona before briefly managing Benfica in 2000. Two years later he returned to Porto, where he won two Portuguese league titles and the UEFA Cup before becoming Europe's most sought-after young manager when his well-drilled side claimed the Champions League trophy in 2004.

• Shortly after this triumph, Mourinho replaced Claudio Ranieri as Chelsea manager, styling himself as a 'Special One' in his first press conference. He certainly lived up to his billing, as his expensively assembled Blues team won back-to-back Premier League titles in 2005 and 2006, the FA Cup in 2007, and the League Cup in both 2005 and 2007.

• After falling out with owner Roman Abramovich, Mourinho left Stamford Bridge in September 2007. He made a sensational return to west London in 2013 and in his second season back with the Blues guided them to both the Premier League and the League Cup, picking up a third Manager of the Year award in the process. However, after a calamitous start to the following campaign Mourinho was sacked in December 2015. Six months later he was appointed Manchester United manager following the departure of Louis van Gaal.

• In between his stints at Chelsea, Mourinho took charge of Italian giants Inter Milan and Real Madrid. He led Inter to the first ever Treble, including the Champions League, by an Italian club in 2010, and guided Real to the Spanish title two years later with record tallies for points (100) and goals (121), making him the only manager to have won the championship in England, Italy and Spain.

'I'll stick my chewing gum on Pep's seat – that'll be a laugh!'

NATIONAL LEAGUE

The pinnacle of the non-league system which feeds into the Football League, the fifth tier of English football was rebranded as the National League in 2015, having previously been called the Football Conference. The league was founded as the Alliance Premier League in 1979 and has been divided into three sections – National, North and South – since 2004.

• **Promotion and relegation between the Football League and the Conference became automatic in 1987, when Scarborough United replaced Lincoln City.**

• However, clubs have to satisfy the Football League's minimal ground requirements before their promotion can be confirmed and Kidderminster Harriers, Macclesfield Town and Stevenage Borough all failed on this count in the mid-1990s after topping the Conference table.

• **Barnet are the only club to have won the Conference three times, lifting the title in 1991, 2005 and 2015. In 2011 Crawley Town won the league with a record 105 points.**

• On 8th April 2017 Tranmere Rovers thrashed Solihull Moors 9-0 to equal the biggest ever win in the division.

THE NETHERLANDS

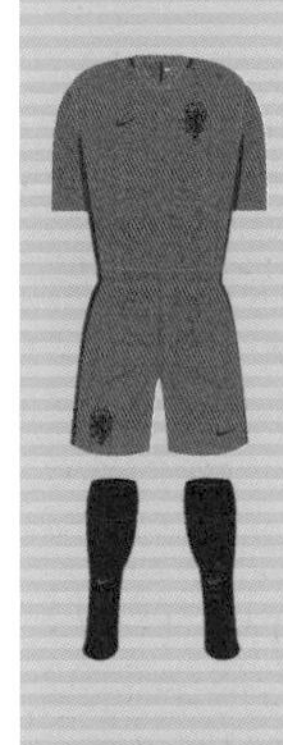

First international: Belgium 1 Netherlands 4, 1905
Most capped player: Wesley Sneijder, 131 caps (2003-)
Leading goalscorer: Robin van Persie, 50 goals (2005-)
First World Cup appearance: Netherlands 2 Switzerland 1, 1934
Biggest win: Netherlands 11 San Marino 0, 2011
Heaviest defeat: England amateurs 9 Netherlands 1, 1909

All Netherlands' home matches are played in an orange haze, matching their famous kit

Long associated with an entertaining style of attacking football, the Netherlands have only won one major tournament, the European Championships in 1988. In the final that year the Dutch beat the USSR with goals from their two biggest stars of the time, Ruud Gullit and Marco van Basten.

• **The Netherlands are the only country to have lost all three World Cup finals they have played in. On the first two of these occasions they had the misfortune to meet the hosts in the final, losing to West Germany in 1974 and Argentina in 1978. Then, in the 2010 final, they went down 1-0 in extra-time to Spain in Johannesburg following a negative, at times brutal, Dutch performance which was totally at odds with the country's best footballing traditions. The Netherlands again did well at the next World Cup, coming third.**

• A professional league wasn't formed in the Netherlands until 1956, and it took some years after that before the country was taken seriously as a football power. Their lowest ebb was reached in 1963 when the Dutch were humiliatingly eliminated from the European Championships by minnows Luxembourg.

• **However, the following decade saw a renaissance in Dutch football. With exciting players like Johan Cruyff, Johan Neeskens and Ruud Krol in their side, the Netherlands were considered the best team in Europe. Pivotal to their success was the revolutionary 'Total Football' system devised by manager Rinus Michels which allowed the outfield players constantly to switch positions during the game.**

• In 2011 the Netherlands strolled to their biggest ever win, 11-0 against San

TOP 10

NETHERLANDS GOALSCORERS

1. Robin van Persie (2005-) 50
2. Klaus-Jan Huntelaar (2006-) 42
3. Patrick Kluivert (1994-2004) 40
4. Dennis Bergkamp (1990-2000) 37
5. Faas Wilkes (1946-61) 35
   Ruud van Nistelrooy (1998-2011) 35
7. Abe Lenstra (1940-59) 33
   Johan Cruyff (1966-77) 33
   Arjen Robben (2003-) 33
10. Wesley Sneijder (2003-) 31

Marino in a Euro 2012 qualifier – just two goals shy of Germany's record European Championships victory against the same hapless opposition five years earlier.

• The Netherlands' all-time record appearance maker is midfielder Wesley Sneijder, who passed goalkeeper Edwin van der Sar's old benchmark of 130 caps when he played and scored in a 5-0 defeat of Luxembourg in June 2017.

HONOURS
European Championships winners
1988
World Cup Record
1930 Did not enter
1934 Round 1
1938 Round 1
1950 Did not enter
1954 Did not enter
1958 Did not qualify
1962 Did not qualify
1966 Did not qualify
1970 Did not qualify
1974 Runners-up
1978 Runners-up
1982 Did not qualify
1986 Did not qualify
1990 Round 2
1994 Quarter-finals
1998 Fourth place
2002 Did not qualify
2006 Round 2
2010 Runners-up
2014 Third place

MANUEL NEUER

Born: Gelsenkirchen, Germany, 27th March 1986
Position: Goalkeeper
Club career:
2004-08 Schalke II 26
2006-11 Schalke 156
2011- Bayern Munich 187
International record:
2009- Germany 74

World Goalkeeper of the Year in 2013, 2014, 2015 and 2016, Bayern Munich's Manuel Neuer is only the second player to win the award four times on the trot (after Real Madrid's Iker Casillas, who won five consecutive awards). In the second of those years Neuer became the first goalkeeper to figure in the top three of the FIFA Ballon d'Or when he came third behind Cristiano Ronaldo and Lionel Messi.

• A magnificent shot-stopper with excellent reflexes and a good distributor of the ball, Neuer signed for Bayern from Schalke for £19 million in 2011, at the time the second biggest transfer fee ever for a goalkeeper. Since then he has helped Bayern Munich win the Champions League in 2013 and a record five consecutive Bundesliga titles between 2013 and 2017.

• In 2012 Neuer's penalty saves from Cristiano Ronaldo and Kaka in the semi-final shoot-out against Real Madrid enabled Bayern to reach the Champions League final, where they faced Chelsea at their home ground, the Allianz Arena. In the subsequent shoot-out that settled the match, Neuer became the first ever goalkeeper to score in a Champions League final, although he still finished on the losing side.

There's a lot of aimless standing around when you're Bayern Munich's goalkeeper...

• Neuer impressed at the 2010 World Cup, helping Germany come third in South Africa. Four years later he was instrumental in Germany's success in Brazil, keeping four clean sheets and collecting the Golden Glove award.

NEWCASTLE UNITED

Year founded: 1892
Ground: St James' Park (52,354)
Nickname: The Magpies
Biggest win: 13-0 v Newport County (1946)
Heaviest defeat: 0-9 v Burton Wanderers (1895)

The club was founded in 1892 following the merger of local sides Newcastle East End and Newcastle West End, gaining election to the Football League just a year later.

• In 1895 Newcastle suffered their worst ever defeat, going down 9-0 to Burton Wanderers in a Second Division match. However, their most embarrassing loss was a 9-1 home hammering by Sunderland in December 1908. The Toon recovered, though, to win the title that season, making that defeat by their local rivals the heaviest ever suffered by the eventual league champions. The Magpies recorded their best ever win in 1946, thrashing Newport County 13-0 to equal Stockport County's record for the biggest ever victory in a Football League match. Star of the show at St James' Park was Len Shackleton, who scored six of the goals on his Newcastle debut to set a club record.

• Newcastle have a proud tradition in the FA Cup, having won the competition on six occasions. In 1908 the Magpies reached the final after smashing Fulham 6-0, the biggest ever win in the semi-final. Then, in 1924, 41-year-

N NEWCASTLE UNITED

Newcastle's Christian Atsu shows off his pace

old defender Billy Hampson became the oldest player ever to appear in the cup final, when he turned out for the Toon in their 2-0 defeat of Aston Villa at Wembley.

• The club's best cup era was in the 1950s when they won the trophy three times, with boss Stan Seymour becoming the first man to lift the cup as a player and a manager. Centre-forward Jackie Milburn was instrumental to Newcastle's success, scoring in every round in 1951 and then notching after just 45 seconds in the 1955 final against Manchester City – the fastest Wembley cup final goal ever at the time. In 1952 Chilean George Robledo notched the winner against Arsenal to become the first foreign player to score in the FA Cup final.

• Milburn is the club's leading goalscorer in league matches with 178 strikes between 1946 and 1957. However, Alan Shearer holds the overall club goalscoring record, finding the net 206 times in all competitions after his then world record £15 million move from Blackburn Rovers in 1996. Shearer's predecessor Andy Cole scored 41 goals in all competitions in 1993/94 to set another club record.

• The club's leading appearance maker is goalkeeper Jimmy Lawrence, who featured in 432 league games between 1904 and 1921. Another goalkeeper, Shay Given, is easily Newcastle's most honoured international with 83 caps for the Republic of Ireland between 1997 and 2009.

• In January 2011 Newcastle sold striker Andy Carroll to Liverpool for a club record £35 million, the highest fee at the time for a British player moving from one Premier League club to another. Michael Owen is Newcastle's most expensive player, joining the club from Real Madrid for £16 million in 2005.

• In 2016, having spent £80 million on new players, Newcastle became the most expensively assembled side ever to be relegated from the Premier League, although the Magpies bounced back the following season as Championship table-toppers.

• When Alan Shearer scored for Newcastle against Manchester City on 18th January 2003 after just 10.4 seconds, it was the second-fastest goal in Premier League history.

HONOURS
Division 1 champions *1905, 1907, 1909, 1927*
Division 2 champions *1965*
First Division champions *1993*
Championship champions *2010, 2017*
FA Cup *1910, 1924, 1932, 1951, 1952, 1955*
Fairs Cup *1969*

NEWPORT COUNTY

Year founded: 1912
Ground: Rodney Parade (7,850)
Nickname: The Ironsides
Biggest win: 10-0 v Merthyr Town (1930)
Heaviest defeat: 0-13 v Newcastle United (1946)

Founded in 1912, Newport County joined the Football League eight years later. After finishing bottom of the old Fourth Division in 1988 the club dropped into the Conference, only to be expelled in February 1989 for failing to fulfil their fixtures. The club reformed later that year in the Hellenic League, four divisions below the Football League.

• The road back for Newport was a long one, but they eventually returned to the Football League after beating Wrexham 2-0 in the Conference play-off final in 2013, in the first ever final at Wembley between two Welsh clubs.

• The club's greatest days came in the early 1980s when, after winning the Welsh Cup for the only time, County reached the quarter-finals of the European Cup Winners' Cup in 1981 before falling 3-2 on aggregate to eventual finalists Carl Zeiss Jena of East Germany.

• The Ironsides seemed almost certain to lose their league status again in 2017, but an exceptional run of seven wins in 12 matches, including a 2-1 victory over Notts County on the final day of the season, saw them survive by the skin of their teeth.

HONOURS
Division 3 (S) champions *1939*
Welsh Cup *1980*

NEYMAR

In August 2017 Brazilian superstar Neymar became the most expensive

footballer ever when he moved from Barcelona to Paris Saint-Germain for an incredible £200 million – more than double the previous record.

• A superbly talented player who is stronger than his slight frame suggests, Neymar shot to fame soon after making his debut for Santos in 2009 when he scored five goals in a cup match against Guarani. Two years later he helped Santos win the Copa Libertadores for the first time since 1963, scoring against Penarol in the final and earning the Man of the Match award. He was named South American Footballer of the Year in 2011 and 2012 before joining Barcelona in 2013 for £48.6 million - making him the most expensive ever export from South America.

• After a mediocre first season with Barcelona, Neymar was on fire throughout 2014/15, impressing as part of a three-pronged strikeforce with Lionel Messi and Luis Suarez, nicknamed MSN. He scored a total of 39 goals, including one against Juventus in the Champions League final and another in the final of the Copa del Rey against Athletic Bilbao as Barcelona stormed to a superb Treble. The following season he had to be satisfied with just a domestic Double, but again he scored in the Copa del Rey final, this time against Sevilla. In 2017 Neymar equalled a record set by the great Ferenc Puskas in 1962 when he scored in a third consecutive Copa Del Rey final, a 3-1 win over Alaves.

• First capped by Brazil in 2010, Neymar has gone on to become the pin-up boy of Brazilian football and is now his country's fourth highest scorer of all time. At the 2014 World Cup he was Brazil's top scorer with four goals, despite missing his country's last two matches through injury. Two years later he scored the winning goal in the shoot-out against Germany as Brazil won Olympic Gold on home soil.

Neymar, the world's most expensive player, is so good he can balance the ball on just a single tuft of hair!

NORTHAMPTON TOWN

Year founded: 1897
Ground: Sixfields Stadium (7,724)
Nickname: The Cobblers
Biggest win: 11-1 v Southend United (1909)
Heaviest defeat: 0-11 v Southampton (1901)

The club was founded at a meeting of local schoolteachers at the Princess Royal Inn in Northampton in 1897. After turning professional in 1901 Northampton were founder members of the Third Division in 1920.

• The club's first full-time manager was Herbert Chapman (1907-12), who later became the first manager to win the league title with two different clubs, Huddersfield and Arsenal.

• Despite being injured fighting in France during the Second World War, winger Tommy Fowler went on to make a record 552 appearances for the Cobblers between 1946 and 1961. His team-mate Jack English is the club's record scorer with a total of 143 goals.

• The Cobblers enjoyed a rollercoaster decade in 1960s, rising from the old Fourth Division to the First in just six seasons. In the process they became the first club to rise through the three lower divisions to the top flight, before plummeting back down by 1969.

• Defender Edwin Lloyd Davies made a club record 12 appearances for Wales between 1908 and 1914, and is the Cobblers' oldest ever player, turning out for the last time aged 42 in 1920.

HONOURS
Division 3 champions *1963*
Division 4 champions *1987*
League Two champions *2016*

NORTHERN IRELAND

First international: Northern Ireland 2 England 1, 1923
Most capped player: Pat Jennings, 119 caps (1964-86)
Leading goalscorer: David Healy, 36 goals (2000-13)
First World Cup appearance: Northern Ireland 1 Czechoslovakia 0 (1958)
Biggest win: Northern Ireland 7 Wales 0, 1930
Heaviest defeat: England 9 Northern Ireland 2, 1949

Until Trinidad and Tobago appeared at the 2006 tournament, Northern Ireland were the smallest country to qualify for a World Cup finals tournament. They have made it on three occasions, reaching the quarter-finals in 1958 and beating the hosts Spain in 1982 on their way to the second round.

• **Northern Ireland's Norman Whiteside is the youngest player ever to appear at the World Cup. He was aged just 17 years and 42 days when he played at the 1982 tournament in Spain, beating the previous record set by Pelé in 1958.**

• During the Euro 2008 qualifying campaign Northern Ireland's highest ever scorer David Healy banged in a competition best 13 goals.

• **Under manager Michael O'Neill Northern Ireland qualified for the European Championships for the first time in 2016. They did it in fine style too, becoming the first ever country from the fifth pot in the draw to top their qualifying group. At the finals they enjoyed their first ever win, beating Ukraine 2-0, before going out to Wales in the last 16.**

• In June 2016 defender Aaron Hughes became the first outfield player for Northern Ireland to reach 100 caps when he came on as a sub in a friendly against Slovakia.

World Cup Record
1930 Did not enter
1934 Did not enter
1938 Did not enter
1950 Did not qualify
1954 Did not qualify
1958 Quarter-finalists
1962 Did not qualify
1966 Did not qualify
1970 Did not qualify
1974 Did not qualify
1978 Did not qualify
1982 Round 2
1986 Round 1
1990 Did not qualify
1994 Did not qualify
1998 Did not qualify
2002 Did not qualify
2006 Did not qualify
2010 Did not qualify
2014 Did not qualify

Life just keeps getting better and better for Northern Ireland!

NORWICH CITY

Year founded: 1902
Ground: Carrow Road (27,244)
Nickname: The Canaries
Biggest win: 10-2 v Coventry City (1930)
Heaviest defeat: 2-10 v Swindon Town (1908)

Founded in 1902 by two schoolteachers, Norwich City soon found themselves in hot water with the FA and were expelled from the FA Amateur Cup in 1904 for being 'professional'. The club joined the Football League as founder members of the Third Division in 1920.

• **Norwich were originally known as the Citizens, but adopted the nickname Canaries in 1907 as a nod to the longstanding popularity of canary-keeping in the city – a result of 15th-century trade links with Flemish weavers who had brought the birds over to Europe from Dutch colonies in the Caribbean. Soon afterwards, the club changed their colours from blue and white to yellow and green.**

• City fans enjoyed the greatest day in their history when Norwich beat Sunderland 1-0 at Wembley in 1985 to win the League Cup. However, joy soon turned to despair when the Canaries were relegated from the top flight at the end of the season, the first club to experience this particular mix of sweet and sour.

• **Ron Ashman is the club's leading appearance maker, turning out in 592 league matches between 1947 and 1964. The Canaries' leading scorer is Ashman's team-mate John Gavin, who notched 122 league goals between 1948 and 1958.**

• Now under the ownership of cook and recipe book author Delia Smith, Norwich came a best ever third in the inaugural Premiership season in 1992/93 – albeit with a goal difference of -4, the worst ever by a team finishing in the top three in the top flight. The following season the Canaries played in Europe for the first and only time, famously beating Bayern Munich away in the second round of the UEFA Cup – the only time a British club has won in the Olympic Stadium.

• **In January 2016 the Canaries splashed out a club record £9.1 million to bring Everton striker Steven Naismith to Carrow Road. In January**

Norwich fans hope the Canaries will be singing again soon

2017 Norwich received a club record £13 million when they sold midfielder Robbie Brady to Burnley.

• Along with Crystal Palace, Middlesbrough and Sunderland, Norwich have been relegated from the Premier League a record four times, most recently taking the plunge in 2016.

HONOURS
Division 2 champions *1972, 1986*
First Division champions *2004*
Division 3 (S) champions *1934*
League One champions *2010*
League Cup *1985*

NOTTINGHAM FOREST

Year founded: 1865
Ground: The City Ground (30,445)
Nickname: The Reds
Biggest win: 14-0 v Clapton (1891)
Heaviest defeat: 1-9 v Blackburn Rovers (1937)

One of the oldest clubs in the world, Nottingham Forest were founded in 1865 at a meeting at the Clinton Arms in Nottingham by a group of former players of 'shinty' (a form of hockey), who decided to switch sports to football.

• Over the following years the club was at the forefront of important innovations in the game. For instance, shin guards were invented by Forest player Sam Widdowson in 1874, while four years later a referee's whistle was first used in a match between Forest and Sheffield Norfolk. In 1890, a match between Forest and Bolton Wanderers was the first to feature goal nets.

• Forest enjoyed a golden era under legendary manager Brian Clough, who sat in the City Ground hotseat from 1975 until his retirement in 1993. After winning promotion to the top flight in 1977, the club won the league championship the following season – a feat that no promoted team has achieved since. Forest also won the League Cup to become the first side to win this particular double. Even more incredibly, the Reds went on to win the European Cup in 1979 with a 1-0 victory over Malmo in the final. The next year Forest retained the trophy, beating Hamburg 1-0 in the final in Madrid, to become the first and only team to win the European Cup more times than their domestic league.

• Those glory days, however, felt very distant in 1999 when Forest became the first club to suffer the indignity of finishing rock bottom of the Premier League on three separate occasions.

• In 1959, in the days before subs, Forest won the FA Cup despite being reduced to 10 men when Roy Dwight, an uncle of pop star Elton John, was carried off with a broken leg after 33 minutes of the final against Luton Town. It was the first time that a club had won the cup with fewer than 11 players.

Nottingham Forest had a pretty 'dread'-ful season in 2016/17

• Defender Bobby McKinlay, a member of that 1959 team, is Forest's longest serving player, turning out in 614 league games in 19 seasons at the club. The Reds' record scorer is Grenville Morris, who fell just one short of a double century of league goals for the club in the years before the First World War.

• In 1950/51 striker Wally Ardron scored a club record 36 league goals as Forest won the Division Three (South) championship, scoring a club best 110 goals in total.

• Nottingham Forest's City Ground is just 330 yards from Notts County's Meadow Lane, making the two clubs the nearest neighbours in the Football League.

HONOURS
Division 1 champions *1978*
Division 2 champions *1907, 1922*
First Division champions *1998*
Division 3 (S) champions *1951*
FA Cup *1898, 1959*
League Cup *1978, 1979, 1989, 1990*
European Cup *1979, 1980*
European Super Cup *1979*

NOTTS COUNTY

Year founded: 1862
Ground: Meadow Lane (20,229)
Nickname: The Magpies
Biggest win: 15-0 v Rotherham (1885)
Heaviest defeat: 1-9 v Aston Villa (1888), v Blackburn (1889) and v Portsmouth (1927)

Notts County are the oldest professional football club in the world. Founded in 1862, the club were founder members of the Football League in 1888 and have since played a record 4,894 matches in the competition (losing a record 1,893 games).

• In their long history County have swapped divisions more often than any other league club, winning 13

promotions and suffering the agony of relegation 16 times, most recently dropping into League Two in 2015.

• The club's greatest ever day was way back in 1894 when, as a Second Division outfit, they won the FA Cup – the first time a team from outside the top flight had lifted the trophy. In the final at Goodison Park, County beat Bolton 4-1, with Jimmy Logan scoring the first ever hat-trick in the FA Cup final.

• **Striker Henry Cursham scored a competition record 48 goals for Notts County in the FA Cup between 1880 and 1887, playing alongside his two brothers in the same County team.**

• In their long and distinguished history Notts County have had 65 different managers, a record for an English club.

• **During the 2016/17 season County lost a club record 10 consecutive league games.**

HONOURS
Division 2 champions *1897, 1914, 1923*
Division 3 (S) champions *1931, 1950*
Division 4 champions *1971*
Third Division champions *1998*
League Two champions *2010*
FA Cup *1894*

NUMBERS

Shirt numbers were first used in a First Division match by Arsenal against Sheffield Wednesday at Hillsborough on 25th August 1928. On the same day Chelsea also wore numbers for their Second Division fixture against Swansea at Stamford Bridge.

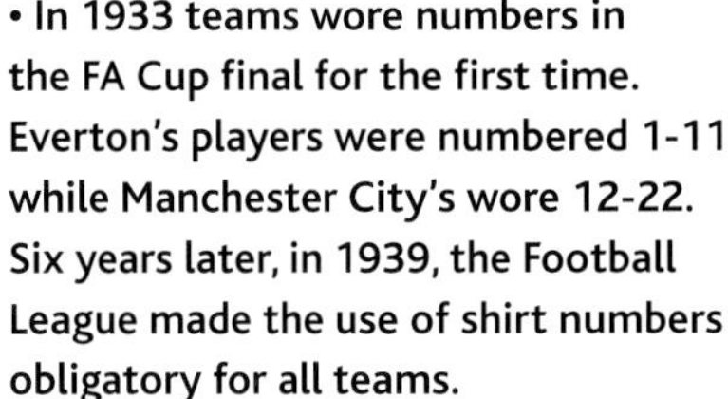

• **In 1933 teams wore numbers in the FA Cup final for the first time. Everton's players were numbered 1-11 while Manchester City's wore 12-22. Six years later, in 1939, the Football League made the use of shirt numbers obligatory for all teams.**

• England and Scotland first wore numbered shirts on 17th April 1937 for the countries' Home International fixture at Hampden Park. Scotland won 3-1. The following year numbers were introduced for the World Cup tournament in France.

• **A number of clubs have 'retired' certain shirt in tribute to past or current players who have died. These include West Ham (6, Bobby Moore), Manchester City (23, Marc-Vivien Foe) and QPR (31, Ray Jones).**

• Squad numbers were adopted by Premier League clubs at the start of the 1993/94 season. The highest number worn to date by a Premier League player is 78 by Manchester City's Jose Angel Pozo in the 2014/15 season.

• **According to Sports Direct, the most popular Premier League replica shirt in the 2016/17 season was a Manchester United one with 'Pogba' and '6' on the back.**

• In July 2015 Atletico Mineiro goalkeeper Victor wore the highest ever shirt number in football history, 2019, in a match against Sao Paulo to commemorate the fact that he had signed a new contract with the club until 2019.

• **In 2010 Australia's Thomas Oar set a world record for a high shirt number in an international match when he sported '121' on his back for an Asian Cup qualifier against Indonesia.**

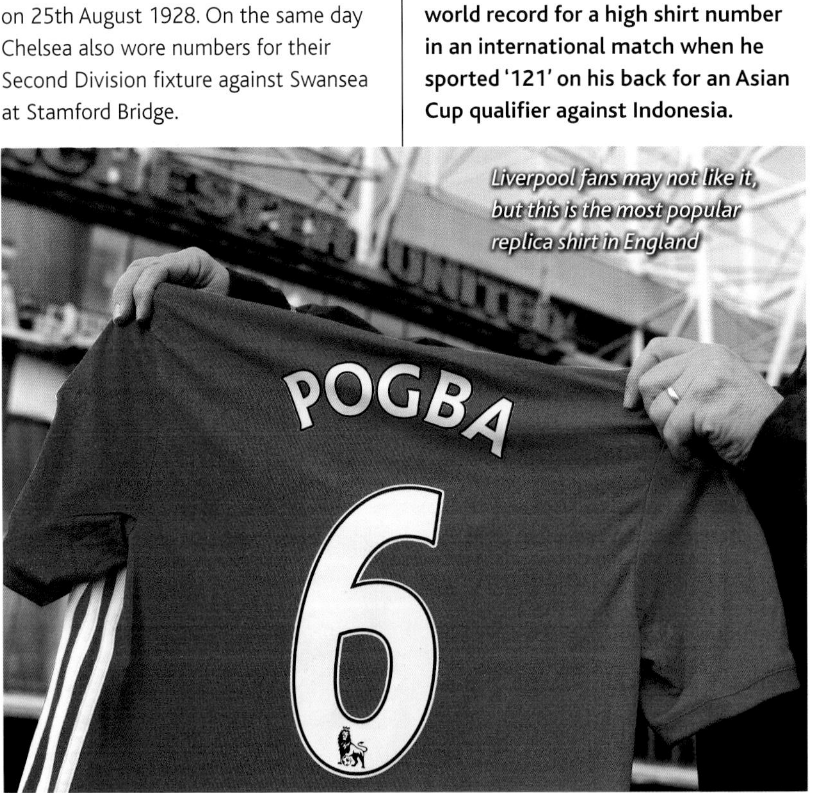

Liverpool fans may not like it, but this is the most popular replica shirt in England

OLDHAM ATHLETIC

Year founded: 1895
Ground: Boundary Park (13,512)
Previous name: Pine Villa
Nickname: The Latics
Biggest win: 11-0 v Southport (1962)
Heaviest defeat: 4-13 v Tranmere Rovers (1935)

Originally known as Pine Villa, the club was founded by the landlord of the Featherstone and Junction Hotel in 1895. Four years later the club changed to its present name and in 1907 Oldham joined the Second Division.

• **The Latics enjoyed a golden era in the early 1990s under manager Joe Royle, reaching the League Cup final (in 1990), two FA Cup semi-finals (1990 and 1994) and earning promotion to the top flight (1991). The club were founder members of the Premier League in 1992 but were relegated two years later.**

• In 1997 Oldham dropped into the third tier and have remained there ever since – the longest stay of any club in the same division outside the Premier League.

• **In 1989 Oldham striker Frankie Bunn scored six of his side's goals in a 7-0 hammering of Scarborough in the third round of the League Cup. He remains the only player to have notched a double hat-trick in the competition.**

• In 1989 Oldham striker Frankie Bunn scored a competition best six goals in the Latics' 7-0 trouncing of Scarborough in the League Cup third round.

HONOURS
Division 2 champions *1991*
Division 3 (N) champions *1953*
Division 3 champions *1974*

MARTIN O'NEILL

Born: Kilrea, 1st March 1952
Managerial career:
1990-95 Wycombe Wanderers
1995 Norwich City
1995-2000 Leicester City
2000-05 Celtic
2006-10 Aston Villa
2011-13 Sunderland
2013- Republic of Ireland

Manager of the Republic of Ireland since 2013, Martin O'Neill led his team to the Euro 2016 finals after a play-off win over Bosnia and into the last 16 before a 2-1 defeat to hosts France ended their dreams of glory. He then guided the Irish to an impressive start to their 2018 World Cup qualifying campaign, which saw them unbeaten in their first six matches.

• One of the most articulate managers in the game, O'Neill started out at Wycombe Wanderers in 1990, taking the Chairboys out of the Conference and into the Football League before spending a short period at Norwich. He left Carrow Road in 1995 to move to Leicester, who he guided into the Premier League the following year. He then led the Foxes to the League Cup in 1997, and won the competition again three years later.

• In 2000 O'Neill joined Celtic, with whom he won the Treble in his first season. Dubbed 'Martin the Magnificent' by the fans, O'Neill led the Glasgow giants to two more league titles, four more cups and to the final of the UEFA Cup in 2003 before leaving the club to look after his sick wife in 2005. He returned to management the following year with Aston Villa, making the Villans a regular top six side during his four-year tenure. In December 2011 he was appointed manager of Sunderland, the club he had supported as a boy, but a poor run of results saw him sacked after just 16 months.

• A one-time law student at Queen's University in Belfast, O'Neill spent most of his playing career with Nottingham Forest, with whom he won the league championship and two European Cups. A hard-working midfielder, O'Neill also played for Norwich, Manchester City and Notts County, and captained Northern Ireland at the 1982 World Cup in Spain.

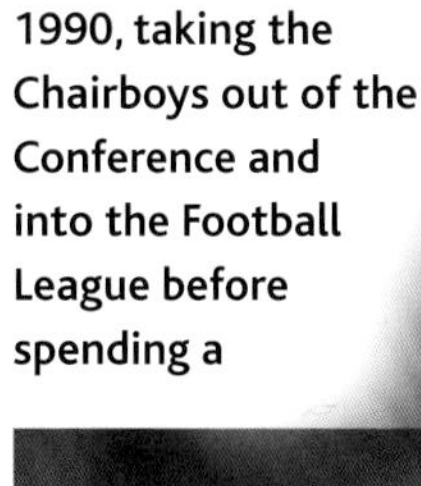

Republic of Ireland manager Martin O'Neill

MICHAEL O'NEILL

Born: Portadown, 5th July 1969
Managerial career:
2006-08 Brechin City
2009-11 Shamrock Rovers
2011- Northern Ireland

A surprise choice as his country's manager in December 2011, Michael O'Neill led Northern Ireland to their first ever European Championships when they topped their Euro 2016 qualifying group – the first time a country from the fifth pot of seeds had achieved this feat.

• To the delight of their fans, O'Neill took his side into the last 16 of the competition where they narrowly lost 1-0 to Wales in the first ever meeting between two British nations at the knock-out stage of a major tournament. He then guided Northern Ireland to their best ever start to a World Cup qualifying campaign, with four wins in their first six group games giving them a great chance of making it to Russia in 2018.

• After a spell in charge of Brechin City, O'Neill rose to prominence as manager of Shamrock Rovers, who he guided to the League of Ireland title in 2010 and the Setanta Sports Cup the following year. In 2011 he became the first manager to lead a League of Ireland side into the group stage of a European competition when Rovers beat Partizan Belgrade in the final qualifying round of the Europa League.

• In his playing days O'Neill turned out for a number of clubs, including Dundee United, Hibs and Newcastle, for whom he was the club's leading scorer in the old First Division in 1987/88.

OWN GOALS

The first ever own goal in the Football League was scored on the opening day of the inaugural 1888/89 season, the unfortunate George Cox of Aston Villa putting through his own net in his team's 1-1 draw with Wolves.

• The record number of own goals in a single match is, incredibly, 149. In 2002 Madagascan team Stade Olympique l'Emyrne staged a predetermined protest against alleged refereeing bias by constantly whacking the ball into their own net, their match against AS Adema finishing in a 149-0 win for their opponents. The Madagascan FA took a dim view of the incident and promptly handed out long suspensions to four SOE players and their coach.

IS THAT A FACT?

The first of seven own goals in the FA Cup final was scored by nine-times finalist Arthur Kinnaird in 1877. Playing in goal for Wanderers rather than his normal position as a forward, Kinnaird caught a corner but stepped over the line with the ball to gift a goal to Oxford University. Despite this howler, Wanderers won the match 2-1.

• The fastest ever own goal in English football was scored by Torquay's Pat Kruse, who headed past his own keeper after just six seconds against Cambridge United on 3rd January 1977. The Gulls scored another own goal later in the same match, so were presumably extremely relieved to earn a point in a 2-2 draw.

• During the 1934/35 season Middlesbrough's Bobby Stuart scored five own goals – a record for a single campaign. The Premier League record is held by former Liverpool defender Martin Skrtel with four in 2013/14.

• The hapless Richard Dunne, formerly of QPR, holds the individual Premier League own goal record, with an amazing 10 strikes at the wrong end.

• However, Dunne's record may one day be under threat from an unexpected source: Tottenham striker Harry Kane! The England captain already has three Premier League own goals to his name, plus another one in the Europa League against Gent in February 2017.

• A total of 41 own goals have been scored at the World Cup finals, the first by Mexico's Manuel Rosas against Chile in 1930.

OXFORD UNITED

Year founded: 1893
Ground: Kassam Stadium (12,500)
Previous name: Headington, Headington United
Nickname: The U's
Biggest win: 9-1 v Dorchester Town, 1995
Heaviest defeat: 0-7 v Sunderland, 1998

The club was founded by a local vicar and doctor in 1893 as Headington, primarily as a way of allowing the cricketers of Headington CC to keep fit during the winter months. The name Oxford United was adopted in 1960, six years before Oxford were elected to the Football League.

• In 1964 Oxford became the first Fourth Division side to reach the quarter-finals of the FA Cup. However, despite being backed by a record crowd of 22,750 at their old Manor Ground, the U's went down 2-1 to eventual finalists Preston.

• The club enjoyed a golden era under controversial owner Robert Maxwell in the 1980s, although the decade began badly when the newspaper proprietor proposed that Oxford and Reading should merge as the 'Thames Valley Royals'. The fans' well-organised campaign against the idea was successful, and their loyalty was rewarded when Oxford became the first club to win consecutive third and second-tier titles to reach the top flight in 1985.

• The greatest day in the club's history, though, came in 1986 when Oxford defeated QPR 3-0 at Wembley to win the League Cup. The following two decades saw a period of decline, however, and by 2006 Oxford had become the first major trophy winners to sink down into the Conference.

• Midfielder Ron 'The Tank' Atkinson, who later found fame as the manager of West Brom, Manchester United and Aston Villa, played in a club record 509 games for the U's between 1959 and 1971. His brother Graham scored a club record 97 goals during the same period.

HONOURS
Division 2 champions *1985*
Division 3 champions *1968, 1984*
League Cup *1986*

MESUT OZIL

Born: Gelsenkirchen, Germany, 15th October 1988
Position: Midfielder
Club career:
2006-08 Schalke 30 (0)
2008-10 Werder Bremen 71 (13)
2010-13 Real Madrid 102 (19)
2013- Arsenal 114 (23)
International record:
2009- Germany 84 (21)

When he won the FA Cup with Arsenal in 2014 Mesut Ozil became the first player to win the major domestic cup competition in England, Germany and Spain, having previously triumphed with Werder Bremen (2009) and Real (2011). Following Arsenal's win in the final against Chelsea in 2017, Ozil became the first German (along with his team-mate Per Mertesacker) to win the cup three times.

• One of the most creative midfielders in the game, Ozil set a new Premier League record in the 2015/16 season when he provided an assist for a goal in seven consecutive matches. In the same season Ozil was credited with 19 assists in total, just one short of Thierry Henry's record of 20 set in 2002/03.

• Ozil became Arsenal's record signing at the time when he joined the Gunners for £42.4 million from Real Madrid in September 2013. He had previously won the Copa del Rey (2011) and La Liga (2012) with the Spanish titans after starting his career in his native Germany with Schalke and Werder Bremen.

Arsenal's, Mesut Ozil in a cheerful mood

• Ozil first captured global attention in the summer of 2009 when was named as Man of the Match after the German Under-21 side smashed their English counterparts 4-0 in the European Championships final, prompting the manager of the team to hail him as 'the German Messi'.

• Ozil was Germany's top scorer with eight goals during qualification for the 2014 World Cup and he played a full part in his country's success in Brazil, notably scoring the decisive second goal in a last 16 victory over Algeria.

PARIS SAINT-GERMAIN

Year founded: 1970
Ground: Parc des Princes (48,712)
Nickname: PSG
League titles: 6
Domestic cups: 11
European cups: 1

Founded as recently as 1970 following a merger between Paris FC and Stade Saint-Germain, Paris Saint-Germain are now one of the richest clubs in the world after being bought by the Qatar Investment Authority in 2011. In August 2017 PSG splurged £200 million on Barcelona superstar Neymar, completing obliterating the old world transfer record.

• In 1996 PSG became only the second French club to win a European trophy when they beat Rapid Vienna 1-0 in the final of the Cup Winners' Cup. The Paris outfit had a good chance to become the only club to retain the trophy the following year, but lost in the final to Barcelona.

• In running away with the French title in 2015/16 PSG set numerous Ligue 1 records, including most points (96), best ever goal difference (+83), most wins (30), fewest goals conceded (19) and longest unbeaten run (36 matches).

• In 2017 PSG won the French Cup for a record 11th time, beating Angers 1-0 in the final thanks to a last-minute own goal.

TOP 10

FRENCH CUP WINNERS

1.	Paris Saint-Germain	11
2.	Marseille	10
3.	Lille	6
	Saint-Etienne	6
5.	Lyon	5
	Monaco	5
	RC Paris	5
	Red Star	5
9.	Auxerre	4
	Bordeaux	4

With new boy Neymar on their books, PSG are expecting fun times ahead!

HONOURS
French League champions *1986, 1994, 2013, 2014, 2015, 2016*
French Cup *1982, 1983, 1993, 1995, 1998, 2004, 2006, 2010, 2015, 2016, 2017*
European Cup Winners' Cup *1996*

PARTICK THISTLE

Year founded: 1876
Ground: Firhill (10,102)
Nickname: The Jags
Biggest win: 16-0 v Royal Albert (1931)
Heaviest defeat: 1-10 v Dunfermline (1959)

Founded in 1876, the club adopted the name Partick Thistle to distinguish themselves from local rivals Partick FC.

• The club emerged from the shadows of giant Glasgow neighbours Celtic and Rangers to win the Scottish Cup in 1921, and in 1972 Partick enjoyed the greatest day in their history when they thrashed Celtic 4-1 in the League Cup final at Hampden Park.

• The club's longest serving player is goalkeeper Alan Rough, who made 410 league appearances between 1969 and 1982. Rough is also the club's most decorated international, winning 51 caps.

• Partick's record scorer is the prolific Willie Sharp, who banged in 226 goals for the Jags including one in 1947

against Queen of the South after just seven seconds – the fastest ever goal in Scottish football.

• In 1995 Partick became the first Scottish club to compete in the InterToto Cup, a feeder competition for the UEFA Cup, but were knocked out in the group stage after defeats to Metz and NK Zagreb.

HONOURS
Division 2 champions *1897, 1900, 1971*
First Division champions *1976, 2002, 2013*
Second Division champions *2001*
Scottish Cup *1921*
League Cup *1972*

PEDRO

Born: Santa Cruz de Tenerife, Spain, 28th July 1987
Position: Winger
Club career:
2005-07 Barcelona C 70 (10)
2007-09 Barcelona B 55 (17)
2008-15 Barcelona 204 (58)
2015- Chelsea 62 (16)
International record:
2010- Spain 63 (17)

A £19 million signing from Barcelona in August 2015, Chelsea winger Pedro played an important role in the Blues' Premier League title success in 2016/17, chipping in with nine goals and nine assists.

• Born Pedro Eliezer Rodriguez Ledesma on the island of Tenerife, Pedro joined the Barcelona youth team when he was 17. He came through the ranks to win five league titles with the Catalans and also won the Champions League three times, scoring in the 2011 final against Manchester United at Wembley.

• A busy and dynamic figure who packs a blistering shot on either foot, Pedro became the first player ever to score at least one goal in six different official club competitions – league, Spanish Cup, Spanish Super Cup, Champions League, European Super Cup and Club World Cup – in the same season in 2009/10.

• Just weeks after making his debut for Spain, Pedro started for his country in the 2010 World Cup final and finished on the winning side after a 1-0 win against the Netherlands. Two years later he enjoyed more success in the European Championships, coming on as a sub in Spain's 4-0 thrashing of Italy in the final in Kiev.

Pedro loves a spot of fancy dress, even when he's playing for Chelsea!

PELÉ

Born: Tres Coracoes, Brazil, 23rd October 1940
Position: Striker
Club career:
1956-74 Santos 412 (470)
1975-77 New York Cosmos 56 (31)
International record:
1957-71 Brazil 92 (77)

Born Edson Arantes do Nascimento, but known throughout the world by his nickname, Pelé is generally recognised as the greatest footballer ever to play the game.

• In 1957, aged just 16 years and nine months, he scored on his debut for Brazil against Argentina to become the youngest international goalscorer ever. The following year he made headlines around the globe when he scored twice in Brazil's 5-2 World Cup final defeat of hosts Sweden, in the process making history as the youngest ever World Cup winner.

Pele, scorer of an incredible 1,281 career goals

• Four years later he missed most of Brazil's successful defence of their trophy through injury but was later awarded a winner's medal by FIFA. After being kicked out of the 1966 World Cup, he was back to his best at the 1970 tournament in Mexico, opening the scoring in the final against Italy and inspiring a magnificent Brazilian side to a comprehensive 4-1 victory. He remains the only player in the world with three World Cup winner's medals.

• Fast, strong, tremendously skilful and powerful in the air, Pelé was the complete footballer. He was also a phenomenal goalscorer who remains Brazil's top scorer of all time with an incredible 77 goals (in just 92 games), a record only surpassed in international football by five players. Twelve of those goals came at the World Cup, making him the fifth highest scorer in the history of the tournament.

• Pelé's career total of 1,281 goals in 1,365 top-class matches is officially recognised by FIFA as a world record, although many of his goals came in friendlies for his club Santos. The Brazilian ace's most prolific patch saw him score in 14 consecutive games, to set another world record.

If Yaya Toure is taking a penalty, this is the almost inevitable result!

PENALTIES

Penalty kicks were first proposed by goalkeeper William McCrum of the Irish FA in 1890 and adopted the following year. Wolves' John Heath was the first player to take and score a penalty in a Football League match, in a 5-0 win against Accrington at Molineux on 14th September 1891.

• **Francis Lee holds the British record for the most penalties in a league season, scoring 15 for Manchester City in Division One in 1971/72. He earned many of the penalties himself, leading fans to dub him 'Lee Won Pen'. In the Premier League era, Andy Johnson scored a record 11 penalties for Crystal Palace in 2004/05, but to no avail as the Eagles were still relegated.**

• Three players have scored a record four penalties each at the World Cup finals: Eusebio (Portugal, 1966), Rob Resenbrink (Netherlands, 1978) and Gabriel Batistuta (Argentina, two penalties each in 1994 and 1998).

• **Alan Shearer is the most prolific penalty-taker in the Premier League era, scoring 56 times from the spot.**

• The most penalties ever awarded in a British match is five in the game between Crystal Palace and Brighton at Selhurst Park in 1989. Palace were awarded four penalties (one scored, three missed) while Brighton's consolation goal in a 2-1 defeat also came from the spot.

• **Argentina's Martin Palermo missed a record three penalties in a Copa America match against Colombia in 1999. His first effort struck the crossbar, his second penalty sailed over, but remarkably Palermo still insisted on taking his side's third spot-kick of the match. Perhaps he shouldn't have bothered, as his shot was saved by the goalkeeper.**

• Manchester City midfielder Yaya Toure holds the record for the most Premier League penalties taken (11) without missing once.

• **Witton Albion were awarded the fastest ever penalty in an FA Trophy match against Chester City on 13th December 2016. The time on the ref's watch when he pointed to the spot for a foul on winger Tolani Omotola was just 6.18 seconds.**

PENALTY SHOOT-OUTS

Penalty shoot-outs were first used in England as a way to settle drawn matches in the Watney Cup in 1970. In the first ever shoot-out Manchester United beat Hull City in the semi-final of the competition, United legend George Best being the first player to take a penalty while his team-mate Denis Law was the first to miss.

• **The third/fourth place play-off between Birmingham and Stoke in 1972 was the first FA Cup match to be decided by penalties, Birmingham winning 4-3 after a 0-0 draw. However, spot-kicks weren't used to settle normal FA Cup ties until the 1991/92 season, Rotherham United becoming the first team to progress by this method when they beat Scunthorpe United 7-6 in the shoot-out after their first-round replay finished 3-3. In 2005 Arsenal became the first team to win the final on penalties, defeating Manchester United 5-4 after a 0-0 draw.**

• The first World Cup match to be settled by penalties was the 1982 semi-final between France and West Germany. The Germans won 5-4 on spot-kicks and have the best overall record in the competition with four wins out of four. In 1994 the final was settled by penalties for the first time, Brazil defeating Italy 3-2 on spot-kicks after a dull 0-0 draw. The 2006 final also went to penalties, Italy beating France 5-3 after a 1-1 draw.

• **The first major international tournament to be settled on penalties was the 1976 European Championships final between Czechoslovakia and West Germany in Belgrade. Following a 2-2 draw, the Czechs won 5-3 in the shoot-out, Antonin Panenka scoring the decisive penalty with a cheeky dinked shot down the middle.**

• The longest FA Cup shoot-out saw Scunthorpe defeat Worcester City 14-13 after 32 penalties had been taken to settle their second-round tie in December 2014.

• **The longest ever penalty shoot-out was between fifth-tier Czech sides SK Batov and FC Frystak in a regional championship match in June 2016. After an incredible total of 52 kicks, SK Batov emerged victorious 22-21.**

• When Bradford City beat Arsenal in the 2012/13 League Cup quarter-final, they did so in their ninth straight penalty shoot-out win – a record for English football. However, the Bantams' astonishing run came to an end when they lost on penalties to York City in the League Cup in August 2015.

• **The first European tie to be settled by penalties was the first round European Cup Winners' Cup clash between Aberdeen and Honved in September 1970, the Hungarian outfit progressing after a 5-4 victory.**

• In a rare case of a penalty shoot-out lasting the minimum six kicks in total, Chile beat Portugal 3-0 on spot-kicks in the 2017 Confederations Cup semi-final in the Russian city of Kazan after the South Americans' goalkeeper, Claudio Bravo, saved all three of Portugal's efforts.

• **After criticisms that teams taking the first penalty in a shoot-out had an unfair advantage, a new format was trialled in youth competitions early in 2017. The so-called 'ABBA' system – modelled on the tennis tie-break – was first used in England for the 2017 Community Shield when Arsenal beat Chelsea 4-1 on spot-kicks after a 1-1 draw.**

PETERBOROUGH UNITED

Year founded: 1934
Ground: London Road (15,314)
Nickname: The Posh
Biggest win: 9-1 v Barnet (1998)
Heaviest defeat: 1-8 v Northampton Town (1946)

Peterborough were founded in 1934 at a meeting at the Angel Hotel to fill the void left by the collapse of local club Peterborough and Fletton United two years earlier.

• The club's unusual nickname, The Posh, stemmed from Peterborough and Fletton manager Pat Tirrel's remark in 1921 that the club wanted "Posh players for a Posh team". When the new club played its first game against Gainsborough Trinity in 1934 there were shouts of "Up the Posh!" and the nickname stuck.

• Peterborough were finally elected to the Football League in 1960 after numerous failed attempts. The fans' long wait was rewarded when Peterborough stormed to the Fourth Division title in their first season, scoring a league record 134 goals. Striker Terry Bly notched an amazing 52 of the goals to set a record for the fourth tier.

• In July 2013 Peterborough sold striker Dwight Gayle to Crystal Palace for a club record £6 million. In the same month the Posh splashed £1.2 million on their most expensive ever purchase, Watford striker Britt Assombalonga.

• Winger Terry Robson played in a club record 482 games for Peterborough between 1969 and 1981 while his team-mate Jim Hall scored a record 122 goals for the Posh.

HONOURS
Division 4 champions *1961, 1974*
Football League Trophy *2014*

JORDAN PICKFORD

Born: Washington, 7th March 1994
Position: Goalkeeper
Club career:
2011-17 Sunderland 31
2012 Darlington (loan) 17
2013 Alfreton Town (loan) 12
2013 Burton Albion (loan) 12
2014 Carlisle United (loan) 18
2014-15 Bradford City (loan) 33
2015 Preston North End (loan) 24
2017- Everton

In June 2017 Jordan Pickford became the most expensive British goalkeeper ever and the third most expensive in the world when he joined Everton from Sunderland for £25 million.

• An excellent shot-stopper, Pickford enjoyed a breakthrough season with the Black Cats in 2016/17, his impressive performances earning him a nomination for the PFA Young Player of the Year award – the first player from a relegated club to appear on the shortlist since West Ham's Jermain Defoe in 2003.

• After joining the Sunderland academy aged eight and signing his first pro contract in 2011, Pickford learned his trade with a number of loans to clubs lower down the football pyramid. His final loan with Championship outfit Preston North End in 2015 saw him keep six consecutive clean sheets to equal the club record.

• Pickford was part of the England Under-21 team that won the Toulon Tournament in 2016, and the following year he helped the Young Lions reach the semi-finals of the European Under-21 Championships in Poland where they lost on penalties to eventual winners Germany.

PITCHES

According to FIFA rules, a football pitch must measure between 100 and 130 yards in length and 50 and 100 yards in breadth. It's no surprise, then, that different pitches vary hugely in size.

• Of Premier League clubs, Stoke City have the smallest pitch at just 6,400 square metres. The largest pitches

Something about this stripy pitch suggests it might just belong to Newcastle!

in the league are at Bournemouth, Manchester City and Swansea – all of which come in at 7,140 square metres.

• The highest national stadium is the Estadio Hernando Siles in La Paz. Used by Bolivia for home matches, it is 2,500 metres above sea level. In Europe the highest stadium is the Ottmar Hitzfeld Stadium, home of FC Gspon, in Switzerland. At 2,000 metres above sea level players and fans need to take a cable car to reach the three-quarter-size artificial turf pitch.

• The world's largest floating football pitch is the full-size 'The Float' in Marina Bay, Singapore. Owned by the Singapore Sports Council, the stadium can seat 30,000 spectators.

• At the start of the 1981/82 season QPR became the first English club to install an artificial pitch, with Oldham, Luton Town and Preston soon following suit. By 1994, however, Preston were the last club still playing on 'plastic' and at the start of the 1994/95 season the Football League banned all artificial surfaces on the grounds that they gave home clubs an unfair advantage. In Scotland, Premiership clubs Hamilton and Kilmarnock both play on 3G artificial pitches.

• In 2014 Maidstone entertained Stevenage in the first FA Cup tie played on a 3G pitch. Home side Maidstone made use of their greater experience on the artificial surface to win 2-1.

PLAY-OFFS

The play-off system was introduced by the Football League in the 1986/87 season. Initially, one club from the higher division competed with three from the lower division at the semi-final stage but this was changed to four teams from the same division in the 1988/89 season. The following season a one-off final at Wembley replaced the original two-legged final.

• Blackpool have been promoted from the play-offs a record five times, and share with Huddersfield Town the distinction of having won all three divisional play-off finals. The Seasiders have also scored a record total of 47 goals in the play-offs.

Huddersfield will tell you that the best way to go up is via the play-offs

IS THAT A FACT?
Nottingham Forest and MK Dons have featured a record four times each in the play-offs without once reaching the final.

• Preston have participated in the play-offs a record 10 times, but have only once won promotion – in 2015 when they beat Swindon 4-0 in the League One final.

• The Championship play-off final is the most financially rewarding sporting event in the world, its worth to the winners in prize money, TV and advertising revenue, and increased gate receipts, being estimated at nearly £200 million.

• In 2015 Swindon Town and Sheffield United drew 5-5 in the League One play-off semi-final second leg, the highest ever score in a play-off match.

PLYMOUTH ARGYLE

Year founded: 1886
Ground: Home Park (17,800)
Previous name: Argyle FC
Nickname: The Pilgrims
Biggest win: 8-1 v Millwall (1932) and v Hartlepool (1994)
Heaviest defeat: 0-9 v Stoke City (1960)

The club was founded as Argyle FC in 1886 in a Plymouth coffee house, the name deriving from the Argyll and Sutherland Highlanders who were stationed in the city at the time. The current name was adopted in 1903, when the club became fully professional and entered the Southern League.

• After joining the Football League in 1920, Plymouth just missed out on promotion from the Third Division (South) between 1922 and 1927, finishing in second place in six consecutive seasons – a record of misfortune no other club can match.

• Sammy Black, a prolific marksman during the 1920s and 1930s, is the club's leading goalscorer with 185 league goals. The Pilgrims' longest serving player is Kevin Hodges, with 530 appearances between 1978 and 1992.

• The largest city in England never to have hosted top-flight football, Plymouth have won the third tier of English football a record four times, most recently topping the Second Division in 2004.

• On their way to gaining promotion from League Two in 2016/17 Plymouth won a club record 13 away league games.

HONOURS
Division 3 (S) champions 1930, 1952
Division 3 champions 1959
Second Division champions 2004
Third Division champions 2002

MAURICIO POCHETTINO

Born: Murphy, Argentina, 2nd March 1972
Managerial career:
2009-12 Espanyol
2013-14 Southampton
2014- Tottenham Hotspur

Appointed boss of Tottenham in May 2014, Mauricio Pochettino led the north Londoners to their best ever Premier League finish, second, three years later. The Argentinian's team also set numerous other club records during an impressive 2016/17 campaign, including most points (86), most wins (26) and fewest defeats (4).

• Pochettino began his managerial career with Spanish side Espanyol in 2009, but was sacked three years later when the Barcelona-based club slipped to the bottom of La Liga.

• Later that season, however, he was a surprise choice to replace Nigel Adkins at Southampton. Despite never speaking to the press in English, Pochettino soon won over the Saints fans by introducing a vibrant and entertaining attacking style of play. In his only full season at St Mary's in 2013/14, Pochettino led Southampton to a then best ever eighth place finish in the Premier League.

• A central defender in his playing days, Pochettino twice won the Copa del Rey with Espanyol. He also represented Argentina at the 2002 World Cup, famously fouling Michael Owen in the penalty area to allow England captain David Beckham to score the only goal of the group game between the sides from the spot.

PAUL POGBA

Born: Lagny-sur-Marne, France, 15th March 1993
Position: Midfielder
Club career:
2011-12 Manchester United 3 (0)
2012- Juventus 124 (28)
2016- Manchester United 30 (5)
International record:
2013- France 47 (8)

In August 2016 France midfielder Paul Pogba became the most expensive player in football history at the time when he rejoined his first club, Manchester United, from Juventus for a staggering £89.3 million. In his first season at Old Trafford he paid back some of that fee by helping United win the League Cup and then scoring in the Red Devils' 2-0 defeat of Ajax in the Europa League final in Stockholm.

• Pogba won four successive Scudetto titles with Juve after joining the Turin giants from Manchester United in 2012. His best season was in 2015/16 when he scored a personal best eight goals and topped the Serie A assists chart with 12. His outstanding performances for club and country saw him win the 2013 Golden Boy award for the best young player in Europe.

• Pogba started out with Le Havre before moving to England in 2009 aged just 16. However, he only made a handful of appearances for United and frustrated with his lack of progress at Old Trafford decided to move to Italy.

• A combative midfielder whose tentacle-like long legs have earned him the nickname 'Paul the Octopus', Pogba made his debut for France in 2013 and the following year was his country's most impressive performer as Les Bleus reached the quarter-finals of the World Cup in Brazil. He was part of the French team that reached the final of Euro 2016, but had to settle for a runners-up medal after a 1-0 defeat to Portugal.

Paul Pogba, the most expensive Premier League player ever – for now, at least

PORT VALE

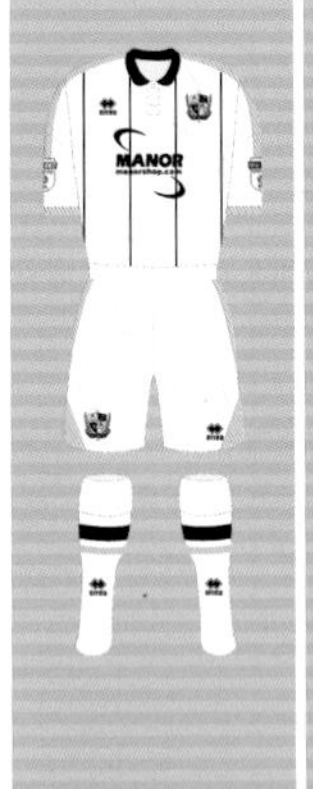

Year founded: 1876
Ground: Vale Park (19,052)
Previous name: Burslem Port Vale
Nickname: The Valiants
Biggest win: 9-1 v Chesterfield (1932)
Heaviest defeat: 0-10 v Sheffield United (1892) and v Notts County (1895)

Port Vale's name derives from the house where the club was founded in 1876. Initially, the club was known as Burslem Port Vale – Burslem being the Stoke-on-Trent town where the Valiants are based – but the prefix was dropped in 1911.

• In their first season as a league club, in 1892/93, Port Vale suffered the worst ever home defeat in Football League history when Sheffield United hammered them 10-0. However, Vale's defence was in much better nick in 1953/54 when they kept a league record 30 clean sheets on their way to the Third Division (North) championship.

• In the same season the Valiants came desperately close to being the first third-tier club to reach the FA Cup final. Having knocked out holders Blackpool in the fifth round, Vale took the lead against West Brom in the semi-final at Villa Park but eventually lost 2-1.

• After a 12-year gap Port Vale returned to the Football League in October 1919, replacing the disbanded Leeds City. Bizarrely, the Valiants inherited the Yorkshiremen's playing record (won four, lost two, drawn two) and went on to finish in a respectable 13th position.

• Relegated from League One in 2017, Port Vale's longest serving player is loyal defender Roy Sproson, appearing in a phenomenal 761 league games between 1950 and 1972. Only two other players in the history of league football have made more appearances for the same club.

HONOURS
Division 3 (N) champions *1930, 1954*
Division 4 champions *1959*
Football League Trophy *1993, 2001*

FC PORTO

Year founded: 1893
Ground: Estadio do Dragao (50,434)
Nickname: The Dragons
League titles: 27
Domestic cups: 19
European cups: 5
International cups: 2

One of the giants of Portuguese football, Porto were founded in 1893 by a local wine salesman who had been introduced to football on his regular business trips to England.

• **Porto's total of 27 domestic championships is second only to arch rivals Benfica, who have 36 to their name. The club's most successful decade was in the 1990s when they won an impressive eight titles, while they have since twice gone through a whole season unbeaten in the league – in 2010/11 and 2012/13. In the first of those campaigns Porto won the league by a record 21 points.**

• Porto have the best record in Europe of any Portuguese side, with two victories in the European Cup/Champions League (in 1987 and 2004) and two in the UEFA Cup (in 2003 and 2011), the latter of these triumphs coming under Andre Villas-Boas – at 33, the youngest coach ever to win a European competition.

• **Porto are the only Portuguese club to have been crowned world champions, claiming the Intercontinental Cup in both 1987 and 2004.**

• Porto's total of 19 wins in the Portuguese Cup is second to Benfica's 29.

HONOURS
Portuguese League champions *1935, 1939, 1940, 1956, 1959, 1978, 1979, 1985, 1986, 1988, 1990, 1992, 1993, 1995, 1996, 1997, 1998, 1999, 2003, 2004, 2006, 2007, 2008, 2009, 2011, 2012, 2013*
Portuguese Cup *1922, 1925, 1932, 1937, 1956, 1958, 1968, 1977, 1984, 1988, 1991, 1994, 1998, 2000, 2001, 2003, 2006, 2009, 2011*
European Cup/Champions League *1987, 2004*
UEFA Cup/Europa League *2003, 2011*
European Super Cup *1987*
Intercontinental Cup *1987, 2004*

PORTSMOUTH

Year founded: 1898
Ground: Fratton Park (20,620)
Nickname: Pompey
Biggest win: 9-1 v Notts County (1927)
Heaviest defeat: 0-10 v Leicester City (1928)

Portsmouth were founded in 1898 by a group of sportsmen and businessmen at a meeting in the city's High Street. After starting out in the Southern League the club joined the Third Division in 1920.

• **In 1949 the club became the first team to rise from the third tier to claim the league championship, and the following year became the first of just five clubs to retain the title since the end of the Second World War.**

• The most influential player in that team was half-back Jimmy Dickinson, who went on to play a record 764 times for Pompey, the second highest number of Football League appearances with any single club. Dickinson is also Portsmouth's most decorated international, winning 48 caps for England.

• **The club won the FA Cup for the first time in 1939, when Pompey thrashed favourites Wolves 4-1 in the final at Wembley. In 2008 they lifted the cup for a second time when a single goal from Nigerian striker Kanu was enough to beat Cardiff City in only the second final at the new Wembley.**

• In the same season Portsmouth were involved in the highest-scoring Premier League match ever, thrashing Reading 7-4 at Fratton Park.

• **Pompey made their record signing in July 2008, bringing lanky striker Peter Crouch to Fratton Park from Liverpool for £11 million. Six months later the club sold midfielder Lassana Diarra to Real Madrid for a record £18 million.**

• An ongoing financial crisis saw Portsmouth slide all the way down to the fourth tier in 2013, but there was better news for their long-suffering fans in 2017 when Pompey won the League Two title to become only the fifth club to win all four divisions of English football. Incredibly, the south coast club only topped the table for the final 32 minutes of the season – the shortest length of time of any champions of any division ever.

HONOURS
Division 1 champions *1949, 1950*
First Division champions *2003*
Division 3 (South) champions *1924*
Division 3 champions *1962, 1983*
League Two champions *2017*
FA Cup *1939, 2008*

PORTUGAL

First international: Spain 3 Portugal 1, 1921
Most capped player: Cristiano Ronaldo, 143 caps (2003-)
Leading goalscorer: Cristiano Ronaldo, 75 goals (2003-)
First World Cup appearance: Portugal 3 Hungary 1, 1966
Biggest win: Portugal 8 Liechtenstein 0, 1994 and 1999
Heaviest defeat: Portugal 0 England 10, 1947

Never rule out Portugal – they've got Cristiano Ronaldo!

P PORTUGAL

After a number of near misses, Portugal won their first major trophy in 2016 when an extra-time goal from Lille striker Eder secured them a 1-0 win over hosts France in the final of the European Championships. The Portuguese had reached the final of the same competition on home soil 12 years earlier, but went down to a surprise 1-0 defeat to Greece.

• **Portugal's best showing at the World Cup was in 1966 when they finished third after going out to hosts England in the semi-finals. Much of their success was down to legendary striker Eusebio, who topped the goalscoring charts with nine goals.**

• The southern Europeans also reached the semi-finals of the World Cup in 2006, after beating Holland in 'The Battle of Nuremburg' in the last 16 and England on penalties in the quarter-finals. A 1-0 defeat to France, though, ended their hopes of appearing in the final.

• **With 75 goals to his name Portugal captain Cristiano Ronaldo is the second highest scoring European international ever behind Hungary legend Ferenc Puskas.**

HONOURS
European Championships winners 2016
World Cup Record
1930-38 Did not enter
1950-62 Did not qualify
1966 Third place
1970-82 Did not qualify
1986 Round 1
1990-98 Did not qualify
2002 Round 1
2006 Fourth place
2010 Round 2
2014 Round 1

PREMIER LEAGUE

The Premier League was founded in 1992 and is now the most watched and most lucrative sporting league in the world, boasting record revenues of £3.6 billion in the 2015/16 season.

• **Initially composed of 22 clubs, the Premier League was reduced to 20 teams in 1995. A total of 49 clubs have played in the league but just six – Manchester United, Blackburn Rovers, Arsenal, Chelsea, Manchester City and Leicester City – have won the title. Of this group, United are easily the most successful, having won the league 13 times.**

To the joy of the money men, the Premier League is the most watched sporting league in the world

• Reflecting their historical dominance of the league, Manchester United have accumulated the most points in total (2,021), won the most games (604) and scored the most goals (1,856).

• **Alan Shearer scored a Premier League record 260 goals for Blackburn and Newcastle. The former England captain also scored a record 11 hat-tricks and, with Newcastle's Andy Cole, holds the record for the most goals in a season (34).**

• Chelsea hold the record for most points in a Premier League season (95 in 2004/05), most goals (103 in 2009/10) and most games won (30 in 2016/17).

• **Between 1992 and 2014 Manchester United winger Ryan Giggs played in a record 632 Premier League games and collected a record 13 winner's medals.**

PREMIER LEAGUE APPEARANCES

1.	Ryan Giggs (1992-2014)	632
2.	Gareth Barry (1998-)	628
3.	Frank Lampard (1996-2015)	609
4.	David James (1992-2010)	572
5.	Gary Speed (1992-2008)	535
6.	Emile Heskey (1996-2012)	516
7.	Mark Schwarzer (1996-2015)	514
8.	Jamie Carragher (1997-2013)	508
9.	Phil Neville (1995-2013)	505
10.	Rio Ferdinand (1996-2015)	504
	Steven Gerrard (1998-2015)	504

PRESTON NORTH END

Year founded: 1879
Ground: Deepdale (23,404)
Nickname: The Lilywhites
Biggest win: 26-0 v Hyde (1887)
Heaviest defeat: 0-7 v Blackpool (1948)

Preston were founded in 1879 as a branch of the North End Cricket and Rugby Club, playing football exclusively from 1881.

• **Founder members of the Football League in 1888, Preston won the inaugural league title the following year, going through the entire 22-game season undefeated and conceding just 15 goals (a league record). For good measure the club also won the FA Cup, beating Wolves 3-0 in the final, to become the first club to win the Double. During their cup run, Preston demolished Hyde 26-0 to record the biggest ever win in any English competition, striker Jimmy Ross scoring seven of the goals to set a club record that has never been matched. Ross went on to score a record 19 goals in the cup that season.**

• Of the 12 founder members of the league, Preston are the only club still playing at the same ground, making

Deepdale the oldest league football stadium anywhere in the world.

• Tom Finney is Preston's most capped international, turning out for England in 76 games. The flying winger is also the club's highest scorer, with 187 strikes between 1946 and 1960. North End's leading appearance maker is Alan Kelly, who played in goal for the club in 447 league games between 1958 and 1973.

• Preston are one of just five clubs to have won all four divisions of English football, achieving this feat in 1996 when they topped the Third Division (now League Two).

• Preston have participated in the play-offs a record 10 times, but have only once managed to go on to win promotion. Mind you, the Lilywhites did so in fine style, thrashing Swindon 4-0 in the League One final in 2015, thanks partly to Jermaine Beckford's hat-trick – only the third ever in a play-off final.

• In 1922 Preston goalkeeper James Mitchell became the first (and last) player to wear spectacles in the FA Cup final. Perhaps it wasn't the greatest idea as the Lilywhites went down 1-0 to Huddersfield at Stamford Bridge.

HONOURS
***Division 1 champions** 1889, 1890*
***Division 2 champions** 1904, 1913, 1951*
***Division 3 champions** 1971*
***Second Division champions** 2000*
***Third Division champions** 1996*
***FA Cup** 1889, 1938*
***Double** 1889*

PROMOTION

Automatic promotion from the Second to First Division was introduced in the 1898/99 season, replacing the 'test match' play-off-style system. The first two clubs to go up automatically were Glossop North End and Manchester City.

• Birmingham City, Leicester City and Notts County have gained a record 13 promotions, while the Foxes have gone up to the top flight on a record 12 occasions – most recently in 2014, after winning the Championship.

• Crystal Palace, Leicester, Sunderland and West Brom have all been promoted to the Premier League a record four times.

• The best finish by a promoted club in the Premier League the following season is third – by Newcastle in 1993/94 and Nottingham Forest in 1994/95. Less impressively, all three promoted clubs – Barnsley, Bolton Wanderers and Crystal Palace – were relegated from the Premier League in 1997/98.

• Between 2010 and 2014 SV Rodinghausen won a world record five consecutive promotions in German regional football.

QUEENS PARK RANGERS

Year founded: 1882
Ground: Loftus Road (18,489)
Nickname: The R's
Biggest win: 9-2 v Tranmere Rovers (1960)
Heaviest defeat: 1-8 v Mansfield Town (1965) and v Manchester United (1969)

Founded in 1882 following the merger of St Jude's and Christchurch Rangers, the club was called Queens Park Rangers because most of the players came from the Queens Park area of north London.

• A nomadic outfit in their early days, QPR have staged home matches at no fewer than 19 different venues, a record for a Football League club.

• The club enjoyed its finest moment in 1967 when Rangers came from two goals down to defeat West Bromwich Albion 3-2 in the first ever League Cup final to be played at Wembley. In the same season the R's won the Third Division title to pull off a unique double.

• Loftus Road favourite Rodney Marsh hit a club record 44 goals that season, 11 of them coming in the League Cup. George Goddard, though, holds the club record for league goals with 37 in 1929/30. Goddard is also the club's leading scorer, notching 174 league goals between 1926 and 1934. Meanwhile, no other player has pulled on Rangers' famous hoops more often than Tony Ingham, who made 519 league appearances between 1950 and 1963.

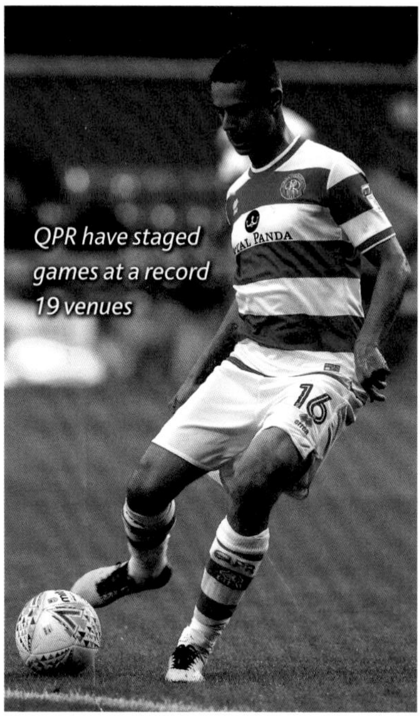

QPR have staged games at a record 19 venues

• In 1976 QPR finished second in the old First Division, being pipped to the league championship by Liverpool. The following season Rangers enjoyed their best ever European campaign, reaching the quarter-finals of the UEFA Cup before losing on penalties to AEK Athens.

• In 1982 Rangers reached the FA Cup final for the only time in their history but went down 1-0 to Tottenham in a replay after the original match finished 1-1.

• Striker Charlie Austin scored 18 Premier League goals in QPR's relegation season of 2014/15 – the best return ever for a player at a club finishing bottom of the league.

• QPR's record signing is defender Christopher Samba, who cost £12.5 million when he moved to west London from Anzhi Makhachkala in January 2013. Just six months later Samba boosted Rangers' coffers by a record £12 million when he returned to the Russian side following the Superhoops' relegation from the Premier League.

HONOURS
***Division 2 champions** 1983*
***Championship champions** 2011*
***Division 3 (S) champions** 1948*
***Division Three champions** 1967*
***League Cup** 1967*

SERGIO RAMOS

Born: Camas, Spain, 30th March 1986
Position: Defender
Club career:
2003-04 Sevilla B 26 (2)
2004-05 Sevilla 39 (2)
2005- Real Madrid 364 (49)
International record:
2005- Spain 143 (10)

In 2017, following Real Madrid's 4-1 thrashing of Juventus in Cardiff, Sergio Ramos became the first player to captain a side to back-to-back Champions League titles. Previously, Ramos had scored in two other Champions League finals: in 2014 he headed a last-minute equaliser against city rivals Atletico Madrid which enabled Real to go on and win the cup; then, in 2016, he put Real ahead against the same opposition and also scored in his team's ultimately successful penalty shoot-out.

• **A strong tackler who can play either in central defence or at right-back, Ramos started out at Sevilla before joining Real for around £20 million in 2005 – aged 19 at the time, he was the most expensive teenager in Spanish football history.**

• As well as his three Champions League triumphs, Ramos has won four La Liga titles and two Spanish cups. He also scored in the semi-final and final of the 2014 FIFA Club World Cup in Marrakesh, and was voted Player of the Tournament. Less impressively, he has been sent off in the Spanish league an incredible 17 times, just one short of the record for La Liga.

• **Ramos has enjoyed huge success at international level, winning two European Championships (2008 and 2012) and the World Cup in South Africa in 2010. He is the youngest European player ever to win 100 caps for his country, reaching three figures a week before his 27th birthday when Spain played Finland in a World Cup qualifier in March 2013. Ramos marked the occasion in style, scoring his side's goal in a 1-1 draw, and he has gone on to become Spain's second highest capped player behind Iker Casillas.**

RANGERS

Year founded: 1873
Ground: Ibrox Stadium (50,817)
Nickname: The Gers
Biggest win: 14-2 v Blairgowrie (1934)
Heaviest defeat: 2-10 v Airdrieonians (1886)

The most decorated club in the history of world football, Rangers were founded by a group of rowing enthusiasts in 1873. The club were founder members of the Scottish League in 1890, sharing the inaugural title with Dumbarton.

• **Rangers have won the league title 54 times, a record of domestic success which is unmatched by any club on the planet. Between 1989 and 1997**

Sergio Ramos shows off the Champions League trophy yet again in 2017 – and he didn't drop it this time!

On Rangers' long journey back to the top their opponents have tried to stop them by fair means or foul!

the Gers topped the league in nine consecutive seasons, initially under Graeme Souness and then under Walter Smith, to equal a record previously set by arch rivals Celtic.

• In 2000 Rangers became the first club in the world to win 100 major trophies. The Glasgow giants have since extended their tally to 115, most recently adding the League Cup and SPL title in 2011. The club's tally of seven domestic Trebles is also unequalled anywhere in the world.

• Way back in 1898/99 Rangers enjoyed their best ever league season, winning all 18 of their matches to establish yet another world record.

• The club's record goalscorer is former Rangers manager Ally McCoist. In a 15-year Ibrox career between 1983 and 1998 McCoist banged in an incredible 251 goals (355 in all competitions), including a record 28 hat-tricks. McCoist is also the club's most capped international, winning 59 of his 61 Scotland caps while with the Gers.

• Rangers also hold two important records in the Scottish League Cup, with more wins (27) and more appearances in the final (34) than any other club. The Gers' first win in the competition came in its inaugural year when they thrashed Aberdeen 4-0 in the final in 1947.

• The club's record in the Scottish Cup is not quite as impressive, the Gers' 33 triumphs in the competition being bettered by Celtic's 37. However, it was in the Scottish Cup that Rangers recorded their biggest ever victory, thrashing Blairgowrie 14-2 in 1934. Striker Jimmy Fleming scored nine of the goals on the day to set a club record.

• Former Rangers boss Bill Struth is the most successful manager in the history of the British game, winning an incredible 18 league titles in a 34-year stint in the Ibrox hotseat between 1920 and 1954.

• No player has turned out in the royal blue shirt of Rangers more often than former captain John Greig, who made 755 appearances in all competitions between 1961 and 1978. Famously, Greig led the Gers to their one success in continental competition, the European Cup Winners' Cup in 1972 when they beat Dynamo Moscow in the final.

• Rangers are the only club to have won four different Scottish divisional titles, completing this feat in 2016 when the Gers topped the Championship table – the last stage of their return to the top flight after they were forced into liquidation in 2012 and made to start from scratch in the bottom tier.

• In November 2000 Rangers splashed out a club record £12 million on Chelsea's Norwegian international striker Tore Andre Flo.

HONOURS

***Division 1 champions** 1891 (shared), 1899, 1900, 1901, 1902, 1911, 1912, 1913, 1918, 1920, 1921, 1923, 1924, 1925, 1927, 1928, 1929, 1930, 1931, 1933, 1934, 1935, 1937, 1939, 1947, 1949, 1950, 1953, 1956, 1957, 1959, 1961, 1963, 1964, 1975*

***Premier League champions** 1976, 1978, 1987, 1989, 1990, 1991, 1992, 1993, 1994, 1995, 1996, 1997*

***SPL champions** 1999, 2000, 2003, 2005, 2009, 2010, 2011*

***Championship champions** 2016*

***League One champions** 2014*

***Third Division champions** 2013*

***Scottish Cup** 1894, 1897, 1898, 1903, 1928, 1930, 1932, 1934, 1935, 1936, 1948, 1949, 1950, 1953, 1960, 1962,1963, 1964, 1966, 1973, 1976, 1978, 1979, 1981, 1992, 1993, 1996, 1999, 2000, 2002, 2003, 2008, 2009*

***Scottish League Cup** 1947, 1949, 1961, 1962, 1964, 1965, 1971, 1976, 1978, 1979, 1982, 1984, 1985, 1987, 1988, 1989, 1991, 1993, 1994, 1997, 1999, 2002, 2003, 2005, 2008, 2010, 2011*

***European Cup Winners' Cup** 1972*

Marcus Rashford, the youngest ever scorer in the Manchester derby

MARCUS RASHFORD

Born: Manchester, 31st October 1997
Position: Striker
Club career:
2014- Manchester United 43 (10)
International record:
2016- England 9 (1)

When, aged 18 and 208 days, Marcus Rashford opened the scoring for England in a 2-1 friendly win over Australia at the Stadium of Light in May 2016 he became the youngest ever scorer for his country on his debut, beating the record previously set by Tommy Lawton way back in 1938.

• On the books of Manchester United since the age of seven, Rashford enjoyed a sensational start to his Old Trafford career, scoring twice in a 5-1 thrashing of Danish side Midtjylland in the Europa League on 25th February 2015 to become the club's youngest ever scorer in European competition, eclipsing a record previously held by the legendary George Best.

• Three days later Rashford scored twice in a 3-2 home win over Arsenal, putting himself in third place in the list of United's youngest ever Premier League scorers behind Federico Macheda and Danny Welbeck. He then set another record by notching the winner away to Manchester City to become the youngest ever scorer in the Manchester derby.

• After enduring a disappointing 20-match run without a goal, Rashford ended the 2016/17 season on a high after helping United win the Europa League. The young striker's winning goal in the semi-final first leg away to Celta Vigo was probably the most important yet of his fledgling career.

• Fast, strong and a composed finisher in front of goal, Rashford was a surprise choice by England manager Roy Hodgson for the 2016 European Championships, and when he came on in a 2-1 win against Wales became his country's youngest ever player at the finals, aged 18 and 229 days.

READING

Year founded: 1871
Ground: Madejski Stadium (24,161)
Nickname: The Royals
Biggest win: 10-2 v Crystal Palace (1946)
Heaviest defeat: 0-18 v Preston (1894)

Reading were founded in 1871, making them the oldest Football League club south of Nottingham. After amalgamating with local clubs Reading Hornets (in 1877) and Earley FC (in 1889), the club was eventually elected to the new Third Division in 1920.

• The oldest club still competing in the FA Cup never to have won the trophy, Reading have got as far as the semi-finals just twice, losing to Cardiff City in 1927 and Arsenal in 2015.

• In the 1985/86 season Reading set a Football League record by winning their opening 13 matches, an outstanding start which provided the launch pad for the Royals to go on to top the old Third Division at the end of the campaign.

• Reading's greatest moment, though, came in 2006 when, under manager Steve Coppell, they won promotion to the top flight for the first time in their history. They went up in fine style, too, claiming the Championship title with a Football League record 106 points and going 33 matches unbeaten (a record for the second tier) between 9th August 2005 and 17th February 2006.

• Prolific marksman Ronnie Blackman holds two scoring records for the club, with a total of 158 goals between 1947 and 1954 and a seasonal best of 39 goals in the 1951/52 campaign. Defender Martin Hicks played in a record 500 league games for the Royals between 1978 and 1991.

• During the 1978/79 season Reading goalkeeper Steve Death went 1,074 minutes without conceding a goal – a Football League record until 2009, when Manchester United's Edwin van der Sar beat it.

• Reading's 18-0 defeat by Preston in the first round of the FA Cup in 1894 is the second worst in the history of English football – although it still fell a little way short of Hyde's 26-0 humiliation, also at the hands of the Lilywhites, in the cup seven years earlier.

• When Reading were beaten on penalties by Huddersfield Town in the 2017 Championship play-off final they matched Sheffield United's record of having lost four play-off finals.

HONOURS
Championship champions 2006, 2012
Division 3 (S) champions 1926
Division 3 champions 1986
Second Division champions 1994
Division 4 champions 1979

TOP 10

POINTS IN A SEASON

1.	Reading (2005/06)	106
2.	Sunderland (1998/99)	105
3.	Wolverhampton Wanderers (2013/14)	103
4.	Leicester City (2013/14)	102
	Newcastle United (2009/10)	102
	Plymouth Argyle (2001/02)	102
	Swindon Town (1985/86)	102
8.	Charlton Athletic (2011/12)	101
	Fulham (1998/99)	101
	Fulham (2000/01)	101
	York City (1983/84)	101

REAL MADRID

Year founded: 1902
Ground: Estadio Bernabeu (81,044)
Previous name: Madrid
Nickname: Los Meringues
League titles: 33
Domestic cups: 18
European cups: 17
International cups: 5

Founded by students as Madrid FC in 1902, the title 'Real' (meaning 'Royal') was bestowed on the club by King Alfonso XIII in 1920.

• One of the most famous names in world football, Real Madrid won

When Real Madrid regained the Champions League in 2017 it literally rained silver!

the first ever European Cup in 1956 and went on to a claim a record five consecutive victories in the competition with a side featuring greats such as Alfredo di Stefano, Ferenc Puskas and Francisco Gento. Real's total of 12 victories in the European Cup/Champions League is also a record, and following their most recent success – an emphatic 4-1 defeat of Juventus in the final in Cardiff in 2017 – Real became the first club to retain the trophy in the Champions League era.

• The club have dominated Spanish football over the years, winning a record 33 league titles (nine more than nearest rivals Barcelona), including a record five on the trot on two occasions (1961-65 and 1986-90).

• On their way to winning the title in 2016/17 Real scored in every league match – a first for a 38-match La Liga season. For good measure Los Meringues also found the net at least once in their other 22 matches of the campaign.

• Real have participated in the Champions League for a record 21 consecutive seasons since 1997/98.

HONOURS

***Spanish League** 1932, 1933, 1954, 1955, 1957, 1958, 1961, 1962, 1963, 1964, 1965, 1967, 1968, 1969, 1972, 1975, 1976, 1978, 1979, 1980, 1986, 1987, 1988, 1989, 1990, 1995, 1997, 2001, 2003, 2007, 2008, 2012, 2017*

***Spanish Cup** 1905, 1906, 1907, 1908, 1917, 1934, 1936, 1946, 1947, 1962, 1970, 1974, 1975, 1980, 1982, 1989, 1993, 2011, 2014*

***European Cup/Champions League** 1956, 1957, 1958, 1959, 1960, 1966, 1998, 2000, 2002, 2014, 2016, 2017*

***UEFA Cup** 1985, 1986*

***European Super Cup** 2002, 2014, 2016*

***Intercontinental Cup/Club World Cup** 1960, 1998, 2002, 2014, 2016*

REFEREES

In the 19th century Colonel Francis Marindin was the referee at a record nine FA Cup finals, including eight on the trot between 1883 and 1990. His record will never be beaten as the FA now appoints a different referee for the FA Cup final every year.

• The first referee to send off a player in the FA Cup final was Peter Willis, who dismissed Manchester United defender Kevin Moran in the 1985 final for a foul on Everton's Peter Reid. Video replays showed that it was a harsh decision.

• 2010 World Cup final referee Howard Webb holds the record for the most Premier League matches refereed in a single season, with 35 in 2008/09.

• On 9th February 2010 Amy Fearn became the first woman to referee a Football League match when she took charge of the last 20 minutes of Coventry's home game with Notts Forest after the original ref, Tony Bates, limped off with a calf injury.

• Bobby Madley dished out the most bookings in the 2016/17 Premier League season, brandishing his yellow card 124 times. However, Kevin Friend had the highest yellow card count per match, with an average of 4.7.

• In one of the most bizarre incidents ever in the history of football, a referee scored in a Division Three fixture between Plymouth and Barrow in 1968. A shot from a Barrow player was heading wide until it deflected off the boot of referee Ivan Robinson and into the Pilgrims' net for the only goal of the match.

RELEGATION

Birmingham City boast the unwanted record of having been relegated from the top flight more often than any other club, having taken the drop 12 times – most recently in 2010/11. However, the Blues have not experienced that sinking feeling as often as Notts County, who have suffered 16 relegations in total. Meanwhile, Bristol City were the first club to suffer three consecutive relegations, dropping from Division One to Division Four between 1979/80 and 1981/82.

• In the Premier League era Crystal Palace, Middlesbrough, Norwich City and Sunderland have dropped out of the top flight on a joint-record four occasions. In 1993 the Eagles were desperately unlucky to go down with a record 49 points, a tally matched by Norwich in 1985 in the old First Division. Southend in 1988/89 and Peterborough in 2012/13 were even more unfortunate, being relegated from the old Third Division and the Championship respectively despite amassing 54 points.

• Manchester City are the only club to be relegated a year after winning the league title. Following their championship success in 1937 City went down in 1938 despite being top scorers in the First Division with 80 goals.

• When Derby County went down from the Premier League in 2008, they did so with the lowest points total of any club in the history of English league football. The Rams accumulated only 11 points in a miserable campaign, during which they managed to win just one match out of 38.

• SV Lohhof (2000-2003) and FC Kempton (2008-2011) have both suffered a record four consecutive relegations in German regional football.

REPLAYS

In the days before penalty shoot-outs, the FA Cup fourth qualifying round tie between Alvechurch and Oxford City went to a record five replays before Alvechurch reached the first round proper with a 1-0 win in the sixth match between the two clubs.

• The first FA Cup final to go to a replay was the 1875 match between Royal Engineers and Old Etonians, Engineers winning 2-0 in the second match. The last FA Cup final to require a replay was the 1993 match between Arsenal and Sheffield Wednesday, the Gunners triumphing 2-1 in the second game. In 1999 the FA scrapped final replays, ruling that any drawn match would be settled on the day by penalties.

• In 1912 Barnsley required a record six replays in total before getting their hands on the FA Cup. Fulham also played six replays in their run to the FA Cup final in 1975, but the extra games appeared to have taken their toll as they lost limply 2-0 to West Ham at Wembley.

• Four Scottish Cup finals required second replays before they were decided, the most recent in 1979 when Rangers finally beat Hibs 3-2 in the third match at Hampden Park.

REPUBLIC OF IRELAND

First international: Republic of Ireland 1 Bulgaria 0, 1924
Most capped player: Robbie Keane, 146 caps (1998-2016)
Leading goalscorer: Robbie Keane, 68 goals (1998-2016)
First World Cup appearance: Republic of Ireland 1 England 1, 1990
Biggest win: 8-0 v Malta (1983)
Heaviest defeat: 0-7 v Brazil (1982)

The Republic of Ireland enjoyed their most successful period under English manager Jack Charlton in the late 1980s and early 1990s. 'Big Jack' became a legend on the Emerald Isle after guiding the Republic to their first ever World Cup in 1990, taking the team to the quarter-finals of the tournament – despite not winning a single match – before they were eliminated by hosts Italy.

• Ireland have a tremendous recent record against England, and following a 0-0 draw in Dublin with the Three Lions in June 2015 are undefeated in six of these derbies dating back to

The Republic of Ireland have an experienced squad, as Jonathan Walters' grey hairs suggest!

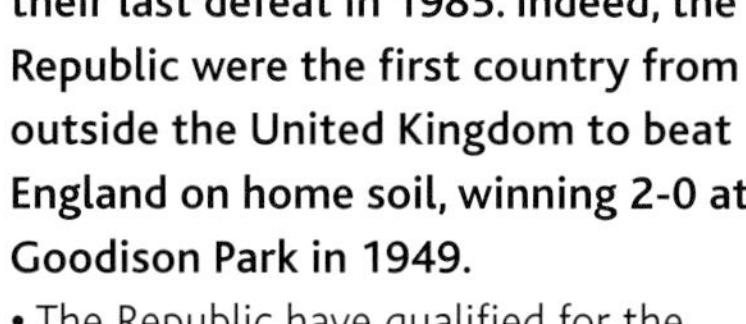

their last defeat in 1985. Indeed, the Republic were the first country from outside the United Kingdom to beat England on home soil, winning 2-0 at Goodison Park in 1949.

• The Republic have qualified for the European Championships on three occasions, reaching the knock-out stages for the first time at Euro 2016 thanks to a famous 1-0 win over Italy. However, a 2-1 defeat against hosts France ended their hopes of further progress.

• In 2009, in a World Cup play-off against France, the Republic were on the wrong end of one of the worst refereeing decisions of all time when Thierry Henry's blatant handball went unpunished before he crossed for William Gallas to score the goal that ended Ireland's hopes of reaching the 2010 finals in South Africa.

• Republic of Ireland striker Robbie Keane has won more caps (146) and scored more international goals (68) than any other player from the British Isles.

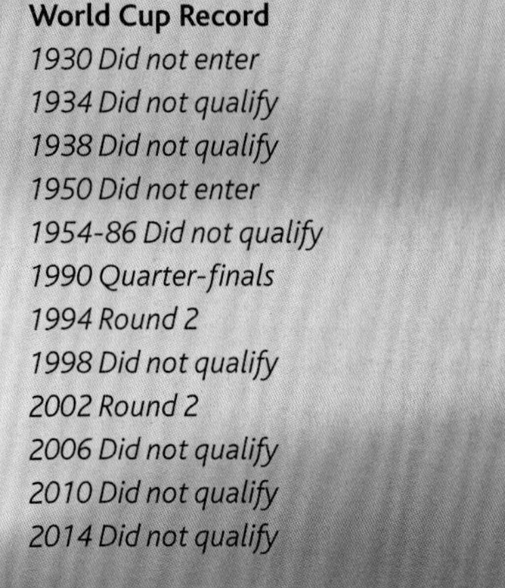

World Cup Record
1930 Did not enter
1934 Did not qualify
1938 Did not qualify
1950 Did not enter
1954-86 Did not qualify
1990 Quarter-finals
1994 Round 2
1998 Did not qualify
2002 Round 2
2006 Did not qualify
2010 Did not qualify
2014 Did not qualify

ARJEN ROBBEN

Born: Bedum, Netherlands, 23rd June 1984
Position: Winger
Club career:
2000-02 Groningen 50 (8)
2002-04- PSV 56 (17)
2004-07 Chelsea 67 (15)
2007-09 Real Madrid 50 (11)
2009- Bayern Munich 168 (90)
International record:
2003- Netherlands 92 (33)

Flying winger Arjen Robben is one of a handful of players to have won the domestic league title with four clubs in four different countries, having finished top of the pile with PSV (2003), Chelsea (2005 and 2006), Real Madrid (2008) and Bayern Munich (2010, 2013-17).

Arjen Robben's long stride makes him almost impossible to catch

• After starting out with Groningen, Robben made his name with PSV, with whom he was named Dutch Young Player of the Year in 2003. The following year he joined Chelsea where, despite suffering a number of injuries and a testicular cancer scare during his three years in London, he enjoyed huge success, collecting five winner's medals before departing for Real Madrid in 2007 for £24 million.

• After two years he was on the move again, to Bayern Munich, where he won the domestic Double in his first season and was also voted Player of the Year in Germany – the first Dutchman to receive the honour. Robben, though, was denied a Treble when Bayern were beaten in the final of the Champions League by Inter Milan. Two years later, in 2012, he suffered more heartbreak in the same tournament when Bayern were beaten by Chelsea in the final in Munich, but the following year he finally got his hands on the trophy when he scored a last-minute winner against Borussia Dortmund in the final at Wembley.

• The pacy wideman has also experienced much disappointment at international level, being part of the Netherlands team that lost in the 2010 World Cup final to Spain. Four years later he starred in his country's 5-1 hammering of world champions Spain at the World Cup in Brazil, but he was denied another chance to win the trophy when Argentina beat the Netherlands in the semi-final.

ROCHDALE

Year founded: 1907
Ground: Spotland Stadium (10,249)
Nickname: The Dale
Biggest win: 8-1 v Chesterfield (1926)
Heaviest defeat: 1-9 v Tranmere Rovers (1931)

Founded at a meeting at the town's Central Council Office in 1907, Rochdale were elected to the Third Division (North) as founder members in 1921.

• The proudest day in the club's history came in 1962 when they reached the League Cup final. Rochdale lost 4-0 on aggregate to Norwich City, then in the Second Division, but took pride in becoming the first team from the bottom tier to reach a major cup final. The Dale's manager at the time was Tony Collins, the first ever black boss of a league club.

• Rochdale failed to win a single game in the FA Cup for 18 years from 1927 – the longest period of time any club has gone without victory in the competition. The appalling run finally came to an end in 1945 when the Dale beat Stockport 2-1 in a first-round replay.

• There was more misery for fans of the Dale in 1973/74 when their heroes won just two league games in the old Third Division – the worst ever return in a 46-match campaign.

• Rochdale made their record signing in 2001 when they bought striker Paul Connor from Stoke City for £150,000. In July 2014 the Dale sold striker Scott Hogan to Brentford for a club record £750,000.

MARCOS ROJO

Born: La Plata, Argentina, 20th March 1990
Position: Defender
Club career:
2008-11 Estudiantes 43 (3)
2011-12 Spartak Moscow 8 (0)
2012-14 Sporting Lisbon 49 (5)
2014- Manchester United 59 (1)
International record:
2011- Argentina 54 (2)

One of the toughest and most competitive defenders in the Premier League, Marcos Rojo has helped Manchester United win the FA Cup (2016) as well as the League Cup and Europa League (both in 2017) since his £16 million move from Sporting Lisbon in August 2014.

• The Argentinian, whose surname means 'red' in Spanish, began his career with Estudiantes with whom he won the Copa Libertadores in 2009. In the same year he played in the Club World Cup final, but finished on the losing side after a narrow 2-1 defeat to Barcelona.

• Rojo made his debut for Argentina in a friendly against Portugal in 2011. He scored his first goal for his country in a 3-1 win against Nigeria at the 2014 World Cup and was part of the Argentina team which reached the final of the tournament, losing 1-0 to Germany.

• The following year Rojo endured more disappointment when Argentina reached the final of the Copa America but lost to hosts Chile on penalties after a 0-0 draw. And it was a case of deja vu in 2016, as Rojo finished on the losing side in the same competition after Argentina failed in the shoot-out for a second time against Chile.

CRISTIANO RONALDO

Born: Madeira, Portugal, 5th February 1985
Position: Winger/Striker
Club career:
2001-03 Sporting Lisbon 25 (3)
2003-09 Manchester United 196 (84)
2009- Real Madrid 265 (285)
International record:
2003- Portugal 143 (75)

Cristiano Ronaldo is the all-time leading scorer in the Champions League with a total of 105 goals for Manchester United and Real Madrid, including a record 52 in the knock-out stages and a record 17 in the 2013/14 season. He is also Real's all-time leading scorer with an incredible 406 goals in all competitions, a total which includes a record 32 hat-tricks in La Liga.

• Born on the Portuguese island of Madeira, Ronaldo began his career with Sporting Lisbon before joining Manchester United in a £12.25 million deal in 2003. The following year he won his first trophy with the Red Devils, opening the scoring as United beat Millwall 3-0 in the FA Cup final. He later helped United win a host of major honours, including three Premiership titles and the Champions League in 2008 before signing for Real for a then world record £80 million in 2009.

• In 2007 Ronaldo was voted PFA Player of the Year and Young Player of the Year, the first man to achieve this double since Andy Gray in 1977. The following season he scored a remarkable 42 goals for United in all competitions, and won the European Golden Boot. Three years later, in his second season with Real, he became the first player ever to win the award in two different countries. He has gone on to win two La Liga titles and the Champions League three times with Real, in 2014, 2016 and 2017, and is the only player in the modern era to score in three finals.

IS THAT A FACT?
Cristiano Ronaldo is the only player ever to score at seven consecutive major international tournaments: the European Championships in 2004, 2008, 2012 and 2016 and the World Cup in 2006, 2010 and 2014.

• Arguably the most exciting talent in world football today, Ronaldo is the only player from the Premier League to have been voted World Footballer of the Year, having collected this most prestigious of awards in 2008. After playing second fiddle for some years to his great rival Lionel Messi, he was delighted to win the award again in both 2013 and 2014, and in 2016 he was the first winner of the Best FIFA Men's Player award.

• Captain of Portugal since 2008, Ronaldo is his country's all-time top scorer with 75 goals in a record 143 appearances. After coming close a number of times, he finally led his nation to glory at Euro 2016, although he had to limp off in the first half of Portugal's eventual 1-0 defeat of hosts France in the final in Paris. His tally of nine goals at the European Championships is a joint record, and he has also made a record 21 appearances at the finals.

Cristiano Ronaldo, the all-time leading scorer in the Champions League

WAYNE ROONEY

Born: Liverpool, 24th October 1985
Position: Striker/Midfielder
Club career:
2002-04 Everton 67 (15)
2004-17 Manchester United 393 (183)
2017- Everton
International record:
2003-16 England 119 (53)

With 53 goals for England and 253 in all competitions for Manchester United, Wayne Rooney is the leading all-time scorer for both the Red Devils and the Three Lions. In both cases, he passed longstanding benchmarks set in the early 1970s by another United and England legend, Sir Bobby Charlton. Rooney's total of 119 England caps, meanwhile, is a record for an outfield player and only surpassed by Peter Shilton.

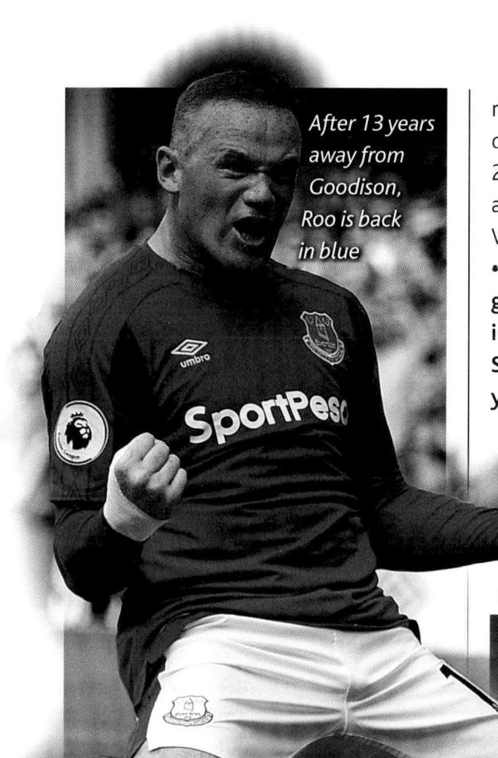
After 13 years away from Goodison, Roo is back in blue

• Rooney burst onto the scene with Everton in 2002, scoring his first league goal for the Toffees with a magnificent 20-yarder against reigning champions Arsenal at Goodison Park just five days before his 17th birthday. At the time he was the youngest ever Premiership scorer, but his record has since been surpassed by both James Milner and James Vaughan.

• After starring for England at Euro 2004 Rooney signed for Manchester United later that summer for £25.6 million, to become the world's most expensive teenage footballer. He started his Old Trafford career in sensational style with a hat-trick against Fenerbahce and until he returned on a free transfer to Everton in July 2017 played a pivotal role for the Red Devils, winning five Premier League titles, three League Cups, the FA Cup, the Champions League and, in his last match for United, the Europa League.

• Rooney's total of 198 Premier League goals is only bettered by Alan Shearer, while he is also one of just four players to have passed the century mark in assists. During the 2016/17 season he also became United's record scorer in European football, when he banged in his 39th goal against Feyenoord. His total of 30 goals in the Champions League is a record for a British player.

• Rooney is the youngest ever England player to play 100 times for his country, reaching the landmark against Slovenia on 15th November 2014 aged 29 and 22 days. He marked the occasion with a goal from the penalty spot in a 3-1 Wembley win.

• When Wayne Rooney scored his first goal for England, against Macedonia in a Euro 2004 qualifier on 6th September 2003, he was aged just 17 years and 317 days – the youngest player ever to find the net for the Three Lions.

DANNY ROSE

Born: Doncaster, 2nd July 1990
Position: Defender
Club career:
2006-07 Leeds United 0 (0)
2007- Tottenham Hotspur 108 (8)
2009 Watford (loan) 7 (0)
2009 Peterborough United (loan) 6 (0)
2010-11 Bristol City (loan) 17 (0)
2012-13 Sunderland (loan) 27 (1)
International record:
2016- England 12 (0)

Danny Rose's consistent performances for a resurgent Tottenham in the last couple of seasons have seen him voted into the PFA Team of the Year in both 2016 and 2017.

• A solid and reliable left-back who loves to bomb forward and fire in dangerous crosses, Rose was a product of the Leeds United academy but never figured in the club's first team line-up before joining Spurs for £1 million in July 2007. Following loan spells at Watford and Peterborough, he eventually made his Premier League debut in April 2010 and immediately endeared himself to Spurs fans with a stunning 25-yard volley against arch rivals Arsenal. However, Rose still had to go out on loan again, to Bristol City and Sunderland, before finally establishing himself at White Hart Lane.

• Despite his long club apprenticeship, Rose was a regular for the England Under-21 side, winning an impressive total of 29 caps. He made his senior debut for the Three Lions in a famous 3-2 friendly win in Germany in March 2016, and later that year started in three of England's four matches at the European Championships in France.

• Rose's younger brother Mitch is also a footballer, playing for Newport County in League Two.

ROSS COUNTY

Year founded: 1929
Ground: Global Energy Stadium (6,541)
Nickname: The Staggies
Biggest win: 11-0 v St Cuthbert Wanderers (1993)
Heaviest defeat: 1-6 v Alloa (1968) and v Meadowbank (1991)

Founded in 1929, Ross County played in the Highland league until 1994 when they were elected to the Scottish Third Division along with Inverness Caledonian Thistle.

• Ross County enjoyed the greatest day in their history in 2016 when they beat Hibs 2-1 in the final of the Scottish League Cup thanks to a late winner by Dutch striker Alex Schalk. Six years earlier the Staggies reached the Scottish Cup final for the only time in their history after sensationally beating Celtic in the semi-final. However, there was to be no fairytale ending as they went down 3-0 to Dundee United in the final at Hampden Park.

• In 2012 the club won promotion to the SPL for the first time in their history after a glorious campaign which ended with them being a record 24 points clear at the top of the Scottish First Division. The Staggies also put together an incredible 34-match unbeaten run, matching a record for the Scottish second tier set by Airdrieonians way back in 1955. The following season County finished fifth in the SPL, their best showing to date.

• Midfielder Michael Gardyne is the Staggies top appearance maker and leading scorer with 63 goals in all competitions in 318 games since making his debut in 2006.

HONOURS
First Division champions 2012
Second Division champions 2008
Third Division champions 1999
League Cup 2016

ROTHERHAM UNITED

Year founded: 1925
Ground: New York Stadium (12,021)
Nickname: The Millers
Biggest win: 8-0 v Oldham Athletic (1947)
Heaviest defeat: 1-11 v Bradford City (1928)

The club had its origins in Thornhill FC (founded in 1878, later becoming Rotherham County) and Rotherham Town, who merged with County to form Rotherham United in 1925.

• **The club's greatest moment came in 1961 when they reached the first ever League Cup final, losing 3-2 on aggregate to Aston Villa. Six years earlier Rotherham had missed out on goal average on promotion to the First Division... the closest they've ever been to playing top-flight football.**

• Gladstone Guest scored a record 130 goals for the Millers between 1946 and 1956, while his team-mate Danny Williams played a club best 459 games in midfield.

• **Rotherham paid a club record £500,000 for Peterborough winger Jon Taylor in August 2016, but he was unable to prevent the Millers from sliding out of the Championship at the end of the season.**

HONOURS
Division 3 (N) champions 1951
Division 3 champions 1981
Division 4 champions 1989
Football League Trophy 1996

IAN RUSH

Born: St Asaph, 20th October 1961
Position: Striker
Club career:
1979-80 Chester City 34 (18)
1980-87 Liverpool 224 (139)
1987-88 Juventus 29 (8)
1988-96 Liverpool 245 (90)
1996-97 Leeds United 36 (3)
1997-98 Newcastle United 10 (2)
1998 Sheffield United (loan) 4 (0)
1998-99 Wrexham 18 (0)
1999 Sydney Olympic 2 (0)
International record:
1980-96 Wales 73 (28)

One of the most prolific strikers ever, Ian Rush is Liverpool's leading scorer of all time with a total of 346 goals for the club in two spells at Anfield.

• **Rush has scored more goals in the FA Cup final than any other player, with a total of five for Liverpool in the 1986, 1989 and 1992 finals. His strikes helped the Reds win all three games, two of them against local rivals Everton. With 44 goals in the competition as a whole, Rush is the second highest scorer in the history of the tournament and the leading FA Cup marksman of the 20th century.**

• 'Rushie', as he was known to fans, is also the joint leading scorer in the League Cup with Geoff Hurst, the pair both ending their careers on 49 goals. He enjoyed huge success in the tournament, winning the trophy in 1981, 1982, 1983, 1984 and 1995 to become the first player to collect five League Cup winner's medals.

• **Rush tops the scoring charts for Wales, with 28 goals in 73 matches. However, he never played in the finals of either the World Cup or the European Championships.**

• Rush is the all-time leading scorer in the Merseyside derby with 25 goals against Everton, including a post-war record four goals in a 5-0 thrashing of the Toffees at Goodison Park in 1982.

• **In 1987 Rush moved from Liverpool to Juventus but had a hard time settling in Turin, telling one reporter, "It's like living in a foreign country." After just one season in Serie A he returned to Anfield for a then British record £2.7 million.**

RUSSIA

First international: Soviet Union 3 Turkey 0, 1924
Most capped player: Sergei Ignashevich, 120 caps (2002-)
Leading goalscorer: Oleg Blokhin, 42 goals (1972-88)
First World Cup appearance: Soviet Union 2 England 2, 1958
Biggest win: Soviet Union 11 India 1, 1955
Heaviest defeat: Germany 16 Russian Empire 0, 1912

The successor to the old Soviet Union which broke up into its constituent parts in the early 1990s, Russia has a distinctly mediocre record in international football but will be hoping to impress their home fans when the country hosts the World Cup for the first time in 2018.

• **Russia gained its only major success as the Soviet Union way back in 1960 when they came from behind to beat Yugoslavia 2-1 in the final of the inaugural European Championships in Paris. The Soviets also reached the final of the same competition in 1988 but lost 2-0 to the Netherlands in Munich.**

• The country's best showing at the World Cup was in 1966 when a Soviet team featuring legendary black-clad goalkeeper Lev Yashin reached the semi-finals of the tournament in England before losing 2-1 to West Germany at Goodison Park.

• **Four years later the Soviet Union became the first country ever to use a substitute at the World Cup finals when Anatoliy Puzach replaced Viktor Serebryanikov at half-time during the tournament's opening fixture, a drab 0-0 draw with hosts Mexico.**

• Since the demise of the Soviet Union, Russia have performed disappointingly for such a large country, although they did reach the semi-finals of Euro 2008 before falling 3-0 to eventual winners Spain.

• **Russia hosted the Confederations Cup for the first time in 2017, but made an early exit after failing to qualify from the group stages. The eventual winners were Germany who beat Chile 1-0 in the final in St Petersburg.**

HONOURS
European Championships winners 1960
World Cup Record
1930-54 Did not enter
1958 Quarter-finals
1962 Quarter-finals
1966 Fourth place
1970 Quarter-finals
1974 Disqualified
1978 Did not qualify
1982 Round 2
1986 Round 2
1990 Round 1
1994 Round 1
1998 Did not qualify
2002 Round 1
2006 Did not qualify
2010 Did not qualify
2014 Round 1

SACKINGS

A record 58 managers were sacked during the 2015/16 season, including big names like Jose Mourinho (Chelsea), Brendan Rodgers (Liverpool) and Steve McClaren (Newcastle United).

• In 1959 Bill Lambton got the boot from Scunthorpe United after just three days in the managerial hotseat, an English league record. His reign at the Old Showground took in just one match – a 3-0 defeat at Liverpool in a Second Division fixture. The shortest Premier League reign, meanwhile, was Les Reed's seven-game stint at Charlton in 2006.

• In May 2007 Leroy Rosenior was sacked as manager of Conference side Torquay United after just 10 minutes in charge! No sooner had the former West Ham and QPR striker been unveiled as the Gulls' new boss when he was told that the club had been bought by a business consortium and his services were no longer required.

• Notts County have sacked more managers than any other Football League club. When Kevin Nolan took over at Meadow Lane in January 2017 he was the Magpies' 65th boss in their 149-year history.

• Sam Allardyce had the shortest reign of any permanent England manager, quitting the Three Lions after just 67 days and one match in charge. His departure in September 2016 came following newspaper allegations that he offered advice to reporters posing as businessmen on how to break FA third party ownership rules.

• However, the most sensational sacking of an England manager came in 1999 when Glenn Hoddle quit after his comments to a newspaper reporter that disabled people were somehow paying for deeds committed in a previous life provoked widespread outrage.

ST JOHNSTONE

Year founded: 1884
Ground: McDiarmid Park (10,696)
Nickname: The Saints
Biggest win: 13-0 v Tulloch (1887)
Heaviest defeat: 0-12 v Cowdenbeath (1928)

St Johnstone were founded in 1884 by a group of local cricketers in Perth who wanted to keep fit in winter.

• The Saints enjoyed their best ever day in 2014, when they beat Dundee United 2-0 in the Scottish Cup final at Celtic Park. Previously, the club had appeared in two League Cup finals, but lost in 1969 to Celtic and again in 1998 to Rangers.

• The Saints' record signing is striker Billy Dodds, who joined the club in 1994 from Dundee for £400,000. The most expensive player to leave McDiarmid Park is defender Callum Davidson, who moved to Blackburn Rovers in 1998 for £1.75 million.

• Along with Falkirk, St Johnstone have won the Scottish second tier a record seven times, most recently claiming the First Division title in 2009 while going on a club record unbeaten run of 21 games.

• In 1946 Saints striker Willie McIntosh scored a club record six goals in a 9-0 hammering of Albion Rovers in a Scottish League Cup tie.

HONOURS
Division 2 champions *1924, 1960, 1963*
First Division champions *1983, 1990, 1997, 2009*
Scottish Cup *2014*

Mohamed Salah, Liverpool's record signing

MOHAMED SALAH

Born: Basyoun, Egypt, 15th June 1992
Position: Winger/striker
Club career:
2010-12 El Mokawloon 38 (11)
2012-14 Basel 47 (9)
2014-16 Chelsea 13 (2)
2015 Fiorentina (loan) 16 (6)
2015-16 Roma (loan) 34 (14)
2016-17 Roma 31 (15)
2017- Liverpool
International record:
2011- Egypt 53 (29)

Egypt international Mohamed Salah became Liverpool's record signing and the most expensive African player ever when he joined the club from Roma for £36.9 million in June 2017.

• A speedy and direct winger who can also play as a central striker, Salah started out with Cairo club El Mokawloon before moving to Basel in 2012. After winning consecutive Swiss championships, Salah joined Chelsea in 2014, having impressed the Londoners' hierarchy by scoring in three European matches against the Blues.

• However, he failed to establish himself at Stamford Bridge and in February 2015 he was loaned out to Fiorentina. Another loan at Roma followed, and after Salah topped the club's scoring charts with 14 Serie A goals in 2015/16 the move was made permanent in a £16 million deal.

• **First capped by Egypt in 2011, Salah was joint-top scorer in the African section of the 2014 World Cup qualifiers with six goals. In 2017 he was part of the Egypt team which reached the final of the Africa Cup of Nations, losing 2-1 to Cameroon.**

ALEXIS SANCHEZ

Born: Tocopilla, Chile, 19th December 1988
Position: Winger/striker
Club career:
2005-06 Cobreloa 47 (12)
2006-07 Colo-Colo 32 (5)
2007-08 River Plate 23 (4)
2008-11 Udinese 95 (20)
2011-14 Barcelona 88 (39)
2014- Arsenal 105 (53)
International record:
2006- Chile 115 (38)

Dynamic Chilean forward Alexis Sanchez is the only South American to score in two FA Cup finals. The Arsenal star hit a superb effort in the Gunners' 4-0 demolition of Aston Villa in 2015 and two years later opened the scoring in his side's 2-1 defeat of London rivals Chelsea.

• **Sanchez made his name with Italian side Udinese, before joining Barcelona in 2011. He won the Copa del Rey with the Catalan giants in 2012 and La Liga the following year.**

• When he scored three goals for Arsenal in a 5-2 win at Leicester in September 2015 Sanchez became the first ever player to score hat-tricks in the Premier League, La Liga and Serie A. His impressive tally of 15 league goals away from home in 2016/17 was the best return for an Arsenal player for 82 years.

Alexis Sanchez is Chile's all-time top scorer

• **Sanchez made his debut for Chile against New Zealand in 2006 and is now his country's highest scorer of all time with 38 goals, while his tally of 115 caps is a record shared with goalkeeper Claudio Bravo. In 2015 he starred in Chile's first ever Copa America triumph, scoring the winning penalty as the hosts beat Argentina on spot-kicks in the final, and the following year he was named Player of the Tournament as Chile retained the trophy in the USA.**

LEROY SANE

Born: Essen, Germany, 11th January 1996
Position: Winger
Club career:
2014-16 Schalke 47 (11)
2016- Manchester City 25 (5)
International record:
2015- Germany 6 (0)

A talented winger who can race past defenders with a sudden blistering burst of acceleration, Leroy Sane chipped in with nine goals in all competitions in his first season for Manchester City following his £37 million move from Schalke in August 2016.

• **After a relatively slow start at the Etihad, Sane's form improved to such an extent that he was nominated for the PFA Young Player of the Year award, although he was pipped in the final poll by Tottenham's Dele Alli.**

• Sane can thank both his parents for providing him with excellent sporting genes. His father was an international footballer for Senegal, while his mother was a gymnast who competed for West Germany at the 1984 Olympics.

• **After representing Germany at both Under-19 and Under-21 level, Sane made his full international debut in a 2-0 friendly defeat by France in Paris in November 2015 – a match which was overshadowed by a series of terrorist attacks in the French capital on the same night.**

'C'mon, somebody dance with me!'

KASPER SCHMEICHEL

Born: Copenhagen, Denmark, 5th November 1986
Position: Goalkeeper
Club career:
2005-09 Manchester City 8
2006 Darlington (loan) 4
2006 Bury (loan) 29
2007 Falkirk (loan) 15
2007-08 Cardiff City (loan) 14
2008 Coventry City (loan) 9
2009-10 Notts County 43
2010-11 Leeds United 37
2011- Leicester City 230
International record:
2013- Denmark 24

Kasper Schmeichel became the first biological son of a Premier League-winning father to also lift the trophy when he helped surprise package Leicester City top the table in 2016, playing every minute of the campaign. His father, Peter, had previously won the title five times with Manchester United, a record for a goalkeeper. The following season he became the first goalkeeper in Champions League history to save a penalty in both legs of a knock-out tie when he twice denied Sevilla from the spot in the Foxes' 3-2 aggregate last-16 win.

• **Schmeichel started out with Manchester City but failed to hold down a first-team place and was loaned out to five other clubs before moving to Notts Country in 2009, with whom he won the League Two title the following year.**

• After spending a season with Leeds United in 2010/11, Schmeichel joined Leicester and began to impress with some tremendous performances between the goalposts. He was voted into the Championship Team of the Year in 2013 and the next season was in fine form again as the Foxes won the Championship with a club record 102 points.

• Like his father, who won the European Championships with Denmark in 1992, Schmeichel is a Danish international, making his debut in a 6-0 rout of Malta in 2013.

SCOTLAND

First international: Scotland 0 England 0, 1872
Most capped player: Kenny Dalglish, 102 caps (1971-86)
Leading goalscorer: Denis Law (1958-74) and Kenny Dalglish (1971-86), 30 goals
First World Cup appearance: Scotland 0 Austria 1, 1954
Biggest win: Scotland 11 Ireland 0, 1901
Heaviest defeat: Scotland 0 Uruguay 7, 1954

Along with England, Scotland are the oldest international team in the world. The two countries played the first official international way back in 1872, the match at Hamilton Crescent, Partick, finishing 0-0. Since then, honours have been more or less even between the 'Auld Enemies', with England winning 48 matches, Scotland winning 41, and 25 ending in a draw.

• It took the Scots a while to make an impression on the world scene. After withdrawing from the 1950 World Cup, Scotland competed in the finals for the first time in 1954 but were eliminated in the first round after suffering their worst ever defeat, 7-0 to reigning champions Uruguay.

• Scotland have taken part in the World Cup finals on eight occasions but have never got beyond the group stage – a record for the tournament. They have been unlucky, though, going out in 1974, 1978 and 1982 only on goal difference.

• Scotland have a pretty poor record in the European Championships, only qualifying for the finals on two occasions, in 1992 and 1996. Again, they failed to reach the knockout stage both times, although they were unfortunate to lose out on the 'goals scored' rule to Holland at Euro '96.

• Scotland had a good record in the Home Championships until the tournament was scrapped in 1984, winning the competition 24 times and sharing the title another 17 times. Only England (34 outright wins and 20 shared) have a better overall record.

• A European record crowd of 149,415 watched Scotland beat England 3-1 at Hampden Park in the Home Championships in 1937.

• Scotland's oldest player is former Rangers defender David Weir, who made his last appearance for his country against Spain in October 2010 aged 40 and 155 days.

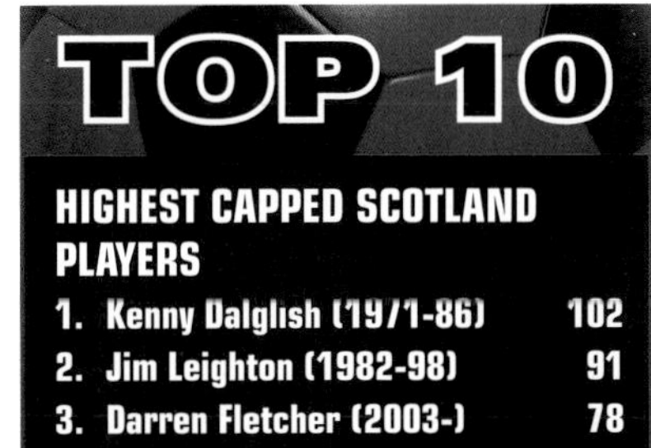

HIGHEST CAPPED SCOTLAND PLAYERS

1.	Kenny Dalglish (1971-86)	102
2.	Jim Leighton (1982-98)	91
3.	Darren Fletcher (2003-)	78
4.	Alex McLeish (1980-93)	77
5.	Paul McStay (1983-97)	76
6.	Tommy Boyd (1990-2001)	72
7.	Kenny Miller (2001-13)	69
	David Weir (1997-2010)	69
9.	Christian Dailly (1997-2008)	67
10.	Willie Miller (1975-89)	65

HONOURS
World Cup Record
1930-38 Did not enter
1950 Withdrew
1954 Round 1
1958 Round 1
1962-70 Did not qualify
1974 Round 1
1978 Round 1
1982 Round 1
1986 Round 1
1990 Round 1
1994 Did not qualify
1998 Round 1
2002 Did not qualify
2006 Did not qualify
2010 Did not qualify
2014 Did not qualify

SCOTTISH CUP

The Scottish Cup was first played for in 1873/74, shortly after the formation of the Scottish FA. Queen's Park, who the previous year had competed in the English FA Cup, were the first winners, beating Clydesdale 2-0 in the final in front of a crowd of 3,000 at the original Hampden Park.

• Queen's Park were the dominant force in the early years of the competition, winning 10 of the first 20 finals, including one in 1884 when their opponents, Vale of Leven, failed to turn up! Since then, Celtic (37 wins) and Rangers (33 wins) have ruled the roost, although Queen's Park (10 wins) remain third in the list of all-time winners ahead of Hearts (eight wins).

• Celtic boss Willie Maley is the most successful manager in the history of the competition with 14 triumphs between 1899 and 1937.

• Incredibly, the biggest ever victories in the history of British football took place in the Scottish Cup on the same day, 12th September 1885. Dundee Harp beat Aberdeen Rovers 35-0 and were confident that they had set a new record. Yet, no doubt to their utter amazement, they soon discovered that Arbroath had thrashed Bon Accord, a cricket club who had been invited to take part in the competition by mistake, 36-0!

• Celtic legend Jimmy McGrory is the all-time leading scorer in the competition with 77 goals between 1922 and 1937, including three while on loan at Clydebank.

SCOTTISH LEAGUE CUP

The Scottish League Cup came into being in 1946, some 14 years before the English version. The following April, Rangers won the first final by thrashing Aberdeen 4-0 at Hampden Park.

• Surprisingly, minnows East Fife were the first club to win the trophy three times (in 1947, 1949 and 1953) but since those early years the Glasgow giants have predictably dominated the competition, Rangers leading the way with 27 triumphs to Celtic's 16.

• Ayr United (1952) and Partick Thistle (1993) jointly hold the record for the biggest win in the competition, with 11-1 hammerings of Dumbarton and Albion Rovers respectively. Celtic hold the record for the most emphatic win in the final, demolishing Rangers 7-1 at Hampden Park in 1957 in the biggest ever margin of victory in a major British final.

• In 1987 Rangers beat Aberdeen 5-3 on penalties after a thrilling 3-3 draw at Hampden Park to win the first major British final to be settled by a penalty shoot-out.

• Prolific striker Joe Harper is the top scorer in the competition with 74 goals for Morton, Aberdeen and Hibs between 1963 and 1981.

SCUNTHORPE UNITED

Year founded: 1899
Ground: Glanford Park (9,088)
Previous name: Scunthorpe & Lindsey United
Nickname: The Iron
Biggest win: 9-0 v Boston United (1953)
Heaviest defeat: 0-8 v Carlisle United (1952)

The club was founded in 1899 when Brumby Hall linked up with some other local teams. Between 1910 and 1958 they were known as Scunthorpe and Lindsey United after amalgamating with the latter team.

• Elected to the Third Division (North) when the league expanded in 1950, Scunthorpe won the division eight years later. In 1962 the Iron finished a best ever fourth in the old Second Division, missing out on promotion to the top flight by just five points.

• In two spells at Scunthorpe between 1979 and 1987, Steve Cammack scored a club record 110 goals for the Iron. Defender Jack Brownswood made a record 597 appearances for the club between 1947 and 1965.

• In the 2013/14 season Scunthorpe boss Russ Wilcox made the best ever start of a manager in Football League history, remaining unbeaten in his first 28 matches in charge as the Iron secured promotion to League One.

• Beaten in the League One play-off semi-finals in 2017, Scunthorpe made their record signing in 2009 when giant defender Rob Jones moved from Hibs for around £350,000. Striker Billy Sharp became the most expensive player to leave Glanford Park when he joined Sheffield United for £2 million in 2007.

HONOURS
Division 3 (North) champions *1958*
League One champions *2007*

ALAN SHEARER

Born: Newcastle, 13th August 1970
Position: Striker
Club career:
1988-92 Southampton 118 (23)
1992-96 Blackburn Rovers 138 (112)
1996-2006 Newcastle United 303 (148)
International record:
1992-2000 England 63 (30)

Alan Shearer's incredible total of 260 Premiership goals (including a record 11 hat-tricks) for Blackburn and Newcastle is easily a record for the league, none of his rivals having passed the double-century mark. No fewer than 20 of his goals came against Leeds United, a Premier League record for one player against the same opponents.

• Shearer began his career with Southampton, marking his full debut for the Saints in 1988 by scoring three goals in a 4-2 victory over Arsenal. Aged just 17 years and 240 days, he was the youngest ever player to score a top-flight hat-trick.

• In 1992 Shearer moved to Blackburn for a then British record £3.3 million. He helped Rovers win the Premiership title in 1994/95, his record tally of 34 goals that campaign earning him one of his three Golden Boots.

• A then world record £15 million move to Newcastle followed in 1996, to the delight of the Geordie faithful. An instant hit at St James' Park, Shearer eventually became the club's all-time record goalscorer, his total of 206 goals in all competitions for the Magpies eclipsing the 49-year-old record of another Toon legend, Jackie Milburn.

• Strong, good in the air and possessing a powerful shot with both feet, Shearer proved a real handful for international defences, too. He scored a record 13 goals for the England Under-21 side and his five goals at Euro '96 powered England to the semi-finals of the tournament and won him the competition's Golden Boot. By the time he quit international football after Euro 2000 he had scored 30 goals for his country, a figure only surpassed by five other England players.

• Shearer became a pundit for the BBC after hanging up his boots in 2006, but three years later he sensationally returned to his beloved St James' Park as Newcastle caretaker manager. However, in his eight matches in charge he was unable to prevent the Geordies from dropping out of the Premier League for the first time.

IS THAT A FACT?
On 12th September 2016 a 9ft 6in tall statue of Alan Shearer, right arm aloft in his trademark goal celebration, was unveiled outside St James' Park. 'I like it because it has hair,' quipped the now-bald TV pundit.

SHEFFIELD UNITED

Year founded: 1889
Ground: Bramall Lane (32,702)
Nickname: The Blades
Biggest win: 10-0 v Port Vale (1892) and v Burnley (1929)
Heaviest defeat: 0-13 v Bolton (1890)

The club was founded at a meeting at the city's Adelphi Hotel in 1899 by the members of the Sheffield United Cricket Club, partly to make greater use of the facilities at Bramall Lane.

• The Blades enjoyed their heyday in the late Victorian era, winning the title in 1898, and lifting the FA Cup in both 1899 and 1902. The club won the FA Cup again in 1915, beating Chelsea 3-0 at Old Trafford, in what was to be the last final to be played before the First World War brought a halt to the sporting calendar. They chalked up another victory in 1925.

• The club's leading scorer is Harry Johnson, who bagged 201 league goals between 1919 and 1930. His successor at centre-forward, Jimmy Dunne, scored in a Football League record 12 consecutive games in the 1931/32 season.

• The Blades' home, Bramall Lane, is one of the oldest sporting arenas in

Sheffield United's promotion party got a bit fiery...

the world. It first hosted cricket in 1855, before football was introduced to the ground in 1862. Sixteen years later, in 1878, the world's first ever floodlit match was played at the stadium between two sides picked from the Sheffield Football Association, the lights being provided by two generators.

• During an 18-year career with the club between 1948 and 1966, Joe Shaw made a record 631 appearances for the Blades. Goalkeeper Jack Smith made a record 203 consecutive appearances for the Blades between 1936 and 1947, and also saved 11 penalties to establish another club record.

• Sheffield United hold the record for the most number of points, 90 in 2011/12, for a team failing to win promotion from the third tier.

• To the dismay of their fans, United have appeared in four play-off finals and lost them all – a miserable record only matched by Reading. Most recently, the Blades lost the 2012 League One play-off final to Huddersfield on penalties after all 22 players on the pitch had been required to take a spot-kick – the first time this had happened in a Wembley final.

• However, in 2017 United won the League One title with a club record 100 points to become one of just five clubs to have topped all four English divisions.

HONOURS
Division 1 champions *1898*
Division 2 champions *1953*
League One champions *2017*
Division 4 champions *1982*
FA Cup *1899, 1902, 1915, 1925*

SHEFFIELD WEDNESDAY

Year founded: 1867
Ground: Hillsborough (39,732)
Previous name: The Wednesday
Nickname: The Owls
Biggest win: 12-0 v Halliwell (1891)
Heaviest defeat: 0-10 v Aston Villa (1912)

The club was formed as The Wednesday in 1867 at the Adelphi Hotel in Sheffield by members of the Wednesday Cricket Club, who originally met on that particular day of the week. In 1929 the club added 'Sheffield' to their name, but are still often referred to simply as 'Wednesday'.

• In 1904 the Owls became the first club in the 20th century to win consecutive league championships. They did so again in 1929/30, but have not won the league since.

• In 1935 Wednesday won the FA Cup for the third and last time, striker Ellis Rimmer scoring in every round of the competition.

• In 1961/62 the Owls enjoyed their best ever run in European competition, reaching the quarter-finals of the Fairs Cup before losing 4-3 on aggregate to mighty Barcelona.

• In 1991, while residing in the old Second Division, the Owls won the League Cup for the first and only time in their history, beating Manchester United 1-0 at Wembley. It was the last time that a club from outside the top flight has lifted a major domestic cup.

• Beaten in the Championship play-off semi-finals by Yorkshire rivals Huddersfield in 2017, Wednesday made their record signing a year earlier when Middlesbrough winger Adam Reach moved to Hillsborough for £6 million.

• On the opening day of the 2000/01 season Wednesday goalkeeper Kevin Pressman was sent off after just 13 seconds at Molineux for handling a Wolves shot outside the penalty area... the fastest dismissal ever in British football.

HONOURS
Division 1 champions *1903, 1904, 1929, 1930*
Division 2 champions *1900, 1926, 1952, 1956, 1959*
FA Cup *1896, 1907, 1935*
League Cup *1991*

PETER SHILTON

Born: Leicester, 18th September 1949
Position: Goalkeeper
Club career:
1966-75 Leicester City 286 (1)
1975-78 Stoke City 110
1978-82 Nottingham Forest 202
1982-87 Southampton 188
1987-92 Derby County 175
1995-96 Bolton Wanderers 1
1997 Leyton Orient 9
International record:
1970-90 England 125

Peter Shilton is the only player in the history of English football to have played 1,000 league games. He reached the landmark, aged 47, while keeping a clean sheet for Leyton Orient in their 2-0 win over Brighton on 22nd December 1996.

• **Shilton is England's highest capped player with 125 appearances to his name. In his 20-year international career he played at three World Cups, where he kept 10 clean sheets – a goalkeeping record shared with France's Fabien Barthez.**

• A losing FA Cup finalist with Leicester City in 1969 at the age of 19, Shilton had to wait almost 10 years before he collected his first honour, the league championship with Nottingham Forest in 1978. He went on to win two European Cups with Forest before moving on to Southampton in 1982.

• **Shilton is the last goalkeeper to be voted PFA Player of the Year, collecting the award in 1978. The only other keeper to be so honoured was Tottenham's Pat Jennings, two years earlier.**

SHREWSBURY TOWN

Year founded: 1886
Ground: Montgomery Waters Meadow (9,875)
Nickname: The Shrews
Biggest win: 11-2 v Marine (1995)
Heaviest defeat: 1-8 v Norwich City (1952) and v Coventry City (1963)

Founded at the Lion Hotel in Shrewsbury in 1886, the club played in regional football for many years until being elected to the Football League in 1950.

• **Prolific striker Arthur Rowley is the club's record scorer, hitting 152 goals between 1958 and 1965 to complete his all-time league record of 434 goals (he also turned out for West Bromwich Albion, Fulham and Leicester City). His best season for the Shrews was in 1958/59 when he banged in a club best 38 goals.**

• In May 2006 the Shrews sold future England goalkeeper Joe Hart to Manchester City for a club record £600,000. Two years later Shrewsbury splashed out a record £170,000 on Nottingham Forest striker Grant Holt.

• **In 1971 Shrews striker Alf Wood became the first player in the post-war era to score four headers in a Football League match. He ended the game with five goals in a 7-1 drubbing of Blackburn Rovers.**

• Shrewsbury have won the Welsh Cup six times – a record for an English club.

HONOURS
Division 3 champions *1979*
Third Division champions *1994*
Welsh Cup *1891, 1938, 1977, 1979, 1984, 1985*

DAVID SILVA

Born: Las Palmas, Spain, 8th January 1986
Position: Winger
Club career:
2003-04 Valencia B 14 (1)
2004-10 Valencia 119 (21)
2004-05 Eibar (loan) 35 (5)
2005-06 Celta (loan) 34 (4)
2010- Manchester City 214 (39)
International record:
2006- Spain 113 (32)

A tricky winger who can wriggle out of the tightest of situations, David Silva became the first Spanish player to win the Premier League twice after helping his club Manchester City top the table in both 2012 and 2014.

• **Prior to moving to the Etihad stadium, Silva was a key player in the Valencia side that regularly managed to upset Real Madrid and Barcelona. His best moment with the Spanish side came in 2008, when Valencia won the Copa del Rey after beating Getafe 3-1 in the final.**

• Nicknamed 'El Mago' (The Magician) for his sublime skills on the ball, Silva joined City for £24 million in 2010 and in his first season in Manchester helped the Sky Blues win their first trophy for 35 years when they beat Stoke City 1-0 in the FA Cup final at Wembley. His most prolific campaign with City was in 2014/15 when he scored 12 goals in the Premier League to help his team finish second behind champions Chelsea.

• **First capped by his country in 2006, Silva was an integral figure in the Spain side that won Euro 2008, but was restricted to just two appearances as the Spanish became world champions in South Africa two years later. However, he returned to the starting line-up at Euro 2012, heading the first goal in Spain's 4-0 thrashing of Italy in the final. Silva has won 61 of his 113 caps with Manchester City, making him the club's most decorated international.**

David Silva has lost his hair...but not his skills!

TOP 10

WORLD'S TALLEST FOOTBALLERS

1.	Kristof van Hout (Westerlo, Belgium)	2.08m
2.	Paul Millar (Deveronvale, Scotland)	2.07m
3.	Yang Changpeng (Henan Jianye, China)	2.05m
	Vanja Ivesa (NK Istra 1961, Croatia)	2.05m
	Daniel Muller (Augsburg II, Germany)	2.05m
6.	Jason Mooney (Cliftonville, N. Ireland)	2.04m
7.	Oyvind Hoas (Kristiansund, Norway)	2.03m
	Kjell Petter Opheim (Stryn, Norway)	2.03m
	Costel Pantilimon (Watford, England)	2.03m
	Lacina Traore (Monaco, France)	2.03m

SIZE

The heaviest player in the history of the professional game was Willie 'Fatty' Foulke, who played in goal for Sheffield United, Chelsea and Bradford City. By the end of his career, the tubby custodian weighed in at an incredible 24 stone.

• At just 5ft tall, Fred Le May is the shortest player ever to have appeared in the Football League. He played for Thames, Clapton Orient and Watford between 1930 and 1933. The shortest England international ever was Frederick 'Fanny' Walden, a 5ft 2in winger with Tottenham who won the first of his two caps in 1914.

• No prizes for guessing who the tallest ever England international is. It is, of course, towering striker Peter Crouch, who stands 6ft 7in in his socks. Crouch, though, is a full inch shorter than Watford goalkeeper Costel Pantilimon, who claims the record as the tallest ever Premier League player.

• The smallest Premier League player in 2016/17 was Bournemouth's pint-sized winger Ryan Fraser, who is just 5ft 4in tall.

SON HEUNG-MIN

Born: Chuncheon, South Korea, 8th July 1992
Position: Winger/striker
Club career:
2010 Hamburg II 6 (1)
2010-13 Hamburg 73 (20)
2013-15 Bayer Leverkusen 62 (21)
2015- Tottenham Hotspur 62 (18)
International record:
2010- South Korea 55 (17)

A hard-working frontman who loves to run at defenders before unleashing a powerful shot, Tottenham's Son Heung-Min became the first Asian player to collect the Premier League Player of the Month award in September 2016. The South Korean continued to enjoy an excellent season, and his total of six goals in the FA Cup made him the competition's joint-top scorer for 2016/17.

• Son began his career in Germany, setting a record as the youngest player to score a league goal for Hamburg when he hit the target against Cologne, aged 18, in 2010. Three years later he moved on to Bayer Leverkusen for a club record fee of around £8 million.

• In 2015 Son became the most expensive Asian player ever when he signed for Tottenham for £22 million, and in the same year he was named Asian International Footballer of the Year – the first South Korean to win this award.

• Son played for South Korea at the 2014 World Cup, scoring in a 4-2 defeat against Algeria, and the following year he was on the scoresheet in the Asian Cup final but had to settle for a runners-up medal after Australia won 2-1 in extra-time.

Son Heung-Min, the most expensive Asian player ever

SOUTHAMPTON

Year founded: 1885
Ground: St Mary's (32,505)
Previous name: Southampton St Mary's
Nickname: The Saints
Biggest win: 14-0 v Newbury (1894)
Heaviest defeat: 0-8 v Tottenham (1936) and v Everton (1971)

Founded as Southampton St Mary's by members of St Mary's Church Young Men's Association in 1885, the club joined the Southern League in 1894 and became simply 'Southampton' the following year.

• The Saints won the Southern League six times in the decade up to 1904 and also appeared in two FA Cup finals during that period, losing to Bury in 1900 and to Sheffield United two years later.

• The club finally won the cup in 1976. Manchester United were hot favourites to beat the Saints, then in the Second Division, but the south coast side claimed the trophy thanks to Bobby Stokes' late strike. As scorer of the first (and only) goal in the final, Stokes was rewarded with a free car... unfortunately, he still hadn't passed the driving test!

• Mick Channon, a member of that cup-winning team and now a successful racehorse trainer, is the Saints' leading scorer with a total of 185 goals in two spells at The Dell, the club's old ground. Incredibly, Channon was top scorer in the old First Division in the 1973/74 season with 21 goals

but Southampton were still relegated – the first club to go down after finishing third bottom under the then new 'three up, three down' system.

• Winger Terry Paine, a member of England's 1966 World Cup-winning squad, is Southampton's longest serving player. Between 1956 and 1974 he wore the club's colours in no fewer than 713 league games before moving to Hereford United. Paine's amazing total of 824 league games puts him fourth in the all-time list, behind Peter Shilton, Tony Ford and Graham Alexander.

• England goalkeeper Shilton is the club's most capped player, winning 49 of his record 125 caps while at The Dell.

• In August 2017 the Saints forked out a record £18 million to buy Gabon international midfielder Mario Lemina from Juventus. A year earlier they received a club record £34 million when Senegalese striker Sadio Mane left the south coast to join Liverpool.

• The Saints enjoyed their best European run in 1977, reaching the quarter-finals of the Cup Winners' Cup before bowing out to Belgian giants Anderlecht 3-2 on aggregate.

• Southampton are one of just four clubs to have lost both League Cup finals they have appeared in, going down 3-2 to Nottingham Forest in 1979 and ending up on the wrong end of the same scoreline against Manchester United in 2017.

HONOURS
Division 3 (South) champions 1922
Division 3 champions 1960
FA Cup 1976
Football League Trophy 2010

SOUTHEND UNITED

Year founded: 1906
Ground: Roots Hall (12,392)
Nickname: The Shrimpers
Biggest win: 10-1 v Golders Green (1934), v Brentwood (1968) and v Aldershot (1990)
Heaviest defeat: 1-9 v Brighton and Hove Albion (1965)

Southend United were founded in 1906 at the Blue Boar pub, just 50 yards away from the club's home, Roots Hall.

• After joining the Football League in 1920 the Shrimpers remained in the third tier for a record 46 years, before dropping into the Fourth Division in 1966.

• The club's top appearance maker is Sandy Anderson, who turned out in 452 league games between 1950 and 1962. His team-mate Roger Hollis is Southend's leading marksman, rifling in 120 league goals in just six years at the club between 1954 and 1960.

• Southend were relegated from the third tier in 1988/89 despite amassing a record points total for a demoted team (54). In all, the Shrimpers have dropped down to the fourth tier a record seven times.

• Southend were the only Football League club managed by England World Cup-winning captain Bobby Moore, who was in charge at Roots Hall between 1984 and 1986, and also served on the club's board until his untimely death in 1993.

• In January 2017 Southend sold 13-year-old defender Finley Burns to Manchester City for £175,000 – a record fee for a player of that age.

HONOURS
League One champions 2006
Division 4 champions 1981

GARETH SOUTHGATE

Born: Watford, 3rd September 1970
Managerial career:
2006-09 Middlesbrough
2013-16 England Under-21
2016- England

'Don't worry, England fans, I won't be taking any more penalties!'

Having played 57 times for his country between 1995 and 2004, Gareth Southgate is the second highest capped England manager ever after Kevin Keegan (63 caps). However, unfortunately for Southgate, his international career is best remembered for a penalty shoot-out miss against Germany which cost England a possible place in the final of Euro '96.

• **Southgate became England manager, initially on a four-match temporary basis, following the sudden resignation of Sam Allardyce in September 2016. Two months later he was appointed full-time boss of the Three Lions on a four-year contract. He had previously been in charge of the England Under-21 team for three years.**

• Southgate began his managerial career with Middlesbrough in 2006. Two years earlier he had become the first Boro' captain to lift a major trophy when the Teesiders beat Bolton 2-1 in the League Cup final. However Southgate's long association with the club ended in the sack in October 2009, a few months after Boro' lost their Premier League place.

• **A ball-playing centre-back, Southgate started out with Crystal Palace before moving to Aston Villa in 1995. The following year he helped Villa win the League Cup for a then joint-record fifth time and in 2000 he captained the Birmingham outfit in their 1-0 FA Cup final defeat to Chelsea. During a six-year spell at Villa Park he won a club record 42 caps for England.**

SPAIN

First international: Spain 1 Denmark 0, 1920
Most capped player: Iker Casillas, 167 caps (2000-)
Leading goalscorer: David Villa, 59 goals (2005-14)
First World Cup appearance: Spain 3 Brazil 1, 1934
Biggest win: Spain 13 Bulgaria 0, 1933
Heaviest defeat: Italy 7 Spain 1, 1928 and England 7 Spain 1, 1931

Spain are the first country in football history to win three major international titles on the trot following their successes at Euro 2008, the 2010 World Cup in South Africa and Euro 2012 in Poland and Ukraine.

• **Spain secured their first ever World Cup triumph with a 1-0 victory over Holland at Soccer City Stadium in Johannesburg, midfielder Andres Iniesta drilling home the all-important goal four minutes from the end of extra-time. Despite their entertaining close passing style of play, Spain only managed to score eight goals in the tournament – the lowest total ever by the winning nation at a World Cup.**

• Along with Germany, Spain have won the European Championships a record three times. Their first success came in 1964 when they had the advantage of playing the semi-final and final, the latter against holders the Soviet Union, on home soil at Real Madrid's Bernabeu Stadium. Then, in 2008, a single Fernando Torres goal was enough to see off Germany in the final in Vienna. Finally, in 2012, Spain made it a hat-trick of victories after annihilating Italy 4-0 in the final in Kiev.

Spain's Gerard Pique

• **Between 2007 and 2009 Spain went 35 matches without defeat (winning 32 and drawing just three) to equal the world record set by Brazil in the 1990s. The run came to an end when Spain lost 2-0 to USA at the 2009 Confederations Cup, but the Spanish were soon back on form, going into the 2010 World Cup on the back of 18 consecutive victories – including a record 10 in qualification – before they surprisingly lost their opening match at the finals against Switzerland. That setback, though, was soon forgotten as Vicente del Bosque's men went on to lift the trophy, sparking jubilant scenes across Spain from Santander to Seville.**

• With 167 caps for Spain goalkeeper Iker Casillas is the second highest capped European international of all time, behind fellow custodian Gianluigi Buffon of Italy.

HONOURS
World Cup winners
2010
European Championships winners *1964, 2008, 2012*
World Cup Record
1930 Did not enter
1934 Quarter-finals
1938 Did not enter
1950 Fourth place
1954 Did not qualify
1958 Did not qualify
1962 Round 1
1966 Round 1
1970 Did not qualify
1974 Did not qualify
1978 Round 1
1982 Round 2
1986 Quarter-finals
1990 Round 2
1994 Quarter-finals
1998 Round 1
2002 Quarter-finals
2006 Round 2
2010 Winners
2014 Round 1

SPONSORSHIP

Manchester United's £53 million-a-year shirt sponsorship deal with US car manufacturers Chevrolet, which started in 2014, is a record for the Premier League. In European football, Barcelona's new deal with Japanese company Rakuten is the most lucrative, being worth around £47 million a year.

• **On 24th January 1976 Kettering Town became the first senior football club in the UK to feature a sponsor's logo on their shirts, Kettering Tyres, for their Southern League Premier Division match against Bath City. The Football Association ordered the removal of the logo, but finally accepted shirt sponsorship in June 1977. Two years later Liverpool became the first top-flight club to sport a sponsor's logo after signing a deal with Hitachi.**

• In the 2017/18 season Premier League clubs were permitted to sport shirt sleeve sponsorship for the first time. The first club to sign such a deal were Manchester City, who teamed up with Korean tyre manufacturers Nexen Tire.

• **The League Cup was the first major English competition to be sponsored, being renamed the Milk Cup after receiving backing from the Milk Marketing Board in 1982. It has since been rebranded as the Littlewoods Cup, the Rumbelows Cup, the Coca-Cola Cup, the Worthington Cup, the Carling Cup, the Capital One Cup, the EFL Cup and, from 2017, the Carabao Cup. Since 1994 the FA Cup has been sponsored by Littlewoods, AXA, E.ON, Budweiser, and from the 2015/16 season, Emirates. Meanwhile, the Premier League has been sponsored by Carling, Barclaycard and Barclays, but has had no sponsor since 2016.**

• The first competition in England to be sponsored was the Watney Cup in 1971, a pre-season tournament between the highest scoring teams in the different divisions of the Football League.

• **Arsenal's shirt sponsorship deal with Emirates airline, which began in 2006, is the longest running in the Premier League.**

IS THAT A FACT?

The first FA Cup final to feature sponsored shirts was in 1984 between Everton and Watford. The Toffees wore the logo of canned meat company Hania, while the Hornets advertised industrial vehicles manufacturer Iveco.

STADIUMS

With a capacity of 150,000 the Rungrado 1st of May Stadium in Pyongyang, North Korea is the largest football stadium anywhere in the world. As well as football matches, the stadium also hosts athletic meetings and mass displays of choreographed gymnastics. In the late 1990s a number of North Korean army generals were burned to death in the stadium after being implicated in a plot to assassinate the country's then dictator, Kim Jong-il.

• **Barcelona's Nou Camp is the largest football stadium in Europe and the second largest in the world with a capacity of 99,354. Old Trafford (75,643) has the largest capacity of any dedicated Premier League ground, followed by the Emirates Stadium (60,432).**

• Built at a cost of £798 million, Wembley Stadium is the most expensive sporting venue in the world. After years of delays, the stadium finally opened to the public in 2007 and has since hosted 54 England internationals, 10 FA Cup finals and nine League Cup finals. During the 2017/18 season it hosted Premier League football for the first time when Spurs moved in while their new ground in north London was under construction.

• **With a capacity of just 11,464 Bournemouth's Vitality Stadium is the smallest ever to host Premier League football.**

The Rungrado 1st of May Stadium in North Korea is the largest in the world

RAHEEM STERLING

Born: Kingston, Jamaica, 8th December 1994
Position: Winger
Club career:
20012-15 Liverpool 91 (18)
2015- Manchester City 64 (13)
International record:
2012- England 32 (2)

Speedy winger Raheem Sterling became the most expensive English player ever when he moved from Liverpool to Manchester City for £49 million in July 2015. He struggled to justify the huge fee in his first season at the Etihad but did help City win the 2016 League Cup final against his old club.

• **Jamaican-born Sterling started his career with QPR, before switching to Liverpool for a bargain £600,000 in 2010. He became the third youngest player ever to make his debut for the Reds when he came on as a sub in a 2-1 home defeat against Wigan Athletic on 24th March 2012. Seven months later he became the club's second youngest goalscorer at the time (behind Michael Owen) when he notched his first goal for the Merseysiders in a 1-0 win against Reading.**

• Sterling was a star of Liverpool's magnificent 2013/14 Premier League campaign, during which he chipped in with a career-best nine league goals. At the end of the year he became only the second English player (after Wayne

Sterling work by Raheem

Rooney in 2004) to win the Golden Boy award for the most promising player aged under-21 in European football. However, Sterling's performances the following season were affected by a contract dispute with Liverpool, which ended with him demanding to leave Anfield.

• **Sterling rose through the England youth ranks to make his senior debut in a 4-2 friendly defeat away to Sweden in November 2012. In only his fourth game for the Three Lions he was sent off in a pre-2014 World Cup friendly against Ecuador to become the youngest ever England player to see red.**

STEVENAGE

Year founded: 1976
Ground: Broadhall Way (6,722)
Previous name: Stevenage Borough
Nickname: The Boro
Biggest win: 7-0 v Merthyr (2006)
Heaviest defeat: 1-6 v Farnborough (2002)

The club was founded in 1976 as Stevenage Borough, following the bankruptcy of the town's former club, Stevenage Athletic. In 2010 the club decided to become simply 'Stevenage'.

• **Stevenage rose through the football pyramid to gain promotion to the Conference in 1994. Two years later they won the title but were denied promotion to the Football League as their tiny Broadhall Way Stadium did not meet the league's standards.**

• Stevenage finally made it into the league in 2010 after topping the Conference table with an impressive 99 points. If the club's two victories against Chester City, who were expelled from the league during the season, had not been expunged then Stevenage would have set a new Conference record of 105 points. The following season Stevenage were promoted again, after beating Torquay United 1-0 in the League Two play-off final at Old Trafford, but their three-year stay in League One ended in 2014 when they finished bottom of the pile.

• **In 2007 Stevenage became the first club to lift a trophy at the new Wembley, beating Kidderminster Harriers 3-2 in the final of the FA Trophy watched by a competition record crowd of 53,262.**

• Veteran goalkeeper Chris Day has made a record 223 appearances in the Football League for the Boro since 2010.

HONOURS
Conference champions 1996, 2010

STOKE CITY

Year founded: 1863
Ground: Bet365 Stadium (27,902)
Previous name: Stoke Ramblers, Stoke
Nickname: The Potters
Biggest win: 11-0 v Stourbridge (1914)
Heaviest defeat: 0-10 v Preston (1889)

IS THAT A FACT?
Stoke defender Ryan Shawcross has conceded a total of 10 penalties – more than any other player in Premier League history.

Founded in 1863 by employees of the North Staffordshire Railway Company, Stoke are the second oldest league club in the country. Between 1868 and 1870 the club was known as Stoke Ramblers, before simply becoming Stoke and then adding the suffix 'City' in 1925.

• **Stoke were founder members of the Football League in 1888 but finished bottom of the table at the end of the season. After another wooden spoon in 1890 the club dropped out of the league, but returned to the big time after just one season.**

• The club's greatest moment came in 1972 when they won the League Cup, beating favourites Chelsea 2-1 in the final at Wembley, thanks to a late winner by George Eastham – aged 35 and 161 days at the time, the oldest player ever to score in the League Cup final. The Potters had a great chance to add to their meagre haul of silverware in 2011 when they reached the FA Cup final for the first time, but they lost 1-0 to Manchester City. At least their fans enjoyed the semi-final, when Stoke thrashed Bolton 5-0 in the joint-biggest win yet by a club side at the new Wembley.

• **While playing in his second spell at Stoke, the great Stanley Matthews became the oldest player ever to appear in the top flight. On 6th February 1965 Matthews played his last game for the club against Fulham five days after celebrating his 50th birthday.**

• Midfielder Greg Whelan is Stoke's most capped player, with 81 appearances for the Republic of Ireland since 2008.

• **Freddie Steele is Stoke's leading scorer with 140 league goals between 1934 and 1949, including a club record 33 in the 1936/37 season. Stalwart defender Eric Skeels played in a record 507 league games for the Potters between 1960 and 1976.**

• The Potters enjoyed their best run in Europe in the 2011/12 season, when they reached the last 32 of the Europa League before going out 2-0 on aggregate to Valencia.
• In February 2016 Stoke splashed out a club record £18.3 million to bring French midfielder Giannelli Imbula to the Potteries from Porto. The club received a record £20 million in July 2017 when Austrian winger Marko Arnautovic joined West Ham.
• On 27th January 1974 Stoke became the first top-flight club to host Sunday football when they played Chelsea at their former home, the Victoria Ground. Ignoring the complaints of religious groups, a crowd of nearly 32,000 turned up to see Stoke win 1-0.
• On the final day of the 2016/17 season Stoke striker Peter Crouch became the first player ever to score 50 headers in the Premier League when he nodded in the only goal in a 1-0 win at Southampton.

HONOURS
Division 2 champions *1933, 1963*
Division 3 (North) champions *1927*
Second Division champions *1993*
League Cup *1972*
Football League Trophy *1992, 2000*

JOHN STONES

Born: Barnsley, 28th May 1994
Position: Defender
Club career:
2012-13 Barnsley 24 (0)
2013- Everton 77 (1)
2016- Manchester City 27 (0)
International record:
2014- England 18 (0)

An elegant ball-playing defender who loves to launch attacks from deep inside his own half, John Stones became the second most expensive defender in the world at the time (after David Luiz) when he signed for Manchester City from Everton for £47.5 million in July 2016. He had a decent first season at the Etihad, helping City finish third in the Premier League and qualify automatically for the Champions League.
• Stones started out with his hometown club, Barnsley, coming through the Tykes' academy before making his first-team debut against Reading in March 2012. At the start of the following year he moved to Everton for £3 million, but had to wait until August 2013 before he made his first appearance for the Toffees.
• The young defender scored his first goal for Everton in a 3-0 home defeat of Manchester United in April 2015 and that summer was the subject of three large bids from reigning Premier League champions Chelsea, all of which were rejected by the Goodison club despite Stones reportedly handing in a transfer request.
• Stones made his debut for England in a 3-0 friendly win against Peru at Wembley in May 2014. He missed out on that summer's World Cup but was an unused squad player at Euro 2016.

GORDON STRACHAN

Born: Edinburgh, 9th February 1957
Managerial career:
1996-2001 Coventry City
2001-04 Southampton
2005-09 Celtic
2009-10 Middlesbrough
2013- Scotland

Appointed as Scotland manager in January 2013, Gordon Strachan has endured a difficult time in his role, failing so far to lead his country to a first major finals since the 1998 World Cup. However, in June 2017 he came close to being the first Scotland boss since Jock Stein in 1985 to deliver a home win over arch rivals England, only for an injury-time goal from Harry Kane to level the sides' World Cup qualifier at Hampden Park.

A rare laugh for Scotland boss Gordon Strachan

• Strachan's managerial career began at Coventry in 1996 when he was still playing. The following year he became the first outfield player to appear in the Premier League aged 40. He was sacked by the Sky Blues after taking them down in 2001, but soon moved to Southampton, guiding them to their first FA Cup final in 27 years in 2003.
• In 2005, Strachan was appointed boss of Celtic. Despite losing his first match, a Champions League qualifier against Artmedia Bratislava, 5-0, the little Scot went on to enjoy huge success in Glasgow. Between 2006 and 2008 he won three successive SPL titles, a feat previously only matched by two other Celtic managers. He resigned his position after Celtic were pipped to the SPL title by arch rivals Rangers on the last day of the 2008/09 season, and then spent an unsuccessful year as Middlesbrough boss before quitting in October 2010.
• Strachan won a host of honours in his playing days as a tireless midfielder, including the European Cup Winners' Cup with Aberdeen, the FA Cup with Manchester United in 1983 and 1985 and the league title with Leeds in 1992. He also won 50 caps with Scotland.

LUIS SUAREZ

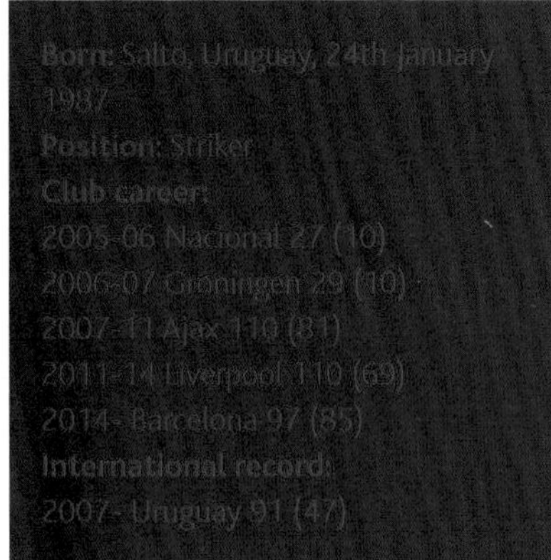
Born: Salto, Uruguay, 24th January 1987
Position: Striker
Club career:
2005-06 Nacional 27 (10)
2006-07 Groningen 29 (10)
2007-11 Ajax 110 (81)
2011-14 Liverpool 110 (69)
2014- Barcelona 97 (85)
International record:
2007- Uruguay 91 (47)

A quick-witted striker who is famed for his ability to score from the tightest of angles, Luis Suarez became the third most expensive player in football history at the time when he joined Barcelona from Liverpool in July 2014 for £75 million. He helped the Catalan giants win the Treble in 2015, scoring in the Champions League final against Juventus, and the following season won the European Golden Shoe after scoring 40 goals as Barca won another Double.

Watch out! Luis Suarez is searching for his next prey...

• Suarez enjoyed a rollercoaster three years with Liverpool after signing for the Merseysiders from Ajax for £22.8 million in January 2011. In his first full season with the Reds he helped them win the Carling Cup but, less impressively, was given an eight-match ban by the FA and fined £40,000 for racially abusing Manchester United defender Patrice Evra.

• The following season Suarez was in hot water again after he bit Chelsea defender Branislav Ivanovic on the arm in an unprovoked attack. The striker, who had been banned for seven games after a similar incident while playing for his previous club Ajax, was hit with a 10-game ban – the fifth longest in Premier League history.

• However, the Uruguayan appeared to turn over a new leaf in 2013/14 when he topped the Premier League scoring charts with 31 goals, won both Player of the Year awards and became the first player ever to score 10 Premier League goals in a month in December 2013.

• The temperamental Suarez was involved in another shocking incident at the 2014 World Cup when he bit Italy defender Giorgio Chiellini, earning a four-month ban from all football activities in the stiffest ever sanction handed out by FIFA at the World Cup for on-field misconduct. In happier days with Uruguay, Suarez was named Player of the Tournament when his country won the 2011 Copa America, and two years later he became the South Americans' all-time leading scorer.

SUBSTITUTES

Substitutes were first allowed in the Football League in the 1965/66 season. The first player to come off the bench was Charlton's Keith Peacock, who replaced injured goalkeeper Mike Rose after 11 minutes of the Addicks' match away to Bolton on 21st August 1965. On the same afternoon Barrow's Bobby Knox became the first substitute to score a goal when he notched against Wrexham.

• The fastest ever goal scored by a substitute was by Arsenal's Nicklas Bendtner, who headed in a corner against Tottenham at the Emirates on 22nd December 2007, just 1.8 seconds after replacing Emmanuel Eboue.

• The most goals ever scored in a Premier League game by a substitute is four by Ole Gunnar Solskjaer in Manchester United's 8-1 win at Nottingham Forest in 1999. Incredibly, the Norwegian striker was only on the pitch for 19 minutes. However, Jermain Defoe has scored the most Premier League goals as a sub with 23 for his various clubs. Former Newcastle forward Shola Ameobi made a record 138 appearances as a sub in the Premier League, while Bradley Wright-Phillips' first 30 appearances for Manchester City in the league were as a sub.

• Substitutes were first allowed at the World Cup in 1970, with Holland's Dick Nanninga becoming the first sub to score in the final eight years later. The most goals scored by a sub at the tournament in a single match is three by Hungary's Lazlo Kiss against El Salvador in 1982. Brazilian winger Denilson made a record 11 appearances as a substitute at the finals in 1998 and 2002.

• West Brom striker Hal Robson-Kanu made a record 24 appearances as a sub in the 2016/17 Premier League season, while Sunderland midfielder Steed Malbranque was subbed off a record 26 times in 2009/10.

TOP 10

PREMIER LEAGUE SUBSTITUTE APPEARANCES

1.	Shola Ameobi (2000-15)	138
2.	Peter Crouch (2002-)	135
3.	Jermain Defoe (2001-)	132
4.	Carlton Cole (2002-15)	121
5.	Nwankwo Kanu (1999-2010)	118
6.	Joe Cole (1999-2015)	117
7.	Ryan Giggs (1992-2014)	110
8.	Victor Anichebe (2006-17)	107
9.	Paul Scholes (1994-2013)	101
10.	Adam Johnson (2005-16)	100

• Jermain Defoe has made a record 35 substitute appearances for England since making his debut in 2004, scoring a record seven goals for the Three Lions off the bench.

• In the 2014/15 season Manchester City became the first club to use all three of their permitted substitutions in every one of their 38 Premier League matches.

SUNDERLAND

Year founded: 1879
Ground: Stadium of Light (49,000)
Previous name: Sunderland and District Teachers' AFC
Nickname: The Black Cats
Biggest win: 11-1 v Fairfield (1895)
Heaviest defeat: 0-8 v Sheffield Wednesday (1911), v West Ham (1968), v Watford (1982) and v Southampton (2014)

The club was founded as the Sunderland and District Teachers' AFC in 1879 but soon opened its ranks to other professions and became simply 'Sunderland' the following year.

• Sunderland were the first 'new' club to join the Football League, replacing Stoke in 1890. Just two years later they won their first league championship and they retained the title the following year, in the process becoming the first club to score 100 goals in a league season. In 1895 Sunderland became the first club ever to win three championships, and their status was further enhanced when they beat Scottish champions Hearts 5-3 in a one-off 'world championship' match.

• In 1958 Sunderland were relegated after a then record 57 consecutive seasons in the top flight – a benchmark which lasted until Arsenal went one better in 1983/84.

• Sunderland were the first Second Division team in the post Second World War era to win the FA Cup, beating Leeds 1-0 at Wembley in 1973 in one of the biggest upsets of all time thanks to a goal by Ian Porterfield. Incredibly, their line-up featured not one international player. The following season the Wearsiders had their one and only experience of European football, reaching the second round of the Cup Winners' Cup before losing 3-2 on aggregate to Sporting Lisbon.

• Goalkeeper Jim Montgomery, a hero of that cup-winning side, is the Black Cats' record appearance maker, turning out in 537 league games between 1960 and 1977.

• Sunderland's record victory was an 11-1 thrashing of Fairfield in the FA Cup in 1895. However, the club's best ever league win, a 9-1 demolition of eventual champions and arch rivals Newcastle at St James' Park in 1908, probably gave their fans more pleasure. To this day, it remains the biggest ever victory by an away side in the top flight.

• Sunderland last won the league championship in 1935/36, the last time, incidentally, that a team wearing stripes has topped the pile. The Wearsiders' success, though, certainly wasn't based on a solid defence... the 74 goals they conceded that season is more than any other top-flight champions before or since.

• Sunderland midfielder Jack Rodwell started a record 39 Premier League games (including two for his previous club Manchester City) over 1,370 days without once finishing on the winning side. At least his miserable run ended in fine style when the Black Cats thumped Crystal Palace 4-0 at Selhurst Park in February 2017.

• Inside forward Charlie Buchan is Sunderland's record scorer with 209 league goals between 1911 and 1925. Dave Halliday holds the record for a single season, hitting the target 43 times in 1928/29.

• Sunderland have finished rock bottom of the Premier League on three occasions – in 2003, 2006 and 2017 – to match a record first set by Nottingham Forest in the 1990s. The Black Cats are also one of just four clubs to have been relegated from the league on four separate occasions.

• The club's record signing is midfielder Didier Ndong, who cost £14 million from Lorient in August 2016.

HONOURS
Division 1 champions *1892, 1983, 1895, 1902, 1913, 1936*
Division 2 champions *1976*
Championship champions *2005, 2007*
Division 3 champions *1988*
FA Cup *1937, 1973*

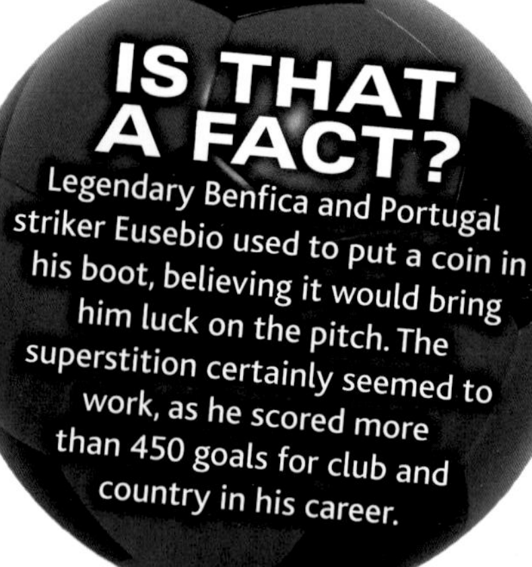

SUPERSTITIONS

Many footballers, including some of the great names of the game, are highly superstitious and believe that performing the same personal routines before every game will bring them good luck. Former England striker Gary Lineker, for instance, never shot during the warm-up as he thought it was a waste of a goal.

• Kolo Toure's superstition almost cost his then club Arsenal dear in their 2009 Champions League clash with Roma. Believing that it would be bad luck to walk out of the dressing room before team-mate William Gallas, who was receiving treatment, Toure failed to appear for the start of the second half, leaving the Gunners to restart the match with just nine players!

• Real Madrid star Cristiano Ronaldo has a number of pre-match superstitions, including always sitting in the same spot on the team bus, insisting on being the last player out on the pitch (unless he is playing for Portugal, when he is always first) and taking a slug of water after the official team photo.

• John Terry is equally superstitious. The former England captain has admitted to 'about 50' pre-match rituals, including always playing the same Usher CD in his car while driving to the stadium, parking in the same spot and wearing the same pair of shin pads.

• At the 2002 Africa Cup of Nations Cameroon coach Winfried Schafer and his assistant Thomas Nkono were arrested by police after placing a lucky charm on the pitch ahead of their team's semi-final against hosts Mali. However, the 'magic' still worked as Cameroon won the match 3-0 and went on to win the final against Senegal on penalties.

• Some superstitions are not entirely irrational. For example, Arsenal always

make sure that a new goalkeeper's jersey is washed before it is used for the first time. The policy stems from the 1927 FA Cup final, which the Gunners lost when goalkeeper Dan Lewis let in a soft goal against Cardiff. He later blamed his mistake on the ball slipping from his grasp and over the line as it brushed against the shiny surface of his new jumper.

SWANSEA CITY

Year founded: 1912
Ground: Liberty Stadium (21,088)
Previous name: Swansea Town
Nickname: The Swans
Biggest win: 12-0 v Sliema Wanderers (1982)
Heaviest defeat: 0-8 v Liverpool (1990) and v Monaco (1991)

The club was founded as Swansea Town in 1912 and entered the Football League eight years later. The present name was adopted in 1970.

• **Under former Liverpool striker John Toshack the Swans climbed from the old Fourth Division to the top flight in just four seasons between 1978 and 1981, the fastest ever ascent through the Football League. The glory days soon faded, though, and by 1986 Swansea were back in the basement division.**

• In 2011, though, Swansea beat Reading 4-2 in the Championship play-off final at Wembley to become the first Welsh club to reach the Premier League. Again, their rise was a rapid one as they had been in the basement tier just six years earlier.

• **The club's greatest day came in 2013 when they won their first major trophy, the League Cup. The Swans triumphed in fine style, too, demolishing League Two outfit Bradford City 5-0 at Wembley in the biggest ever victory in the final.**

• Ivor Allchurch is the Swans' leading scorer, banging in 166 goals in two spells at the club between 1949 and 1968. One-club man Wilfred Milne is the Swans' leading appearance maker, turning out in 586 league games between 1920 and 1937.

• **In 1961 the club became the first from Wales to compete in Europe, but were knocked out of the Cup Winners' Cup in the first round by East German side Carl Zeiss Jena. In the same competition the Swans recorded their biggest ever win over Maltese minnows Sliema Wanderers 12-0 in 1982.**

• Former skipper Ashley Williams is the Swans' most capped player, appearing 64 times for Wales between 2008 and 2016.

• **Iceland midfielder Gylfi Sigurdsson is the most expensive player to leave the Swans, signing for Everton for £45 million in August 2017.**

HONOURS
Division 3 (South) champions 1925, 1949
League One champions 2008
Third Division champions 2000
League Cup 2013
Football League Trophy 1994, 2006
Welsh Cup 1913, 1932, 1950, 1961, 1966, 1981, 1982, 1983, 1989, 1991

No player traps the ball better on his nose than Swansea's Martin Olsson

SWINDON TOWN

Year founded: 1879
Ground: The County Ground (15,728)
Previous name: Swindon Spartans
Nickname: The Robins
Biggest win: 10-1 v Farnham United Breweries (1925)
Heaviest defeat: 1-10 v Manchester City (1930)

The club was founded by the Reverend William Pitt in 1879, becoming Swindon Spartans two years later before adopting the name Swindon Town in 1883. In 1920 Swindon were founder members of the Third Division, kicking off their league career with a 9-1 thrashing of Luton.

• **The Robins' finest moment came in 1969 when, as a Third Division club, they beat mighty Arsenal 3-1 in the League Cup final on a mud-clogged Wembley pitch. Legendary winger Don Rogers was the star of the show, scoring two of Swindon's goals.**

• In 1993, three years after being denied promotion to the top flight for the first time because of a financial scandal, Swindon earned promotion to the Premiership via the play-offs. The following campaign, though, proved to be a miserable one as the Robins finished bottom of the pile and conceded 100 goals... a record for the Premier League.

• **Relegated to League Two in 2017, Swindon won the Fourth Division title in 1985/86 with a then Football League best 102 points, a total which remains a record for the bottom tier.**

• John Trollope is Swindon's longest serving player, appearing in 770 league games for the club between 1960 and 1980 – a record for a single club.

HONOURS
Second Division champions 1996
Division 4 champions 1986
League Two champions 2012
League Cup 1969

JOHN TERRY

Born: Barking, 7th December 1980
Position: Defender
Club career:
1998-2017 Chelsea 492 (41)
2000 Nottingham Forest (loan) 6 (0)
2017- Aston Villa
International record:
2003-12 England 78 (6)

John Terry is the most successful captain in the history of the Premier League, skippering Chelsea to five title triumphs before leaving the club in May 2017 after a final table-topping campaign. Two years earlier, in 2014/15, he became only the second outfield player (after Manchester United defender Gary Pallister in 1992/93) to play every minute of a Premier League-winning campaign.

• Now on the books of Aston Villa, JT, as he is known to fans and team-mates alike, also won five FA Cups and three League Cups in his 19-year career with the Blues. In 2012, despite being suspended for the final against Bayern Munich, he added the Champions League to that list, making up for his disappointment four years earlier when he slipped and put his penalty wide in the shoot-out against Manchester United in the final in Moscow.

• A superb tackler who reads the game well, Terry was voted PFA Player of the Year in 2005 after leading the Blues to the first of their back-to-back Premiership titles. His total of 717 games for Chelsea in all competitions is only bettered by Peter Bonetti (729) and Ron 'Chopper' Harris (795).

IS THAT A FACT?
With 41 goals to his name, John Terry is the highest-scoring defender in Premier League history.

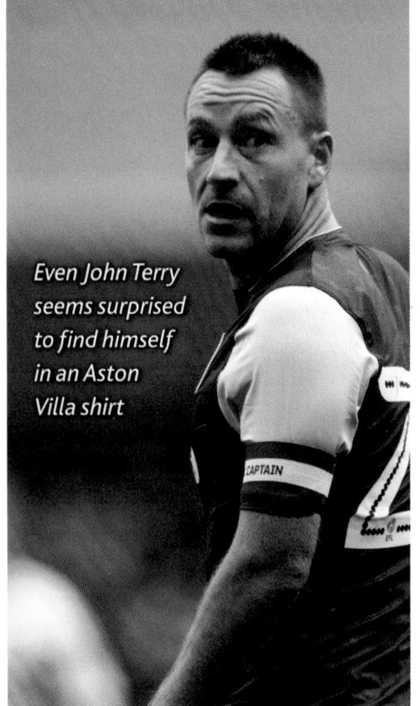

Even John Terry seems surprised to find himself in an Aston Villa shirt

• After making his England debut in 2003, Terry went on to represent his country at Euro 2004 and Euro 2012, the 2006 World Cup – where he was the only England player to be selected for the all-star FIFA squad at the end of the tournament – and the 2010 World Cup.

• He was first appointed England captain by Steve McClaren in 2006 and retained the role under Fabio Capello. However, in February 2010 Terry was sensationally stripped of the armband following newspaper revelations about his private life. The following year, though, he reclaimed the captaincy only for the FA to take it off him again in February 2012 after he was charged by police for racially abusing QPR defender Anton Ferdinand earlier in the season. Terry was acquitted at his trial, but when the FA charged him with the same offence he decided to retire from international football.

THROW-INS

Thomas Gronnemark from Denmark holds the world record for the longest ever throw. Employing a forward hand spring technique he hurled the ball an incredible 51.33 metres on 18th June 2010.

• The player with the longest throw in football is former Serbian Under-21 international Ljubo Baranin, who can easily hurl the ball beyond the far post from a position near a corner flag. In England, the most famous long throw specialist in the Premier League era is former Stoke midfielder Rory Delap, a one-time schoolboy javelin champion, who could hurl the ball deep into the opposition box from as far away as the halfway line.

• The most bizarre goal from a throw-in came in a derby between Birmingham City and Aston Villa in 2002. Villa defender Olof Mellberg threw the ball back to goalkeeper Peter Enckelman and it dribbled under his foot and into the net. Despite Villa's protests, referee David Elleray ruled that the goal should stand because Enckelman had made contact with the ball.

• In the 2016/17 season Leicester City made the least effective use of their throw-ins, gifting the ball back to the opposition an incredible 297 times. At the other end of the scale, Arsenal only threw the ball to their opponents 71 times in total.

TOTTENHAM HOTSPUR

Year founded: 1882
Ground: Wembley stadium (90,000)
Previous name: Hotspur FC
Nickname: Spurs
Biggest win: 13-2 v Crewe (1960)
Heaviest defeat: 0-8 v Cologne (1995)

The club was founded as Hotspur FC in 1882 by a group of local cricketers, most of whom were former pupils of Tottenham Grammar School. Three years later the club decided to add the prefix 'Tottenham'.

• Tottenham were members of the Southern League when they won the FA Cup for the first time in 1901, defeating Sheffield United 3-1 in a replay at Bolton's Burnden Park. Spurs' victory meant they were the first (and, so far, only) non-league club to win the cup since the formation of the Football League in 1888.

• In 1961 Tottenham created history when they became the first club in the 20th century to win the fabled league and cup Double. Their title success was based on a storming start to the season, Bill Nicholson's side winning their first 11 games to set a top-flight record which has not been matched since. By the end of the campaign, the north Londoners had won 31 of their 42 league matches to create another record for the top tier.

• As Arsenal fans like to point out, Tottenham have failed to win the league since those 'Glory, Glory' days of skipper Danny Blanchflower, Dave Mackay and Cliff Jones. Spurs, though, have continued to enjoy cup success, and their total of eight victories in the FA Cup is only surpassed by the Gunners and Manchester United. Remarkably, five of those triumphs came in years ending in a '1', giving rise to the legend that these seasons were particularly lucky for Spurs.

• Tottenham have also enjoyed much success in the League Cup, winning the competition four times. The last of these triumphs, in 2008 following a 2-1 defeat of holders Chelsea in the final, saw Tottenham become the first club to win the League Cup at the new Wembley.

• Spurs have a decent record in Europe, too. In 1963 they thrashed Atletico Madrid 5-1 in the final of the European Cup Winners' Cup, striker Jimmy Greaves grabbing a brace, to become the first British club to win a European trophy. Then, in 1972, Tottenham defeated Wolves 3-2 on aggregate in the first ever UEFA Cup final and the first European final to feature two English clubs. A third European triumph followed in 1984 when Tottenham beat Anderlecht in the first UEFA Cup final to be settled by penalties. Spurs' average of 2.1 goals per game in Europe is the best of any English club.

• Ace marksman Jimmy Greaves holds two goalscoring records for Tottenham. His total of 220 league goals between 1961 and 1970 is a club best, as is his impressive tally of 37 league goals in 1962/63. Clive Allen, though, struck an incredible total of 49 goals in all competitions in 1986/87, including a record 12 in the League Cup.

• Stalwart defender Steve Perryman is the club's longest serving player, pulling on the famous white shirt in 655 league games between 1969 and 1986, including 613 in the old First Division – a top-flight record for a player at a single club. His team-mate Pat Jennings is the club's most decorated international, winning 74 of his record 119 caps for Northern Ireland while at the Lane.

• In August 2013 Spurs received a then world record transfer fee of £86 million from Real Madrid for Welsh winger Gareth Bale. The club's record buy is Colombian defender Davinson Sanchez, who cost £42 million from Ajax in August 2017.

• Tottenham's first title success was in 1950/51 when Arthur Rowe's stylish 'Push and Run' team topped the table just one year after winning the Second Division championship. In the years since, only Ipswich Town (in 1961 and 1962) have managed to claim the top two titles in consecutive seasons.

• Spurs finished a best ever second in the Premier League in 2016/17 with a goal difference of +60 – a record for a club not winning the title.

• Spurs' incredible 9-1 trouncing of Wigan on 22nd November 2009 was only the second time a club had scored nine goals in a Premier League game. Jermain Defoe struck five times after half-time to set a Premier League record for the most goals scored in a single half.

• In 2017 Tottenham moved to Wembley for a season while the finishing touches were put to their new 61,559-capacity stadium at White Hart Lane. Previously, only Leyton Orient, in 1930, had played home league matches at the national stadium.

HONOURS

Division 1 champions *1951, 1961*
Division 2 champions *1920, 1950*
FA Cup *1901, 1921, 1961, 1962, 1967, 1981, 1982, 1991*
League Cup *1971, 1973, 1999, 2008*
Double *1961*
European Cup Winners' Cup *1963*
UEFA Cup *1972, 1984*

Forget 'big club'... Tottenham are giant-sized!

After splashing out a world record £200 million on Neymar, PSG couldn't actually afford any other players...

PREMIER LEAGUE TRANSFERS

1. **Paul Pogba (Juventus to Manchester United, 2016) £89.3 million**
2. **Romelu Lukaku (Everton to Manchester United, 2017) £75 million**
3. **Alvaro Morata (Real Madrid to Chelsea, 2017) £60 million**
4. **Angel Di Maria (Real Madrid to Manchester United, 2014) £59.7 million**
5. **Kevin De Bruyne (Wolfsburg to Manchester City, 2015) £54.5 million**
6. **Benjamin Mendy (Monaco to Manchester City, 2017) £52 million**
7. **Fernando Torres (Liverpool to Chelsea, 2011) £50 million**
8. **Raheem Sterling (Liverpool to Manchester City, 2015) £49 million**
9. **John Stones (Everton to Manchester City, 2016) £47.5 million**
10. **Alexandre Lacazette (Lyon to Arsenal, 2017) £46.5 million**

TRANSFERS

The world's most expensive player is Brazilian striker Neymar, who moved from Barcelona to Paris Saint-Germain in August 2017 for an incredible £200 million, more than double the previous record set a year earlier when Paul Pogba joined Manchester United from Juventus for £89.3 million.

• Premier League clubs spent £1.4 billion on new players during the summer of 2017, a record for a single transfer window. The total of £210 million spent by Premier League clubs on deadline day eclipsed the previous record of £155 million set in the summer of 2016.

• The world's most expensive goalkeeper is Ederson Moraes, who joined Manchester City from Benfica for £35 million in June 2017.

• In the summer of 2011 Chelsea paid Porto £13.3 million in compensation to Porto after appointing Andre Villas-Boas as their new boss. The record transfer fee for a manager proved to be a bit of a waste of money, as Villas-Boas was sacked early the following year.

• Milene Domingues, the then wife of Brazil star Ronaldo, became the most expensive female footballer in the world when she moved from Italian side Fiamma Monza to Atletico Madrid Feminas for £200,000 in September 2002. Chelsea Ladies set a new British transfer record in July 2015 when they bought striker Fran Kirby from Reading for around £60,000.

TV AND RADIO

The first ever live radio broadcast of a football match was on 22nd January 1927 when the BBC covered the First Division encounter between Arsenal and Sheffield United at Highbury. The *Radio Times* printed a pitch marked into numbered squares, which the commentators used to describe where the ball was at any given moment (which some suggest gave rise to the phrase 'back to square one').

• The 1937 FA Cup final between Sunderland and Preston was the first to be televised, although only parts of the match were shown by the BBC. The following year's final between Preston and Huddersfield was the first to be screened live and in full, although the audience was only around 10,000 as so few people had TV sets at the time.

• The biggest British TV audience ever for a football match (and, indeed, the biggest ever for any TV broadcast in this country) was 32.3 million for the 1966 World Cup final between England and West Germany. The viewing figures for the match, which was shown live by both BBC and ITV, were all the more remarkable as only 15 million households in the UK had TV sets. The biggest worldwide TV audience for any football match is 3.2 billion for the 2014 World Cup final between Germany and Argentina.

• The BBC's *Match of the Day* is the longest-running football programme in the world. It was first transmitted on 22nd August 1964 when highlights of Arsenal's trip to Liverpool were broadcast to an audience estimated to be around 20,000.

• The TV deal between Sky, BT and the Premier League which started in the 2016/17 season is the biggest in the history of the game. Under the terms of the deal the two companies will pay £5.136 billion over three years to show 168 live games per season – a 71 per cent increase on the previous three-year agreement. The Premier League's biggest deal outside of the UK is with Chinese digital broadcaster PPTV, who will pay £564 million over three years from the start of the 2019/20 season.

TWITTER

Cristiano Ronaldo has more followers on Twitter than any other footballer in the world, with over 56 million at the last count – putting him ahead of the likes of Ariana Grande, Shakira and even US President Donald Trump. Ronaldo, though, can't compete with the world's most popular Twitter celebrity, the singer Katy Perry, who has more than 100 million followers.

• The 2014 World Cup semi-final between hosts Brazil and Germany generated an incredible 35.6 million tweets – a record for a sporting event.

• Arsenal midfielder Mesut Ozil is the most popular Premier League footballer on Twitter, his 15.7 million followers putting him just ahead of Wayne Rooney (14.8 million).

• Chelsea defender Ashley Cole was fined a record £90,000 for a tweet in October 2012, when he posted abusive comments about the FA after the governing body had questioned the truth of his statements in the John Terry race abuse inquiry.

• The most popular football club on Twitter are Real Madrid, with 24 million followers, followed by Barcelona (22 million).

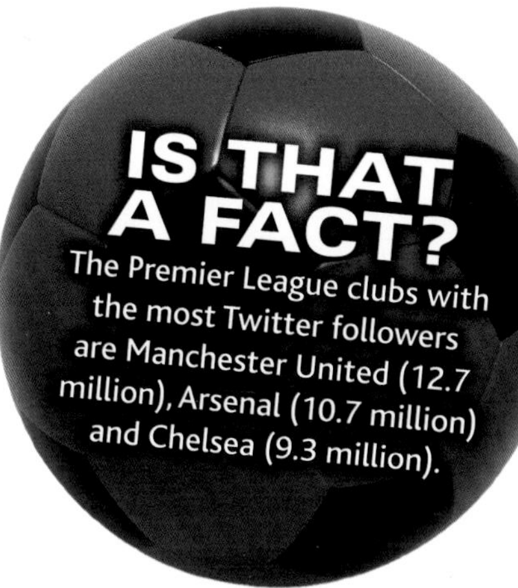

IS THAT A FACT?

The Premier League clubs with the most Twitter followers are Manchester United (12.7 million), Arsenal (10.7 million) and Chelsea (9.3 million).

UEFA

UEFA, the Union of European Football Associations, was founded in 1954 at a meeting in Basel during the Swiss World Cup. Holding power over all the national FAs in Europe, with 55 members it is the largest and most influential of the six continental confederations of FIFA.

• UEFA competitions include the Champions League (first won as the European Cup by Real Madrid), the Europa League (formerly the UEFA Cup) and the UEFA Super Cup.

• The longest serving UEFA President is Sweden's Lennart Johansson, who did the job for 17 years between 1990 and 2007. In 2015 the then President, former French international Michel Platini, was forced to step down after an investigation by FIFA's Ethics Committee and was replaced the following year by Slovenian lawyer Aleksander Ceferin.

• Controversial UEFA decisions in the past include the introduction of penalty kicks to decide drawn European ties (from 1970) and the ban on English clubs competing in European competitions for five years from 1985 after the Heysel tragedy.

URUGUAY

First international: Uruguay 2 Argentina 3, 1901
Most capped player: Maxi Pereira, 120 caps (2005-)
Leading goalscorer: Luis Suarez, 47 goals (2007-)
First World Cup appearance: Uruguay 1 Peru 0, 1930
Biggest win: Uruguay 9 Bolivia 0, 1927
Heaviest defeat: Uruguay 0 Argentina 6, 1902

In 1930 Uruguay became the first winners of the World Cup, beating arch rivals Argentina 4-2 in the final on home soil in Montevideo. The match was a repeat of the Olympic final of 1928, which Uruguay had also won. In terms of population, Uruguay is easily the smallest nation ever to win the World Cup.

• In 1950 Uruguay won the World Cup for a second time, defeating hosts Brazil 2-1 in 'the final' (it was actually the last and decisive match in a four-team final group). The match was watched by a massive crowd of 199,854 in the Maracana Stadium in Rio de Janeiro, the largest ever to attend a football match anywhere in the world.

• Uruguay set a record at the 1970 World Cup when they started their group game with Italy with no fewer than eight players from the same club, Montevideo outfit Nacional. Although they only managed to draw 0-0 the South Americans went on to reach the semi-finals before losing 3-1 to neighbours Brazil.

• At the 2010 World Cup in South Africa Uruguay again finished fourth. However, their campaign is mostly remembered for a blatant handball on the line by striker Luis Suarez, which denied their opponents Ghana a certain winning goal in the teams' quarter-final clash.

• Uruguay are the most successful team in the history of the Copa America. Winners of the inaugural tournament in 1916, Uruguay have won the competition a total of 15 times, most recently lifting the trophy in 2011 after beating Paraguay 3-0 in the final.

HONOURS
***World Cup winners** 1930, 1950*
***Copa America winners** 1916, 1917, 1920, 1923, 1924, 1926, 1935, 1942, 1956, 1959, 1967, 1983, 1987, 1995, 2011*
World Cup Record
1930 Winners
1934 Did not enter
1938 Did not enter
1950 Winners
1954 Fourth place
1958 Did not qualify
1962 Round 1
1966 Quarter-finals
1970 Fourth place
1974 Round 1
1978 Did not qualify
1982 Did not qualify
1986 Round 2
1990 Round 2
1994 Did not qualify
1998 Did not qualify
2002 Round 1
2006 Did not qualify
2010 Fourth place
2014 Round 2

JAMIE VARDY

Born: Sheffield, 11th January 1987
Position: Striker
Club career:
2007-10 Stocksbridge Park Steels 107 (66)
2010-11 Halifax Town 37 (27)
2011-12 Fleetwood Town 36 (31)
2012- Leicester City 168 (62)
International record:
2015- England 16 (6)

In 2016 Jamie Vardy became the first ever Leicester City player to be voted Footballer of the Year by the football writers after his 24 goals helped fire the Foxes to the Premier League title. He also scored in 11 consecutive Premier League games to set a new record for the league.

• Vardy struggled to replicate that form the following season, but he still ended up with a respectable 13 Premier League goals, including a first ever professional hat-trick in a 4-2 win against Manchester City.

• Vardy started out on £30 per week with non-league Stocksbridge Park Steels after being rejected by Sheffield Wednesday for being too short. Following spells with Halifax Town and Fleetwood Town, with whom he was top scorer in the Conference in 2011/12 with 31 goals, the Sheffield-born striker moved to Leicester City in the summer of 2012 for £1 million – a record fee for a non-league player. After initially struggling to adjust to higher level football, Vardy enjoyed a superb season in 2013/14, scoring 16 league goals as the Foxes claimed the Championship title.

• A hard-working, pacy and clinical striker who loves to chase after long balls, Vardy made his England debut as a sub in a 0-0 friendly draw with the Republic of Ireland in June 2015. The following year he scored his first goal for his country with a clever backheel flick in a 3-2 win against Germany in Berlin, and he was also on the scoresheet in England's 2-1 victory over Wales at Euro 2016.

Jamie Vardy never stops chasing the ball – even when it goes completely out of focus!

THEO WALCOTT

Born: Stanmore, 16th March 1989
Position: Winger/striker
Club career:
2005-06 Southampton 21 (4)
2006- Arsenal 260 (65)
International record:
2006- England 47 (8)

Arsenal winger Theo Walcott is the youngest ever player to represent England, making his debut as a substitute against Hungary at Old Trafford in 2006 when he was aged just 17 years and 75 days.

• The speedy wideman was soon setting more records for England, becoming the youngest player to notch a hat-trick for his country when he banged in three goals against Croatia in a World Cup qualifier in Zagreb in 2008, and finishing on the winning side in his first 14 internationals – the best ever such run by an England player. However, his inconsistent performances have seen him left out of the England squads for a number of tournaments, including the 2016 European Championships.

• Walcott began his career at Southampton and is the youngest player ever to appear for the Saints, making his debut as a sub against Wolves in 2005 when he was still 16.

Thanks to players like Gareth Bale, Wales have been flying in recent years

• After impressing with some dynamic displays for the south coast club, Walcott moved to Arsenal in 2006 for an eventual fee of £9.1 million, making him the most expensive 16-year-old in the history of the British game. He opened his account for the Gunners the following year in the League Cup final against Chelsea, to become the second youngest scorer in the final of the competition.

• However, Walcott didn't earn his first silverware with the Gunners until 2015, when Arsenal thrashed Aston Villa 4-0 in the FA Cup final at Wembley. It was the England man, too, who opened the scoring with a superb left-foot volley that flew past Villa keeper Shay Given. Two years later Walcott scored his 100th goal for the Gunners in the same competition in a 2-0 win against non-league Sutton United, but he was only an unused substitute when Arsenal beat Chelsea in the final.

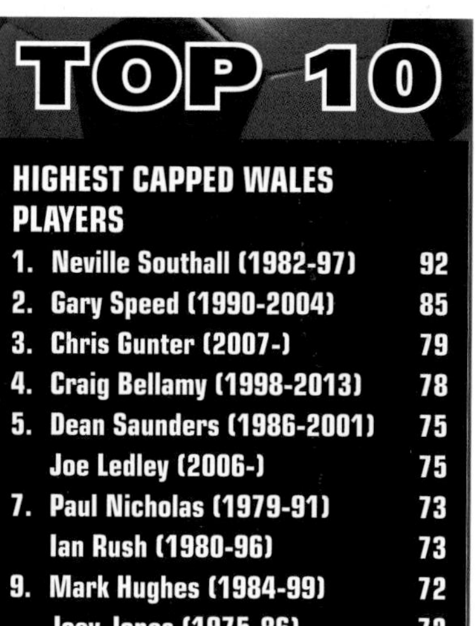

TOP 10

HIGHEST CAPPED WALES PLAYERS

1.	Neville Southall (1982-97)	92
2.	Gary Speed (1990-2004)	85
3.	Chris Gunter (2007-)	79
4.	Craig Bellamy (1998-2013)	78
5.	Dean Saunders (1986-2001)	75
	Joe Ledley (2006-)	75
7.	Paul Nicholas (1979-91)	73
	Ian Rush (1980-96)	73
9.	Mark Hughes (1984-99)	72
	Joey Jones (1975-86)	72

WALES

First international: Scotland 4 Wales 0, 1876
Most capped player: Neville Southall, 92 caps (1982-98)
Leading goalscorer: Ian Rush, 28 goals (1980-96)
First World Cup appearance: Wales 1 Hungary 1, 1958
Biggest win: Wales 11 Ireland 0, 1888
Heaviest defeat: Scotland 9 Wales 0, 1878

Wales have only qualified for two major international tournaments, but on both occasions did their loyal fans more than proud. The country's finest moment came at Euro 2016 in France when a Welsh side including the likes of Gareth Bale, Aaron Ramsey and skipper Ashley Williams defied the odds to reach the last four.

• Despite losing to England in their second match, Wales topped their group after impressive victories against Slovakia and Russia. Following a narrow 1-0 win over Northern Ireland in the last 16, Wales produced a superb performance against Belgium in the quarter-finals, coming from a goal down to triumph 3-1. However, they were unable to repeat those heroics in the semi-final, losing 2-0 to eventual winners Portugal.

• Wales' only other tournament experience came in 1958 when a side including such great names as John Charles, Ivor Allchurch, Cliff Jones and Jack Kelsey qualified for the World Cup finals in Sweden after beating Israel in a two-legged play-off. After drawing all three of their group matches, Wales then beat Hungary in a play-off to reach the quarter-finals where they lost 1-0 to eventual winners Brazil.

• Wales winger Billy Meredith is the oldest international in the history of British football. He was aged 45 years and 229 days when he won the last of

his 48 caps against England in 1920, a quarter of a century after making his international debut. Six months earlier he scored in a 2-1 win against England, to set a record for the oldest scorer in an international match (45 years and 73 days) which still stands today.

• Wales' youngest player is Liverpool's Harry Wilson, who was aged 16 and 207 days when he made his debut as a sub against Belgium in October 2013. Having spotted his interest in football when he was just 18 months old, Wilson's grandfather had put a £50 bet on him playing international football at odds of 2,500/1 – and collected a cool £125,000 when the youngster made his three-minute cameo appearance for the Dragons!

World Cup Record
1930-38 Did not enter
1950-54 Did not qualify
1958 Quarter-finals
1962-2014 Did not qualify

KYLE WALKER

Born: Sheffield, 28th May 1990
Position: Defender
Club career:
2008-09 Sheffield United 2 (0)
2008 Northampton Town (loan) 9 (0)
2009-17 Tottenham Hotspur 183 (4)
2009-10 Sheffield United (loan) 26 (0)
2010-11 QPR (loan) 20 (0)
2011 Aston Villa (loan) 15 (1)
2017- Manchester City
International record:
2011- England 27 (0)

An athletic right-back who enjoys surging forward from deep, Kyle Walker became the second most expensive British defender ever (after John Stones) when he moved from Tottenham to Manchester City for an initial £45 million in July 2017.

• Walker joined Sheffield United, his local club, when he was aged just seven, eventually going on to make his first-team debut in an FA Cup tie against Leyton Orient in January 2009. Later that year he became the youngest ever Blades player to appear at Wembley, when he turned out for United in their Championship play-off final defeat against Burnley three days short of his 19th birthday.

• That summer he joined Tottenham along with team-mate Kyle Naughton for a combined fee of £9 million, but was immediately loaned back to the Yorkshire outfit. Further loans at QPR and Aston Villa followed before Walker cemented his place in the Tottenham line-up at the start of the 2011/12 season. At the end of the campaign he was voted PFA Young Player of the Year.

• While representing England at Under-21 level Walker was named in the Team of the Tournament at the 2011 European Under-21 Championships. Later that year he made his senior debut as a sub in a 1-0 friendly win over Spain at Wembley and he is now established as England's first-choice right-back.

WALSALL

Year founded: 1888
Ground: Banks's Stadium (11,300)
Previous name: Walsall Town Swifts
Nickname: The Saddlers
Biggest win: 10-0 v Darwen (1899)
Heaviest defeat: 0-12 v Small Heath (1892) and v Darwen (1896)

The club was founded in 1888 as Walsall Town Swifts, following an amalgamation of Walsall Swifts and Walsall Town. Founder members of the Second Division in 1892, the club changed to its present name three years later.

• Walsall have never played in the top flight, but they have a history of producing momentous cup shocks, the most famous coming back in 1933 when they sensationally beat eventual league champions Arsenal 2-0 in the FA Cup. The Saddlers' best run in the League Cup, meanwhile, came in 1984 when they reached the semi-finals before losing 4-2 on aggregate to eventual winners Liverpool.

• Two players share the distinction of being Walsall's all-time leading scorer: Tony Richards, who notched 184 league goals for the club between 1954 and 1963, and his strike partner Colin Taylor, who banged in exactly the same number in three spells with the Saddlers between 1958 and 1973.

• After 127 years Walsall finally made it to Wembley in 2015 when they reached the final of the Football League Trophy. Sadly for their fans, the day did not end happily as the Saddlers lost 2-0 to Bristol City.

• Goalkeeper Mick Kearns played in a club record 15 internationals for the Republic of Ireland while with Walsall between 1973 and 1979.

HONOURS
***Division 4 champions** 1960*
***League Two champions** 2007*

WATFORD

Year founded: 1881
Ground: Vicarage Road (21,500)
Previous name: Watford Rovers, West Herts
Nickname: The Hornets
Biggest win: 10-1 v Lowestoft Town (1926)
Heaviest defeat: 0-10 v Wolves (1912)

Founded as Watford Rovers in 1881, the club changed its name to West Herts in 1893. Five years later, following a merger with Watford St Mary's, the club became Watford FC.

• The club's history was fairly nondescript until pop star Elton John became chairman in 1976 and invested a large part of his personal wealth in the team. With future England manager Graham Taylor at the helm, the Hornets rose from the Fourth to the First Division in just five years, and reached the FA Cup final in 1984. In the late 1990s Taylor returned to the club and worked his magic again, guiding the Hornets to two successive promotions and a brief taste of life in the Premiership.

• After finishing second in the old First Division in 1983, Watford made their one foray into Europe, reaching the third round of the UEFA Cup before losing 7-2 on aggregate to Sparta Prague.

• Luther Blissett, one of the star players of that period, is the club's record appearance maker. In three spells at Vicarage Road the energetic striker notched up 415 league appearances and scored 148 league goals (also a club record).

• In the 1959/60 season striker Cliff Holton scored a club record 42 league goals for the Hornets, helping them gain promotion from the third tier.

• England winger John Barnes and Wales defender Kenny Jackett made a club record 31 appearances each for their respective countries while with Watford in the 1980s.

• In August 2017 the Hornets splashed out £18.5 million on Burnley striker Andre Gray, their most expensive signing ever. In January 2017 the Hertfordshire side received a record £20 million when striker Odion Ighalo joined Chinese Super League side Changchun Yatai.

For the first time ever, Wembley hosted Premier League football in 2017

• In May 2007 Watford goalkeeper Alec Chamberlain became the second oldest player in Premier League history when he came off the bench against Newcastle aged 42 years and 327 days.

• In 2015 Watford became the first club to gain promotion to the Premier League after employing four managers during the season. Giuseppe Sannino, Oscar Garcia and Billy McKinlay were all briefly in the Vicarage Road hotseat before former Chelsea midfielder Slavisa Jokanovic steadied the ship and guided the Hornets to second place in the Championship.

HONOURS
Division 3 champions *1969*
Second Division champions *1998*
Division 4 champions *1978*

WEMBLEY STADIUM

Built at a cost of £798 million, the new Wembley Stadium is the most expensive sporting venue ever. With a capacity of 90,000, it is also the second largest in Europe and the largest in the world to have every seat under cover.

• The stadium's most spectacular feature is a 315m-wide arch, the world's longest unsupported roof structure. Wembley also boasts a staggering 2,618 toilets, more than any other venue in the world.

• Originally scheduled to open in 2003, the stadium was not completed until 2007 due to a variety of financial and legal difficulties. The first professional match was played at the new venue on 17th March 2007 when England Under-21s met their Italian counterparts, with the first goal arriving after just 28 seconds when Giampaolo Pazzini struck for the visitors. Half an hour later, David Bentley became the first Englishman to score at the new stadium.

• Chelsea have played at the new stadium a record 17 times, while Arsenal played a record 41 times at the old stadium.

• The first Wembley Stadium was opened in 1923, having been constructed in just 300 days at a cost of £750,000. The first match played at the venue was the 1923 FA Cup final between Bolton and West Ham, although the kick-off

was delayed for nearly an hour when thousands of fans spilled onto the pitch because of overcrowding in the stands.

• **Tottenham moved into Wembley for the 2017/18 season on a full-time basis while construction work continued on their new stadium at White Hart Lane. Spurs had previously played four European games at Wembley during the 2016/17 campaign, but only managed to win one of these encounters.**

• Arsenal and England defender Tony Adams played a record 60 games at Wembley between 1987 and 2000, a total boosted by the fact that the Gunners used the stadium for their home games in the Champions League in the late 1990s.

ARSÈNE WENGER

Born: Strasbourg, France, 22nd October 1949
Managerial career:
1984-87 Nancy
1987-94 Monaco
1995-96 Nagoya Grampus Eight
1996- Arsenal

Arsenal boss Arsène Wenger is the most successful manager in the history of the FA Cup, having won the trophy a record seven times, most recently guiding the Gunners to victory over Chelsea in the 2017 final. However, after overseeing an English record run of 19 consecutive participations in the Champions League he had to be satisfied with a Europa League slot for the 2017/18 season when Arsenal could only finish fifth in the Premier League.

• **After a modest playing career which included a stint with his local club Strasbourg, Wenger cut his managerial teeth with Nancy before moving to Monaco in 1987. He won the league title in his first season there, with a team including English stars Glenn Hoddle and Mark Hateley, and the French Cup in 1991.**

• Following a year in Japan with Nagoya Grampus Eight, Wenger arrived in north London in September 1996. In his first full season at Highbury he became the first non-British manager to win the league and cup Double, and he repeated this accomplishment in 2002.

• **His greatest achievement, though, came in 2004 when his Arsenal side won the title for a third time after going through the entire Premiership season undefeated. Wenger's 'Invincibles', as they were dubbed, were hailed as the greatest team in English football history, not only for their record 49-game unbeaten run but also for their fluid attacking style of play which made the most of exceptional talents like Thierry Henry, Dennis Bergkamp and Patrick Vieira.**

Arsène Wenger shows off his keepy-uppy skills

• Easily the longest serving manager in England, Wenger is one of just four managers in English post-war football to be in charge for 1,000 matches with the same club. He reached the landmark when Arsenal played at Chelsea on 22nd March 2014 – but it turned out to be a day to forget as the Gunners crashed to a humbling 6-0 defeat.

WEST BROMWICH ALBION

Year founded: 1878
Ground: The Hawthorns (26,852)
Previous name: West Bromwich Strollers
Nickname: The Baggies
Biggest win: 12-0 v Darwen (1892)
Heaviest defeat: 3-10 v Stoke City (1937)

Founded as West Bromwich Strollers in 1878 by workers at the local Salter's Spring Works, the club adopted the suffix 'Albion' two years later and were founder members of the Football League in 1888.

• **The Baggies were the first club to lose two consecutive FA Cup finals, going down to Blackburn Rovers in 1886 and Aston Villa the following year. In 1888, though, West Brom recorded the first of their five triumphs in the cup, beating favourites Preston 2-1 in the final.**

• In 1931 West Brom became the first and only club to win promotion and the FA Cup in the same season. The Baggies came close to repeating this particular double in 2008 when they topped the Championship, but were beaten in the FA Cup semi-final by eventual winners Portsmouth.

• **West Brom claimed their only league title in 1920, in the first post-First World War season. The 60 points they amassed that season and the 104 goals they scored were both records at the time. The club's manager at the time, Fred Everiss, was in charge at** the Hawthorns from 1902-48, his 46-year stint being the longest in English football history.**

• In 1966 West Brom won the last League Cup final to be played over two legs, overcoming West Ham 5-3 on aggregate. The next year they appeared in the first one-off final at Wembley, but surprisingly lost 3-2 to Third Division QPR after leading 2-0 at half-time.

• The Baggies, though, returned to Wembley the following season and beat Everton 1-0 in the FA Cup final. West Brom's winning goal was scored in extra-time by club legend Jeff Astle, who in the process became one of just 12 players to have scored in every round of the competition. Astle also found the target in his side's 2-1 defeat by Manchester City in the 1970 League Cup final to become the first player to score in both domestic cup finals at Wembley.

• In 1892 West Brom thrashed Darwen 12-0 to record their biggest ever win. The score set a record for the top flight which has never been beaten, although Nottingham Forest equalled it in 1909.

• Cult hero Tony 'Bomber' Brown is West Brom's record scorer with 218 league goals to his name. The attacking midfielder is also the club's longest serving player, turning out in 574 league games between 1963 and 1980.

• The Baggies' most capped player is midfielder Chris Brunt, who has played 47 times for Northern Ireland since joining the club from Sheffield Wednesday in 2007.

• West Brom's record purchase is Belgian international midfielder Nacer Chadli, who joined the Baggies from Tottenham Hotspur for £13 million in August 2016. The club's bank balance was boosted by a record £15 million when striker Saido Berahino joined Stoke City in January 2017.

• With an average age of 29 and 322 days, West Brom's team was the oldest in the Premier League in the 2016/17 season.

HONOURS
Division 1 champions *1920*
Division 2 champions *1902, 1911*
Championship champions *2008*
FA Cup *1888, 1892, 1931, 1954, 1968*
League Cup *1966*

WEST HAM UNITED

Year founded: 1895
Ground: London Stadium (60,000)
Previous name: Thames Ironworks
Nickname: The Hammers
Biggest win: 10-0 v Bury (1983)
Heaviest defeat: 2-8 v Blackburn (1963)

The club was founded in 1895 as Thames Ironworks by shipyard workers employed by a company of the same name. In 1900 the club was disbanded but immediately reformed under its present name.

• The biggest and best supported club in east London, West Ham have a proud tradition in the FA Cup. In 1923 they reached the first final to be played at the original Wembley Stadium, losing 2-0 to Bolton Wanderers.

• The Hammers experienced a more enjoyable Wembley 'first' in 1965 when they became the first English side to

West Ham want to enjoy that soaring feeling a bit more often

win a European trophy on home soil, defeating Munich 1860 2-0 in the final of the Cup Winners' Cup.

• The following year West Ham were the only club to provide three members – Bobby Moore, Geoff Hurst and Martin Peters – of England's World Cup-winning team. Between them Hurst and Peters scored all four of England's goals in the final against West Germany while Moore, as captain, collected the trophy.

• Striker Vic Watson holds three significant goalscoring records for the club. He is West Ham's leading scorer, with an impressive 298 league goals between 1920 and 1935, including a record 42 goals in the 1929/30 season. In the same campaign Watson hit a record six goals in a match, a feat later equalled by Geoff Hurst in an 8-0 drubbing of Sunderland at Upton Park in 1968.

• No West Ham player has turned out more often for the club than former manager Billy Bonds. Between 1967 and 1988 'Bonzo', as he was dubbed by fans and team-mates alike, appeared in 663 league games.

• In 1980 West Ham became the last club from outside the top flight to win the FA Cup. The Hammers, then residing in the old Second Division, beat favourites Arsenal 1-0 thanks to a rare headed goal by Trevor Brooking.

• The legendary Bobby Moore is the club's most capped international. He played 108 times for England to set a record that has since only been passed by Peter Shilton, David Beckham, Wayne Rooney and Steven Gerrard.

• In their long and distinguished history West Ham have had just 15 managers, fewer than any other major English club. The longest serving of the lot was Syd King, who held the reins for 31 years from 1901 to 1932.

• On Boxing Day 2006 Teddy Sheringham became the oldest player ever to score in the Premier League when he netted for West Ham against Portsmouth aged 40 years and 266 days. Four days later he made his last appearance for the Hammers at Manchester City, stretching his own record as the oldest outfield player in the league's history.

• The Hammers spent a club record £20.5 million on Swansea City striker Andre Ayew in August 2016. Six months later they sold former fans' favourite Dimitri Payet to Marseille for a record £25 million.

HONOURS
***Division 2 champions** 1958, 1981*
***FA Cup** 1964, 1975, 1980*
***European Cup Winners' Cup** 1965*

WIGAN ATHLETIC

Year founded: 1932
Ground: DW Stadium (25,138)
Nickname: The Latics
Biggest win: 7-1 v Scarborough (1997)
Heaviest defeat: 1-9 v Tottenham Hotspur (2009)

The club was founded at a public meeting at the Queen's Hotel in 1932 as successors to Wigan Borough, who the previous year had become the first ever club to resign from the Football League. After 34 failed attempts, including a bizarre application to join the Scottish Second Division in 1972, Wigan were finally elected to the old Fourth Division in 1978 in place of Southport.

• The greatest day in the club's history came in 2013 when Wigan won their first major trophy, the FA Cup, after beating hot favourites Manchester City 1-0 in the final at Wembley thanks to a last-minute header by Ben Watson. Sadly for their fans, Wigan's eight-year stay in the Premier League ended just three days after that triumph, meaning that they became the first club ever to win the FA Cup and be relegated in the same season.

• In November 2009 Wigan were hammered 9-1 at Tottenham, only the second time in Premier League history that a side had conceded nine goals. The eight goals the Latics let in after the break was a record for a Premier League half.

• The club's record goalscorer is Andy Liddell, who hit 70 league goals between 1998 and 2003. No player has pulled on Wigan's blue-and-white stripes more often than Kevin Langley, who made 317 league appearances in two spells at the club between 1981 and 1994.

• Midfielder Jimmy Bullard made a club record 123 consecutive league appearances for Wigan between January 2003 and December 2005.

• Relegated to League One in 2017, Wigan's most decorated international is goalkeeper Ali Al Habsi who played 42 times for Oman between 2010 and 2015.

HONOURS
***Second Division champions** 2003*
***League One champions** 2016*
***Third Division champions** 1997*
***FA Cup** 2013*
***Football League Trophy** 1985, 1999*

ASHLEY WILLIAMS

Born: Wolverhampton, 23rd August 1984
Position: Defender
Club career:
2001-03 Hednesford Town 60 (0)
2003-08 Stockport County 162 (3)
2008 Swansea City (loan) 3 (0)
2008-16 Swansea City 319 (4)
2016- Everton 36 (1)
International record:
2008- Wales 71 (2)

At Euro 2016 Ashley Williams became the first player to captain his country to a semi-final of a major tournament. The veteran centre-back played a major role in his team's run to the final four, scoring in Wales' dramatic 3-1 quarter-final victory over Belgium with a powerful header from a corner and earning rave reviews for his defensive prowess.

• Born in Wolverhampton, Williams was a youth player at West Brom but was released by the Baggies when he was 16. He then spent two years with non-league Hednesford Town, also working at a petrol station and as a waiter, before joining Stockport County in 2003.

• Five years later Williams moved on to Swansea City for a then club record fee of £400,000. In 2011 he was part of the Swans team that gained promotion to the Premier League for the first time and in 2013 he became the first Swansea captain to lift a major trophy, following his side's 5-0 demolition of fourth-tier Bradford City in the League Cup final. In August 2016 he joined Everton for around £12 million.

• Williams qualified for Wales through his maternal grandfather, making his international debut in 2008. The 64 international caps he won with Swansea make him the club's highest-capped player ever.

Wolves will be stretching every sinew to get back to the Premier League

WOLVERHAMPTON WANDERERS

Year founded: 1877
Ground: Molineux (31,700)
Previous name: St Luke's
Nickname: Wolves
Biggest win: 14-0 v Cresswell's Brewery
Heaviest defeat: 1-10 v Newton Heath

Founded as St Luke's by pupils at a local school of that name in 1877, the club adopted its present name after merging with Blakenhall Wanderers two years later. Wolves were founder members of the Football League in 1888, finishing the first season in third place behind champions Preston and Aston Villa.

• The Black Country club enjoyed their heyday in the 1950s under manager Stan Cullis, a pioneer of long ball 'kick and rush' tactics. After a number of near misses, Wolves were crowned league champions for the first time in their history in 1954 and won two more titles later in the decade to cement their reputation as the top English club of the era. Incredibly, the Black Country outfit scored a century of league goals in four consecutive seasons between 1958 and 1961.

• When Wolves won a number of high-profile friendlies against foreign opposition in the 1950s in some of the first ever televised matches they were hailed as 'champions of the world' by the national press, a claim which helped inspire the creation of the European Cup. In 1958 Wolves became only the second English team to compete in the competition, following in the footsteps of trailblazers Manchester United.

• The skipper of that great Wolves team, centre-half Billy Wright, is the club's most capped international. Between 1946 and 1959 he won a then record 105 caps for England, captaining his country in 90 of those games (another record).

• Steve Bull is Wolves' record scorer with an incredible haul of 250 league goals between 1986 and 1999. His impressive total of 306 goals in all competitions included a record 18 hat-tricks for the club.

• Stalwart defender Derek Parkin pulled on the famous gold shirt more often than any other player, making 501 appearances in the league between 1967 and 1982.

• Wolves won the first of their four FA Cups in 1893 when they beat Everton 1-0 at the Fallowfield Stadium in Manchester. The Merseysiders complained that spectators in the 60,000 crowd had frequently encroached from the sidelines onto the pitch, but their demands for a replay were rejected.

• Wolves were the first team in the country to win all four divisions of the Football League, completing the

'full house' in 1989 when they won the old Third Division title a year after claiming the Fourth Division championship.

• Wolves splashed out a Championship record £15.8 million on Porto midfielder Ruben Neves in July 2017. With his previous club he became the youngest player ever to start a Champions League match as captain, when he wore the armband against Maccabi Tel Aviv in October 2015 aged just 18 and 221 days.

HONOURS
Division 1 champions *1954, 1958, 1959*
Division 2 champions *1932, 1977*
Championship champions *2009*
Division 3 (North) champions *1924*
Division 3 champions *1989*
League One champions *2014*
Division 4 champions *1988*
FA Cup *1893, 1908, 1949, 1960*
League Cup *1974, 1980*
Football League Trophy *1988*

WOMEN'S FOOTBALL

The first recorded women's football match took place between the north and south of England at Crouch End, London in 1895. The north won the game 7-1.

• **The Women's FA was founded in 1969 and the first Women's FA Cup final took place two years later, Southampton beating Stewart and Thistle 4-1. The most successful side in the competition are Arsenal with 14 victories, and the holders are Manchester City who thrashed Birmingham City 4-1 in the 2017 final watched by a record crowd of 35,271 at Wembley.**

• In a bid to attract more fans to games, the top flight was reorganised in 2011 as a semi-professional summer league consisting of eight clubs, the FA Women's Super League. However, the FA decided to return to a winter league in 2017 with Chelsea finishing top of that year's one-off bridging competition, the Spring Series.

• **The first British international women's match took place in 1972 when England beat Scotland 3-2. In 2005 England recorded their biggest ever win, thrashing Hungary 13-0. Their worst defeat was in 2000 when Norway won 8-0.**

• Midfielder Fara Williams has won a record 165 caps for England, while striker Kelly Smith scored a record 46 goals between 1995 and 2015.

• **Between 1987 and 2010 Kristine Lilly won a world record 354 caps for the USA. Powerfully built American striker Abby Wambach is the leading scorer in women's international football with an incredible 184 goals between 2001 and 2015.**

• In 2016 27-year-old Chan Yuen Ting became the first female coach to lead a men's team to their domestic title when she won the Hong Kong championship with Eastern AA.

WOMEN'S WORLD CUP

Since it was first competed for in China in 1991 there have been seven Women's World Cup tournaments. The USA won the first World Cup and have gone on to lift the trophy a record three times, most recently beating Japan 5-2 in the 2015 final in Vancouver at the

England's Jodie Taylor was top scorer at the 2017 European Championships

USA players celebrate their third Women's World Cup triumph in 2015

first tournament to be played entirely on artificial turf. Germany have won the tournament twice, while Norway (1995) and Japan (2011) are the only two other nations to take the trophy home.

• **The top scorer in the World Cup is Marta (Brazil) with 15 goals between 2003 and 2015. Michelle Akers of the USA scored a record 10 goals at the 1991 tournament, including a record five in one game against Chinese Taipei.**

• The USA's Kristine Lilly played in a record 30 games at the World Cup between 1991 and 2007.

• **Germany hold the record for the biggest win at the Women's World Cup, thrashing Argentina 11-0 in 2007.**

• The youngest player at the finals is Nigeria's Ifeanyi Chiejine, who was aged just 16 and 34 days when she played against North Korea in 1999.

WORLD CUP

The most successful country in the history of the World Cup is Brazil, who have won the competition a record five times. Germany and Italy are Europe's leading nation with four wins each, the Germans becoming the first European nation to triumph in South America when they beat Argentina 1-0 in the 2014 final in Brazil. Neighbours Argentina and Uruguay have both won the competition twice, the Uruguayans emerging victorious when the pair met in the first ever World Cup final in Montevideo in 1930. The only other countries to claim the trophy are England (1966), France (1998) and Spain (2010).

• **Including both Japan and South Korea, who were joint hosts for the 2002 edition, the World Cup has been held in 15 different countries. The first nation to stage the tournament twice was Mexico (in 1970 and 1986), while Italy (1934 and 1990), France (1938 and 1998), Germany (1974 and 2006) and Brazil (1950 and 2014) have also welcomed the world to the planet's biggest football festival on two occasions each.**

• Brazil are the only country to have played at all 20 tournaments and have recorded the most wins (70). Germany, meanwhile, have reached a record eight finals, have played the most games (106) and have scored the most goals (224).

• **However, Hungary hold the record for the most goals scored in a single tournament, banging in 27 in just five games at the 1954 finals in Switzerland. Even this incredible tally, though, was not quite sufficient for the 'Magical Magyars' to lift the trophy as they went down to a 3-2 defeat in the final against West Germany, a team they had beaten 8-3 earlier in the tournament.**

• Hungary also hold the record for the biggest ever victory at the finals, demolishing El Salvador 10-1 in 1982. That, though, was a desperately close encounter compared to the biggest win in qualifying, Australia's 31-0 annihilation of American Samoa in 2001, a game in which Aussie striker Archie Thompson helped himself to a record 13 goals.

TOP 10

APPEARANCES AT WORLD CUP FINALS

1.	Brazil	20
2.	Germany	18
	Italy	18
4.	Argentina	16
5.	Mexico	15
6.	England	14
	France	14
	Spain	14
9.	Belgium	12
	Uruguay	12

• The legendary Pelé is the only player in World Cup history to have been presented with three winner's medals. The Brazilian superstar enjoyed his first success in 1958 when he scored twice in a 5-2 rout of hosts Sweden in the final, and was a winner again four years later in Chile despite hobbling out of the tournament with a torn leg muscle in the second match. He then made it a hat-trick in 1970, setting a sparkling Brazil side on the road to an emphatic 4-1 victory against Italy in the final with a bullet header.

• The leading overall scorer in the World Cup is Germany's Miroslav Klose with 16 goals between 2002 and 2014. He is followed by Brazil legend Ronaldo with 15, including two in the 2002 final against Germany.

• England's Geoff Hurst had previously gone one better in 1966, scoring a hat-trick as the hosts beat West Germany 4-2 in the final at Wembley. His second goal, which gave England a decisive 3-2 lead in extra-time, was the most controversial in World Cup history and German fans still argue to this day that his shot bounced on the line after striking the crossbar, rather than over it. Naturally, England fans generally agree with the eagle-eyed Russian linesman, Tofik Bahramov, who awarded the goal.

• Germany midfielder Lothar Matthaus made a record 25 World Cup appearances for his country between 1982 and 1998. Argentina legend Diego Maradona captained his country in a record 16 matches between 1986 and 1994.

• England's Peter Shilton kept a record 10 clean sheets between 1982 and 1990, his tally later being matched by France's Fabien Barthez.

• Turkey striker Hakan Sukur scored the fastest goal at the finals after just 11 seconds of the play-off for third place against South Korea in 2002.The fastest goal in the final itself was scored by Netherlands midfielder Johan Neeskens from the penalty spot after 90 seconds against hosts West Germany in 1974.

• The oldest player to appear in the qualifying rounds is MacDonald Taylor Sr, who was aged 46 and 175 days when he lined up for the US Virgin Islands against Saint Kitts and Nevis in 2004. The youngest player is Togo midfielder Souleymane Mamam, who was only 13 and 310 days when he played against Zambia in 2001.

• Brazil suffered the worst ever defeat by a host nation when they were trounced 7-1 by Germany in 2014 – also the biggest ever win in a semi-final. However, four years earlier South Africa fared even worse, becoming the first hosts to be eliminated in the first round.

• Oleg Salenko scored a record five goals for Russia in their 6-1 hammering of Cameroon in 1994.

• The record goalscorer in qualifying is Guatemala striker Carlos Ruiz with 39 goals between 2002 and 2016.

'Top tekkers' from Zabivaka, the 2018 World Cup mascot

World Cup Finals

1930 Uruguay 4 Argentina 2 (Uruguay)
1934 Italy 2 Czechoslovakia 1 (Italy)
1938 Italy 4 Hungary 2 (France)
1950 Uruguay 2 Brazil 1 (Brazil)
1954 West Germany 3 Hungary 2 (Switzerland)
1958 Brazil 5 Sweden 2 (Sweden)
1962 Brazil 3 Czechoslovakia 1 (Chile)
1966 England 4 West Germany 2 (England)
1970 Brazil 4 Italy 1 (Mexico)
1974 West Germany 2 Netherlands 1 (West Germany)
1978 Argentina 3 Netherlands 1 (Argentina)
1982 Italy 3 West Germany 1 (Spain)
1986 Argentina 3 West Germany 2 (Mexico)
1990 West Germany 1 Argentina 0 (Italy)
1994 Brazil 0 Italy 0 (USA)*
1998 France 3 Brazil 0 (France)
2002 Brazil 2 Germany 0 (Japan/ South Korea)
2006 Italy 1 France 1 (Germany)*
2010 Spain 1 Netherlands 0 (South Africa)
2014 Germany 1 Argentina 0 (Brazil)
* Won on penalties

WORLD CUP 2018

The 2018 World Cup will take place in Russia – the first time that the competition has been held in Eastern Europe. Russia was chosen as the venue in December 2010 after beating off rival bids by Spain/Portugal, Belgium/Netherlands and England.

• As at all previous World Cups since 1998, 32 countries will compete at the finals. A total of 12 venues will host matches, with the final being played at the 81,000-capacity Luzhniki Stadium in Moscow on 15 July.

• The total budget for the tournament is an eye-watering £23.7 billion, making Russia 2018 easily the most expensive World Cup in history.

• On 12th March 2015 East Timor striker Chiquito do Carmo scored the first goal of the qualification process in a 4-1 defeat of Mongolia. Two years later Brazil became the first nation to secure their place at the finals when they beat Paraguay 3-0 in the South American qualifying section.

• In the European qualifying section, new FIFA members Gibraltar and Kosovo took part in the World Cup for the first time.

WORLD CUP GOLDEN BALL

The Golden Ball is awarded to the best player at the World Cup following a poll of members of the global media. The first winner was Italian striker Paolo Rossi, whose six goals at the 1982 World Cup helped the Azzurri win that year's tournament in Spain.

• Rossi was followed in 1986 by another World Cup winner, Argentina captain Diego Maradona, but since then only one player has claimed the Golden Ball and a winner's medal at the same tournament, Brazilian striker Romario in 1994.

• The only goalkeeper to win the award to date is Germany's Oliver Kahn, who finished on the losing side in the final against Brazil in 2002. The most controversial winner, meanwhile, was France's mercurial midfielder Zinedine Zidane, who was named as the outstanding performer at the 2006 World Cup before the final – a game which ended in disgrace for Zidane after he was sent off for headbutting Italian defender Marco Materazzi.

• Another much-debated winner of the Golden Ball was Argentina's Lionel Messi, who failed to sparkle in the knock-out rounds at the 2014 finals after a good start to the tournament. Even fellow countryman Diego Maradona described the award as "unfair".

World Cup Golden Ball Winners
1982 Paolo Rossi (Italy)
1986 Diego Maradona (Argentina)
1990 Salvatore Schillaci (Italy)
1994 Romario (Brazil)
1998 Ronaldo (Brazil)
2002 Oliver Kahn (Germany)
2006 Zinedine Zidane (France)
2010 Diego Forlan (Uruguay)
2014 Lionel Messi (Argentina)

WORLD CUP GOLDEN BOOT

Now officially known as the 'adidas Golden Shoe', the Golden Boot is awarded to the player who scores most goals in a World Cup finals tournament. The first winner was Guillermo Stabile, whose eight goals helped Argentina reach the final in 1930.

• French striker Just Fontaine scored a record 13 goals at the 1958 tournament in Sweden. At the other end of the scale, nobody managed more than four goals at the 1962 World Cup in Chile, so the award was shared between six players.

• Surprisingly, it wasn't until 1978 that the Golden Boot was won outright by a player, Argentina's Mario Kempes, whose country also won the tournament. Since then only Italy's Paolo Rossi in 1982 and Brazil's Ronaldo in 2002 have won both the Golden Boot and a World Cup winner's medal in the same year.

• The only English player to win the Golden Boot is Gary Lineker, whose six goals in 1986 included a famous hat-trick against Poland.

• At the 2010 World Cup in South Africa Germany's Thomas Muller was one of four players to top the scoring charts with five goals, but FIFA's new rules gave him the Golden Boot because he had more assists than his three rivals for the award, David Villa, Wesley Sneijder and Diego Forlan.

• The 2014 award went to Colombia's James Rodriguez, who scored six goals, including a brilliant volley against Uruguay which was later voted the best of the tournament by fans on FIFA's website.

WYCOMBE WANDERERS

Year founded: 1887
Ground: Adams Park (10,284)
Nickname: The Chairboys
Biggest win: 15-1 v Witney Town (1955)
Heaviest defeat: 0-8 v Reading (1899)

Wycombe Wanderers were founded in 1887 by a group of young furniture-makers (hence the club's nickname, The Chairboys) but had to wait until 1993 before earning promotion to the Football League.

Watch out defenders, Wycombe's Adebayo Akinfenwa will have you for breakfast!

• **Under then manager Martin O'Neill the club went up to the Second Division (now League One) in their first season, beating Preston in the play-off final.**
• In 2001 the Chairboys caused a sensation by reaching the semi-finals of the FA Cup where they lost 2-1 to eventual winners Liverpool at Villa Park. Wycombe also reached the semi-finals of the League Cup in 2007, but were beaten 5-1 on aggregate by eventual winners Chelsea.
• **On 23rd September 2000 Wycombe's Jamie Bates and Jermaine McSporran set a new Football League record for the shortest time between two goals when they both scored against Peterborough within nine seconds of each other either side of half-time.**
• Midfielder Steve Brown played in a record 371 league games for Wycombe between 1994 and 2004. Defender Mark Rogers won a record seven international caps for Canada while at Adams Park between 2000 and 2003.

HONOURS
Conference champions 1993
FA Amateur Cup 1931

YEOVIL TOWN

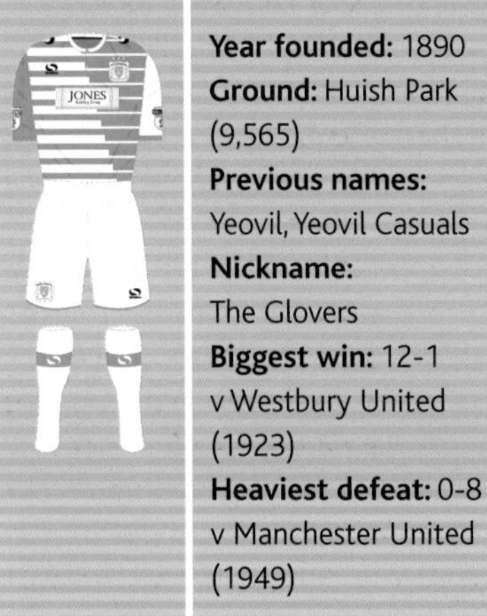

Year founded: 1890
Ground: Huish Park (9,565)
Previous names: Yeovil, Yeovil Casuals
Nickname: The Glovers
Biggest win: 12-1 v Westbury United (1923)
Heaviest defeat: 0-8 v Manchester United (1949)

Founded in 1890, initially as Yeovil and then as Yeovil Casuals (1895-1907), the club had to wait until 2003 before finally entering the Football League when they were promoted as Conference champions by a then record 17 points margin.
• **The Glovers adapted well to league football, beating Rochdale 3-1 away in their opening fixture – the last time a newcomer to the Football League has won on their debut. After two more promotions Yeovil reached the heady heights of the Championship in 2013, but the glory years were short-lived and following two consecutive relegations the Somerset club were back in the basement division two years later.**
• Before they made it into the Football League, Yeovil were famed FA Cup giant-killers, knocking out no fewer than 20 league clubs – a record for a non-league outfit. Their most notable scalp came in 1949 when they beat Sunderland 2-1 in the fourth round on their famously sloping Huish Park pitch.
• **Stalwart defender Terry Skiverton played in a record 328 league games for the Glovers between 1999 and 2010. Striker Phil Jevons scored a record 42 goals for the club, including a seasonal best of 27 when Yeovil won the League Two title in 2005.**

HONOURS
League Two champions 2005
Conference champions 2003

WILFRIED ZAHA

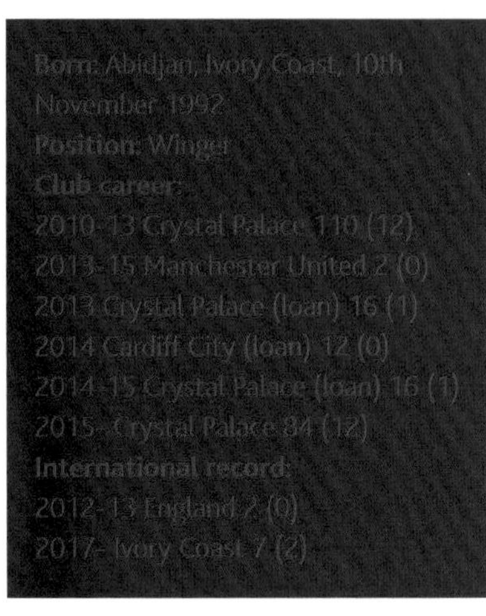

Born: Abidjan, Ivory Coast, 10th November 1992
Position: Winger
Club career:
2010-13 Crystal Palace 110 (12)
2013-15 Manchester United 2 (0)
2013 Crystal Palace (loan) 16 (1)
2014 Cardiff City (loan) 12 (0)
2014-15 Crystal Palace (loan) 16 (1)
2015- Crystal Palace 84 (12)
International record:
2012-13 England 2 (0)
2017- Ivory Coast 7 (2)

Wilfried Zaha chose the Ivory Coast over England, but still isn't sure if he made the right decision

After making two non-competitive appearances for England back in the 2012/13 season, pacy Crystal Palace winger Wilfried Zaha disappointed Three Lions boss Gareth Southgate by switching his allegiance to his birth nation, Ivory Coast, ahead of the 2017 Africa Cup of Nations. Zaha went on to figure in all three of the reigning champions group matches at the tournament but couldn't prevent Ivory Coast from being dumped out at the first stage.

• **Zaha moved from Africa to London with his family aged four. He came through the ranks of the Crystal Palace academy to make his debut, aged 17, in April 2010, and the following year gained national prominence when he starred in the Eagles' shock 2-1 victory away to Manchester United in the League Cup quarter-final. At the end of the 2011/12 campaign he was voted the Football League's Young Player of the Year.**

• A £15 million move to Manchester United followed in January 2013, making Zaha the most expensive player to leave Selhurst Park at the time. However, he was immediately loaned back to the Eagles, helping them gain promotion to the Premier League via the play-offs. When he eventually pitched up at Old Trafford Zaha soon fell out of favour with then United boss David Moyes and was loaned out to Cardiff City.

• **A further loan to Palace resulted in a permanent move back to Selhurst Park, and the familiar south London atmosphere sparked a revival in Zaha's form. He was an instrumental figure in Palace's run to the 2016 FA Cup final – which ironically they lost to United – and in some of the Eagles' best displays of an up-and-down 2016/17 season.**

ZINEDINE ZIDANE

Born: Marseille, France, 23rd June 1972
Position: Midfielder
Club career:
1988-92 Cannes 61 (6)
1992-96 Bordeaux 139 (28)
1996-2001 Juventus 151 (24)
2001-06 Real Madrid 155 (37)
International record:
1994-2006 France 108 (31)

Zinedine Zidane – the first manager to win the Champions League in consecutive seasons

In 2017 Real Madrid boss Zinedine Zidane became the first manager in the Champions League era to lift the trophy in consecutive seasons after his side smashed Juventus 4-1 in the final in Cardiff. In the same campaign, the Frenchman also guided Real to their first La Liga title for five years.

• **An extravagantly gifted midfielder, Zidane started out with Cannes and Bordeaux before gaining worldwide attention with Juventus, with whom he won the Serie A title in 1997 and 1998. After five years with the Italian giants he moved to Real Madrid for a then world record fee of £46 million in 2001, and the following year scored a spectacular volleyed winner for his new club in the Champions League final against Bayer Leverkusen. The next season he won his only league title with Real.**

• In 2003 Zidane became only the second player (after Brazilian striker Ronaldo) to win the old World Player of the Year award three times and the following year he was voted the best European Footballer of the past 50 years in a poll as part of UEFA's 50th anniversary celebrations.

• **Although of Algerian descent, Zidane chose to play for his native France and he became a hero to his fellow countrymen at the 1998 World Cup when he headed two goals in his side's surprisingly comfortable 3-0 defeat of favourites Brazil in the final in Paris. Two years later 'Zizou', as he was known to his team-mates, was voted Player of the Tournament as France beat Italy 2-1 in the final of the European Championships in Rotterdam.**

• Zidane came out of international retirement to help a struggling French team qualify for the 2006 World Cup. However, his magnificent career ended on a sour note when he was sent off in the final for headbutting Italian defender Marco Materazzi in the chest after his opponent had made derogatory comments about Zidane's family. Nonetheless, Zidane's sublime performances in the finals ensured that he was awarded the Golden Ball as the outstanding player of the tournament.

• **Zidane's record in his first 70 games as Real Madrid manager is the best ever in the history of the club – 51 ganes won, 14 drawn and just 5 defeats with 194 goals scored and 71 conceded.**

'Noooooo!' Poor old Cristiano Ronaldo can't believe this book has come to an end already!